This book is divided into three main parts: (1) parent–child coconstruction of narrative, which focuses on aspects of the social interaction that facilitate oral narrative development in Spanish-speaking children; (2) development of independent narration by Spanish-speaking children; and (3) narrative links between Latino children's oral narration and their early literacy and other school achievements. Chapters address narration to and by Latino children aged 6 months to 11 years old and in low, middle, and upper socioeconomic groups. Nationalities of speakers include Costa Rican, Dominican, Ecuadorian, Mexican, Peruvian, Puerto Rican, Venezuelan, and Spanish–English bilingual children who are citizens or residents of the United States. Narratives studied include those in conversations, personal and fictional stories, and those prompted by wordless picture books or videos. Thus, the current project makes central diversity in nationality, socioeconomic background, and genre of narrative.

ALLYSSA McCABE, Ph.D., is Professor of Psychology at the University of Massachusetts, Lowell. She founded and coedits the journal *Narrative Inquiry* and has researched how narrative develops with age, the way parents can encourage narration, and cultural differences in narration, as well as interrelationships among the development of narrative, vocabulary, and phonological awareness. She is the recipient (with L. S. Bliss and A. Covington) of the Editor's Award from *Contemporary Issues in Communication Science and Disorders,* presented at the 1999 Annual Convention of the American Speech-Language-Hearing Association in San Francisco, California, for the article, "Assessing the Narratives of African American Children." Her current work concerns a theoretical approach to early literacy called the Comprehensive Language Approach, which looks at ways that the various strands of oral and written language affect each other in the acquisition of full literacy. With Lynn Bliss, she most recently published *Patterns of Narrative Discourse: A Multicultural Lifespan Approach.*

ALISON L. BAILEY, Ed.D., is Associate Professor and a former Division Head of the Psychological Studies in Education Program in the Department of Education, University of California, Los Angeles, in addition to being a faculty associate researcher for the National Center for Research on Evaluation, Standards, & Student Testing (CRESST). Dr. Bailey, a graduate of Harvard University, focuses her research primarily on language and sociocommunicative development in both first- and second-language learners, as well as early literacy development and assessment. Her work has been supported by the National Science Foundation among others. She serves on the advisory boards of the California Department of Education, the consortia of numerous other states, and commercial publishers developing language and literacy assessments for English learners. Dr. Bailey is coauthor of the new Pre-Kindergarten–Kindergarten *IPT Assessment of English Language Development,* editor of and contributing author to *The Language Demands of School: Putting Academic English to the Test,* and coauthor with Margaret Heritage of *Formative Assessment for Literacy K-6: Building Reading and Academic Language Skills Across the Curriculum.* She was the 2005–2006 Fellow of the Sudikoff Family Institute at UCLA, which expands public awareness of critical issues related to education and information studies.

GIGLIANA MELZI, Ph.D., is Associate Professor and Director of Undergraduate Studies in the Department of Applied Psychology at New York University's Steinhardt School of Culture, Education, and Human Development. Dr. Melzi obtained her doctoral degree from Boston University. She has published articles and chapters focusing on the early literacy and language development of Spanish-speaking Latino children living in the United States and in their countries of origin. In one line of research, she has investigated through qualitative methodologies the daily literacy activities of immigrant parents and their impact on children's school performance. She also conducted studies on various discourse and linguistic features of Spanish-speaking mother–child dyads from nonimmigrant and immigrant Latin American families across various socioeconomic groups. Currently, Dr. Melzi is funded by the National Institutes of Health and the Administration for Children and Families (ACF) in the U.S. Department of Health and Human Services for her wo̶ ̶ ̶ ̶ ̶ ̶ ̶ ̶ ̶ ̶ ̶ment of Latino Head Start families.

T0381638

Spanish-Language Narration and Literacy

CULTURE, COGNITION, AND EMOTION

Edited by

Allyssa McCabe
University of Massachusetts, Lowell

Alison L. Bailey
University of California, Los Angeles

Gigliana Melzi
New York University, New York

CAMBRIDGE
UNIVERSITY PRESS

University Printing House, Cambridge CB2 8BS, United Kingdom

One Liberty Plaza, 20th Floor, New York, NY 10006, USA

477 Williamstown Road, Port Melbourne, VIC 3207, Australia

314-321, 3rd Floor, Plot 3, Splendor Forum, Jasola District Centre, New Delhi - 110025, India

103 Penang Road, #05-06/07, Visioncrest Commercial, Singapore 238467

Cambridge University Press is part of the University of Cambridge.

It furthers the University's mission by disseminating knowledge in the pursuit of education, learning and research at the highest international levels of excellence.

www.cambridge.org
Information on this title: www.cambridge.org/9780521710046

© Cambridge University Press 2008

First published 2008

A catalogue record for this publication is available from the British Library

Library of Congress Cataloging in Publication data

McCabe, Allyssa.
Spanish-language narration and literacy development : culture, cognition, and emotion / Allyssa McCabe, Lowell Alison Bailey [and] Gigliana Melzi.
   p.   cm.
Includes bibliographical references and index.
ISBN 978-0-521-88375-7 (hardcover : alk. paper) – ISBN 978-0-521-71004-6 (pbk. : alk. paper)
1. Spanish language – Study and teaching (Early childhood)   I. Bailey, Alison L.   II. Melzi, Gigliana.   III. Title.
PC4074.85.M34   2008
372.656'1–dc22   2008027125

ISBN 978-0-521-88375-7 Hardback
ISBN 978-0-521-71004-6 Paperback

CONTENTS

LIST OF CONTRIBUTORS

ALISON L. BAILEY is Associate Professor and a former Division Head of the Psychological Studies in Education Program in the Department of Education, University of California, Los Angeles, in addition to being a faculty associate researcher for the National Center for Research on Evaluation, Standards, & Student Testing (CRESST). Dr. Bailey, a graduate of Harvard University, focuses her research primarily on language and sociocommunicative development in both first- and second-language learners, as well as early literacy development and assessment. She directed the Academic English Language Proficiency Project at CRESST, which has conducted research to provide an empirical basis for the operationalization of the academic language construct for assessment, curriculum, and teacher professional development. Dr. Bailey's research on narrative development has focused on parental support of young children's narration and ties between narrative development and later literacy outcomes for both first- and second-language learners. Dr. Bailey serves on the advisory boards of the California Department of Education and numerous other states and commercial publishers developing language and literacy assessments for English learners. Dr. Bailey is coauthor of the new Pre-Kindergarten–Kindergarten *IPT Assessment of English Language Development*, from Ballard and Tighe Publishers, editor of and contributing author to *The Language Demands of School: Putting Academic English to the Test*, from Yale University Press, and coauthor with Margaret Heritage of *Formative Assessment for Literacy K-6: Building Reading and Academic Language Skills Across the Curriculum*, from Corwin/Sage Press.

SARAH W. BECK is Assistant Professor of English Education in the Department of Teaching and Learning in New York University's Steinhardt School of Culture, Education, and Human Development. She obtained her doctorate in human development and psychology with a focus on language and literacy development from Harvard Graduate School of Education in 2002, where she also worked with students in the Teacher Education Programs. Her research interests include the development, instruction, and assessment of literacy skills among adolescents; urban education; and discourse analysis development. Her research on the teaching and learning of subject-specific literacy has been supported by the Spencer Foundation, which is also supporting her current investigation into the nature of academic writing in U.S. high schools. Dr. Beck has published articles and chapters on these topics in *Research in the Teaching of English*, *Educational Researcher*, and the *Yearbook of the National Reading Conference*.

MARGARET CASPE is Survey Researcher at Mathematica Policy Research, Inc., where she works on both early childhood and international projects. Her research interests focus on cultural variations in children's narrative development and how relationships among families and early childhood programs promote early narrative competence. As a 2005–2007 Head Start Graduate Research Scholar, Dr. Caspe investigated how family literacy and narrative practices within low-income immigrant Latino communities are related to children's later language and literacy. In 2007, she received her Ph.D. in developmental psychology from New York University's Steinhardt School of Culture, Education, and Human Development.

TONIA N. CRISTOFARO is Research Consultant for University Settlement, where she provides training and educational consultation to the Early Childhood Center. Among her responsibilities, she is working on a reading and writing research project examining children's literacy development and school readiness over time. Dr. Cristofaro completed her doctorate in developmental psychology at New York University's Steinhardt School of Culture, Education, and Human Development in 2007. Her research has focused on understanding the ways in which parent–child and teacher–child engagements and discourse shape and support children's language and autobiographical narratives, with a particular emphasis on the experiences of children from ethnically diverse, low-income families. As a recipient of a Head Start Graduate Student Research Grant, funded by the ACF from 2002 to 2004, Dr. Cristofaro was involved in research and community outreach activities with three Head Start programs on the Lower East Side of New York City. This project enabled her to examine teachers' encouragement of pre-kindergarteners' language and narrative competencies.

C. NICHOLAS CUNEO is a Phi Beta Kappa graduate of Duke University, where he majored in biology and biological anthropology and anatomy. While at Duke, Mr. Cuneo published an essay on Ralph Ellison's *Invisible Man* and completed a distinction thesis on lemur comparative immunology. A Fulbright Scholarship recipient and Rhodes Scholarship finalist, Mr. Cuneo studied abroad in Costa Rica and South Africa, where he worked on issues ranging from indigenous education and biodiversity conservation to linguistic evolution and rural health. He is currently working with a medical relief organization in rural Haiti and plans to become a physician focusing on global health and development issues.

MARY DINGLE is Associate Professor in the Department of Educational Leadership and Special Education at Sonoma State University (SSU), where she teaches core courses in the educational specialist credential programs. Prior to arriving at SSU, Dr. Dingle taught in the public school system for 14 years in both general education and special education classrooms. Currently, her research interests include studying the outcomes of early intervention programs on the early literacy skills of English language learners, professional development in the use of assessment data to inform instruction, and classroom observations to identify effective instructional strategies for English language learners and students with learning disabilities.

CAMILA FERNÁNDEZ is Assistant Professor in the Department of Psychology at Universidad de los Andes in Bogotá, Colombia. She obtained her doctoral degree in developmental psychology in 2007 from New York University's Steinhardt School of Culture, Education, and Human Development. Dr. Fernández's research focuses on the intersection of social cognition and language development, specifically on the evaluative aspects of children's narrative discourse in relation to their social development during the early school years. Currently, Dr. Fernández directs a research group in early childhood development at the Universidad de los Andes and serves as a consultant for large-scale funded projects in education and early childhood development housed in the university's research center for economic development (Centro de Estudios para el Desarrollo Económico [CEDE]).

COLLEEN GALLAGHER is a specialist in the field of language education. She earned her master's degree in applied linguistics at Georgetown University, where she is also a doctoral candidate. Colleen's research interests include biliteracy and bilingual education, language socialization, child narrative development and language assessment. She is a lecturer in the Department of Curriculum and Instruction at the University of Maryland, College Park and coordinates the Teaching English to Speakers of Other Languages master's program within the Department's Second Language Education and Culture Program. Previously, she worked as a research assistant at the Center for Applied Linguistics in Washington, DC and as a teacher in Spanish, English as second language and dual language classrooms in Virginia and Arizona.

ALISON WISHARD GUERRA is Assistant Professor in the Education Studies Program at the University of California, San Diego. She received her Ph.D. in Education from UCLA with an emphasis in Psychological Studies in Education. Dr. Wishard Guerra's research focuses on social and language development in early childhood, with particular focus on developmental competencies among Latino children from low-income families. She studies within group variations related to immigration and acculturation experiences and their associations to children's longitudinal developmental outcomes. Specifically in her narrative work she has sought to describe the normative development of narrative competencies among Mexican-heritage children. Dr. Wishard Guerra was a member of the expanded research consortia that helped to develop the California Preschool Learning Foundations on English-Language Development.

KENDALL A. KING has taught in the areas of bilingualism, second language acquisition, and language policy at New York University, Stockholm University, and Georgetown University, where she was Associate Professor until 2008. She is currently an Associate Professor in the Second Languages and Cultures Program at the University of Minnesotta in Minneapolis. She has published widely on Quichua (the variety of Quechua spoken in Ecuador) and Spanish bilingualism and bilingual education policy in Andean countries in journals such as *Annual Review of Applied Linguistics*, the *International Journal of the Sociology of Language*, and the *International Journal of Bilingualism and Bilingual Education*, as well as a 2001 book, *Language Revitalization Processes and Prospects: Quichua in the Ecuadorian Andes.*

ALLYSSA McCABE is Professor of Psychology at the University of Massachusetts, Lowell. She founded and coedits the journal *Narrative Inquiry* and has researched how narrative develops with age, the way parents can encourage narration, and cultural differences in narration, as well as interrelationships among the developments of narrative, vocabulary, and phonological awareness. Her most recent work concerns a theoretical approach to early literacy called the Comprehensive Language Approach, which looks at ways that the various strands of oral and written language (e.g., vocabulary, phonological awareness, and print knowledge) affect each other in the acquisition of full literacy. A key concern is with assessment of preschool-aged children, especially preventing misdiagnosis of cultural differences in oral narration as deficits. Allyn & Bacon Publishers recently published Dr. McCabe's *Patterns of Narrative Discourse: A Multicultural Lifespan Approach,* coauthored by Lynn Bliss.

GIGLIANA MELZI is Associate Professor of Applied Psychology and Director of Undergraduate Studies in Applied Psychology at New York University's Steinhardt School of Culture, Education, and Human Development. Dr. Melzi was born and raised in Lima, Perú. She came to the United States in 1985 to pursue her undergraduate degree at Clark University, where she majored in Spanish literature and psychology. She continued her studies in developmental psychology, focusing on language development, at Boston University, where she obtained her Ph.D. Dr. Melzi's research has examined the language development and literacy experiences of Spanish-speaking children within and outside the United States. In her narrative work specifically, she has focused on various aspects of mother–child narrative discourse across Latin American communities, including, most recently, middle-class Brazilian mothers from Porto Alegre. Currently, Dr. Melzi is funded by the National Institutes of Health and the Administration for Children and Families (ACF) in the U.S. Department of Health and Human

Services for her work on the educational involvement of Latino Head Start families. Dr. Melzi also acts as a consultant for various educational projects, including the PBS program *Between the Lions.*

ANI C. MOUGHAMIAN received her Ph.D. in educational psychology from the University of California, Los Angeles in 2005. She was an Educational Research Analyst at the Los Angeles Unified School District for two years, where she focused on the implementation and evaluation of various district language and literacy programs. Dr. Moughamian is currently an Assistant Research Professor at the University of Houston, where she works in the Texas Institute for Research, Evaluation, and Statistics (TIMES). She is working under a Center on Instruction grant, providing research support and technical assistance to regional centers across the United States. In addition, she is pursuing her research interests in narrative, language, and literacy development in English language learners and Armenian American student outcomes.

MARTHA SHIRO is Professor at the Universidad Central de Venezuela and obtained her doctoral degree at Harvard Graduate School of Education. She is the director of the Instituto de Filología Andres Bello, a research center within the Facultad de Humanidades y Educación, which specializes in language studies, particularly Venezuelan Spanish. Her research interests, reflected in her publications, lie in the areas of first- and second-language development, discourse analysis, and grammar. Dr. Shiro is the author or co-editor of three books recently published by Universidad Central de Venuezuela: *Haciendo lingüística, La modalidad epistémica en narraciones infantiles,* and *Analizando discurso.* Currently, she is also the editor of the journal *Boletín de Lingüística.* Dr. Shiro's research in narrative development focuses on children's abilities to produce different narrative genres and on the ways sociocultural differences affect their discourse. Dr. Shiro lectures in several graduate programs. Her courses include Psycholinguistics, Discourse and Cognition, Narrative Discourse, Evaluative Language in Discourse, and Functional Grammar.

ALISON SPARKS is Project Manager for the Preschool Language Project, a longitudinal intervention study funded by the National Institute of Child Health and Human Development (NICHD), at Clark University. She is also a Five College Associate at Amherst College. Her research focuses on developing language and literacy in culturally and linguistically diverse populations. She is a speech language pathologist with extensive clinical experience with Spanish-speaking children in urban settings and is currently a doctoral candidate in developmental psychology at Clark University.

PABLO A. STANSBERY is Early Childhood Development Senior Advisor for International Programs at Save the Children. He received his doctorate in human development and psychology from Harvard University and completed his postdoctoral training at the Child Development Unit at Boston Children's Hospital (Harvard Medical School). Dr. Stansbery also consults with early childhood development programs throughout the United States and directs a longitudinal research project in Costa Rica. The purpose of the Costa Rican Child Development Project is to identify early interactions and home environmental conditions that may be linked to school success. The cohort has been followed from birth to the present (10 years). His research is both qualitative and quantitative in exploring the impact of culture on child-rearing practices and how those tacit day-to-day interactive strategies influence developmental trajectories of children beginning at the earliest ages.

CATHERINE S. TAMIS-LeMONDA is Professor of Applied Psychology at New York University's Steinhardt School of Culture, Education, and Human Development. Her research focuses on children's cognitive, language, and social development in the first four years of life, with attention to parental influences on early learning and school readiness. Dr. Tamis-LeMonda has conducted research with families from different ethnic groups in the United States as well as internationally. She is currently Director of NYU's Center for Research on Culture, Development, and Education, where she is examining cultural views and practices relative to children's learning outcomes in Mexican, Dominican, African American, and Chinese families living in New York City. Her research has been funded by the NICHD, ACYF, NSF, and the Ford Foundation. She has published numerous articles and chapters and coedited four books on topics of children's development and parenting.

PAOLA UCCELLI is Assistant Professor in Language and Literacy at the Harvard Graduate School of Education. Her research focuses on socio-cultural and individual differences in language and literacy development in Spanish and English. She studied linguistics at the Pontificia Universidad Católica in Perú, her country of origin, and then pursued graduate studies in human development and psychology at the Harvard Graduate School of Education. Two main lines of research characterize her work. First, she investigates early language development with a particular focus on understanding how children learn to translate experience into narrative. Second, she carries out research on reading comprehension instruction and assessment with a special interest in the challenges faced, as well as the strengths displayed, by language minority children. In both lines of research she explores how different language skills (lexical, grammatical, and discourse) interact with each other to either promote or hinder the meaning-making processes of expression and comprehension, within and across languages. Currently, she is also investigating the challenges involved in academic language development and instruction. She has written articles and chapters on these topics for the *Cambridge Handbook of Literacy, the Handbook of Educational Linguistics, Child Psychology: A Handbook of Contemporary Issues,* and in several journals. Her postdoctoral work was supported by the Institute of Education Sciences (IES).

PREFACE

The initial idea for this book was simple: Alison suggested an edited volume that would recognize the impact Allyssa McCabe has had on two generations of researchers focusing on the study of narrative development. From the start, it seemed critical that Allyssa should be part of the editorial process – who better to make the book a strong contribution to the field? The extension of much of the pioneering work of Allyssa and her colleagues in the 1980s to populations of preschool and school-age children who do not have English as a first language made the choice of Spanish-language narration a natural one. Many of Allyssa's former students were concentrating on both the formal and informal contexts of narrative development in children from diverse backgrounds outside the U.S. mainstream – indeed, some outside the United States entirely. Contacting them and others who have been influenced by Allyssa's work to contribute chapters to the proposed volume set the book in motion.

AUDIENCE: FOR WHOM IS THIS BOOK WRITTEN?

We see a number of audiences for this book: students of language development in speech-language pathology, linguistics, and psychology, as well as those involved in literacy acquisition in preschool and elementary education. The book could readily serve as the main text of a graduate-level seminar devoted to the study of narrative development in Spanish-speaking children, as well as function as an auxiliary text in a course on narrative development or language development more broadly written.

Preschool and elementary schoolteachers and the staff who support them (i.e., principals and school psychologists) in the United States and elsewhere should find the descriptions of narrative diversity presented in the chapters critical to their own understanding of the stories told to them by the Spanish-speaking children they educate. The text can play a key role in the preparation of preservice teachers who will be working with Spanish-speaking children who hail from all over the Americas, as well as be a catalyst for comparison and discussion during the continued professional development of more experienced teachers.

ACKNOWLEDGMENTS

First, we thank all the chapter writers for their excellent contributions to the volume. Their dedication to the project has meant that we have kept everyone we initially invited and we have managed to stay on publication schedule. On everyone's behalf, we also want to say a special "gracias" and "thank you" to the children, parents, and teachers all across the Americas whose narrative skills and experiences are at the very heart of this book.

Storytelling through its various media – oral, written, and visual – has a long-standing tradition across the Spanish-speaking Americas. In this book, we honor the unique ways in which oral stories are woven and shared by and with children. In choosing the cover for our book, we also wanted to honor the cultural heritage of visual storytelling; therefore, we chose to present an *arpillera*, a contemporary form of textile art created by Latin American women. The arpilleras, sometimes called *cuadros parlantes* (talking portraits) are three-dimensional sewn cloths that portray scenes of everyday life, much like personal narratives of everyday experience. The arpilleras began as a form of underground communication and political protest in the Chile of Pinochet, most notably as a way in which mothers protested *without words* the disappearance of their sons and daughters. Since then, this form of art has traveled north to give voice to the hands of other Latin American women. The arpillera on the cover is the work of Doña Julia Rosa Huaranga Vilchez from Lima, Peru, who was gracious enough to weave for us this tale of children playing in the streets of an Andean city. We thank her for her talent and generosity. We would also like to thank Carlos Fernández Loayza for helping us photograph Doña Julia Rosa's work.

At Cambridge University Press, we wish to thank Eric Schwartz, April Potenciano, and Ken Karpinski, who handled the creation of this volume so skillfully and painlessly from start to finish.

Finally, we gratefully thank our families and all of our friends for their continued support. Alison thanks Frank, Nick, and Will Ziolkowski for their love and abiding interest in absolutely everything. Gigliana gives heartfelt gracias to Jaime for his unconditional support and dedicates her work in this book to the memory of her sister, Cecilia, *con mucho amor, estés donde estés.* Allyssa thanks Charlie, Nick, and Jessamyn for many reasons.

1

Introduction

ALISON L. BAILEY, ALLYSSA McCABE, AND GIGLIANA MELZI

A first task is to define the term used to describe the individuals we are talking about in this book. The primary term we have chosen is *Latino*; as the broadest and most inclusive term (Suárez-Orozco & Páez, 2002), it reflects the complex issues involved in the identities of Spanish-speaking people – issues such as citizenship, ethnicity, race, native language(s), politics, gender, social class, and generation. The term *Latino* has all too often been used in American research to refer exclusively to individuals immigrating to the United States from a country in the Spanish-speaking regions of the Americas and the Caribbean. Instead, in this book we are expanding the use of the term to also include individuals who are still living in their country of origin across Spanish-speaking Latin America. In this way, we align ourselves with the use of the term *Latino* in Latin America itself (i.e., as an abbreviation of *Latino Americano*). In choosing the primary term *Latino,* we in no way mean to minimize the ethnic, political, social preference, and ideological orientations of individual authors and/or Spanish-speaking communities across the United States who may call themselves Chicano, Hispanic, Mexicano/Mejicano, and so forth. For an insightful personal discussion of these nomenclature issues, see Shorris (1992).

The common thread of the contributions to this volume is that they portray the development of narrative in Spanish either in monolingual or bilingual settings. All participants have a rich and complex background involving a mix of cultures, a strong sense of the importance of family, and numerous other cultural values that are identified in this introduction and concluding chapters. All chapters also involve children who are developing typically. Our decision to focus on these children stems from a real need to provide detailed information about typical narrative development in Spanish-speaking children to teachers, researchers, speech-language pathologists, and other professionals working with children. There is far too little information about narrative development in Latino children despite its identification as a critical precursor to literacy development in English-speaking children (e.g., Scarborough, 2001; Snow, Burns, & Griffin, 1998; Tabors, Snow, & Dickinson, 2001) and, therefore, a cornerstone of academic success. As we mentioned earlier, without such knowledge, Latino children are at risk of having their cultural differences from European American culture mistaken for deficits and their deficits not properly identified. Moreover, practitioners need to work with the cultural grain of students who genuinely lag behind their peers in order to optimize chances for successful treatment. This volume makes explicit which aspects of narration are valued in the broad Latino community.

In the context of the United States, some argue that there is an overrepresentation of Spanish-speaking children enrolled in special education programs (Artiles & Trent, 1994). Much of the research conducted on Spanish-speaking children has looked at those who are identified using labels such as Specific Language Impaired or Delayed. This volume is an explicit effort to redress that tendency.

That said, Spanish-speaking children are not a monolithic group by any means. Lipski (1994) has a detailed discussion of linguistic variation in *The World's Spanishes*. Thus, our book includes diverse populations, including (1) U.S. Americans whose families come from Puerto Rico, Mexico, Dominican Republic, and El Salvador; and (2) Latin Americans in Peru, Puerto Rico, Costa Rica, Ecuador, and Venezuela. We also have some participants from mixed backgrounds. This diversity is representative of Latino communities around the world. We include a range of Spanish varieties spoken as a first language, along with diverse bilingual and trilingual communities, whose linguistic repertoires might include Spanish, English and indigenous languages such as Quechua (as used in Peru) or Quichua (as used in Ecuador).

REFERENCES

Artiles, A. J., & Trent, S. C. (1994). Overrepresentation of minority students in special education: A continuing debate. *Journal of Special Education, 27*(4), 410–437.

Lipski, J. M. (1994). *Latin American Spanish.* New York: Longman.

Scarborough, H. S. (2001). Connecting early language and literacy to later reading (dis)abilities: Evidence, theory, and practice. In S. B. Neuman & D. K. Dickinson (Eds.), *Handbook of early literacy research, Vol. 1.* NY: Guilford.

Shorris, E. (1992). *Latinos.* NY: Norton.

Snow, C. E., Burns, M. S., & Griffin, P. (1998). *Preventing reading difficulties in young children.* Washington, DC: National Academy Press.

Suárez-Orozco, M. M., & Páez, M. M. (2002). *Latinos: Remaking America.* Berkeley: University of California Press.

Tabors, P. O., Snow, C. E., & Dickinson, D. K. (2001). Homes and schools together: Supporting language and literacy development. In D. K. Dickinson & P. O. Tabors (Eds.), *Beginning literacy with language* (pp. 313–334). Baltimore: Brookes.

PART ONE

PARENT–CHILD NARRATIVES

GIGLIANA MELZI

Children develop narrative abilities through the interactions they have with others on a daily basis. The conversations shared between caregivers and children during these interactions serve as a primary sociolinguistic context in which children gain mastery of the skills necessary to produce and share a coherent story in later years. The language used during these conversations both reflects cultural norms and serves to socialize children into culture-specific practices (Ochs & Capps, 2001; Schieffelin & Ochs, 1986).

Interest in family narrative practices across cultures has increased in the last few decades and studies from various disciplines have contributed to our understanding of the multiple ways in which children across the world develop narrative skills (e.g., Fivush & Haden, 2003; Ochs & Capps, 2001). Despite this interest, however, few studies have investigated Latino families' narrative interactions (e.g., Eisenberg, 1985; Schecter & Bayley, 2002; Torres, 1997) and, to our knowledge, even fewer have gone beyond U.S. borders. The first five chapters of this volume address these gaps by examining the multiple ways in which Latin American and U.S. Latino parents contribute to their children's development.

In chapter 2, Caspe and Melzi examine how mothers from three different countries – Peru, Puerto Rico, and the United States– share a wordless book and support their 3-year-olds' participation in the creation of the story. Like personal narrative conversations, book-sharing interactions constitute an everyday context in which mothers and children share stories together. However, book-sharing interactions have received relatively less attention from investigators interested in children's development of narrative skills. Caspe and Melzi's results show that mothers from each cultural group support their children's interactions in distinct ways. Not only were there the expected cultural differences in the narrative discourse used by the U.S. American and Latin American dyads, but there were also differences between the two Spanish-speaking groups. Their findings underscore the heterogeneity of Spanish-speaking Latin American populations.

3

Narrative is a genre of oral discourse and thus has its origins in the earliest social exchanges between the child and important others. In chapter 3, Stansbery examines these origins by investigating cultural differences in the everyday routines between Costa Rican and U.S. American mothers and their 6-month-old infants. Stansbery's microanalysis of both the verbal and nonverbal content of routine interactions, such as bathing and feeding, shows cultural differences in early sociocommunicative patterns, setting the stage for later culture-specific discourse and narrative practices.

Most of the research on the social origins of children's narrative skills has focused on mother–child conversations. The lack of research with other family members, such as fathers, gives us an incomplete picture of family narrative practices. The few studies with U.S. European American fathers' discourse have shown differences in the ways mothers and fathers engage their children as well as in the topics they choose to highlight during narrative conversations (Buckner & Fivush, 2000; Reese, Haden, & Fivush, 1996). In chapter 4, Cristofaro and Tamis-LeMonda address the neglected contribution of fathers in children's narrative development. Their results show both similarities and differences in the topics mothers and fathers choose to discuss with their preschool children and draw our attention to the role of narratives in children's cultural socialization.

The seminal work of Labov and Waletzky (1967) on conversational narratives has served as a springboard for contemporary studies on children's narratives. In their work, they identified two major functions in the stories we create and share with others: referential and evaluative. The final two chapters in this part address the evaluative function of the narratives shared by mothers and children from two South American communities. The evaluative function of narratives – that which transmits subjective interpretation of the experienced event – plays a critical role in various socioemotional and cognitive aspects of children's development (Fivush, Haden, & Reese, 2006). In chapter 5, Fernández and Melzi examine gender and age variations in the use of one type of evaluation – internal-state language – across two narrative contexts. In chapter 6, King and Gallagher examine the use of evaluative morphology and emotion words in the narratives shared by Andean Ecuadorian mothers and their preschool-aged children. Taken together, these two studies illustrate how culture-specific expectations about gender are embedded and transmitted in the narratives shared by parents and children.

REFERENCES

Buckner, J. P., & Fivush, R. (2000). Gendered themes in family reminiscing. *Memory*, 8(6), 401–412.

Eisenberg, A. R. (1985). Learning to describe past experience in conversation. *Discourse Processes*, 8(2), 177–204.

Fivush, R., & Haden, C. A. (2003). *Autobiographical memory and the construction of a narrative self: Developmental and cultural perspectives.* Mahwah, NJ: Lawrence Erlbaum.

Fivush, R., Haden, C. A., & Reese, E. (2006). Elaborating on elaborations: Role of maternal reminiscing style in cognitive and socioemotional development. *Child Development, 77*(6), 1568–1588.

Labov, W., & Waletzky, J. (1967). Narrative analysis: Oral versions of personal experience. In J. Helm (Ed.), *Essays on the verbal and visual arts* (pp. 12–44). Seattle: University of Washington Press.

Ochs, E., & Capps, L. (2001). *Living narrative: Creating lives in everyday storytelling.* Cambridge, MA: Harvard University Press.

Reese, E., Haden, C., & Fivush, R. (1996). Mothers, father, daughters, sons: Gender differences in reminiscing. *Research on Language and Social Interaction, 29,* 27–56.

Schieffelin, B. B., & Ochs, E. (1986). Language socialization. *Annual Review of Anthropology, 15,* 163–191.

Schecter, S. R., & Bayley, R. (2002). *Language as cultural practice: Mexicanos en el Norte.* Mahwah, NJ: Lawrence Erlbaum.

Torres, L. (1997). *Puerto Rican discourse: A sociolinguistic study of a New York City suburb.* Mahwah, NJ: Lawrence Erlbaum.

2

Cultural Variations in Mother–Child Narrative Discourse Style

MARGARET CASPE AND GIGLIANA MELZI

Key Words: mother-child narratives, Latino children, Spanish, mother-child book sharing, cultural variations

ABSTRACT

Children develop narrative ability in the context of the conversations they have with significant others, mainly family members. Within these conversations, children acquire language and literacy and become socialized to the discourse patterns, beliefs, and values of the community in which they live. Recent research has begun to highlight that Latino mothers scaffold their children's narratives differently than might mothers from other cultures. The goal of the current study was to explore how Peruvian, European American, and Puerto Rican mothers of comparable socioeconomic backgrounds, living in their country of origin, scaffolded their children's narratives in a semistructured book-sharing paradigm. Specifically, the study addressed two main questions: (1) Do variations exist in the styles that Puerto Rican, European American, and Peruvian mothers use to engage their children while sharing a wordless children's picture book? (2) Are there cultural preferences in these styles?

As part of a larger study, 45 mothers were visited in their home and asked to share a wordless children's picture book with their children. Book-sharing interactions were audiotaped, transcribed, and verified using a standardized format and coded at the utterance level. Results of a cluster analysis revealed two book-sharing styles that hinged on the degree to which mothers provided or requested narrative information from their children. Storytellers provided rich narrative information to their children and took control of the narrative, whereas storybuilders coconstructed the story with their children, creating a story together. The book-sharing style that mothers adopted was associated with culture. Peruvian mothers were more likely to adopt a storytelling style, whereas European American and, to a lesser extent, Puerto Rican mothers were more likely to adopt the storybuilding style. Findings demonstrate the heterogeneity and similarities among different Latino groups and are discussed in relation to implications for educational programs for families and their young children.

INTRODUCTION

Mother:	*Había una vez un niño que cuidaba mucho a su ranita, ¿verdad?*	Once upon a time, there was a boy that took care of his frog, right?
Child:	*Sí.*	Yes.
Mother:	*Y el perrito estaba jugando con la ranita. Está pensativo. Parece que le dejaron abierta la jarra y la ranita se salió. Y el nene estaba durmiendo. ¿Con quién está durmiendo el nene aquí?*	And the dog was playing with the frog. He looks thoughtful. It seems like they left the jar open and the frog left. And the boy is sleeping. Who is the little boy sleeping with here?
Child:	*Con el perrito.*	With the dog.
Mother:	*Y ¿qué pasó?*	And what happened?
Child:	*Se cayó.*	He fell.
Mother:	*No, mira lo que pasó.*	No, look what happened.
Child:	*Se rompió.*	It broke.
Mother:	*¿A la ranita qué le paso? Se fue, ¿verdad?*	And to the frog, what happened? He left, right?
Child:	*Y estaba ahí.*	And he's there.
Mother:	*Sí, pero la ranita se escapó. El nene comienza a buscar a la ranita.*	Yes, but the frog escaped. The boy then begins to look for his frog.

In the previous excerpt, Rosalie, a 3-year-old Puerto Rican girl, and her mother begin to tell the adventures of a young boy and his dog as they search for the boy's mischievous frog, who escaped from a jar. In conversational contexts such as this one, young children around the world begin to develop the ability to construct and share stories. Narrative is a language-based tool that helps humans organize thoughts and past events in memory, ultimately aiding individuals in the understanding and interpretation of their experiences and surrounding world. Early narrative is important because it is linked to the knowledge and skills young children need to transition into conventional readers (Griffin, Hemphill, Camp, & Wolf, 2004; Snow, Tabors, Nicholson, & Kurland, 1995). Narrative is also important for development in other cognitive and socioemotional areas, such as abstract thinking and self-concept (Dickinson & Tabors, 2001; Fivush & Nelson, 2006; Nelson & Fivush, 2004). Yet there is great individual and cultural variation in the manner and style in which narrative contexts are structured and the discourse adult conversational partners use to scaffold children's storytelling abilities. Adult scaffolding styles, in turn, influence greatly children's expectations of a meaningful story and the ways in which they organize and share their narratives. The purpose of this chapter is to examine how Spanish-and English-speaking monolingual mothers living in three different countries – Peru, Puerto Rico, and the United States – guided their children's narratives as they shared a wordless children's picture book. In particular, we consider the similarities and differences in the ways that two groups of Latino mothers scaffold their preschoolers' narrative skills.

Sociocultural View of Narrative Development

Children's narrative competence emerges in the context of the conversations and stories children have with significant others in their life, primarily those in their family. Based on a Vygotskian (1978) developmental perspective, parents' linguistic contributions scaffold their children's participation in conversations, allowing children to take part in interactions that are richer and more complex than those children could handle alone (Fivush, 1991; McCabe & Peterson, 1991; Reese, Haden, & Fivush, 1993). Over time, children begin to internalize these patterns of narrative discourse and construct their own stories based on the styles utilized by their parents and their community.

Research has examined the ways that parents, mainly mothers, scaffold children's narratives in a variety of conversational contexts – most commonly in personal narrative conversations and book-reading exchanges. Results from studies investigating middle-class European American mothers' personal narrative conversational styles have shown individual differences in the ways that mothers support children's narrative construction. For example, some mothers adopt an elaborative style, engaging in long, richly embellished conversations even when their children do not provide much in the way of spontaneous recall (Fivush & Fromhoff, 1988; McCabe & Peterson, 1991; Peterson & McCabe, 1994; Reese et al., 1993). They ask many questions and offer many details about the events experienced, continually adding new information to cue memory or sequence events for the novice narrator (Bailey, Moughamian, McCabe, & Reynolds, 2005). Other mothers adopt a repetitive (or low elaborative) style, engaging in short conversations during which they provide little descriptive information. In contrast to the highly elaborative mothers, these mothers use a redundant, test-like mode of questioning and probe children for specific pieces of information in the absence of many cues (Fivush & Fromhoff, 1988; Haden, 1998; McCabe & Peterson, 1991; Peterson & McCabe, 1994; Reese et al., 1993). These differences in parental style have been shown to influence both the quantity and quality of narratives produced by preschool children. Researchers have found, for instance, that a more elaborative style is related to children's production of longer narratives and better memory about the past (Fivush, Haden, & Reese, 2006). Moreover, mother–child conversations that are characterized by demanding, decontextualized utterances also enhance children's literacy skills, especially print concepts, vocabulary, and story comprehension (Reese, 1995).

Similarly, researchers have observed individual variations in maternal narrative styles during other narrative contexts – namely, mother–child picture-book reading interactions. Like personal narrative conversations, book-reading interactions provide an opportunity for researchers to understand how mothers and children share stories together. However, unlike personal narratives, book-reading interactions are textual or pictorial. Thus, they are more structured and governed by a predetermined plot that allows researchers to investigate the extent to which mothers adhere to and orate the story at hand or deviate from the prescribed plot through extratextual and nonnarrative comments. For example, Haden, Reese, and Fivush (1996) examined a sample of European American middle-class mothers reading books with their young children and found that maternal book-reading styles fell into one of three types: describers (who describe and elaborate), collaborators (who invite their children's participation), and comprehenders (who ask children for predictions and inferences). These maternal styles of reading were linked to children's later literacy. Controlling for children's initial language skills, children of mothers using a comprehender style had higher vocabulary and story comprehension skills $2\frac{1}{2}$ years later compared with children of mothers using a describer style, whereas children of collaborators had stronger decoding skills in comparison to describers (Haden et al., 1996).

Taken together, research on maternal scaffolding across different contexts has helped build a case that the use of positive feedback, the asking of many questions and fewer directives, and an emphasis on discussion and elaboration of concepts are beneficial for children's development (Eisenberg, 2002; Lonigan & Whitehurst, 1998; Sénéchal, 1997; Whitehurst et al., 1988). This question-and-answer style is usually considered important because it prepares children for the cognitive style emphasized in American schooling (Heath, 1983). However, these characteristics of effective maternal instruction are most commonly observed in middle-class European American families and have been derived from studies with families of this background. Cultural variations must be considered.

Cultural Variations in Maternal Narrative Scaffolding

Interest in family narrative practices has increased in recent decades and across various disciplines, contributing to our understanding of the multiple ways in which children across cultures are socialized to construct and share stories (Fivush et al., 2006; Miller, Cho, & Bracey, 2005; Ochs & Capps, 2001). Preferred communicative patterns of a particular culture or group reflect important differences in beliefs, values, norms, and practices. Therefore, as children become communicatively competent, they are learning not only the structure of their language but also a set of conventions for language interaction embedded in and reflective of the values, attitudes, and beliefs of their community (Garret & Baquedano-López, 2002; Schieffelin & Ochs, 1986a). Subsequently, children develop a general communicative competence that is appropriate to their community. They can then use these competencies like other forms of tacit cultural knowledge.

The cultural differences in communicative patterns are especially salient in situations that include children. These interactions are influenced not only by general norms and values upheld in the larger community but also by the specific beliefs and practices related to children and their development (Garret & Baquedano-López, 2002; Ochs & Schieffelin, 1984; Schieffelin & Ochs, 1986a, 1986b). For instance, the status and role of children in particular groups vary (e.g., lower status versus higher status), leading to different ways of socializing children and engaging with them in conversations (e.g., situation-centered versus child-centered). As a specific example, European American families often prefer to adopt a child-centered upbringing style, considering infants from (or even before) birth to be equal conversational partners. Therefore, in linguistic interactions, parents use self-modifying strategies, such as employing simplified language and fine-tuning their speech to children's linguistic abilities. By contrast, the Mayans of Mexico (Brown, 2001) prefer to adopt a situation-centered upbringing style. Mayan children are either not directly addressed by adults or, when engaged in conversation, are expected to adjust to the demands of the situation. Cultural groups can also differ in specific literacy practices and language routines used with and around children. For example, telling stories through picture books with young children is considered an appropriate literacy activity for European American mothers but is considered more of a "school-like" activity for Mexican American immigrant mothers (Reese & Gallimore, 2000). Therefore, daily parent–child book-sharing among certain Latino subcultures might not be a practice that is customary or encouraged.

Much of the research exploring cultural variations in maternal narrative scaffolding style has focused on comparisons between East Asian (e.g., Chinese, Japanese, and Korean) cultural groups and English-speaking Western societies and primarily in personal narrative conversational contexts. Findings from these studies show that East Asian mothers discourage children from producing elaborated and lengthy narratives by limiting the extent to which children are allowed to introduce their own topics. Parents often interrupt children as a way to keep their contributions succinct (Minami & McCabe, 1991, 1995; Mullen & Yi, 1995) or ask repetitive or test-like questions of their children, providing them with little opportunity for elaboration (Wang, Leichtman, & Davies, 2000). East Asian mother–child conversations, as well, tend to be more hierarchical, with the mother taking a more active role in narrating, whereas European American dyads are more likely to coconstruct, with mother and child being equal participants in the conversation (Wang et al., 2000).

The few studies examining a different conversational context (i.e., book-reading) have also noted cultural differences in the types of supports provided to children that stem from variations in cultural ideologies. Kato-Otani (2004), for example, found that in sharing picture books with their children, East Asian mothers attempt to preserve interpersonal harmony with their children by asking questions that children can answer, whereas middle-class European American mothers ask challenging questions that reflect demands of the elementary school classroom.

Latino Mother–Child Narratives

Pertaining to Latin American and U.S. Latino families, research from anthropology and cultural psychology suggest that groups from a Latin American heritage often emphasize the group over individuals and maintain values characterized by a deep sense of loyalty to the family (Suárez-Orozco & Páez, 2002). Latino parents strive to establish warm and nurturing relationships with their children, placing emphasis on close mother–child relationships, interpersonal responsiveness, and development of children's proper demeanor and sense of dignity (García-Coll, Meyer, & Brillon, 1995; Harwood, Miller, & Irizarry, 1995). These deep-rooted cultural beliefs are reflected in the general communication patterns and literacy practices of Latino families. For example, because children are to be respectful of their parents and elders, they are not expected to take part in adult conversations, to interrupt adults, or to express their preferences or opinions (Delgado-Gaitán, 1994; Valdés, 1996). Teaching interactions in which parents ask children direct questions, to which the answers are known or in which children talk about what they are doing, are not emphasized (Eisenberg, 1986; Valdés, 1996). In narrative interactions, Latino mothers often show a situation-centered approach, in contrast to the child-centered approach upheld by European American mothers. That is, whereas European American mothers scaffold children's narratives in much the same way across different narrative contexts to meet the developmental level of the child, Latino mothers seem to adapt their scaffolding style according to the demands of the situation, varying it according to the social roles (i.e., who is expected to be the narrator or the audience) and ownership of knowledge (i.e., who is deemed to be the expert or the novice) (Melzi, 2000; Melzi & Caspe, 2005; Melzi, Schick & Kennedy, 2007). Accordingly, during narrative interactions with their children, Latino mothers prefer to adopt narrative scaffolding styles that create a sharper distance between the roles of narrator (the expert) and audience (the novice) such that the narrator has the luxury and freedom to create and weave a story in whatever ways she chooses and sees fit (see also Wishard Guerra, chapter 7, this volume).

In the personal narrative context, where children are the experts because they have ownership of the experience, mothers adopt the role of a participatory audience. Eisenberg (1985), for example, found that in Mexican American homes, the majority of conversations involving adults and children were triadic rather than dyadic. Rather than asking questions to initiate conversations between themselves and young children, caregivers would help children initiate and maintain conversations with a third individual. Thus, Mexican American mothers create distance by choosing not to ask questions directly but rather to scaffold children to narrate competently with others. Eisenberg (1985) also demonstrated that Mexican American mothers did not guide their children to produce temporally organized narratives, restructure their children's delivery, or engage in the retelling of experiences as much as European American mothers. This apparent laissez-faire style was a way for mothers to ensure their children had control over the flow of the conversation as a narrator and a sense of connectedness to the parent. In a different study, Eisenberg (2002) compared low-income and middle-class Mexican American mothers and found that, regardless of socioeconomic status, mothers preferred not to engage in questioning of their children. This same tendency has been found with other Latino groups. For example, in a study comparing Central American and European American maternal narrative input, Central American mothers were more focused on fostering children's ability to participate in the social aspects of the narrative task, allowing children to take the story in the direction they chose, whereas European American mothers acted as conarrators and emphasized the organizational aspects of the narrative task (Melzi, 2000). Latino mothers prefer a style that makes a clear distinction between narrator and audience, in which the narrator and holder of the experience is deemed the expert and thus has ownership and control of story content.

During book-sharing interactions, these roles are reversed. In this situation, the mother is the expert, holder of knowledge and skills, and the child is the novice. In a study conducted with middle-class Peruvian and European American mothers in their home country, Melzi and Caspe (2005) found that when sharing a wordless children's picture storybook, Peruvian mothers, in fact, tended to adopt a storytelling style with their children in which the mother served as the sole narrator of an engaging story with minimal child participation. European American mothers, by comparison, tended to adopt a storybuilding style in which they coconstructed the story with their children.

In an extension of that study, Caspe (2007) examined the book-sharing styles of low-income Spanish-speaking Dominican and Mexican immigrant families living in New York City. Three main book-sharing styles emerged: (1) storybuilder-labelers, who coconstructed the story with their child by requesting far more narrative and nonnarrative information than they provided; (2) storytellers, who narrated a rich story with minimal requests of their children; and (3) abridged storytellers, who looked much like storytellers but provided a more concise story. The three styles hinged on the extent to which mothers coconstructed the story with their children (e.g., storybuilders) or told their children an engaging story (e.g., storytellers). The majority of mothers (68%) in the study adopted one of the storytelling styles, whereas the remaining mothers adopted the storybuilding style. More important, controlling for various demographic factors including years of maternal education and children's initial developmental competencies, a storytelling style was positively predictive of children's emergent literacy scores at the end of the school year. Children whose mothers adopted an abridged storytelling style and had participated in preschool for the longest duration of time had the highest literacy scores in the sample. These findings run counter to the general assumption that a question-answer-like interaction is most beneficial for children's language and literacy development and instead emphasize the beneficial nature of a style that creates distance between narrator and audience for this group. One plausible explanation for these findings is that children whose mothers adopted the storytelling styles were more likely to hear rich stories, without interruption, and in turn were exposed to the decontextualized language and phonological skills necessary for transitions to conventional literacy. Even when mothers used a more concise storytelling style (e.g., with less language), children still benefited with more years in their early childhood setting, suggesting that early childhood programs were able to build on and complement the home environment that mothers created.

In a study with low-income Latino parents living in the Western United States, researchers have also found that mothers adopted a multitude of styles when reading books with their children (Boyce, Cook, Roggman, Innocenti, Jump, & Akers, 2004), varying in the extent to which children were included in interactions. In a different study, Hammer, Nimmo, Cohen, Draheim, and Johnson (2005) investigated the book-reading behaviors of African American and Puerto Rican mothers and their Head Start children. The authors found that Puerto Rican mothers were the most likely to adopt a child-centered style in which they produced a lower proportion of utterances than their children. That is, in the child-centered style, the children were the primary storytellers. The authors argued that a child-centered style appears to be consistent with Latino parenting tradition, in which the children are to be nurtured and positive emotions are to be expressed (Hammer et al., 2005). Although the roles of narrator and audience in Hammer and colleagues' study (2005) were reversed from the roles of narrator and audience revealed in the studies by Melzi and Caspe (2005) and Caspe (2007), it is noteworthy that the distance between narrator and audience was maintained. Regardless of whether the mother or the child was the narrator, coconstruction was not the adopted style. It is possible that because Hammer and colleagues (2005) asked parents to read a familiar book (e.g., one that children had read before in their Head Start classroom), the mothers felt comfortable asking children to assume the role of the expert. In Melzi and Caspe (2005) and Caspe (2007), the book presented was unfamiliar to both parents and children, rendering the parent as the expert.

In each of these studies, however, the Latino groups under investigation came from a particular region and background and were compared to a non-Latino group. For example, Puerto Rican families living in the United States were compared to African American families (Hammer et al., 2005), or Peruvian families living in their country of origin were compared to European American families (Melzi & Caspe, 2005). None of these studies compared different Latino groups (e.g., Puerto Ricans to Peruvians), which is unfortunate given that Latinos are a heterogeneous group. Although Latinos might share a language and certain cultural values, they might also differ with regard to the beliefs related to parenting and child development that emerge from different local histories. For example, the Puerto Rican experience is defined by U.S. control of political, economic, and educational systems since 1898, when Puerto Rico became a colony of the United States. The circular migration of Puerto Ricans to and from the United States has substantially influenced the cultural practices of this region. Peru, by contrast, is one of the largest countries in South America with a long and unique history of cultural blending (i.e., *mestizaje*) of Indigenous, Spanish, African, and Asian groups. Thus, although one might expect similarities in Latino groups due to this *mestizaje*, one would also expect differences by region (see chapter 10, this volume, for a discussion of *mestizaje* in children's narrative practices).

Summary and Research Questions

The goal of the present study, then, is to explore how Peruvian, European American, and Puerto Rican mothers of comparable socioeconomic backgrounds, living in their country of origin, scaffold their children's narratives in a semistructured book-sharing paradigm. Three decades of research confirm that children develop narrative ability in the context of the conversations they have with significant others, mainly family members. It is within these conversations that children not only develop the structure of language but also become socialized to the communicative patterns, beliefs, and values of the community in which they live. Recent research has begun to highlight that Latino mothers scaffold their children's narratives differently than might mothers from other cultures. Specifically, as has been noted, Latino mothers seem to create a sharper distance between narrator and audience rather than coconstructing stories, as European American mothers tend to do. However, to date, there are no studies that explore – using the same system of analysis and theoretical standpoints – differences and similarities of scaffolding styles among different Latino and European American groups. This study contributes to the growing body of work that demonstrates how Latino parents scaffold and support their children's developing narrative abilities. It also bridges the gap in the literature pertaining to comparisons and contrasts of differing Latino groups. Specifically, the study asks:

1. Do narrator variations exist in the styles that Puerto Rican, European American, and Peruvian mothers use to engage their children while sharing a wordless children's picture book?
2. Are there cultural preferences in these styles?

We chose to investigate mothers' scaffolding styles during a wordless picture book–sharing task for two main reasons. First, because the book had no words, it was naturalistic enough to compel mothers to engage in narrative interactions according to their cultural conceptualization of the task and to their expectations of the roles narrator and audience might take, regardless of the language (e.g., English or Spanish) used. Second, a wordless picture-book paradigm was standardized enough to provide a stimulus that would minimalize the variability in the overall structure and content of the narrative produced. Thus, a wordless picture book–sharing context was the perfect hybrid of a personal narrative conversation and a book-reading interaction.

We hypothesized that, as in previous research, two main book-sharing styles would emerge that would hinge on the distancing between narrator and audience (Caspe, 2007; Melzi & Caspe, 2005; Melzi et al., 2007). We further hypothesized that mothers from the three cultural groups would differ concerning the book-sharing style they adopted. Specifically, we hypothesized that Peruvian mothers would adopt a storytelling style, whereas European American mothers would adopt a storybuilding style. However, we conceived of the Puerto Rican mothers as a "test case" of a culture in close contact with another. Thus, we hypothesized that it would be reasonable for Puerto Rican mothers to adopt a style much like that adopted by European American mothers because of the political and cultural history linking the two regions. However, it would also be reasonable for Puerto Rican mothers to adopt a style in line with that adopted by Peruvian mothers, with whom they share a language and cultural heritage.

METHODS

Participants

Forty-five mothers and their 3-year-olds participated in this study: 16 mothers and children were recruited in Lima, Peru; 16 dyads were recruited from Boston and New York City, United States; and 13 dyads were recruited from Camuy and Moca, Puerto Rico. Peruvian, European American, and Puerto Rican dyads were monolingual speakers of their respective language, either Spanish or Standard American English. All families belonged to middle- to upper-middle-class socioeconomic backgrounds in their respective country of origin and residence.

Children's ages ranged from 35 to 47 months ($M = 42.04$, $SD = 3.39$). The sample was nearly evenly divided by gender across the three countries (i.e., 8 boys and 8 girls from the U.S., 8 boys and 8 girls from Peru, and 6 boys and 7 girls from Puerto Rico). Approximately 62% of the children ($N = 28$) were either an only or a first-born child; 31% were the youngest in their family; and the remaining children had both an older and a younger sibling. On average, parents reported 11 months for the onset of children's first words. According to parental reports, all children were developing normally and none had substantiated cognitive or language delays. Furthermore, 13 children (i.e., 9 from the Peruvian sample, 3 from the U.S. sample, and 1 from the Puerto Rican sample) had been formally assessed as part of a routine daycare assessment and found to have no developmental or language delays. Of the total children in the sample, 82% attended daycare or preschool, either full-time or part-time; 8 children did not (i.e., 1 Peruvian child, 1 European American child, and 6 Puerto Rican children).

Mothers' ages ranged from 24 to 41 years ($M = 33.13$, $SD = 4.70$). All mothers had completed high school and had also attended post–high school institutions ($M = 16.32$, $SD = 2.14$). However, univariate analysis of variance showed significant differences between a mother's total years of education and country of origin [$F(2, 43) = 4.85$; $p < .05$]. Post hoc analysis using the Dunnett T3 test showed significant differences between European American and Puerto Rican mothers' total years of education ($M = 17.56$, $SD = 2.48$ versus $M = 15.65$, $SD = 1.18$, respectively; $p < .05$). Of the 45 dyads, 87% were members of a two-parent home and 13% (6 dyads) were members of a single-parent home headed by mothers; 76% of the sample lived only with members of their nuclear family.

Procedure

As part of a larger study, a female researcher (matched by language and nationality/ethnicity) visited mothers and children in their home. Mothers had been told that the researcher was interested in investigating how children talked with family members. Mothers were first asked to engage in a conversation with their child about six past events the child had recently experienced.

Once the dyad completed the task, mothers were asked to share with their children a wordless book, *Frog, Where Are You?* (Mayer, 1969). This particular wordless book was chosen because it has been used successfully to elicit narratives from children of different cultural and linguistic backgrounds, and it provided a semistandardized context for comparisons among the three cultural/linguistic groups under investigation (e.g., Berman & Slobin, 1994; Melzi & Caspe, 2005). Mothers were instructed to share the book with their children as they normally would. They were allowed to take as much time as they needed and were instructed to engage children and treat their comments as they normally would. The researcher was in the home at the time of the recording but did not interact with either mother or child during the reading session.

Transcription, Segmentation, and Coding of Interactions

Tapes were transcribed using a standardized format, Codes for the Analysis of Human Language (CHAT), which is available through the Child Language Exchange System (CHILDES; MacWhinney, 2000). Tapes were transcribed by native speakers of the respective languages and were verified by English–Spanish bilinguals.

Book-sharing conversations were segmented into three speech events: (1) prereading exchanges, which were identified as the moment the tape began and consisted of all dialogue about the book prior to engaging in the story (e.g., title, author, predictions of what the story is about); (2) reading exchanges, which included all conversation about the pictures in the book, identified by either linguistic (e.g., "one day," "once upon a time," or *"vamos a ver"* ["let's see"]) or pictorial cues (e.g., mention of bedroom, jar, or moon) that are not identifiable from the cover page; and (3) postreading exchanges, which were defined as dialogue that took place after the book had been completed and was not related to the final picture in the book (e.g., questions about how the child liked the story, review questions to test the child's comprehension). Prereading and postreading were not submitted to quantitative analyses because not all dyads engaged in these types of interactions. In instances where mothers read the book multiple times, only the first reading was coded and analyzed.

Each maternal and child utterance was coded for pragmatic functions and narrative content based on an adaptation of coding schemes developed by Melzi and Caspe (2005) and Reese et al. (2003) (Kappa Statistic = .94, calculated on 20% of transcripts). As with personal narratives, utterances were identified at the time of transcription by grammatical closure and intonation. Pragmatic functions were divided into two mutually exclusive codes: provision of information (e.g., declarative statements) and request of information (e.g., questions, fill-in-the-blank statements).

Content was divided into two mutually exclusive categories: narrative and nonnarrative. Narrative content was further divided as referential (e.g., descriptions, events, and labels) or evaluative (e.g., nonevents, descriptions of internal states, intentions, reported speech) (Labov & Waletsky, 1967). Nonnarrative information included related information (e.g., an event brought about by the story, references made about the task of reading, correction of partner's comment, clarifications) and nonrelated information (e.g., talking about the investigator, talking about the child's well-being). Included here were all single-word utterances (e.g., "oh," "yeah," "ya"). Last, book-literacy–related utterances included nonnarrative information such as general factual information (e.g., reciting definitions, counting) as well as knowledge about conventions of books and print (e.g., talk about the book itself, naming characters in the story). Figure 2.1 provides definitions of these codes along with examples.

Book-Sharing Styles

We first read the series of 45 book-sharing transcripts to develop a general sense of the mother–child interactions. Overall, interactions were warm and mothers and children were involved and engaged in the task. There was, however,

CODE	DEFINITION	EXAMPLE
PRAGMATIC FUNCTION		
Provide	Statement or provision of information in "telling" or declarative form.	No podía encontrar a la rana en ningún lugar. [HE COULDN'T FIND THE FROG ANYWHERE)
Request	Elicitation of information in "questioning" form.	¿Dónde está la ranita? [WHERE IS THE LITTLE FROG?]
NARRATIVE CONTENT		
Label	Provision of or request for names of objects and pictures in the book.	Éste es un perro [THIS IS A DOG].
Description	Provision of or request for descriptions, explanations or elaboration of plot information provided in the pictures.	El niño está sentado en la cama [THE BOY IS SITTING ON THE BED].
Event	Provision of or request for actions and occurrences that move the story forward and are therefore told in the past.	El niño y sus amigos caminaron al agua [THE BOY AND HIS FRIENDS WALKED TOWARDS THE WATER].
Evaluation	Provision of or request for judgment, subjective information, or speculations about the story events including nonevents, descriptions of internal states, intentions, predictions, defeats of narrative expectations, conventional onomatopoeic forms, reported speech, and causality.	Ojalá que el niñito encuentre a su rana [LET'S HOPE THAT THE LITTLE BOY FINDS HIS FROG].
NON-NARRATIVE CONTENT		
Conversation	Provision of or request for confirmations, corrections, clarifications or responses to a partner's previous utterance.	Muy bien, tú sabes mucho [VERY GOOD, YOU KNOW A LOT].
Book literacy-related	Provision of or request for general knowledge such as definitions and counting, the process of booksharing, connections to personal experience and the naming of characters.	Las abejas pican [BEES STING].

Figure 2.1. Coding Scheme.

variability in the number of times the story was shared. The majority of dyads read the storybook once (i.e., 10 Peruvian, 14 European American, and 12 Puerto Rican dyads). The remaining dyads read the story at least twice (i.e., 1 European American dyad, 1 Puerto Rican, and 4 Peruvian dyads read the story twice, 2 Peruvian dyads read it three times). There was also variability in the ways in which dyads began and finished the story: 31 dyads engaged

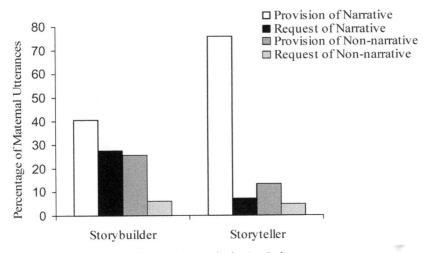

Figurez 2.2. Book-sharing Styles.

in prereading (i.e., 9 Peruvian, 14 European American, and 8 Puerto Rican dyads). During the prereading interaction, mothers and children talked about the cover page, predicted what the story was about, or gave names to the boy and the dog. Likewise, 35 of the dyads engaged in postreading (i.e., 12 Peruvian, 14 European American, and 9 Puerto Rican dyads). During the postreading interaction, mothers asked children whether and what they liked about the story, talked about their general impressions of the story, or asked whether they wanted to read the story again.

To identify maternal narrative styles, a k-means cluster analysis was conducted on proportion of frequencies (i.e., controlling for length of conversation) of four major maternal discourse variables regardless of cultural group: maternal provisions of narrative information, maternal requests for narrative information, maternal provisions of nonnarrative information, and maternal requests for nonnarrative information. Although there were no differences in length of the mothers' narrative contributions by culture, we chose to control for length because we were interested in the proportion of the story that mothers were dedicating to these four narrative components (Hoff-Ginsburg, 1992). We were interested in the style and quality of maternal talk; results identified two narrative clusters and are depicted in Figure 2.2.

Descriptively, the first cluster, labeled "storybuilders," contained 57.8% of the sample ($N = 26$) and was characterized by the highest proportion of requests for narrative and nonnarrative information of the three groups but the lowest proportion of narrative provisions. The second cluster, labeled "storytellers," contained 42.2% of the sample ($N = 19$) and was characterized by providing the highest proportion of narrative and nonnarrative information of the three groups but only making moderate requests for narrative and nonnarrative

Table 2.1. *Means and standard deviations for proportion of maternal variables by style (N = 45)*

	Storybuilder (N = 26)	Storyteller (N = 19)
	M(SD)	M(SD)
Provide Narrative	40.60 (11.15)	75.81 (13.30)**
Request Narrative	27.52 (17.90)	7.23 (6.46)**
Provide Nonnarrative	25.42 (12.12)	13.31 (6.50)**
Request Nonnarrative	6.12 (4.48)	4.85 (3.01)

**$p < .001$

information. The means and standard deviations for each of the four major maternal variables used in the cluster analysis are presented in Table 2.1.

There was a significant difference between the two styles regarding how much narrative information was provided ($F(1, 43) = 92.95$, $p < .001$) and requested ($F(1, 43) = 22.187$, $p < .001$). Storytellers provided significantly more narrative information, whereas storybuilders requested significantly more narrative information. There was also a significant difference between the two styles regarding how much nonnarrative information the mothers provided ($F(1, 43) = 15.60$, $p < .001$). Storybuilders provided more nonnarrative information than storytellers.

Taken together, these data suggest that the two styles differed from each other on two important dimensions: namely, the provision or request of narrative information. Mothers who adopted a storytelling style relied predominantly on telling the story to their children (i.e., providing narrative), whereas mothers who adopted the storybuilder style tended to ask far more questions of their children than the storyteller-style mothers and relied mostly on coconstructing the story (i.e., requesting narrative).

The following excerpts provide qualitative examples of the two book-sharing styles identified. Each excerpt refers to the same series of pages in the story in which the boy searches for his frog in the forest and encounters a variety of different animals along the way, none of which are the frog. The first two excerpts demonstrate the storybuilder style in which European American and Puerto Rican mother–son dyads went through a question-and-answer session of describing the pictures and conjecturing what the characters might have been thinking or how certain events might have happened. The European American mother based her comments on her child's previous utterance and continued to ask him questions about his hypotheses (see Excerpt 1). The Puerto Rican mother in the second example led her child through a series of picture descriptions. She corrected her child's mistakes and asked her child to explain events and actions (see Excerpt 2).

Excerpt 1: A European American Storybuilder

English Original

Mother:	Now what's happening?
Child:	Bees.
Mother:	Yeah. Who's looking at the bees?
Child:	The dog.
Mother:	The dog is looking at the bees. And what's the boy doing?
Child:	Mmm crawling in that hole.
Mother:	You think he thinks the frog is there?
Child:	Yeah.
Mother:	[*Laughs*] Uh oh!
Child:	But is the frog there?
Mother:	Who's there?
Child:	A chipmunk.
Mother:	A chipmunk. I don't think that's what the boy was looking for. Is it?
Child:	No
Mother:	No he's kinda surprised. Isn't he?
Child:	Yep.
Mother:	Boy! That dog and that boy keep looking for that frog! Uh oh! Now what happened with the bees?
Child:	They're flying around.
Mother:	Uh huh. And what happened to their whole house?
Child:	Wrecked.
Mother:	It got wrecked. How did that happen?
Child:	I don't know.
Mother:	You think the bees are happy about that or sad?
Child:	Sad.
Mother:	Yeah. And where'd the boy go? I don't even see the boy. Oh, there he is. What's he doing?
Child:	He's looking for the frog in the tree.
Mother:	Do you think he's gonna find the frog in the tree?
Child:	Maybe he's gonna go in.
Mother:	Do you think the boy would fit in there?
Child:	No.

Excerpt 2: A Puerto Rican Storybuilder

	Spanish Original	English Translation
Mother:	*¿Y aquí que le pasó? ¿Qué es esto que hay aquí?*	And here, what happened to him? What is this here?
Child:	*Un sapo que está triste.*	A frog that is sad.
Mother:	*No, eso es un . . .*	No, this is a . . .
Child:	*Está molesto.*	He's mad.
Mother:	*No, pero eso no es un sapo. ¿Qué es esto?*	No, but this isn't a frog. What is this?

Child:	*Un xx.*	A xx[1].
Mother:	*Un ratoncito. Pero mira, el perro está tratando aquí de coger la . . .*	A little mouse. But look at the dog, he's trying here to get the. . . .
Child:	*¡Las abejas!*	The bees!
Mother:	*Abejas. Sí. Entonces aquí el perro, mira lo que hace. ¿Tratando de qué?*	Bees. Yes. Then, here is the dog. Look, what's he doing? Trying to what?
Child:	*A picar abejas.*	To sting bees.
Mother:	*Que le piquen las abejas. Y el niño, mira, ¡qué hace el niño? ¿Qué le pasa al niño?*	That the bees sting him. And the boy, look, what is the boy doing? What's happening to the boy?
Child:	*[No responde]*	[No answer]
Mother:	*Trepándose en el arbolito.*	He's climbing the little tree.

The next two excerpts provide an example of the storyteller style, in which a Peruvian mother narrated the events of the episode to her daughter in an engaging manner and a Puerto Rican mother narrated the episode to her son. The Peruvian mother asked for her child's contribution at only two points in the story. In the first instance, the mother asked the child to remember a time she herself had been stung by a bee. In the second instance, the mother pauses to ask her child the name of an animal (presumably, because the mother truly did not know what to call the animal). Moreover, the child provided only one spontaneous contribution, when she believed she had thought she might have found the frog. Overall, the narrative is filled with rich evaluations and descriptions, embedding onomatopoeia and reported speech techniques to make the story come alive (see Excerpt 3).

Excerpt 3: A Peruvian Storyteller

	Spanish Original	**English Translation**
Mother:	*Mira. Llegaron a un árbol donde estaba colgado un panal de abejas en una gorrita. ¿Te acuerdas que una vez te picó la abejita?*	Look. They got to a tree where a beehive was hanging from a branch. Do you remember the one time you were stung by a bee?
Child:	*Sí.*	Yes.
Mother:	*Te picó, ¿no es cierto? Estas son las abejitas, mira. Y viven en este panal, redondos grandes. "Zzzz" salen las abejitas, "zzzz" volando. Y Bobby [el perro] está ladrándole al panal y a las abejas. Y Carlitos [el niño] encontró un huequito en el árbol. En el tronquito y gritaba, "¡Ranita,*	It stung you, you remember? These are the bees, look. And they live in this hive, big and round. "Zzzz" the bees go out, "zzzzz" flying. And Bobby [the dog] is barking at the beehive and at the bees. And Carlitos [the boy] found a little hole in the tree. And he called, "Froggie!

---

[1] "xx" refers to a word that was unintelligible.

Spanish Original	English Translation
Ranita!" Pero parece que nadie había. No había ninguna rana. Y Bobby estaba ladrando. Y en eso las abejitas, "zzzz," seguían volando. ¡Uy! Pero mira quién salió del hueco acá ¿Qué es esto? Un ratón [pausa] o ¿qué cosa es?	Froggie!" But it seemed that there wasn't anyone in. There was no frog. And Bobby was barking. And then, the little bees, "zzzz," continue to fly. Oh! But look who came out of that hole here. What is that? A mouse, or [pause], what is it?

Child: *Una ratita.* — A little rat.

Mother: *Una ratita que estaba en el hueco. Parece que le mordió la nariz a Carlitos porque mira como se está sobando su naricita. ¡Entonces de tanto ladrar parece que el panal de abejas se cayó! En eso Carlitos se subió a un árbol. Este árbol tiene un hueco. Entonces se subió al árbol y estaba gritando "¡ranita ranita!" y la ranita no salía. Carlitos estaba triste entonces.* — A little rat was in the hole. It seems that it bit Carlitos' nose because look how he was rubbing his little nose. Then, from all that barking the beehive fell! Suddenly, Carlitos climbed the tree. This tree has a hole. Then he climbed the tree and was yelling, "Froggie! Froggie!" and the froggie was not coming out. Carlitos was therefore sad.

In the final excerpt, a Puerto Rican mother narrated for her son in a story-telling style. For the most part, she elicited little interaction, using a wide variety of onomatopoeia and reported speech devices to add excitement and illustrate action. The mother requested her son's participation in two instances, but it was not clear whether these are rhetorical questions used as a storytelling technique. In the first instance, the child answered the mother's question, but in the second instance, he interpreted the question as a storytelling device and responded by encouraging the mother to continue (see Excerpt 4).

Excerpt 4: A Puerto Rican Storyteller

Spanish Original	English Translation

Mother: *Y entonces Tapeto [el niño] metió la nariz dentro de un hoyo preguntando por Sapito. "¡Sapito! ¡Sapito! ¿Dónde estás?" ¡Ah, y mira! Salió el animalito y "¡Pow!"* — And then Tapeto [the boy] stuck his nose in the hole asking for Froggie. "Froggie! Froggie! Where are you?" Oh, look! A little animal came out and "Pow!"

Child: *Se comió.* — He ate.

Mother: *Le mordió la nariz. Mhmm. Y entonces Tapeto se enojó un poquito pero después le quitó porque estaba bien preocupado. Lo que él quería era encontrar al sapito. Y ¿mira lo que le pasó aquí? ¿A Camio [el perro] qué le paso?* — He bit his nose. Mhmm. And then Tapeto got a little mad but then he let it go because he was very worried. He wanted to find the frog. And look what happened here? What happened to Camio [the dog]?

Child: *Se dio un golpe.* — He got hurt.

Mother:	*El panal de abejas se cayó como el estaba jugando con el panal de abejas, "¡Pow!" Se cayó y todas las abejas se salieron del panal. Pero mira entonces, ¿sabes lo que hizo Tapeto?*	The beehive fell because he was playing with the beehive. "Pow!" It fell and all the bees came out of the hive. But look then. Do you know what happened to Tapeto?
Child:	*¿Qué?*	What?
Mother:	*Se trepó en un árbol y empezó a gritar buscando al sapito, "¡Sapito, sapito amigo mío! ¿A dónde estás Sapito? ¡Por favor regresa!"*	He climbed a tree and began to shout looking for the Froggie, "Froggie, my friend! Where are you, Froggie? Please come back!"

Differences Among Styles for Mothers and Children

To determine whether mothers in the two different book-sharing styles differed in the narrative information discussed, one-way analyses of variance (ANOVAs) were conducted on the mean percentages of total maternal narrative discourse provided (e.g., both provisions and requests of narrative information combined). Bonferonni adjustments were employed as a more conservative control for Type I error rates. There was a statistically significant difference in the mean percentage of evaluations ($F(1, 43) = 11.14$, $p < .01$) and events ($F(1, 43) = 26.49$, $p < .001$) in the two clusters discussed. Specifically, mothers who adopted the storytelling style had a higher mean percentage of evaluations ($M = 25.24$, $SD = 8.37$) than storybuilders ($M = 17.02$, $SD = 7.99$) and a higher mean percentage of events ($M = 20.76$, $SD = 6.62$) than storybuilders ($M = 10.10$, $SD = 7.03$). There were no differences in the number of descriptions the two groups used.

In addition, an analysis was conducted to explore differences in how much and what children talked about by maternal book-sharing style. There was a statistically significant difference in the children's amount of talk between the two maternal styles ($F(1, 43) = 8.95$, $p < .01$). As expected, children of storybuilders ($M = 85.08$, $SD = 61.18$) talked more than children of storytellers ($M = 39.05$, $SD = 31.79$). To determine whether children in the two different book-sharing styles differed in *what* they talked about, four one-way ANOVAs were run to look at differences in percentage of narrative information (including total descriptions, events, and evaluations) that children contributed by book-sharing style. Bonferonni adjustments were employed as a more conservative control for Type I error rates. There were no statistical differences in events or descriptive information children provided by book-sharing style; however, there was a significant difference for evaluations ($F(1, 43) = 4.6$, $p < .05$), indicating that children of storybuilders ($M = 13.76$, $SD = 10.43$) were providing more mean proportions of evaluations than children of storytellers ($M = 7.21$, $SD = 9.62$).

Cultural Comparisons in Narrative Styles

Of storytellers, 69% were from Peru ($N = 13$), 5% were from the United States ($N = 1$), and 26% were from Puerto Rico ($N = 5$). Of storybuilders, 12% were from Peru ($N = 3$), 58% were from the United States ($N = 15$), and 30% were from Puerto Rico ($N = 8$). Stated another way, Peruvian dyads favored the storytelling style, whereas European American and Puerto Rican dyads tended to favor the storybuilding style. Specifically, 81% of Peruvians were storytellers, whereas 94% of European Americans and 62% of Puerto Ricans were story-builders. To determine if there were cultural variations in the distribution of the two narrative styles across the two cultural groups, a chi-square was conducted. Chi-square results showed this distribution to be significantly different across the three cultures ($\chi(2) = 18.55$, $p < .001$). As predicted, the great majority of Peruvian mothers adopted the role of sole narrator, whereas most European American mothers adopted the role of conarrators. The interesting test case of cultures-in-contact showed that the Puerto Rican mothers were more similar to the European American mothers than to the Peruvian mothers.

DISCUSSION

The purpose of this chapter was to investigate the cultural variations in the narrative discourse of Peruvian, Puerto Rican, and European American mothers from comparable socioeconomic backgrounds while sharing a wordless children's picture book with their son or daughter. Our first hypothesis – that two main book-sharing styles would emerge – was supported. As in prior research, we found in our data two book-sharing styles that hinged on the degree to which mothers provided or requested narrative information from their children (Caspe, 2007; Melzi & Caspe, 2005). Storytellers provided rich narrative information to their children and took control of the narrative, whereas storybuilders coconstructed the story with their children, creating a story together. Thus, storytellers promoted distance between the narrator and audience, whereas storybuilders maintained less of a distinction between the two roles. We further hypothesized that the book-sharing style mothers adopted would be associated with culture. We demonstrated that this was, in fact, the case. Peruvian mothers were more likely to adopt a storytelling style, whereas European American and, to a lesser extent, Puerto Rican mothers were more likely to adopt the storybuilding style.

Our findings reflected both the heterogeneity and similarities among different Latin American heritage groups. Most striking, Puerto Rican mothers – our "test case" – were more likely to adopt a storybuilding style like the European American mothers rather than a storytelling style like the Peruvian mothers. That differences exist between Puerto Rican and Peruvian dyads highlights the diversity of Latin American groups. Although, as a group, individuals from Latin American backgrounds share a historical past and speak the same language, they do not necessarily share the same assumptions concerning what constitutes appropriate language use. The term *Latino* as used in the United States, is itself a cultural artifact, developed in the 1970s by the U.S. government as an ethnic category. The term *latino/latina* in Spanish has multiple definitions from describing a type of vessel and sail to identifying members of communities that speak a language derived from Latin[2] (Real Academia Española, 1992). The term *Latino* as an ethnic identification label is not widely used in Latin American and Spanish-speaking Caribbean countries, although it is occasionally used as a shortened version of *latino americano* (Latin American). Research shows that when given the choice, Latinos, both within and outside of the United States, prefer to identify with their country of origin rather than as "Latino" (National Research Council, 2006). Thus, although there are aspects of a larger culture that hold individuals from diverse Latin American backgrounds together (e.g., a sense of strong familialism and commitment to family life), there are specific aspects of social exchanges, routines, and habits that differ by nationality and ethnic group (e.g., Quechua Indigenous, Mestizo). Just as important, not only did cultural differences exist but individual differences also emerged in the study. One European American mother and five Puerto Rican mothers adopted a storytelling style, whereas three Peruvian mothers chose a storybuilding style. Thus, storytelling style is not driven by culture alone but is also related to individual preferences and choices.

The differences in maternal narrative scaffolding style are not simply of academic interest but also have important educational implications. For example, the ability to narrate well is an important precursor to literacy. A growing body of evidence shows that children with relatively better developed narrative skills have an educational advantage over children who enter kindergarten with relatively less well-developed narrative abilities (e.g., Dickinson & Tabors, 2001; Griffin et al., 2004). However, children whose narrative interactions with parents more closely resemble what occurs in the classroom are at an advantage (Au, 2005). They tend to enjoy greater success in school than those children whose prior conceptualization of the role of narrative has been attained through everyday experiences that differ from school-like interactions (e.g., Heath, 1983; Michaels, 1991). A child's failure to perform according to the expectations of the teacher might result in that child being denied access to various activities. It might also affect how the teacher deals with that particular student and, thus, the student's opportunities for success. As an example, a child who might not offer new ideas spontaneously but rather waits until the end of a discussion to add his or her thoughts, or answer only briefly, might be considered lagging rather than courteous.

Thus, schools have a responsibility to broaden their conceptualization of what a narrative is and the role of families in scaffolding the storytelling process. Educators and especially teachers of English-language learners must account for the notion that children will come to school prepared in different ways

---

[2] In Spain, for instance, Latino/a is used to refer to anyone who belongs to a community speaking a language derived from Latin (e.g., French, Italians, Spaniards); whereas Latino Americano/a is used to refer to their counterparts in the Americas (e.g, Bolivians, Colombians, Peruvians).

to listen to and narrate stories. There are certain culture-specific ideals for parent–child interactions and storytelling that vary not only between European Americans and other cultural groups but also between and within different Latino groups. Thus, researchers and educators alike must take care when making recommendations or developing curricula for "Latinos" – for not all Latinos are the same. Family literacy programs, in particular, can build programs specifically around the two styles found in this study. Instead of recommending and teaching just one style of interaction, family literacy programs can focus on expanding parents' reading repertoires to include a diverse array of styles. They can also help parents develop the ability to shift styles depending on the type of book and the child's mood, developmental level, and age. Programs that promote just one blanket style might be well intentioned, but these programs might cause more confusion than good. For example, Whitehurst and colleagues in a series of studies (Lonigan & Whitehurst, 1998; Valdez-Menchaca & Whitehurst, 1992; Whitehurst et al., 1988; Whitehurst, Arnold, et al., 1994; Whitehurst, Epstein, et al., 1994; Whitehurst, Zevenbergen, et al., 1999) demonstrated that training parents and teachers to use a "dialogic" reading approach – whereby parents and teachers both use a series of hierarchical questioning techniques to engage children with the story and encourage them to become the active storytellers – can have a significant impact on children's vocabulary. However, the dialogic reading interventions have been conducted in conjunction with school-based teacher components, or only with teachers, with very few Latino families and children. Thus, caution must be used when considering how these findings will apply to Latino parents or to parents more generally, who are typically not as well trained as teachers.

In fact, a growing body of research has begun to reveal the inherent danger in assuming that all parents should adopt a "question–answer" or "dialogic" approach when reading with their preschoolers. Delgado-Gaitán (2001), for example, designed a family literacy project that encouraged Mexican parents to pose a hierarchy of questions while reading books with their children that promoted active coconstruction of the story (e.g., the storybuilding style). Delgado-Gaitán showed that although there were improvements in parents' and children's literacy, the questioning strategies that parents adopted caused confusion for the parents. Parents were overly concerned with the hierarchy of the questions and unaccustomed to working with academic questioning strategies, most of which were formulated for teachers rather than parents (Delgado-Gaitán, 2001). The results from the current study shed light on the findings obtained in Delgado-Gaitán's family literacy project. Some Latino mothers naturally embrace a storytelling style that offers rich descriptions and creates distance between the narrator and audience.

However, it might not be just Latino parents and children who benefit from a storytelling style. It is interesting that Dickinson and Smith (1994) also noted the positive effects of a storytelling style in their research with European American preschool teachers. Specifically, what they termed a performance-oriented style, characterized by limited interaction with children during a story but with rich discussions before and after reading, was found to have the greatest benefit for children's vocabulary growth, in comparison to a more didactic-interactional style. The authors recommended, in contrast to common pedagogical advice, that teachers need not "feel compelled constantly to stop and discuss books at length" (p. 118).

Future research can continue to look at differences in maternal narrative scaffolding style in different contexts; for example, parent–child personal conversations. It would be interesting to determine whether Puerto Rican mothers resemble European American mothers in a task that is less "school-like." Second, future research can begin to understand how different styles lead to different child outcomes. Caspe (2007), in an investigation of low-income immigrant Mexican and Dominican families living in New York, showed that the storytelling and storybuilding styles had differential relationships with children's outcomes. Storytelling was predictive of print-related literacy, whereas storybuilding was predictive of children's use of evaluations in their own independent narratives 6 months later. To tease apart the impact of culture versus socioeconomic variables, the outcomes of these styles must be explored in a sample of middle-upper-class families living in their country of origin.

Last, future studies can begin to understand whether the storytelling and storybuilding styles exist among different Latino groups or whether there are styles that have yet to be determined. For example, Peru is a country divided almost equally between the highlands and the population centers of the coast. This division marks a sharp cultural as well as geographic divide. The inland regions are marked by extreme poverty and subsistence agriculture, whereas the lowlands have produced a wealthier urban culture. Although Peru's history is marked by political unrest, in recent years its government has become more stable and it is a more economically viable area of South America (Rex, 1992). Puerto Rico, in contrast, is a small Caribbean island whose identity is deeply intertwined with that of the United States. Marked by imperialism and migration, Puerto Rico is an American commonwealth with an easy flow of information between the two countries, especially in the realm of education. These different geographical, societal, and political factors come together to create particular beliefs and practices that result in specific trends and patterns in childrearing. Thus, it is not surprising that these two Latino groups adopted different styles. The question remains, however, as to what style other mothers from the diverse range of other Spanish-speaking countries might adopt.

CONCLUSION

In this chapter, we investigated the cultural variations in the narrative discourse of Peruvian, Puerto Rican, and European American mothers from comparable socioeconomic backgrounds while sharing a wordless children's picture book with their children. We found that two book-sharing styles emerged that hinged on the extent to which mothers created distance between narrator and audience. Peruvian mothers were more likely to adopt a style that provided rich information to their children, whereas European American and Puerto Rican mothers were more likely to adopt a style that coconstructed the story with their children. Findings highlight the diversity and strengths of the Latino population, thus leading to a deeper understanding of how culture permeates narrative and literacy practices.

ACKNOWLEDGMENTS

Support for the collection of the data reported herein was provided to the second author of this chapter by New York University Research Challenge Fund. The authors would like to acknowledge Cecilia Baraybar and Rosalie Báez for their data collection efforts in Peru and Puerto Rico.

REFERENCES

Au, K. (2005). *Multicultural issues and literacy achievement.* Mahwah, NJ: Lawrence Erlbaum.

Bailey, A., Moughamian, A., McCabe, A., & Reynolds, K. (2005). *Parental narrative input: A mechanism for straightening out the leap-frog?* Poster presented at American Psychological Society 17th Annual Convention; Los Angeles, CA: May 26–29.

Berman, R. A., & Slobin, D. I. (1994). *Relating events in narrative: A cross-linguistic developmental study.* Hillsdale, NJ: Lawrence Erlbaum Associates.

Boyce, L. K., Cook, G. A., Roggman, L. A., Innocenti, M. S., Jump, V. K., & Akers, J. F. (2005). Sharing books and learning language: What do Latina mothers and their young children do? *Early Education & Development, 15*(4), 371–385.

Brooks-Gunn, J., & Markman, L. B. (2005). The contribution of parenting to ethnic and racial gaps in school readiness. *The Future of Children, 15*(1), 139–168.

Brown, P. (2001). Learning to talk about motion UP and DOWN in Tzeltal: Is there a language-specific bias for verb learning? In M. Bowerman and S. C. Levinson (Eds.), *Language acquisition and conceptual development* (pp. 512–543). Cambridge: Cambridge University Press.

Caspe, M. (2007). *Family involvement, narrative and literacy practices: Predicting low-income Latino children's literacy development.* Unpublished Dissertation.

Delgado-Gaitán, C. (1994). Consejos: The power of cultural narratives. *Anthropology and Education, 25*(3), 298–316.

Delgado-Gaitán, C. (2001). *The power of community: Mobilizing for family and schooling.* New York: Rowman & Littlefield Publishers, Inc.

Dickinson, D. K., & Smith, M. W. (1994). Long-term effects of preschool teachers' book readings on low-income children's vocabulary and story comprehension. *Reading Research Quarterly, 29*(2), 105–122.

Dickinson, D. K., & Tabors, P. O. (Eds.) (2001). *Beginning literacy with language: Young children learning at home and school.* Baltimore: Paul H. Brookes Publishing Co.

Eisenberg, A. R. (1985). Learning to describe past experience in conversation. *Discourse Processes, 8,* 177–204.

Eisenberg, A. R. (1986). Teasing: Verbal play in two Mexicano homes. In B. Schieffelin & E. Ochs. (Eds.), *Language socialization across cultures.* New York: Cambridge University Press.

Eisenberg, A. R. (1999). Emotion talk among Mexican American and Anglo American mothers and children from two social classes. *Merrill-Palmer Quarterly, 45,* 259–277.

Eisenberg, A. R. (2002). Conversations within Mexican-descent families: Diverse contexts for language socialization and learning. *Hispanic Journal of Behavioral Sciences, 24*(2), 206–224.

Fivush, R. (1991). The social construction of personal narratives. *Merrill-Palmer Quarterly, 37,* 59–82.

Fivush, R., & Fromhoff, F. (1988). Style and structure in mother–child conversation about the past. *Discourse Processes, 11,* 337–355.

Fivush, R., Haden, C. A., & Reese, E. (2006). Elaborating on elaborations: Role of maternal reminiscing style in cognitive and socioemotional development. *Child Development, 77,* 1568–1588.

Fivush, R., & Nelson, K. (2006). Parent–child reminiscing locates the self in the past. *British Journal of Developmental Psychology, 24,* 235–251.

García-Coll, C., Meyer, E., & Brillon, L. (1995). Ethnic and minority parenting. In M. Bornstein. (Ed.), *Handbook of parenting: Biology and ecology of parenting* (pp. 189–209). Mahwah, NJ: Lawrence Erlbaum.

Garrett, P. B., & Baquedano-López, P. (2002). Language socialization: Reproduction and continuity, transformation and change. *Annual Review of Anthropology, 31,* 339–361.

Griffin, T. M., Hemphill, L., Camp, L., and Palmer Wolf, D. (2004). Oral discourse in the preschool years and later literacy skills. *First Language, 24,* 123–147.

Haden, C. A. (1998). Reminiscing with different children: Relating maternal stylistic consistency and sibling similarity in talk about the past. *Developmental Psychology, 34,* 99–114.

Haden, C. A., Reese, E., & Fivush, R. (1996). Mothers' extratextual comments during storybook reading: Stylistic differences over time, and across texts. *Discourse Processes, 21,* 135–169.

Hammer, C. S., Nimmo, D., Cohen, R., Draheim, H. C., & Johnson, A. A. (2005). Book-reading interactions between African American and Puerto Rican Head Start children and their mothers. *Journal of Early Childhood Literacy, 5*(3), 195–227.

Han, J. J., Leichtman, M. D., & Wang, Q. (1998). Autobiographical memory in Korean, Chinese, and American children. *Developmental Psychology, 34*(4), 701–713.

Harwood, R., Miller, J. G., & Irizarry, N. L. (1995). *Culture and attachment: Perceptions of the child in context.* New York: Guilford Press.

Hayne, H., & McDonald, S. (2003). The socialization of autobiographical memory in children and adults: The roles of culture and gender. In R. Fivush & C. A. Haden. (Eds.), *Autobiographical memory and the construction of narrative self: Developmental and cultural perspectives* (pp. 99–201). Mahwah, NJ: Lawrence Erlbaum.

Heath, S. B. (1983). *Ways with words.* New York: Cambridge University Press.

Hoff-Ginsburg, E. (1992). How should frequency of input be measured? *First Language, 12,* 233–244.

Kato-Otani, E. (2004, February). Story time: Mothers' reading practices in Japan and the U.S. *Research Digest*, Harvard Family Research Project. Retrieved April 15, 2008 from http://www.gse.harvard.edu/hfrp/projects/fine/resources/digest/reading.html

Labov, W., & Waletsky, J. (1967). Narrative analysis: Oral versions of personal experience. In J. Helm. (Ed.), *Essays on the verbal and visual art*. Seattle: University of Washington Press.

Lee, V. E., & Burkham, D. T. (2002). *Inequality at the starting gate: Social background differences in achievement as children begin school*. Washington, DC: Economic Policy Institute.

Leichtman, M. D., Wang, Q., & Pillemer, D. B. (2003). Cultural variations in interdependence and autobiographical memory: Lessons from Korea, China, India, and the United States. In R. Fivush & C. A. Haden (Eds.), *Autobiographical memory and the construction of narrative self: Developmental and cultural perspectives*. Mahwah, NJ: Lawrence Erlbaum.

Lonigan, C. J., & Whitehurst, G. J. (1998). Relative efficacy of parent and teacher involvement in a shared-reading intervention for preschool children from low-income backgrounds. *Early Childhood Research Quarterly, 13*(2), 263–290.

MacWhinney, B. (2000). *The CHILDES Project (3rd. ed.), Volume I: Tools for analyzing talk: Transcription format and programs*. Mahwah, NJ: Lawrence Erlbaum.

Mayer, M. (1969). *Frog, where are you?* New York: Penguin Books.

McCabe, A., & Peterson, C. (1991). Getting the story: A longitudinal study of parental styles in eliciting narratives and developing narrative skill. In A. McCabe & C. Peterson. (Eds.), *Developing narrative structure*. Hillsdale, NJ: Lawrence Erlbaum.

Melzi, G. (2000). Cultural variations in the construction of personal narratives: Central American and European American mothers' elicitation styles. *Discourse Processes, 30*(2), 153–177.

Melzi, G., & Caspe, M. (2005). Cultural variations in mothers' storytelling styles. *Narrative Inquiry, 15*(1), 101–125.

Melzi, G., Kennedy, J. & Schick, A. (2007, April). *Cultural variations in mother–child discourse strategies across narrative contexts*. Poster presented at the biennial meetings of the Society for Research in Child Development, Boston, MA.

Michaels, S. (1991). The dismantling of narrative. In A. M. McCabe and C. Peterson (Eds.), *Developing narrative structure* (pp. 303–351). Hillsdale, NJ: Lawrence Erlbaum.

Miller, P. H., Cho, G., & Bracey, J. (2005). Working-class children's experience through the prism of personal storytelling. *Human Development, 48*(3), 115–135.

Minami, M., & McCabe, A. (1991). Haiku as a discourse regulation device: A stanza analysis of Japanese children's personal narratives. *Language in Society, 20*, 577–599.

Minami, M., & McCabe, A. (1995). Rice balls versus bear hunts: Japanese and European North American family narrative patterns. *Journal of Child Language, 22*, 423–446.

Mullen, M. K., & Yi, S. (1995). The cultural context of talk about the past: Implications for the development of autobiographical memory. *Cognitive Development, 10*, 407–419.

National Research Council (2006). Multiple origins, uncertain destinies: Hispanics and the American future. Panel on Hispanics in the United States. M. Tienda & F. Mitchell (Eds), *Committee on Population, Division of Behavioral and Social Sciences and Education*. Washington, DC: The National Academies Press.

Nelson, K., & Fivush, R. (2004). The emergence of autobiographical memory: A social cultural developmental theory. *Psychological Review, 111*(2), 486–511.

Ochs, E., & Capps, L. (2001). *Living narrative: Creating lives in everyday storytelling.* Cambridge, MA: Harvard University Press.

Ochs, E., & Schieffelin, B. B. (1984). Language acquisition and socialization: Three developmental stories. In R. Shweder & R. LeVine. (Eds.), *Culture theory: Essays on mind, self and emotion* (pp. 276–320). New York: Cambridge University Press.

Peterson, C., & McCabe, A. (1994). A social interactionist account of developing decontextualized narrative skill. *Developmental Psychology, 30*(6), 937–948.

Real Academic Española (1992). Diccionario de la lengua española. Madrid: Editorial Espasa Calpe, S.A.

Reese, E. (1995). Predicting children's literacy from mother–child conversations. *Cognitive Development,* 10, 381–405.

Reese, E., Cox, A., Harte, D., & McAnally, H. (2003). Diversity in adults' styles of reading books to children. In A. van Kleeck, S. A. Stahl, & E. B. Bauer (Eds.), *On reading books to children: Parents and teachers* (pp. 58–94). Mahwah, NJ: Lawrence Erlbaum Associates.

Reese, E., Haden, C. A., & Fivush, R. (1993). Mother–child conversations about the past: Relationships of style and memory over time. *Cognitive Development,* 8, 403–430.

Reese, L., & Gallimore, R. (2000). Immigrant Latinos' cultural model of literacy development: An evolving perspective on home-school connections. *American Journal of Education, 108*(2), 103–134.

Rex, A. H. (1992). *Peru: A country study.* Washington, DC: GPO for the Library of Congress. http://lcweb2.loc.gov/frd/cs/petoc.html. Accessed 12/20/06.

Schieffelin, B. B., & Ochs, E. (1986a). Language socialization. *Annual Review of Anthropology,* 15, 163–191.

Schieffelin, B. B., & Ochs, E. (1986b). *Language socialization across cultures.* Cambridge, UK: Cambridge University Press.

Sénéchal, M. (1997). The differential effect of storybook reading on preschoolers' acquisition of expressive and receptive vocabulary. *Journal of Child Language, 24,* 123–138.

Snow, C. E., Tabors, P. O., Nicholson, P. A., & Kurland, B. F. (1995). Oral language and early literacy skills in kindergarten and first-grade children. *Journal of Research in Childhood Education, 10*(1), 37–48.

Suárez-Orozco, M. M., & Páez, M. M. (2002). *Latinos: Remaking America.* Berkeley: University of California Press.

Valdés, G. (1996). *Con respeto: Bridging the distances between culturally diverse families and schools.* New York: Teachers College Press.

Valdez-Menchaca, M. C., & Whitehurst, G. J. (1992). Accelerating language development through picture book reading: A systematic extension to Mexican day care. *Developmental Psychology, 28*(6), 1106–1114.

Vygotsky, L. S. (1978). *Mind in society: The development of higher psychological processes.* Cambridge, MA: Harvard University Press.

Wang, Q. (2001) "Did you have fun?": American and Chinese mother–child conversations about shared emotional experiences. *Cognitive Development,* 16, 693–715.

Wang, Q., Leichtman, M. D., & Davies, K. I. (2000). Sharing memories and telling stories: American and Chinese mothers and their 3-year-olds. *Memory, 8*(3), 159–177.

Whitehurst, G. J., Arnold, D. S., Epstein, J. N., Angell, A. L., Smith, M., & Fischel, J. E. (1994). A picture book reading intervention in day care and home for children from low-income families. *Developmental Psychology, 30(5)*, 679-689.

Whitehurst, G. J., Epstein, J. N., Angell, A. L., Payne, A. C., Crone, D. A., & Fischel, J. E. (1994). Outcomes of an emergent literacy intervention in Head Start. *Journal of Educational Psychology, 86(4)*, 542–555.

Whitehurst, G. J., Falco, F. L., Lonigan, C. J., Fischel, J. E., DeBaryshe, B. D., Valdez-Menchaca, M. C., & Caufield, M. (1988). Accelerating language development through picture-book reading. *Developmental Psychology, 24*(4), 552–559.

Whitehurst, G. J., Zevenbergen, A. A., Crone, D. A. & Schultz, M. D., Vleting, O. N., & Fischel, J. E. (1999). Outcomes of an emergent literacy intervention from Head Start through second grade. *Journal of Educational Psychology, 91(2)* 261–272.

3

Early Sociocommunicative Narrative Patterns During Costa Rican Mother–Infant Interaction

PABLO A. STANSBERY

Key Words: protoconversations, mother-infant interaction, Costa Rica, early language development, and school readiness

ABSTRACT

This chapter examines the relationship between sociocommunicative interactive strategies and child early language. Variation in maternal communicative patterns is well documented (Dickinson & Tabors, 2001; McCabe & Peterson, 1991) and has shown how parents who extend discourse with their children elicit narratives from them. Parents who explain and expand conversation with children seem to provide children with experiences that promote the development of more sophisticated language skills. Most of the available research pertains to young North American children who are able to produce at least one- or two-word utterances. This study contributes to this research by exploring parental interactive styles with preverbal infants in a sample of mother–infant dyads from Costa Rica.

INTRODUCTION

Although infants do not have the capacity to narrate, they do participate in early interactions with primary caregivers. Even in the first few months of life, infants are exposed to routine rituals that provide patterns for interaction with significant adult others. Routines like bathing and feeding provide children with predictable patterns of behavior and speech (Trevarthen & Hubley, 1978; Tronick, Als, & Adamson, 1979). Games played between the infant and caregiver, such as "pat-a-cake" and "I'm-going-to-get-you," offer elements common in emergent conversation including turn-taking and partner engagement, observed through pauses and eye gaze. These subtle sociocommunicative exchanges have been labeled *protoconversations* (Stern, 1985; Trevarthen, 1979).

Exposure to early sociocommunicative experiences and interactions fosters early brain development (Thompson, 2001) and replicates some of the demands of literacy (Dickinson & Tabors, 2001). The level of maternal playfulness, sensitivity to infant behavioral cues, responsiveness to infant solicitations for engagement, expansion of infant utterances, and frequent questions by the caregiver of the infant are associated with better articulation, faster vocabulary acquisition, and more genuinely complex sentences (Bretherton, McNew, Snyder, & Bates, 1983; Nelson, 1981).

Can Infants Participate in Early Conversations?

During the last three decades, enormous gains have been made in our understanding of early brain development and infants' cognitive functioning. One key factor is the recognition of the role that social partners play in learning. Infants have the capacity to interpret adult social behavior very early in their attempts to interpret novel events. Very young infants have the capacity for mutual regulation (Stern, 1971, 1974), intersubjectivity (Trevarthen, 1989), organization (Brazelton, Koslowski, & Main, 1974; Fogel, 1977; Stern, 1974), temporal coordination (Beebe, Jaffe, Feldstein, Mays, & Alson, 1985; Beebe & Jaffe, 1992), emotional sequencing (Fogel, 1982), and interpersonal communication (Field, 1977; Fogel & Thelen, 1987).

Much of this newfound interest in social contributors to a child's cognitive capacity to participate in early conversations can be attributed to two important events in infancy studies. First, researchers began to examine the effect that emotions had on young children. Izard (1977) and Ekman (1972) demonstrated how emotional expressions convey very specific messages and have socially communicative value. Soon, investigators grew interested in how children were able to interpret discreet emotional expressions from significant caregivers. Previously, researchers limited their study of emotions to identifying discreet emotions. For example, early influential studies focused on the classification of primary emotions and measurements of internal reactions (Klinnert, Campos, Sorce, Emde, & Svejda, 1983). These studies ignored the social exchange between the infants and their caregivers.

The second historical influence of significance was a resurgence in popularity of two noteworthy theorists: Lev Vygotsky and Margaret Mead. The availability and wide acceptance of Vygotsky's writings in the late 1960s and 1970s motivated a shift to understand individual development within the larger sociocultural context (Vygotsky, 1978). Briefly, Vygotsky emphasized that any developing skills will first emerge during social interaction and through social assistance by a more skilled member of society, the developing child would actively internalize the skill. Interest in the larger social context was also motivated as developmental psychologists began to search for diverse ways of studying child-rearing within other fields, namely anthropology. Margaret Mead's early cross-cultural investigations, for instance (1931, 1935), prompted psychologists and anthropologists to examine child development in the natural setting rather than in a laboratory. Mead's work led to several cross-cultural studies in human development during the 1970s (e.g., Harkness & Super, 1977; Leiderman, Tulkin, & Rosenfeld, 1977; Super, 1979; Whiting & Whiting, 1975). Much of Mead's work grew out of the sociological perspective, which stresses society's influence on mind and self, and the socially constructed process (Mead, 1934). Subsequently, several cross-cultural developmental studies were conducted that emphasize the importance of the child-rearing environment in child development (Rogoff, 2003; Tobin, Wu, & Davidson, 1989; Tronick, Morelli, & Winn, 1987).

As early as the first year of life, children have been shown to reference adults as a method of interpreting experiences (Ainsworth, Blehar, Waters, & Wall, 1978; Sorce, Emde, Campos, & Klinnert, 1985; Thoman, 1979; Trevarthen & Hubley, 1978). Even during the first week of life, infants are actively engaged with their environment and primary caregiver(s) despite their limited motor and verbal capacities. As early as the first month of life, an infant engages in preconversational exchanges and is especially responsive to the caregiver's voice and face. For example, an infant will gaze at the adult's face and respond (Brazelton et al., 1974; Brazelton, Yogman, Als, & Tronick, 1979; Stern, 1974). An infant has the capacity to imitate tongue protrusions (Bower, 1979), mouth opening (Meltzoff & Moore, 1977), and caregiver pitch and duration of speech sounds (Trevarthen, 1989).

By 6 months of age, a child's interest in toys and objects increases as his or her ability to reach and grasp objects develops. As these capacities unfold, the mother–child communicative interaction shifts toward joint attention, in which partners share communication (i.e., smiles, utterances) about an object beyond the dyad. This underscores the Vygotskian notion of scaffolding, in which appropriate early protoconversations can inspire further exploration and understanding of objects in the child's immediate environment. The discovery of these early infant capacities has helped us to translate preverbal interactions as a key steppingstone toward developing conversation and emergent literacy skills in later years.

THE STUDY

Fifty-two middle-class, Costa Rican primiparous mothers and fifty-two middle-class, primiparous Boston mothers participated in the study with their infants at 6 months of age. All mothers and infants met a set of health and sociodemo-graphic criteria to minimize the effect of confounding risk factors that could obscure ethnic and cultural contributions to caregiving profiles and infant adaptation. That is, the study controlled for variables known to affect parenting and infant outcome (e.g., infant birth order, problem pregnancy, and history of substance abuse).

Maternal and infant characteristics for both the United States and Costa Rican samples are described in Table 3.1. Although an effort was made to control for many factors, there were significant differences in maternal age and maternal education between the two cultures. It is also important to note the variation in the level of maternal education within the Costa Rican sample. Costa Rican mothers

Table 3.1. *Mother–infant home observation sample characteristics*

	United States (N = 52)	Costa Rica (N = 52)
Maternal characteristics		
Primiparous	Yes	Yes
Clinically normal pregnancy	Yes	Yes
Uncomplicated delivery	Yes	Yes
No history of substance abuse	Yes	Yes
Middle class	Yes	Yes
Mean & range of maternal age	31.7 yrs. (22–39)	25.4 yrs. (17–43)***
Mean & range of maternal education	15.9 yrs. (12–20)	10.8 yrs. (3–18)***
Mean & range of paternal age	NA	27.9 yrs. (17–45)
Mean & range of paternal education	NA	9.9 yrs. (1–18)
Infant characteristics		
First born	Yes	Yes
Clinically normal	Yes	Yes
Full-term and healthy	Yes	Yes
Infant age	6 months	6 months

*** $p < .001$.

ranged from a low of 3 years of schooling (i.e., third grade) to completion of a graduate degree (i.e., 18 years of schooling) with an average of 10.8 years. This variation in maternal schooling is important when we explore the relationship between maternal education and key early sociocommunicative exchanges during mother–infant interactions. Table 3.2 provides additional descriptive information about the Costa Rican sample. Data were acquired from interviews conducted with the Costa Rican mothers following a 2-hour videotaped home observation.

Mother-infant interactions during common rituals and/or game-playing activities were videotaped. Similar home-based observations of everyday interactions were previously employed in many cross-cultural, cross-national comparison studies of mother–infant interaction (e.g., France, Japan, and Argentina) (see Bornstein, Azuma, Tamis-LeMonda, & Ogino, 1990; Bornstein et al., 1992). The home-observation procedure captures typical sociocommunicative routines as opposed to interactions in an unfamiliar laboratory setting.

Coding of Mother–Infant Communicative Behaviors

The mother–infant interactions were scored using the Caretaker–Infant Home Observation Coding System, a scoring system designed at the Child Development Unit of Boston Children's Hospital (Tronick & Weinberg, 1992. Although the identification of cultural group (i.e., Costa Rican or U.S.) and infant gender was obvious, coders were blind to maternal level of education. In this chapter, I highlight the types of sociocommunicative exchanges that yield

Table 3.2. *Descriptive statistics of mothers and infants in the Costa Rican sample*
(N = 52)

	Frequency	Percent
Costa Rican mothers' characteristics		
Civil Status		
Married	37	72
Free union	3	6
Single	11	22
Planned Pregnancy		
Yes	25	50
No	25	50
Type of delivery		
Vaginal	34	68
Caesarian, unscheduled	10	20
Caesarian, scheduled	6	12
Someone With You During Delivery		
Yes	16	33
No	33	67
Mother Works (at 6 Months)		
Yes	16	32
No	35	68
Infant Characteristics		
Sleeping Arrangements		
Crib, own room	7	14
Crib, parent room	16	32
Parent bed (entire night)	14	28
Parent bed (part of the night)	13	26
Breastfed (to 6 Months of Age)		
Yes	32	64
No	18	36
Gender		
Female	30	59
Male	21	41
	Mean	**Std Dev**
# Infant Visits to Health Clinic in First 6 Months		
Routine	4.2	1.4
Special ("Illness")	1.0	1.2
Physical Characteristics at Birth		
Birth weight (kg)	31.5	3.5
Length (cm)	49.7	2.3
Apgar 1	8.1	1.3
Apgar 5	8.9	0.4

Table 3.3. *Coding hierarchy for maternal affect*

Maternal affect	Definition
Negative	Withdrawal; unresponsiveness; disengagement in face, body, and/or voice. The mother is generally unresponsive, flat, and disengaged. She may seem to be in her own world. This also includes irritation, marked frowns, pokes/jabs, anger, and sharp commands.
Exaggerated positive	Laughter; exaggerated smiles and faces; exaggerated sounds, vocalizations, and songs; exaggerated and arousing games and play behaviors.
Positive	Bright, happy faces; smiles; motherese; games; songs.
Neutral	Attentiveness and interest but no smiles. Facial expressions range from neutral to interest. No motherese vocalizations.
Unscoreable	The mother's affect cannot be seen or heard.

early protoconversation patterns, such as maternal and infant affect, maternal vocalizations, type of touch, and level of social involvement.

Digital time display was recorded on all videotapes and used to track time intervals. A computerized scoring system allowed for scoring to be accomplished by using a computer keyboard. As the videotaped interactions were viewed on a video monitor, the coder was able to code maternal and infant behaviors by striking designated keys.

Interactions were coded using two distinct coding systems: (1) the *micro-analytic affect coding system*, and (2) the *global affect coding system*. Each system offers unique insights to the early communicative strategies employed by mothers with their young infants.

The micro-analytic affect coding system captures maternal affect at 5-second intervals. Affect includes the mother's face and voice to determine her overall affective state. The mother's body gives additional cues to assess the overall affective state. Affect could be based solely on facial expressions or the voice but not typically on the sole basis of body movements. The micro-analytic affect coding system is able to detect subtle expressions in maternal affect during early mother–infant communicative exchanges. One maternal emotion was recorded for each 5-second interval.

Due to the rapid fluctuation of emotions displayed, it was difficult to maintain high reliability when maternal affect was coded on a second-by-second basis. In general, a single affective expression was expressed during a 5-second interval. However, where two or more emotions were expressed, the rarer occurring expression was scored. For example, if the mother maintained an expression of interest (i.e., "neutral") for most of the 5-second interval and smiled briefly during that same interval, the interval was scored as "positive" rather than "neutral." The hierarchy for coding maternal affect, with definitions, is summarized in Table 3.3.

In this sensitive scoring system, only 12 emotional observations were scored for each minute rather than the 60 observations we would have had if we had coded for every second. Mother–infant dyads were observed for 30 minutes, resulting in a total of 360 affective observations.

In the *global affective rating system*, maternal facial expression and vocal tone were each coded on a minute-by-minute basis. Coders recorded the general emotional state of the mother after each minute for the entire 30-minute observation. To distinguish mothers who are generally neutral in affect from those who are generally positive, the mother's face and voice were rated separately on a 2-point scale for the entire minute. This meant there was a total of 30 global affective rating scores for each mother.

RESULTS

The comparison of U.S. and Costa Rican maternal affective expressions and vocalizations reveals subtle yet significant differences in early sociocommunicative patterns. Both U.S. and Costa Rican mothers display positive affect most of the time when interacting with their infants; however, the U.S. mothers, on average, express positive affect more frequently and intensively than Costa Rican mothers. We also find that U.S. and Costa Rican mothers vary in *how* they express their positive affect through tone of voice and affective facial expression. Lastly, Costa Rican infants were exposed to longer periods with no maternal vocalization.

Results summarize the percentage of time mothers employed affective engagement strategies during early conversational exchanges with their 6-month-old infant. Data summarize micro-analytic affective expressions as well as global maternal affect. Specific examples of maternal interaction are described when we examine the impact of maternal level of education on protoconversation. Where noted, differences between cultural groups were examined using analyses of variance.

Between-Cultural Differences

Maternal Facial Expression and Vocalizations
The micro-analytic affect coding system showed that U.S. mothers, on average, expressed positive and exaggerated affective expression with their infant more than the Costa Rican mothers (Table 3.4). Exaggerated positive exchanges include "over-the-top" high-pitched sounds; laughter; and wide-eyed, open-mouthed facial expressions that are typically used to stimulate an infant and which are more than a social smile or positive vocalization.

The micro-analytic coding system is able to detect subtle differences in maternal affect during early mother–infant communicative exchanges. The U.S. mothers' use of positive and exaggerated affect during routine interactions stimulates the child's motivation to communicate. As an infant vocalizes and/or smiles at his or her mother, the mother typically pauses and then responds with a bright face or high-pitched vocalization; this protoconversation is prolonged and reinforced.

Table 3.4. *Percentage of time mothers displayed positive or exaggerated affect with infant*[1]

	United States	Costa Rica	Significance
Maternal Affective Voice Tone			
Exaggerated positive	8%	7%	<.10
Positive	51%	47%	<.001

[1] Based on the scoreable observations of maternal face and voice. Sometimes a mother's face was not seen and/or her voice could not be heard.

The global affective rating system analyzed maternal affective tone of vocalizations and maternal facial expressions separately. Both U.S. and Costa Rican mothers vocalized positive affective tone most of the time when interacting with their infant. However, U.S. mothers, on average, expressed significantly more positive vocalizations than Costa Rican mothers (i.e., 93% U.S., 79% Costa Rican). Conversely, Costa Rican mothers' vocal tone was more neutral than U.S. mothers' (i.e., 21% Costa Rican, 7% U.S.).

With regard to facial affect expression, Costa Rican mothers were significantly more likely to express positive affect in their facial expression than U.S. mothers (i.e., 17% Costa Rican, 15% U.S.). This means that there were more intervals when Costa Rican mothers displayed smiles and/or an illuminated facial expression than U.S. mothers. Table 3.5 summarizes the percentage of intervals in how maternal affect was expressed.

Frequency of Vocalizations
Costa Rican infants were exposed to longer periods with no maternal vocalization. Table 3.5 shows the difference in the number of maternal vocalizations for the 30-minute observation. Occasional/few vocalizations typically included

Table 3.5. *Percentage of time mothers displayed facial affective expressions, tone of voice, and number of vocalizations with infant*[1]

Engagement strategies	United States	Costa Rica	Significance
Maternal Affective Voice Tone			
Positive	93%	79%	<.01
Neutral	7%	21%	<.05
Maternal Facial Expression			
Positive	15%	17%	<.001
Neutral	85%	73%	<.01
Frequency of Vocalization			
No vocalizations	10%	20%	<.001
Few vocalizations	47%	47%	NS
Many vocalizations	43%	33%	NS

[1] Based on the number of minutes that a coder could view the mother's face and hear her voice. Sometimes a mother's face was not seen and/or her voice could not be heard.

Table 3.6. *Level of maternal education for Costa Rican mothers in sample*

Level of maternal education	Frequency	Percent
<6 Grades	16	31
6 –< High school	15	29
>High school graduate	21	40
Total	52	100

periods of silence and approximately 10 or fewer vocal utterances. The category "many vocalizations" was distinguished by a highly verbal mother during an interval. There were no significant differences in the number of intervals classified as "few" or "many" vocalizations between the two communities. However, Costa Rican mothers were twice as likely to be silent for an entire 1-minute interval.

Within-Group Differences: Maternal Education

As mentioned at the beginning of this chapter, the Costa Rican sample in this study offers a unique opportunity to explore the impact of maternal education on early sociocommunicative interactions within the same cultural context. Previous studies examining the influence of maternal schooling on early communicative interactions used samples from differing societies (Chavajay & Rogoff, 2002; LeVine et al., 1994). This Costa Rican sample consisted of members of the dominant culture (i.e., Spanish-speaking, native Costa Rican), all of whom lived within 7 kilometers of each other. However, maternal education ranged from as little as 3 years of formal schooling to a graduate-school degree. Of the 52 Costa Rican mothers, 16 had completed fewer than 6 years of schooling (31%), whereas 21 of the mothers had completed high school (40%) (Table 3.6).

To examine the relationship between maternal education and sociocommunicative exchange, a Pearson's correlation was used. Maternal education was positively correlated with the use of exaggerated positive affect ($r = .36$, $p < .01$) and global positive affective vocalizations ($r = .29$, $p < .05$) and negatively correlated with the number of "no vocalization" intervals ($r = -.27$, $p < .05$). This suggests that the mother's exposure to schooling influences early sociocommunicative interaction between a mother and her child. Specifically, the engagement strategies employed by Costa Rican mothers with more schooling reflects those that are linked with initial elements of emerging conversation. Characteristics of emerging conversations are consistently linked with early literacy outcomes (Dickinson & Snow, 1987) and subsequent academic achievement (Cunningham & Stanovich, 1997).

To elucidate further how maternal interaction plays out in daily interaction, we highlight two examples of routine mother–infant rituals: bathing and feeding. In each example, a mother with limited schooling is juxtaposed with a mother with substantial schooling. Recall that the study controls for a number of factors that might have confounded outcomes. The level of maternal age and education are detailed. Pseudonyms have been substituted for real names.

Bathing Ritual

María and Teresa. María is 19 years old and has completed 5 years of schooling.

After disrobing Teresa in preparation for her bath, María takes her to the concrete kitchen sink, where she carefully lays her in the basin. María then splashes tap water onto Teresa. Teresa barely shifts as she is doused with the cool water. As María begins to lather Teresa with soap and then shampoo, Teresa remains compliant. At one point, María states sharply to Teresa, *¡Quédese!* [Don't move!] and *¡¡Hmmm!!* [a commonly used light sigh of discontent, such as humph].

The vocal tone is clearly short and negative. During the nearly 4-minute bathing ritual, the previous short comment and sigh are the only utterances from María to Teresa. Other than ambient noise coming from outside the home caused by neighbors or street traffic, the silence is impressive. María's facial expression during the entire episode is attentive (neutral) and never moves past the threshold where she would have been coded "positive." María concludes the bathing ritual by rinsing Teresa with the cool tap water, wrapping Teresa in a towel, and carrying her to another room to be dressed.

Gretel and Katherine. Gretel is 24 years old and has obtained a master's degree, completing a total of 18 years of formal schooling.

Gretel finishes disrobing Katherine and carries her to the bathroom. As they move toward the bathroom, Gretel tells Katherine with exaggerated positive affective tone, *"Vamos al baño para bañarte, Katherine"* Let's go to the bathroom to bathe you, Katherine [as they arrive at the bathroom]. *"Aquí estamos, ¡Ahyeee!"* [Here we are. There!]

Gretel lowers Katherine to a basin placed on the bottom of the stand-up shower stall, where Katherine is bathed. Gretel says, *"¡Ahyeee!, Katherine, ésto es su baño."* [There! Katherine, this is your bath.] Katherine's arm movements results in mild splashes in the basin. Gretel enthusiastically exclaims, *"Ahyeee, Katherine, ésta es el agua. Ésto es su baño."* [There, Katherine, this is water. This is your bath.]

	Tone and Action	Spanish Original	English Translation
Katherine:	Sneezes.		
Gretel:		*Salud.*	Bless you.
Katherine:	Sneezes.		
Gretel:		*Salud. Salud, mi amor. ¿Está muy fria? ¿El agua? Ahyeee. Ahyeee.*	Bless you. Bless you my love. Is it cold? The water? There. There.

Katherine:	Moves her arms in the water and makes mild splashes in the basin.		
Gretel:		*Agua. ¡Katherine, Ahyeee!*	Water. Katherine! There!
Katherine:		Gurgle utterance.	Gurgle utterance.
Gretel:		*Vamos a mover nuestros brazos. Ahyeee. ¡Qué bebé! Aguita. Ahyeee.*	Let's move our arms. There. What a baby! Water. There.
Katherine:	Splashes in the water.		
Gretel:		*Eso bebé. Agua. Ahyeee.*	That's it baby. Water. There.
Katherine:	Glances at a Mickey Mouse bath toy.		
Gretel:		*El Mickey. Katherine, ¿dónde está el Mickey? ¿Dónde está la muñeca?*	The Mickey. Katherine, where is the Mickey? Where's the doll?
Katherine:	Slumps in the basin.		
Gretel:		*Vamos a ver si se puede nadar.*	Let's see if one can swim.
Gretel:	Lays Katherine on her back in the water.	*Vas a nadar, Katherine.*	You're going to swim, Katherine.
Katherine:	Arches her back apparently in an attempt to sit up.		
Gretel:	Immediately supports Katherine to upright, seated position.		
Katherine:	Splashes in the water.		
Gretel:		*Qué rico. Ya vamos a bañarte.*	How great. We're going to bathe you.

In the first dyad, the infant, Teresa, is exposed to only one utterance during the entire bathing episode. That utterance was a directive and negated the child's expression. When Teresa wriggled, her mother responded with a curt response that effectively shut down any future attempt by Teresa to initiate interaction with her mother. Meanwhile, in the second dyad, the infant, Katherine, is exposed to a caregiver who elaborates the bathing experience. Her mother, Gretel, frames the bathing episode by labeling the routine. She has provided a superordinate that contextualizes the other labels applied throughout the episode, such as *agua* and *muñeca* to describe the Mickey Mouse toy. Gretel also employs nonimmediate labels when she refers to *"vamos a nadar"* to reference a learn-to-swim class Katherine has participated in outside of the bathing scene. The number of maternal vocalizations, the positive affect, and the use of superordinates and decontextualized talk have all been associated with facilitating language development.

Feeding Ritual

Ana and Fabián. Ana is 25 years old and has completed 3 years of schooling.

On a sunny, windy day in the foothills of San José, Costa Rica, Ana places Fabián in a walker on the outside patio and then goes inside to retrieve a jar of baby food. When she returns, she sits on a small stool facing Fabián and drags him (in the walker) toward her. As she stirs the glass jar, Fabián's arms flail – presumably with excitement. Fabián does not stray and stays focused on his mother and the food. Ana tastes a spoonful of the baby food and then presents the spoon to Fabián, who opens his mouth to eat the remaining spoonful. After every other spoonful of baby food, Ana uses the spoon to clean Fabián's mouth, chin, and cheeks. Occasionally, Fabián's walker moves away from his mother. It is unclear if the movement away from his mother is intentional or simply a result of his random kicks – again, perhaps from excitement. At first, Ana drags the walker (and Fabián) back toward her so that she can continue to feed him. However, on the next occasion, she lets Fabián stray away: *"¡Fabián! ¡Fabián! ¡Venga acá!"* [Fabián! Fabián! Come here!] Ana quickly stands, crosses the patio, and drags him back to her so she can finish feeding him.

The entire feeding sequence lasts 8 minutes with only that single maternal utterance expressed entirely in a neutral affective tone.

Lisa and José. Lisa is 29 years old and is in graduate school; she has completed a total of 17 years of formal schooling.

Inside the home, next to the dining table, Lisa lowers José into the infant seat in preparation for feeding.

	Tone and Action	Spanish Original	English Translation
Lisa:	Exaggerated positive affective tone.	*¡José, José! Vamos a comer.*	José, José! Let's eat.
Lisa:	Begins to tie a bib around José's neck and sings a common child's song.		
José:	Smiles and draws hands to mouth and then looks up at Lisa.		
Lisa:	Looks directly at José.	*¡José!*	José!

José:	Smiles at Lisa.	Vocalization.	Vocalization.
Lisa:	Smiles eye-to-eye at José	*¿Qué?*	*What?*
José:	Laughs and stretches his arms/hands toward Lisa's face/head.		
Lisa:	Looks eye-to-eye at José	*Te gusta mi pelo, ¿verdad?*	You like my hair, huh?
José:	Laughs with more intensity and again reaches for Lisa's face/head.		
Lisa:	Removes her eyeglasses.	*¡¡Ahyeee!!*	There!
Lisa:	Buries her face in Jose's stomach in an arousing game. She then pulls away from José, still eye-to-eye, and pauses.		
José:	Gleefully reaches for Lisa's face and laughs even louder.		

Lisa repeats the positively charged arousing game for nearly 2 minutes, filled with physical interactions with José, each with exaggerated positive affective expression from both partners. Then Lisa leans away from José and picks up her glasses.

	Tone and Action	Spanish Original	English Translation
José:	Coughs.		
Lisa:	Soothing tone	*¡Qué tos!* *¡Qué tos!*	What a cough! What a cough!
Lisa:	Attempts to feed José with a spoonful of food	*Qué rico.*	That's yummy..
José:	Opens mouth to feed.		
Lisa:		*Qué bueno.*	*That (tastes) good*
José:	Sneezes.		
Lisa:		*Salud.*	*Bless you.*
José:	Sneezes.		
Lisa:		*Salud.*	*Bless you.*

Again, in the two dyads highlighted in the feeding sequence, one observes dramatic differences in parenting style, with the second mother offering considerably more vocalizations and positive affective exchanges with her son. Although the first child described completes the feeding ritual nourished, little or no communicative exchange occurs between the dyad. In the second dyad, one also detects the mother's attempts to disengage her son from the highly charged interaction when she leans back from her infant. She also employs a soothing vocal tone in an attempt to calm her infant in preparation for digesting his dinner.

DISCUSSION AND IMPLICATIONS

In this study, differences in maternal sociocommunicative strategies were found during mother–infant home observations. Cultural differences revealed during the interaction provide empirical evidence to suggest how social partners, through their delicate verbal and nonverbal interactive cues, inadvertently promote or depress emerging communication skills that are related to early literacy. Coding the home-observation scoring system micro-analytically allowed us to uncover subtle interactive differences in maternal affect and behaviors.

Mothers with sensitivity and responsiveness to their infant's behavioral cues are able to moderate the level of stimulation with their infant so as to prolong the communicative dance (Stern, 1985). These early intentional extended conversations that include turn-taking, positively charged facial expressions, and vocalizations prepare the infant for subsequent complex conversations (Stern, Jaffe, Beebe, & Bennett, 1974). Even very young preverbal infants have the capacity to glean communicative patterns when presented with opportunities.

Although there are few studies that describe Latino mother-infant interactions, the cultural differences in maternal sociocommunicative strategies found in the present study corroborate the findings from these investigations. Rogoff and her colleagues (1993), for instance, compared interactions between dyads from Salt Lake City, Utah, and San Pedro, Guatemala. They found that U.S. mothers spoke more frequently to their toddlers and were more likely to use mock expressions of excitement, whereas Guatemalan mothers used nonverbal forms of communication more frequently. The Rogoff study also found that U.S. mothers were more likely to give verbal praise and a positive affective vocalization to their children than the Guatemalan mothers. Richman, Miller and LeVine (1992) reported similar results showing that Mexican mothers are more likely than U.S. mothers to use nonverbal forms of communication before employing vocalizations.

The differences in the early communicative patterns arise from important differences in the general beliefs about child development and child-rearing. It is well established that communities vary regarding the status and role given to children, as well in the overall types of interactional styles, such as situation-centered and child-centered. Ethnographic work with U.S. Latinos, for example, has shown that, as a culture upholding a situation-centered interaction style, pre-verbal infants are not seen as equal conversational partners. Therefore, it is not surprising to find that Latino infants are not engaged in verbal interactions as frequently as they would be if they were raised in a European American home (Schieffelin & Eisenberg, 1984; Zentella, 1997).

The within-culture variation analyses were particularly informative. Costa Rican mothers with more schooling employed interactive strategies that support skills necessary to succeed in school, although it is doubtful that these mothers are aware of the research that links their socioemotional communicative strategies to emergent literacy and school success. These results do raise the question of how schooling might influence the specific interaction and conversation patterns even at this early age.

The current study is in line with global efforts and initiatives, as stated in UNESCO's 2007 Education for All (EFA) monitoring report:

> Time is running out to meet the Education for All (EFA) goals set in 2000. Despite continued overall global progress at the primary level, including for girls, too many children are not in school, drop out early or do not reach minimal learning standards. By neglecting the connections among early childhood, primary and secondary education, and adult literacy, countries are missing opportunities to improve basic education across the board – and in the process, the prospects of children, youth and adults everywhere.

The significance of early-child-rearing environments, those from 0 to 5 years of age, has emerged as a crucial factor in the development of international health, education, and population policies. Myers (1992) points out that after decades of concentrated effort to combat disease and malnutrition in nonindustrialized societies, 12 of 13 infants born in these societies will survive to age 1. This is a result of our success at providing vaccinations, immunizations, and adequate sanitary conditions to prolong life. However, despite having met some basic physiological needs, many children continue to live in less than adequate developmental environments. A growing challenge is to identify early psychosocial phenomena that facilitate robust child development and prepare young children for school in a modern society. In addition, it is of absolute necessity that the phenomena identified are culturally relevant and embedded within the sociocultural reality in which children are raised.

The role of schooling has expanded dramatically in the last half of the 20th century and has continued to reach remote areas around the globe (Fuller, 1991). A current trend for many Ministries of Education in Latin America is to emphasize literacy and language development in primary grades. A large percentage of young children enter school with limited emergent literacy competencies and often repeat the first year of school with an alarming dropout rate. Recently, Latin American governments have looked toward early-childhood-education options as a way to improve education indicators. Educators and policy makers across Latin America might consider the following key findings when they develop programs for preschool-aged children and their families:

1. *Infancy and very young children.* Past research shows that children are ready to participate in early sociocommunicative exchanges very early in life, particularly with significant partners, which prime them for communication patterns, emergent literacy, and, eventually, school success. The present study showed variations in the type of early communicative exchanges to which infants are exposed. School-readiness programs should consider a social marketing component that offers early-brain-development information to communities as part of a design that intentionally focuses on the development of young children.

2. *Role of primary caregivers.* Frequently, early-childhood-development plans focus on center-based preschool programs aimed at children 1 year before they enter primary education. This study highlights the importance of working with primary caregivers as a means of providing early educational experiences. Caregivers, not necessarily the biological parent, spend considerably more time with young children than center-based providers and communicate tacit yet significant messages during early sociocommunicative exchanges. Ideally, early-education programs intentionally consider the involvement of caregivers in an effort to improve education outcomes. No longer can we disregard the importance of early sociocommunicative interactions with young children as just "play." Playful mother–child interactions during routine rituals and game-playing include key foundations for cultivating emerging language and cognitive skills, such as protoconversations. Children who are exposed to a hearty dosage of positive affect and vocal maternal engagement strategies enter school ready to learn.

3. *Definition of robust child development.* There is a global definition of healthy, robust child development to monitor the health and welfare of the world's young children. Most of the indicators of healthy development focus on physical well-being of the infant and include initiation of prenatal care, gestational age at delivery, exposure to substance abuse, Apgar scores (i.e., which assess overall physical health at delivery), and average length and weight of the infant postpartum. If improving educational outcomes is a priority, we must also include early socioemotional communicative indicators.

ACKNOWLEDGMENTS

I would like to acknowledge Ed Tronick and his team at the Child Development Unit at Boston Children's Hospital: Katherine Weinberg, Karen Olson, and Marjorie Beegley Robert LeVine's influence is also noted throughout this examination of early parenting. I also want to acknowledge my Costa Rican colleagues for their insights: Ignacio Dobles, Ana Teresa León, Irma Zuñiga, Norma Naranjo, Michelle Uleman.

REFERENCES

Ainsworth, M., Blehar, M., Waters, E., & Wall, S. (1978). *Patterns of attachment.* Hillsdale, NJ: Erlbaum.

Beebe, B., & Jaffe, J. (1992). Mother–infant vocal dialogues predict attachment, temperament and cognition. *Infant Behavior and Development, 15,* ICIS, Abstracts Issue, 48.

Beebe, B., Jaffe, J., Feldstein, S., Mays, K., & Alson, D. (1985). Interpersonal timing: The application of an adult dialogue model to mother–infant vocal and kinetic interactions. In A. Goldberg, *Frontiers in self psychology.* Hillsdale, NJ: Analytic Press.

Bornstein, M. H., Azuma, H., Tamis-LeMonda, C., & Ogino, M. (1990). Mother and infant activity and interaction in Japan and in the United States: A comparative macro-analysis of naturalistic exchanges. *International Journal of Behavioral Development, 13,* 267–287.

Bornstein, M. H., Haynes, O. M., O'Reilly, A. W., & Painter, K. M. (1996). Solitary and collaborative pretend play in early childhood: Sources of individual variation in the development of representational competence. *Child Development, 67,* 2910–2929.

Bornstein, M. H., Tal, J., Rahn, C., Galperin, C., Pecheux, M., Lamour, M., Toda, S., Azuma, H., Ogino, M., & Tamis-LeMonda, C. (1992). Functional analysis of the contents of maternal speech to infants of 5 and 13 months in four cultures: Argentina, France, Japan, and the United States. *Developmental Psychology, 28*(4), 593–603.

Bower, T. (1979). The infant's discovery of objects and mother. In E. Thoman (Ed.), *Origins of the infant's social responsiveness.* Hillsdale, NJ: Erlbaum.

Brazelton, T. B., Koslowski, B., & Main, M. (1974). The origins of reciprocity: The early mother–infant interaction. In M. Lewis and L. A. Rosenblum (Eds.), *The effect of the infant on its caregiver.* New York: Wiley.

Brazelton, T. B., Yogman, M., Als, H., & Tronick, E. (1979). The infant as a focus for family reciprocity. In M. Lewis and L. A. Rosenblum (Eds.), *The child and its family.* New York: Plenum Press.

Bretherton, I., McNew, S., Snyder, L., & Bates, E. (1983). Individual differences at 20 months: Analytic and holistic strategies in language acquisition. *Journal of Child Language, 10,* 293–320.

Bronfenbrenner, U. (1979). *The ecology of human development.* Cambridge, MA: Harvard University Press.

Chavajay, P., & Rogoff, B. (2002). Schooling and traditional collaborative social organization of problem solving by Mayan mothers and children. *Developmental Psychology, 38,* 55–66.

Cunningham, A. E., & Stanovich, K. E. (1997). Early reading acquisition and its relation to reading experience and ability 10 years later. *Developmental Psychology, 33*(6), 934–945.

Dickinson, D. K., & Snow, C. E. (1987). Interrelationship among prereading and oral language skills in kindergarteners from two social classes. *Early Childhood Research Quarterly, 2,* 1–25.

Dickinson, D. K., & Tabors, P. O. (2001). *Beginning literacy with language.* Baltimore, MD: Brookes Publishing.

Ekman, P. (1972). Universal and cultural differences in facial expression of emotion. *Nebraska Symposium on Motivation, 19,* 207–283.

Field, T. (1977). Effects on early separation, interactive deficits, and experimental manipulations on infant–mother face-to-face interactions. *Child Development, 48,* 763–771.

Fogel, A. (1977). Temporal organization in mother–infant face-to-face interaction. In H. R. Schaffer (Ed.), *Studies in mother–infant interaction.* London: Academic Press.

Fogel, A. (1982). Affect dynamics in early infancy: Affective tolerance. In T. Field & A. Fogel (Eds.), *Emotion and early interaction.* Hillsdale, NJ: Erlbaum.

Fogel, A., and Thelen, E. (1987). Development of early expressive and communicative action: Reinterpreting the evidence from a dynamic systems perspective. *Developmental Psychology, 23*(6), 747–761.

Fuller, B. (1991). *Growing up modern: The Western State builds third-world schools.* New York: Routledge.

Harkness, S., and Super, C. M. (1977). Why African children are so hard to test. In L. L. Adler (Ed.), Issues in cross-cultural research. *Annals of the New York Academy of Sciences, 285,* 326–331.

Izard, C. (1977). *Human emotions.* New York: Plenum Press.

Klinnert, M., Campos, J., Sorce, J., Emde, R., & Svejda, M. (1983). Emotions as behavior regulators in infancy: Social referencing in infancy. In R. Plutchik & H. Kellerman (Eds.), *Emotion: Theory, research and experience* (pp. 57–86). New York: Academic Press.

Leiderman, P. H., Tulkin, S. R., & Rosenfeld, A. (Eds.) (1977). *Culture and infancy: Variations in the human experience.* Orlando, FL: Academic Press.

LeVine, R. (1974). Parental goals: A cross-cultural view. *Teachers College Record, 76,* 2226–2239.

LeVine, R. A., Dixon, S., LeVine, S., Richman, A., Leiderman, P. H., Keefer, C. H., & Brazelton, T. B. (1994). *Childcare and culture: Lessons from Africa.* New York: Cambridge University Press.

McCabe, A., & Peterson, C. (1991). Getting the story: A longitudinal study of parental styles in eliciting narratives and developing narrative skill. In A. McCabe & C. Peterson. (Eds.), *Developing narrative structure* (pp. 217–253). Hillsdale, NJ: Lawrence Erlbaum Associates.

Mead, G. H. (1934). *Mind, self and society: From the standpoint of a social behaviorist.* Chicago: University of Chicago Press.

Mead, M. (1931). The primitive child. In A. C. Murchison (Ed.), *Handbook of child psychology.* Worcester, MA: Clark University Press.

Mead, M. (1935). *Sex and temperament.* New York: William Morrow.

Meltzoff, A. N., & Moore, M. K. (1977). Imitation of facial and manual gestures by human neonates. *Science, 198,* 75–78.

Munroe, R. H., & Munroe, R. L. (1971). Household density and infant care in an East African society. *Journal of Social Psychology, 83,* 3–13.

Munroe, R. L., Munroe, R. H., & Whiting, J. W. M. (Eds.) (1981). *Handbook of cross-cultural human development.* New York: Garland Press.

Myers, R. (1992). *The twelve who survive: Strengthening programs of early childhood development in the third world.* New York: Routledge.

Nelson, K. (1981). Individual differences in language development: Implications for development and language. *Developmental Psychology, 17,* 170–187.

Richman, A. L., Miller, P. M., LeVine, R. A. (1992). Cultural and educational variances in maternal responsiveness. *Developmental Psychology, 28*(4), 614–621.

Rogoff, B. (1990). *Apprenticeship in thinking: Cognitive development in social context.* New York: Oxford University Press.

Rogoff, B. (2003). *The cultural nature of human development.* New York: Oxford University Press.

Rogoff, B., Mistry, J., Goncu, A., & Mosier, C. (1993). Guided participation in cultural activity by toddlers and caregivers. *Monographs of the Society for Research in Child Development, 58*(7).

Schaffer, H. R. (1971). The growth of sociability. Harmondsworth, England: Penguin Press.

Schaffer, H. R. (1977). Early interactive development. In H.R. Schaffer (Ed.), *Studies in mother–infant interaction.* London: Academic Press.

Schieffelin, B. B., & Eisenberg, A. R. (1984). Cultural variation in children's conversations. In R. L. Schiefelbusch & J. Pickar (Eds.), *The acquisition of communicative competence* (pp. 377–420). Baltimore: University Park Press.

Sorce, J. F., Emde, R. N., Campos, J., & Klinnert, M. D. (1985). Maternal emotional signaling: Its effect on the visual cliff behavior of 1-year-olds. *Developmental Psychology, 21*, 195–200.

Stern, D. N. (1971). A micro-analysis of mother–infant interaction: Behaviors regulating social contact between a mother and her three-and-a-half-month-old twins. *Journal of American Academy of Child Psychiatry, 10*, 501–517.

Stern, D. N. (1974). Mother and infant at play: The dyadic interaction involving facial, vocal and gaze behaviors. In M. Lewis and L. A. Rosenblum (Eds.), *The effect of the infant on its caregiver.* New York: Wiley.

Stern, D. N. (1985). *The interpersonal world of the infant.* New York: Basic Books.

Stern, D. N., Jaffe, J., Beebe, B., & Bennett, S. L. (1974). Vocalizing in unison and in alternation: Two modes of communication within the mother–infant dyad. *Annals of the New York Academy of Science, 263*, 89–100.

Super, C. (1979). *A cultural perspective on theories of cognitive development.* Paper presented at the meeting of the Society for Research in Child Development, San Francisco, CA.

Thoman, E. G. (1979). *Origins of the infant's social responsiveness.* Hillsdale, NJ: Erlbaum.

Thompson, R. (2001). Development in the first years of life. *The Future of Children, 11*(1), 20–33.

Tobin, J. J., Wu, D. Y., & Davidson, D. H. (1989). *Preschool in three cultures.* New Haven, CT: Yale University Press.

Trevarthen, C. (1979). Instincts for human understanding and for cultural cooperation: Their development in infancy. In M. von Cronach, K. Foppa, W. Lepenies, & D. Ploog (Eds.), *Human ethology: Claims and limits of a new discipline.* Cambridge: Cambridge University Press.

Trevarthen, C. (1989). Universal cooperative motives: How infants begin to know the language and culture of their parents. In G. Jahoda and I. M. Lewis. (Eds.), *Acquiring culture.* London: Croom Helm.

Trevarthen, C., & Hubley, P. (1978). Secondary intersubjectivity: Confidence, confiders and acts of meaning in the first year. In A. Lock (Ed.), *Action, gesture and symbol: The emergence of language.* London: Academic Press.

Tronick, E., Als, H., & Adamson, L. (1979). Structure of early face-to-face communicative interactions. In M. Bullowa (Ed.), *Before speech: The beginning of interpersonal communication*. New York: Cambridge University Press.

Tronick, E., Morelli, G. A., & Winn, S. (1987). Multiple caretaking of Efe (Pygmy) infants. *American Anthropologist, 89*, 96–106.

Tronick, E., & Weinberg, K. (1992). *Maternal Regulatory Scoring System (MRSS)*. Unpublished manuscript.

UNESCO Report (2007). *Education for All Global Monitoring Report*. Paris: UNESCO. http://www.efareport.unecsco.org.

Vygotsky, L. (1978). *Mind in society*. Cambridge, MA: Harvard University Press.

Whiting, B., & Edwards, C. (1988). *Children of different worlds: The formation of social behavior*. Cambridge, MA: Harvard University Press.

Whiting, B. B., & Whiting, J. W. M. (1975). *Children of six cultures: A psycho-cultural analysis*. Cambridge, MA: Harvard University Press.

Whiting, J. W. M., & Child, I. L. (1953). *Child training and personality*. New Haven, CT: Yale University Press.

Zentella, A. C. (1997). *Growing up bilingual*. Malden, MA: Blackwell.

4

Lessons in Mother–Child and Father–Child Personal Narratives in Latino Families

TONIA N. CRISTOFARO AND CATHERINE S. TAMIS-LEMONDA

Key Words: Parent–child narratives, father–child communication, mother–child communication, preschool children's social-cultural development, preschool children's narrative development, school readiness.

ABSTRACT

Children's early social exchanges, including the oral sharing of personal experiences, play an important role in their development. By talking about personal experiences (i.e., narratives), children come to understand their world and to develop a sense of self within a broader social-cultural context. This chapter describes mother–child and father–child narratives in a sample of 37 low-income Puerto Rican, Mexican, and Dominican immigrant families residing in New York City. We provide a qualitative examination of the major cultural lessons that were communicated by mothers and fathers in their shared stories with their preschoolers.

Between the spring of pre-kindergarten and fall of kindergarten, 16 girls and 21 boys were observed in their home. They were videotaped sharing 2-minute narratives with their mother and father (separately) about a "special memory." Narratives were transcribed verbatim and the thematic content was explored and coded along three major cultural lessons.

First, parents emphasized the central role of family in their children's life, highlighting the importance of children identifying and loving their family members, maintaining ties with the family, and displaying appropriate behaviors toward relatives. Second, shared narratives communicated messages about gender roles, specifically in terms of emotions and activities that are associated with being male and female. Third, parents stressed the value of academic achievement, including the importance of working hard in school and feeling proud about scholastic accomplishments. Both similarities and differences in mother–child and father–child narratives around these themes are discussed. This work has the potential to inform early-childhood programs and intervention affecting social-cultural development and emergent literacy in children from diverse Latino families in the United States.

INTRODUCTION

Mother:	Fourth of July, we went out, so that was a good time we had. We went to the park, we got up real early in the morning, and we said we'd head out to the East River. And then, what you did in the East River? What you were doing?
Child:	Eating. Eating and playing ball.
Mother:	Yeah, and what else we went to?
Child:	I went in the water.
Mother:	Yeah, you got wet, right? And then we did?
Child:	[No response.]
Mother:	What was it?
Child:	[No response.]
Mother:	What else we did over there?
Child:	[No response.]
Mother:	You were playing, remember? We took Grandma into the sprinklers.
Child:	[Nods yes.]
Mother:	And we made sandwiches. Remember?
Child:	[Nods yes.]
Mother:	And what else we did?
Child:	[Shrugs shoulders.]
Mother:	We went around the park, remember? What happened? What else we bought? The colored lights we bought, remember?
Child:	[Nods yes.]
Mother:	And what did they do?
Child:	Glow.
Mother:	Glow when? And when? In the morning or the nighttime?
Child:	Nighttime.
Mother:	In the nighttime you can see them glowing, right? Yeah, then you saw them glowing right?
Child:	[Nods yes.]
Mother:	And all the neighbors stood there in the park. And what else we did? We came home and then what we did? Remember what we were looking out? Where?
Child:	At outside.
Mother:	And what we saw out the window?
Child:	Fireworks.
Mother:	Yeah, we saw the fireworks, right? And what color they were? Remember, what colors were we seeing?
Child:	Green and blue. And pink and red.
Mother:	Yeah.

This narrative between a Latino mother and her 5-year-old son reveals the family's activities during a Fourth of July celebration. This story illustrates the many lessons that underlie otherwise simple, everyday conversations between young children and their parents. In this narrative, a mother and her son reminisce about different aspects of their Fourth of July celebration, from waking up and playing sports in the park, to including the child's grandmother in the festivities, and ending with the evening fireworks. In this narrative, the mother presents a number of nuanced "lessons" to her child, ranging from the proper ways to tell a story to the kinds of shared activities that are valued. For example, in her opening statement, "that was a good time we had," the mother informs her child about the types of events that are memorable and fun. Through the sequenced prompting of events that begin in the morning and end in the evening, she subtly teaches her child how to order temporal events in the retelling of a story. Finally, by choosing to talk about an experience that included the grandmother and neighbors, she is highlighting the roles of family and other people in her child's life.

During the preschool years, children's understanding of the world is typically embedded in their daily interactions with social partners, particularly parents (Astington & Pelletier, 2005). Vygotskian social-interaction theory posits that children develop their language and cognitive skills in the context of interactions with more skilled partners, such as their parents (Rogoff, 1990; Vygotsky, 1978). The sharing of *personal narratives,* or verbalized stories about past experiences (e.g., Nelson & Fivush, 2004; Newcombe & Reese, 2004; Reese & Fivush, 1993), is an essential component of the parent–child relationship. Parent–child narratives during the preschool period support children's language, cognitive, social, emotional, and cultural development by offering children a model for recalling and recounting their autobiographical memories, as well as encouraging children's own contributions to storytelling (Reese & Farrant, 2003; Reese & Fivush, 1993; Reese, Haden, & Fivush, 1993).

Goals of the Chapter

Rooted in social-cultural theory (e.g., Brockmeier, 2001; Bruner, 2002; Nelson & Fivush, 2004; Vygotsky, 1978), this chapter explores the shared narratives of Latino children and their mother and father. Specifically, we provide a qualitative examination of the lessons present in the narratives of 37 mother–child and father–child dyads from diverse Latino families.

The focus on Latino parent–child narratives addresses the need for researchers and educators to better understand the experiences and development of children from this rapidly growing U.S. population. The significant rise in the number of Latino families and children either immigrating to the United States or being born in the country calls for special attention to how parent–child relationships affect children's overall well-being and development. A disconcerting statistic is that the number of Latino children growing up in poverty increased between 2000 and 2004 by about 17% (Current Population Survey, 2005; U.S. Department of Commerce, Bureau of the Census, 2001). Studies reveal that children from low-income families display less advanced language skills than their peers from higher-income backgrounds (Whitehurst, Zevenbergen, Crone, Schultz, Velting, & Fischel, 1999). Children who lag behind their peers in school-readiness abilities tend to experience difficulties in later competencies associated with reading and academic achievement (Bredekamp, 2004; Snow, Burns, & Griffin, 1998). However, children growing up in low-income homes demonstrate great variation in their language and school performance, and they have the opportunity to develop proper literacy skills with adequate environmental support (Burns, Griffin, & Snow, 1999). For example, children who begin kindergarten with more developed narrative skills are at an advantage educationally over children who enter school with less developed narrative skills (e.g., Zevenbergen, Whitehurst, & Zevenbergen, 2003). Thus, children's early conversations with their parents provide a window into language and narrative abilities that may feed into their later educational success.

This chapter begins with an overview of the literature on the major functions of personal narratives for children's development, with an emphasis on the role of both mothers and fathers in children's narrative development. Following this summary, we describe three major lessons, or themes, evidenced in the narratives of Latino mother–child and father–child dyads: (1) the importance of family (*familismo*), (2) gender roles and socialization, and (3) educational achievements.

Children's Narratives

Personal narratives, the focus of this chapter, are stories in which children verbally recount past experiences (Heath, 1994; Hudson & Shapiro, 1991; Uccelli, Hemphill, Pan, & Snow, 1999). For instance, a $4\frac{1}{2}$-year-old child who talks about a visit to her grandparents' house is sharing a personal narrative. Personal narratives require a narrator to draw on a memory of a past episode and to discuss events in the form of a well-structured story (Hudson & Shapiro, 1991). *Autobiographical memories,* therefore, are central to narratives (see Fernández & Melzi, chapter 5, this volume). An autobiographical memory is a particular type of remembrance that involves a child's basic memory skills and an emergent sense of self in relation to others (Nelson, 2003; Nelson & Fivush, 2004). Autobiographical recollections draw on children's language skills, narrative development, and an understanding about self and others (Nelson, 2003; Nelson & Fivush, 2004). Studies demonstrate that in the context of parent–child conversations, preschool children become more capable of reporting memories from their own perspective (Hudson & Shapiro, 1991; Reese & Fivush, 1993).

During the time when children are 3 and 4 years old, their ability to construct a personal narrative reflects their growing capacity to use language as a representational system (Haden, 2003; Nelson, 1996). In the context of personal storytelling, 4-year-olds generally begin to develop a long-term sense of self, a critical prerequisite for autobiographical memory (Nelson & Fivush, 2004). Beyond age four, preschoolers are better able to include multiple components, such as events and evaluations in their narratives (Hudson & Shapiro, 1991). In one longitudinal study of mother–child, father–child, and examiner–child conversations about the past, children between 40 and 70 months increasingly mentioned actions, orientations, evaluations, and descriptions in their narratives (Haden, Haine, & Fivush, 1997). Orientations were comments that provided the listener with information regarding the spatial-temporal context (e.g., participant in narrative), whereas descriptions referred to the provision of or request for details about persons, objects, or events in the narrative (e.g., color of an object) (Haden et al., 1997).

Regarding children's language and cognitive development, narratives serve as contexts for children to build oral-discourse skills. In particular, narratives enable children to practice decontextualized language (or talk about objects and events removed from the present), which has been found to be important for later reading (Dickinson, 1991; Snow & Dickinson, 1990; Watson, 2002). The critical transition from contextualized to decontextualized language is thought to empower children in the acquisition of literacy abilities (Snow, 1983). For example, in one study of 20 White, middle-class mothers sharing narratives and reading books with their children at 40, 46, and 58 months old, the mothers' decontextualized language positively predicted children's print skills at 70 months (Reese, 1995). Children's own participation in their narratives was strongly related to their comprehension of an unfamiliar story and narrative competencies (Reese, 1995). These findings indicate that oral language comprises an important part of children's literacy development and school success (e.g., Aram & Levin, 2001; Beals, De Temple, & Dickinson, 1994; Dickinson & McCabe, 2001; Dickinson, McCabe, Anastasopoulos, Peisner-Feinberg, & Poe, 2003; Shatil, Share, & Levin, 2000) and that early parent–child narratives are building blocks for children's later achievements and school readiness (e.g., Fiorentino & Howe, 2004; Michaels, 1981; Peterson, Jesso, & McCabe, 1999; Roth, Speece, & Cooper, 2002; Snow, 1983; Snow & Dickinson, 1990; Snow, Porche, Tabors, & Harris, 2007; Snow, Tabors, Nicholson, & Kurland, 1995; Zevenbergen et al., 2003).

Cultural Lessons

Most relevant to the current chapter, narratives are a crucial medium for parents to teach their children cultural and social lessons in the form of personal stories. Parent–child reminiscing about meaningful events allows children to make sense of the larger social-cultural contexts of their experiences (e.g., Brockmeier, 2001; Bruner, 2002; Fivush & Haden, 2003; Melzi, 2000; Nelson, 2001). Through shared storytelling, parents both implicitly and explicitly reveal their socialization goals and share their cultural views and expectations of their children, who in turn develop their self-concept in a broader framework (e.g., Ely, Melzi, Hadge, & McCabe, 1998; Pillemer, 1998; Wang, 2006).

Although the majority of studies has investigated the narratives of European American mothers and children from middle-income backgrounds living in the United States, there is some work on the narrative development in children from ethnically and culturally diverse, lower-income U.S. families (e.g., Adams, Kuebli, Boyle, & Fivush, 1995; Benson, 1997; Burger & Miller, 1999; Dunn, Bretherton, & Munn, 1987; Melzi, 2000; Miller & Sperry, 1988; Wiley, Rose, Burger, & Miller, 1998). Among the major findings, research highlights sociocultural variations in parent–child discourse about the past. For instance, a study of working-class and middle-class European American families found that parents and children from working-class families engaged in more co-narrations about past events than did middle-class families (Wiley et al., 1998). In addition, working-class families tended to challenge children's statements (e.g., "No, I didn't"), whereas middle-class families were more likely to reframe their children's provision of information if those facts were incorrect (e.g., "Not a pine cone. Megan was a unicorn.") (Wiley et al., 1998). In another examination of Spanish-speaking Central American and English-speaking European American families, Central American and European American mothers supported their children's narrative contributions in different and specific ways (Melzi, 2000). Whereas Central American mothers encouraged their preschooler's active participation by introducing events not mentioned by the children, European American mothers typically co-narrated stories with their children and guided them in organizing the narratives sequentially.

Parents' Role in Children's Narratives

Parents play a central role in children's discourse abilities and narrative skills (Beals et al., 1994) by creating a "process of coauthorship" (Wahler & Castlebury, 2002, p. 303). Mothers who share experiences with children in the context of personal storytelling provide children with familiarity with literacy activities that will be expected of them in a formal school curriculum (e.g., Uccelli & Páez, 2007). As described by Uccelli and Páez (2007), narrative skills have been shown to be important prerequisites for the literacy achievements of both monolingual (e.g., Dickinson & Tabors, 2001) and bilingual (e.g., Oller & Pearson, 2002) children. As reviewed, children from economically disadvantaged families are at greater risk of literacy delays when compared to their more advantaged peers (e.g., Snow et al., 1998; Whitehurst & Lonigan, 2002). Therefore, understanding the narrative abilities of children drawn from low-income families in our research may shed light on specific oral precursors to their later literacy accomplishments.

Numerous studies (predominantly based on the narratives from middle-income, English-speaking, European American families in the United States) demonstrate that caregivers (primarily mothers) employ unique styles of talking about the past with their children (e.g., McCabe & Peterson, 1991; Newcombe & Reese, 2004; Reese & Farrant, 2003). One style has been referred to as a *highly elaborative* or *narrative* style. Mothers who utilize this style of discourse tend to follow their children's responses and subsequently elaborate on them; mothers generally provide many details (e.g., descriptions, evaluation) about the event in the form of both questions and statements (e.g., "What kind of cake did we have at your birthday party? Where did we go after we opened up gifts? How many toys did you get?") (Reese & Farrant, 2003; Reese & Fivush, 1993). In contrast, mothers with a *low elaborative* or *paradigmatic* style may not consistently follow their children's responses and often repeat their own questions; mothers who exhibit this style usually provide specific points of information for the narrative.

In terms of outcomes, children whose mothers have a high elaborative style are generally better able to report richer details of past experiences concurrently and longitudinally than children whose mothers are less elaborative (Reese & Farrant, 2003). Also, children whose mothers were more elaborative in the preschool years used a more elaborative style themselves later on (i.e., orienting and evaluative style) (Haden et al., 1997). Thus, the way that parents structure conversations about past events influences how young children reflect on the past and how they come to think about themselves (Fivush, 1991; Fivush & Nelson, 2004; Leichtman, 1999).

Nonetheless, most research has focused on mother–child narratives, leaving a gap in knowledge about the personal narratives shared between fathers and their children. Despite an unparalleled growth of interest in fathers' role in children's social-cognitive development and academic achievement in the past 20 years (Lamb, 1997, 2004; Parke, 2004; Tamis-LeMonda & Cabrera, 2002; Tamis-LeMonda, Shannon, Cabrera, & Lamb, 2004), there exists limited research on fathers' influence on children's language development, particularly in Latino families. Little is known about the language and early literacy environments that fathers from low-income families provide their children, and virtually nothing is known about how Latino fathers support their children's developing narrative competencies prior to kindergarten entry and formal schooling.

Regarding a father's role in a young child's language development, mothers and fathers have been found to be similar in their use of different types of language when communicating with their children (e.g., Bellinger & Gleason, 1982). For example, mothers and fathers refer to concrete objects and events at comparable rates during parent–child free play (Bornstein, Vibbert, Tal, & O'Donnell, 1992). However, others have found that mothers and fathers also differ in the frequency and quality of their language use. For instance, mothers engage in longer, more frequent conversational turns than fathers (e.g., Davidson & Snow, 1996; Ely & Berko Gleason, 1995; Ely, Gleason, MacGibbon, & Zaretsky, 2001). On the other hand, fathers produce more language such as directives, requests for clarification, and "wh"-type questions during conversations with their children (e.g., Bellinger & Gleason, 1982; Leaper, Anderson, & Sanders, 1998; Tomasello, Conti-Ramsden, & Ewert, 1990). Because fathers may be less familiar with their children's language abilities, they may be more likely to speak in ways that challenge children's linguistic skills, thus serving as a "bridge" to the outside world (Berko & Gleason, 1975; Ely & Berko Gleason, 1995). In our own work, we have investigated the contributions of both mothers' and fathers' language to toddlers' observed language in 50 ethnically diverse families from low-income backgrounds (Tamis-LeMonda, Cristofaro, & Baumwell, under review). Our research suggests that mother–child and father–child conversations were generally similar in the forms and frequency of language. Both parents predominantly labeled and described objects; likewise, children expressed comparable frequency and types of language with both their mother and father. This study showed that parents provided generally equivalent language environments to their young children, and that both parents' language mattered for toddlers' language.

In the area of narratives, there is tentative evidence for similarities in mothers' and fathers' storytelling styles as well. Among the small number of existing studies of father–child narratives, one examination of 24 mothers and 24 fathers and their 3-year-old children yielded no significant differences between mothers' and fathers' narrative styles (Reese & Fivush, 1993). Mothers and fathers were generally similar in the extent to which they were highly or lowly elaborative. However, differences were found by child gender, in that both mothers and fathers were typically more elaborative with their daughters than with their sons. In a follow-up study of the same children at approximately 5 years of age, mothers and fathers again did not differ greatly in their narrative styles (Reese, Haden, & Fivush, 1996). Yet, by this time, more fathers tended to have a lower elaborative style than mothers (Reese et al., 1996). Therefore, the few past studies on both mothers' and fathers' narrative styles suggest general similarities in parents' styles of reminiscing with their preschoolers.

The Current Study

To address the literature gap on the narratives of Latino parents (in particular, fathers), in the subsequent sections we highlight both similarities and differences in the themes that mothers and fathers develop in their stories with their children. This work emphasizes the role of both parents in children's narrative development and shows how Latino families use narratives as occasions for teaching important cultural lessons.

METHODS

Participants

Participants in this examination were 37 mothers, 37 fathers, and their children (16 girls and 21 boys). Participants were drawn from the New York City site of the national Early Head Start (EHS) Research and Evaluation Project. Families were recruited into the study when they sought EHS services from local community agencies. Because these families participated in a longitudinal study spanning 5 years, it offered us the opportunity to examine shared narratives at the preschool assessment.

On average, mothers were approximately 20 years old at the time of the birth of their child in this study and came from diverse Latino backgrounds: 62% (N = 23) Puerto Rican; 19% (N = 7) Mexican; 11% (N = 4) Dominican; 5% (N = 2) Ecuadorian; and 3% (N = 1) Honduran. At the mothers' request, all mother–child narratives in this study were conducted in English, with the exception of two narratives. Of the mothers, 60% (N = 22) had some high school education, 30% (N = 11) had graduated from high school, and 10% (N = 4) had some college education or were college graduates.

Fathers averaged 21 years old at the time of the birth of their child in this examination. Fathers identified their ethnic backgrounds as 57% (N = 21) Puerto Rican; 22% (N = 8) Dominican; 10% (N = 4) Ecuadorian; 8% (N = 3) Mexican; and 3% (N = 1) Honduran. All father–child narratives were conducted in English (by the fathers' choice) except for two narratives. Of the fathers, 68% (N = 25) had some high school education, 24% (N = 9) had graduated from high school, and 8% (N = 3) had some college education or were college graduates. Of the 37 fathers in this sample, 27 reported living with their children and 8 of those 27 dyads were married.

Children averaged about 57 months ($M = 57.49$ months; *range:* 53.00 to 61.00 months) at the time of their visit with their mother. None of the children had any diagnosed disabilities at the time of the pre-kindergarten home visit, according to maternal reports.

Procedure

Mother–child and father–child dyads were observed in their home on separate visits conducted by teams of research assistants during the spring or summer before children entered kindergarten. As part of the larger protocol, one personal narrative was collected from each dyad. The research assistant told mothers and fathers: "We'd like you to get [child's name] to tell us about something exciting that's happened recently. It could be a family outing, a birthday celebration, or any unusual event that involved [him or her]." Children and their parents were allowed a maximum of 2 minutes and a minimum of 1 minute for the story. If the parent and child completed their narrative before the end of 1 minute, the research assistant said, "You still have a little more time. Have you told us everything about [exciting event]?"

Mother–child and father–child personal narratives at pre-kindergarten were transcribed verbatim from the videotaped interactions. All narratives were examined qualitatively, with a focus on thematic content around the major lessons that parents developed in their story (e.g., Leadbeater & Way, 2007;

Merriam, 2001; Ochs & Capps, 2001; Way, 1998; Way & Chu, 2004). These lessons were generated through an iterative process of closely reading the parent–child narratives and noting the various themes that were present. Then, narratives were read a second time, with an eye toward reading in particular for the target themes. After an iterative process of refining themes, we chose to highlight three of the most prominent for the purpose of this chapter: (1) the importance of family, (2) gender roles, and (3) educational achievements and academic success. These core lessons, or themes, are described in the following section and are based on a total of 74 parent–child narratives (i.e., 37 mother–child and 37 father–child narratives).

RESULTS

In the majority of cases, parents chose the topics of the shared narratives, even though the instructions did not specify who should decide the topic. Specifically, only 3 of the 74 narratives were selected by children (i.e., 1 boy and 1 girl sharing narratives with their mothers and 1 girl sharing a narrative with her father).

In many ways, parents' selection of particular events not only highlighted what was important for children to remember but might also have reflected the parents' child-rearing objective of guiding their child. Others have suggested that through decision making, parents communicate a social hierarchy and their child's role in the parent–child relationship (e.g., Halgunseth, Ispa, & Ruddy, 2006). However, the time limit of the study design might have been a factor as well. Parents may have been aware of the task demands of identifying and elaborating on a shared past experience in a 2-minute window.

As mentioned, three themes were identified in the 37 mother–child and 37 father–child narratives. These themes are now discussed with attention to similarities and differences in mothers' and fathers' shared narratives.

Lesson #1: The Importance of Family

The theme of family (*familismo*) was evident in the majority of narratives. Reminiscing about a family-centered event, experience, or activity that involved either immediate and/or extended family members occurred in about 80% of mother–child and father–child narratives. Specifically, 84% (N = 31) of mother–child narratives were structured around the topic of family; similarly, 78% (N = 29) of fathers talked about family. Of the 31 mother–child narratives, about 10% (N = 3) included the child's sister. An additional 32% of these 31 narratives (N = 10) included an extended family member. Specifically, of these 10 narratives, 5 included the child's grandmother and the child's cousins, 4 included the child's cousins, and 1 included the child's aunt and cousins. Like mothers, about 10% (N = 3) of the 29 father–child narratives included reference to the child's sister. Of the 29 father–child narratives, approximately 48% (N = 14) included extended relatives. Of those 14, 7 included the child's cousins and aunts, 3 included the child's grandmother only, 3 included the child's uncles, and 1 included the child's grandmother and cousins. This pervasive focus on family in Latino narratives emphasized the importance of family affection and ties in the children's life.

Family-focused events included activities such as a cousin's birthday party, a family summer vacation, and weekend activities with either immediate or extended relatives. These family narratives established family networks and relations. For example, mothers and fathers would often encourage their child to recite the names of individuals who comprised the family and to understand how family members were related to one another. In one example, the following excerpt shows the father's interest in his son's ability to list family members. In this narrative, father and son speak of the child's activities at a cousin's birthday party. The father asks his son to name his cousins who were at the party, and the boy responds by listing the people there for his father.[1] Notably, in the father's second and third utterances, he provides his son with the option to either name cousins or discuss the celebration. In response, the child chooses to list his cousins:

Father: Tell them what happened at the birthday party.
Child: I played musical chairs.
Father: Who you went to the party with?
Child: Auntie Carla.
Father: Who else? Which one of your cousins went with you? Tell everything that happened at the birthday party.
Child: I went with my cousin Frank and cousin Michelle and Christina and that's all the people that I came with. I ate cake. And that is what I did.

Similarly, in the next excerpt, a mother requests that her daughter share a story about her and her cousins. As in the previous narrative, the mother directs her child to talk about participants at a pool party:

Mother: Tell them a story about you and your cousins... Remember that time we went to Keith's house? And we had a pool party? Remember that time we went to... Keith's house, who was there? Who was at Keith's house? You don't remember? Who were... the other little girls running around the backyard? Tell me... Natalie and...?
Child: [Smiles.]
Mother: Who else? There's... Tommy, John, Dan, Mark... Right?
Child: [Nods yes.]
Mother: A lot of people there?
Child: [Nods yes.]
Mother: You have fun?
Child: [Nods yes.]

---

[1] Names in all parent–child narratives were changed to maintain confidentiality.

In another mother–daughter dyad, mother and child share a memory about the birth of a new member of the family – a baby cousin. By focusing on the family's addition, the mother teaches her child about family relations and the significance of relatives. The child herself inquires about the baby's name. The mother continues the conversation by helping her child comprehend how her relatives are related. In doing so, the mother verbally creates a family tree for her daughter:

Mother:	Remember when we had the baby shower for Jenny?
Child:	[Nods yes.]
Mother:	When did she have the baby? Today!
Child:	Today!
Mother:	What did she have? What did she have? What did she have?
Child:	A boy!
Mother:	A boy! And who is that going to be to you?
Child:	Um, me . . . my xx.[2]
Mother:	He's going to be your what?
Child:	Um . . .
Mother:	Your cousin!
Child:	He's my cousin!
Mother:	Yeah.
Child:	Who I'm going to call him?
Mother:	His name is gonna be Joseph.
Child:	Joseph?
Mother:	Joseph!
Child:	Like Joseph in my class . . .
Mother:	And what about his brother? What's his brother's name?
Child:	Whose brother?
Mother:	The baby's brother?
Child:	My cousin.
Mother:	What's his name?
Child:	Um . . .
Mother:	Michael!
Child:	Michael!
Mother:	That's your cousin.
Child:	Yeah.

Beyond the listing of family members and creations of "family trees," various subthemes were identified in narratives about families: families are enjoyable; relatives express affection toward each other; ties to family and culture should be maintained; and children should help family members and demonstrate appropriate behaviors in the family context.

An important aspect of family lessons was the characterization of family events as *lots of fun*. This tendency to state the fun of family was slightly greater

---

[2] "xx" indicates unintelligible speech.

in mother–child than in father–child narratives. Specifically, 20 of the 31 (65%) mother–child narratives focused on family and 16 of the 29 (55%) father–child narratives explicitly described the family as enjoyable. The following excerpt, for instance, displays a father and his daughter recounting the exciting experiences they shared while on a family vacation to Sesame Place. In a cheerful tone, the father talks with his daughter about specific relatives who joined them on their family trip. Also, the fun surrounding the trip is evident in the child's tone of voice as she enthusiastically describes the pleasurable vacation:

Father:	Tell them about Sesame Place, when we took you to Sesame Place. Tell them what you saw . . . Big Bird, Ernie . . .
Child:	I saw Big Bird and Elmo.
Father:	Tell them who you went with.
Child:	I went with my Mommy and my sister and Mary and Celia and Aunt Jen and who else?
Father:	Remember Nico?
Child:	Nico. Who else?
Father:	Michael. What did we do over there?
Child:	We went down the slide! I like to twist. I got wet in the water.
Father:	And tell them what you did . . . Remember you saw the parade?

Beyond being fun, children were also taught that *families express affection*, as evident in the next excerpt of a girl and her father. By revealing her love and feelings of affection for her cousins, the child demonstrates her knowledge that families cherish one another:

Father:	Your cousin came down, right? You have fun with Stephanie? And what you did?
Child:	We played together. And um . . . we did a lot of stuff together.
Father:	Like what?
Child:	Like watching movies.
Father:	What else?
Child:	And um . . . Playing together . . . Play Barbies.
Father:	Yeah, you playing outside?
Child:	Yeah, we were playing outside.
Father:	With all your cousins, right?
Child:	With all my cousins that I love and I care about . . .

This value of conveying love for family extended specifically to the *grand-mother*. Approximately 15% of family lessons included talk about grandmother. Of the 31 mother–child narratives that centered on family events, 5 spoke of the child's grandmother; of the 29 father–child narratives centered on family, 4 included the child's grandmother. Common across mother–child and father–child narratives of grandmother was the mention of sentiments of love, respect, and devotion.

For example, the following excerpt exemplifies the child's love and warmth toward her grandmother, as her mother refers to the grandmother's home as the child's "favorite place." The mother and daughter recollect the child's activities at her grandmother's, including bathing and eating there, which reflect the child's comfort and engagement in routine activities at her grandparents' home:

Mother:	What did we do yesterday? Where did we go yesterday?
Child:	To the beach.
Mother:	How did you like it?
Child:	Good.
Mother:	What did you do at the beach?
Child:	Swimming . . .
Mother:	And then what did we do afterwards, after the beach, where did we go?
Child:	Um . . .
Mother:	To your favorite place, where did we go?
Child:	Um, I don't know.
Mother:	You don't know where's your favorite place? I thought Grandma's house was your favorite place. You remember after the beach we went to Grandma's house?
Child:	Yes.
Mother:	And you played there?
Child:	And I pet Sammy. I did and I pet Sammy.
Mother:	Sammy, that's the cat.
Child:	He's big.
Mother:	And you took a bath there. And you played with so many toys.
Child:	Yes, a little bit.
Mother:	And we had pizza for dinner.
Child:	And I had cheese. I like cheese.
Mother:	Then we came home . . .

The next excerpt reveals a father and son's reminiscence about a day in the park and an unexpected meeting with a special person the boy loves – his grandmother. In response to his father's question, the child attempts to quantify his love for this significant person in his life:

Father:	Remember . . . and went to the park?
Child:	[Nods yes.]
Father:	. . . You play soccer, you have a great time. Then what happened?
Child:	Then Mike score!
Father:	You tried the ball on the top and you just slide down. And then after that . . . we met somebody in the park, remember? Coming back from home. And then, we saw somebody in the park. Who?
Child:	Grandmother.
Father:	Oh . . . Grandmother. What she say? She was going to the park. She was going to the park.
Child:	Grandmother.

Father:	She's your grandmother. You love her. How much you love her?
Child:	Ninety-nine hundred.
Father:	Oh, ninety-nine hundred? That's cool.

Beyond lessons of fun and affection, in some father–child narratives (but no mother–child narratives), themes around family also highlighted the importance of *maintaining ties to family and culture,* even when families are geographically distant. In the following example, the father and son talked about a relative who needed to return home. The father offers a creative strategy to help comfort his son, who misses his relative. The father's approach illustrates his effort to preserve ties with the extended family:

Father:	What did Steve do in the airport? What was he doing in the airport? What did he tell you not to do?
Child:	He said "no" . . .
Father:	You wanted to fly with him?
Child:	Yeah.
Father:	But you told him we were gonna come and see him, right?
Child:	Yeah.
Father:	Alright.
Child:	Wanna see Stevie.
Father:	Stevie? . . . You have his picture.
Child:	Stevie, Stevie.
Father:	Alright. Let me bring his picture. Remember when we saw Steve? [Looks at cell phone picture with his son.] Yeah!
Child:	Why?
Father:	Because they took his picture, right? Took each other's pictures. And you were playing with him.
Child:	Ha ha! [Laughs]
Father:	You see? I told you I had Steve's picture. See? Remember now? Want to try it again? See? See? Remember that now?
Child:	[Nods yes.]

Another father–child narrative references the father's country of origin because the father chooses to talk about his daughter's visit to Honduras. This topic selection helps his daughter recognize her cultural heritage and family's roots:

Father:	You went to Honduras?
Child:	[Nods yes.]
Father:	How was that? Huh? So you went to Honduras? You have fun over there? There are a lot of kids over there, or no?
Child:	[Shakes head no.]
Father:	It was hot?
Child:	What?
Father:	It was hot over there? No?
Child:	Yeah.

In other families, conversations centered on family members visiting the United States. The following excerpt between a father and his son provides such an example. In this passage, the father prompts his son to recall their relatives' visit to the United States:

Father: Where did we go with Uncle John and Aunt Mary the other day?
Child: To the zoo.
Father: To the zoo, and what did you see?
Child: A lion . . .
Father: What else did you see? Bears? The whale?
Child: Yeah, the whale.
Father: Where do we go when Great-Grandpa comes to New York? Where do we go?
Child: Big park.
Father: And where at the park do we go?
Child: [Whispers in his father's ear.]
Father: Yeah, and when we go to the park, what do we see? . . .

Finally, the themes of *helping family members* and *demonstrating appropriate conduct* were also observed in family narratives. In particular, 12 (20%) of the 60 family-focused parent–child narratives referred to some aspects of offering help to others and being socially appropriate. Mothers and fathers were equally likely to elaborate these themes with their children (i.e., six mother–child and six father–child narratives).

As one example, in the subsequent excerpt, a mother points out her son's helpfulness during a birthday celebration. She notes her pride in her son's manners and proper behavior at the family event, and she also communicates that being cooperative is both fun and gratifying:

Mother: Remember, yesterday, when we went to Stephanie's house for the barbecue? Did you have fun? What were you doing? What were you doing there? Remember?
Child: Eat.
Mother: You ate. What else were you doing? They were cutting the cake. There were presents and spoons. You were helping with the plates and spoons. You were helping Joseph. Yes. You have fun doing that?
Child: Uh huh.

Similarly, the following conversation is drawn from the family baby shower narrative mentioned previously. In this excerpt, the mother calls attention to her daughter's behavior toward her cousin. The mother–daughter conversation presents the lesson that being well behaved and generous leads to happiness in others (in this example, the child's cousin receiving a baby gift):

Mother: Remember, and we went to the party, when Jenny came inside, what we said to her?
Child: We said, "Surprise!"
Mother: "Surprise!" You remember?

Child:	Yeah!
Mother:	And she was all happy. And what did you give her for her baby shower? . . . Remember, what did you make for her? . . .
Child:	A picture.
Mother:	Yeah! You gave her the picture, right? And she was so happy and she was crying and she said, "Thank you."

The following two excerpts also illustrate lessons about the importance of proper manners. In these conversations, parents express their view about their child obeying rules (see Wishard Guerra, chapter 7, this volume). Both examples illustrate the parents' expectations that their child respects various authority figures, including a police officer and the child's mother, respectively.

In the subsequent narrative, a mother and son talk about their fun-filled day at the park. The mother reminds her son about a specific rule the child needed to follow during their stay at the park – not walking on the grass. This shared memory becomes a vehicle for the mother to convey the value of obedience as a marker of correct upbringing:

Mother:	Remember, we went to that big park? And we sat in that little car that was open? Remember? And I told you it had the lake and the water?
Child:	[Nods yes.]
Mother:	What did you like about that place? You were holding a whole bunch of grass. And I was telling you that you can't get in the grass. And remember I told you the policeman said you can't get in the grass? Remember?

Likewise, in the next conversation about a child's attendance at a cousin's birthday celebration, a father states that he values his son's compliance with his mother's rules about candy. The excerpt also implicitly suggests the father's expectation that his son would share the candy with him. This indicates the father's message that being charitable and thinking about others (in this example, the child's own father) is the acceptable way to behave and is also expected of the child:

Father:	What happened to all the candy? You gave me no candy. Huh?
Child:	I didn't ate all of it.
Father:	What happened to the rest of it?
Child:	My mom put it somewhere . . . else.
Father:	Oh, so you can't eat all of it?
Child:	I'm not gonna eat all of it.
Father:	You would of ate all the candy at the party.

Summary. Family was mentioned in approximately 80% of the shared narratives between Latino parents and their children, with both mothers and fathers selecting family events to discuss with their child. These narratives included lessons about relations among family members, the fun and affection of family, and various examples of helping family members. Although not as frequent, several fathers focused their story on the preservation of family ties, through visits outside of the United States and family visits to the United States. In choosing these family-centered topics, parents communicated to their child that family roots (including members who live a distance away) are fundamental to the child's identities.

Lesson #2: Messages About Gender Roles

A second lesson reflected in parent–child narratives was that of gender roles. Both mothers and fathers often used shared conversations as platforms for conveying messages about gender, albeit in subtle ways. Within the broader category, subthemes were focused on gender-based activities, physical appearance (for girls), and emotions expected of boys and girls.

Gender socialization was evident in the *activities* or *experiences* that parents chose to recollect with their boy versus their girl. Specifically, both mothers and fathers frequently talked about "action-based" experiences with their son, such as camping trips, rides at an amusement park, or action-packed scenes from a movie. This emphasis on action with sons was often nested within the broader context of family-centered activities described previously. In contrast, mothers and fathers alike predominantly shared memories about quieter activities and "socially oriented" experiences with their daughter, such as reading books and ways to befriend others. Again, these topics were often found within narratives about the family.

Figure 4.1 illustrates the parents' main focus on action-based or quieter activities with their son versus their daughter. Only three mother–son dyads and two father–son dyads shared narratives with their son that did not include action-based activities. Reciprocally, only four mother–daughter dyads and two father–daughter dyads reminisced about traditionally active versus quiet or social events.

The following narratives exemplify these trends. The first three excerpts demonstrate the parents' emphasis on their son's sports, winning, and energetic play. In the first, a father and son talk about the child's summer camp activities. The father expresses pride in his son's athletic competencies and implies high expectations of performance for him:

Father:	What you do at camp?
Child:	Watch a movie.
Father:	And what?
Child:	And play a game . . . Play basketball. Play soccer.
Father:	Soccer, basketball. You win?
Child:	I don't know, but I can catch.
Father:	You <u>can catch</u>.
Child:	xx throw the ball xx and it made it to me.
Father:	You <u>can throw</u> the ball.

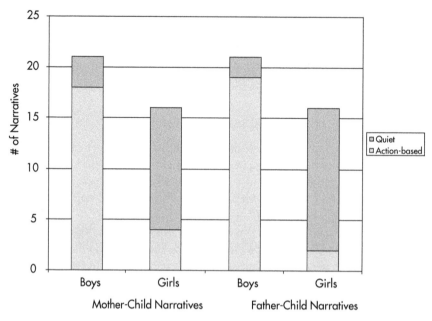

Figure 4.1 Parent–son and parent–daughter narratives by gendered activities (N $=$ 21 boys, N $=$ 16 girls).

In the next example, a father and son discuss the child's bicycle riding during a visit with his aunt and uncle. During the narrative, the father expresses support for his son's bravery. His son in turn talks about his ability to overcome a crushed bike and potential fall, and he notes that it was the other child, not him, who ultimately cried:

Father:	What you do last week when I left you at Auntie's house? Uncle John didn't take you riding your bike? . . . Did you see the bear that was in the backyard?
Child:	[Shakes head no.]
Father:	I thought you did. What did you do that was fun last week?
Child:	Played games.
Father:	And what happened with the game? So you didn't go bike riding? You didn't go bike riding or anything last week?
Child:	He crashed my bike.
Father:	How did he crash your bike?
Child:	(Be)cause he had a big bike, a big giant one.
Father:	And?
Child:	He crashed it.
Father:	And he crashed your bike? Were you on the bike when he crashed it?
Child:	[Nods yes.]
Father:	Did you fall?
Child:	Nope, I jumped off.
Father:	You jumped off! . . .

Child:	He stepped on my training wheels and I couldn't go . . . Then, I stepped on his and he couldn't go. Then he fell down.
Father:	He fell down? He didn't hurt himself, did he?
Child:	Yeah, he was crying.

In the following narrative excerpt, a mother–son dyad shares a memory about a birthday celebration. As the mother prompts her son to list the persons he saw at the party, he begins to name action heroes instead of family or friends. The child appears to be more concerned with the characters who symbolize fortitude and authority, and his mother follows this conversational direction in response to her son's interests:

Mother:	Will you please tell me all about Maria's party? Tell me everything that happened that you know. Who did we see at Maria's party? Who went?
Child:	Spider-Man.
Mother:	Who?
Child:	Spider-Man.
Mother:	And who else?
Child:	X-Men.
Mother:	Did you have fun?
Child:	Yeah.
Mother:	So tell me about the party. What did you do? Who did you see?
Child:	. . . the clown put on Spider-Man costume.

In contrast to these more action-based narratives, the following set of excerpts illustrates the parents' focus on socially oriented and quiet behaviors with their daughter. These passages include messages about the qualities associated with being female (in both manners and physical appearance) and how these characteristics should be enacted in daily life.

For instance, in the following excerpt, a father–daughter dyad talks about the girl's first experiences with her new school. In the complete narrative, the child expresses her sadness about not having friends, and her father uses this opportunity to teach his daughter about connecting with others beyond the family:

Father:	How do you like school? You just started school!
Child:	We didn't go outside.
Father:	It was cold?
Child:	It was sunny.
Father:	Then what?
Child:	Um, I don't have friends.
Father:	You gonna meet friends little by little. You gonna make them once you guys go outside and you gonna make friends.

In the excerpt that follows, a father and his daughter converse about a book that the child read during school. The father thus implicitly conveys to his daughter the enjoyment associated with sharing familiar stories (even though, in reality, the father mixes together pieces of different fairy tales):

Father: Can you tell me about . . . a story in school? Did the teacher ever tell you a story?
Child: [Nods yes.]
Father: About what? *The Three Bears?* Okay, tell me the story of *The Three Bears* . . . Was it the Mamma Bear?
Child: [Nods yes.] The Baby Bear, the Poppa Bear. She was running to the man.
Father: To Grandma's house?
Child: She saw the big bad wolf!
Father: And what did the wolf do?
Child: He ate her!
Father: No way! He ate her?
Child: And he ate the Baby Bear, too!

The next excerpt centers on an action-based memory – a girl's sledding experience with other family members – and is a topic that the child selected to discuss. Although this represents an action-based narrative (more common to the narratives of boys), the father uses this opportunity as a way to speak about his daughter's supposed "fall" during the sledding. Notably, it remains unclear whether his daughter actually did fall because the daughter twice opposes the father's insistence that she had fallen. She claims that she did not succumb to the ice:

Child: Yesterday, I went sledding.
Father: Where?
Child: Sledding . . . I went sledding.
Father: On the ice.
Child: Yeah.
Father: You fall?
Child: No. I was on a thing and I slide down the hill. And then . . .
Father: You didn't fall off?
Child: No! I didn't fell like "boom" in the snow.

The same narrative then ends with the daughter revealing that her father is her "sweetheart" and that he will be her partner at her upcoming school dance. In this particular narrative, as the father expresses his thoughts about his daughter's competencies pertaining to physical, active behaviors such as sledding, his daughter both resists her father's suggestion that she had fallen yet simultaneously communicates her wishes for her father to be her "sweetheart." This term produces images of warmth and protection, with the father assuming a nurturing role in his young daughter's life:

Child: My Mommy said if you wanted to come. You know how to dance.
Father: You gonna be called a sweetheart.
Child: Yeah, it's a sweetheart dance.
Father: So, who you taking?
Child: [Points to her father.]
Father: You taking me?

Beyond the "action" distinction in narratives shared with sons versus daughters, 11 of the 37 mother–child narratives and 9 of the 37 father–child narratives contained lessons about gender roles that included how physical appearance shapes children's identity and the emotions that males and females should express.

Parents who focused on their child's *physical appearance* explicitly commented about the details of "boyhood" or "girlhood" in terms of external qualities. Of the 11 mother–child narratives about gender roles, 3 mentioned children's physical qualities, and all of these were shared by mothers and their daughter. Fathers did not talk about physical appearance with their child. For example, in the subsequent excerpt, a mother and her daughter reminisce about the child's special role as a flower girl at a relative's wedding. The mother notes the color of the child's dress in addition to other observations about physical appearance that create vivid images of "girlhood" for a young daughter:

Mother:	You don't want to talk about the wedding, how you were a flower girl?
Child:	[Nods yes.]
Mother:	And the dress you were wearing and your flower head piece?
Mother:	You walked down the aisle. With who?
Child:	With my sister.
Mother:	And what were you doing?
Child:	Throwing flowers.
Mother:	Did you like it?
Child:	Yeah . . .
Mother:	What color was your dress?
Child:	It was plain, white.
Mother:	But what color skirt and flowers and head piece?
Child:	The head piece was white, purple, blue. Purple with flowers on it.

Similarly, in the next excerpt, a mother and daughter talk about girls' and boys' outward appearance and what they ought to wear:

Mother:	How about when we went to New Jersey? Remember, with Papi, Claudia, and Angela? Remember when we went to eat?
Child:	[Nods yes.]
Mother:	Remember the lady with the big hat?
Child:	[Shakes head no.]
Mother:	You liked that hat?
Child:	[Shakes head no.]
Mother:	What?
Child:	That's for boys, right?
Mother:	No, it's for girls.
Child:	It's for boys.
Mother:	It's for boys?

With respect to gendered messages about *emotions,* 5 of the 11 mother–child narratives about gender socialization and 3 of the 9 father–child narratives moved beyond outward appearance and explicitly included their child's anticipated feelings in terms of socially and culturally approved gender roles. For example, this subsequent excerpt reveals a father's assumption (and expectation) of his daughter's fear in two situations – while swimming in a friend's pool and being frightened of the dark. Although his daughter resists these characterizations, her father insists she was afraid and uses the word "scared" or "scary" four times in his eight conversational turns. Thus, this father implicitly reveals that being scared is acceptable and, in fact, expected:

Father: Did you remember when we went to Martina's house? Do you remember?
Child: Yeah.
Father: Did you like it when she went in the swimming pool with you to swim?
Child: Yeah.
Father: You scared of the water, right?
Child: What?
Father: Was it fun?
Child: Uh huh.
Father: You liked it?
Child: Yup.
Father: What was the best part? What did you like the most? The dark? You was scared of the dark, right?
Child: No! I like the dark.
Father: But I saw the video and it looked like you were scared of the dark. So, tell me.
Child: But me and Margie.
Father: What were you doing? It wasn't scary in the dark? Huh? So tell me. Tell me what happened about the dark.

Likewise, the following excerpt presents a mother and daughter remembering the girl's trip to an amusement park with her cousins. The mother asks her child on several occasions if she was scared on certain rides that seemed to be frightening for the other children. However, this mother also discusses fear in the boys that were at the park. Thus, although there is dialogue about fear, there is a more balanced presentation by child gender. Nonetheless, what is notable is that the topic of fear is again raised with a girl:

Mother: . . . you have fun when we went out with Joey and Robert? Where we went?
Child: Coney Island.
Mother: Did you get on any rides with Joey?
Child: Um, just two.
Mother: Why only two?
Child: Because he was scared on other one . . .
Mother: Which one he was scared on?
Child: The other one that goes around fast.
Mother: You was scared?
Child: No.
Mother: Did you have fun?
Child: Uh huh.

Mother:	What about the one [roller coaster] that you had to turn in circles? Were Robert and you scared of that one?
Child:	No.
Mother:	You wasn't?

In contrast to these narratives, which mention the "presence" of fear, in the following excerpt, a mother notes the "absence" of fear in her son during an amusement park trip:

Mother:	How was the ride?
Child:	Fun.
Mother:	What ride did you go on?
Child:	I got on the motorcycle, the fireman, and uh . . . the . . . house thing that goes up.
Mother:	The spinning wheel?
Child:	[Nods yes.]
Mother:	Was it fun?
Child:	[Nods yes.] And it goes all the way up and you can see the beach.
Mother:	Really?
Child:	[Nods yes.]
Mother:	You weren't scared?
Child:	[Shakes head no.]

Summary. Parent–child narratives provided a venue for parents to socialize their child's gender role. This was expressed in both the activities selected for discussion – being "action-based" for boys versus quiet or "socially based" for girls. Additionally, gendered themes were evident in the mothers' attention to physical appearance when they talked with their girl, and both mothers and fathers stressed emotions such as fear with girls but bravery with boys. Although these specific themes were expressed in relatively smaller numbers of narratives, they are based on only 2 minutes of conversation. When these snapshots of gendered talk are extrapolated across the course of days, weeks, and months, they reflect powerful socialization tools for communicating gendered expectations to young boys and girls.

Lesson #3: Educational Achievements and Academic Success in Latino Families

Finally, a focus on educational achievements was a third cultural lesson evident in shared parent–child narratives. Of the 74 parent–child narratives, 16 emphasized the importance of education in their child's life. In particular, seven mothers and nine fathers referred to the value of school and their expectations of academic success for their boy and girl. Of the 16 narratives about school experiences, 9 were between parents and their daughter (i.e., 4 mother–daughter and 5 father–daughter dyads), and 7 of the 16 school-focused narratives were between parents and their son (i.e., 3 mother–son and 4 father–son narratives). Subthemes under the broader category of educational achievement included personal pride around success, school being enjoyable, and working hard yields positive consequences.

As an example, in the subsequent excerpt, the mother initiates a conversation about her daughter's perfect score on a spelling test. This excerpt contains a main message that *academic success is related to the child's growing self-concept and sense of pride.* Beyond that, however, is explicit mention of a functional link between academic success and family, in that the mother's pride in her child is an important outcome of doing well:

Mother: Let's talk about your spelling test, your score of the spelling test. It was exciting?
Child: [Nods yes.]
Mother: Why?
Child: Because I got a hundred percent.
Mother: Because you had a hundred percent or because . . . you learned your words?
Child: I learned my words.
Mother: Yeah and you study hard.
Child: [Nods yes.]
Mother: It was exciting for you?
Child: Yes.
Mother: You like it.
Child: A hundred percent.
Mother: Why?
Child: Because you, you get so proud of me when I do a hundred percent.
Mother: I, because I get so proud of you when you get a hundred percent?

Similarly, another mother–daughter dyad talks about the child's first day at a new school. In this excerpt, the mother speaks of different aspects of the school experiences, such as the recognition that school requires some undesirable consequences (as in waking up early). Nevertheless, the mother highlights affirmative features of school, including a connection to teachers:

Mother: Tell me about your first day of school. How did you like it?
Child: Fine.
Mother: Yeah . . . what did you do?
Child: Good.
Mother: What did you do in school? Were you excited to go to school?
Child: No.
Mother: Why?
Child: Uh huh. I got hard things.
Mother: Yeah.
Child: Yeah.
Mother: What? In the morning you got to get up to go to school. You excited? You like the teachers?
Child: Yes.

Mother:	Yeah. So, what else you like? Tell me what you like about school.
Child:	Playing.
Mother:	Playing. And what else?
Child:	Nothing else.
Mother:	You don't like nothing else? You not happy that you gotta wake up early to go to school. What else don't you like about school?
Child:	Yeah, I like it.
Mother:	You like school?
Child:	Yeah.
Mother:	You like it a lot?
Child:	Yeah. I like lunch.
Mother:	What about your teachers?
Child:	Yeah.
Mother:	Do you like your teachers?
Child:	Yeah.
Mother:	What are your teachers' names?
Child:	I don't know.
Mother:	You don't know your teachers' names?
Child:	No.
Mother:	You don't know their names? Mr. Morgan.
Child:	Yeah.
Mother:	Who else? What did you do that was exciting that made you happy in school?
Child:	Sing!

Next, a father explicitly states his expectation that his daughter will perform well in school. Although the child does not respond to her father verbally, she responds nonverbally with positive gestures, indicating her concurrence with his school perspectives:

Father:	What happened in school today?
Child:	[Smiles.]
Father:	How did it go in school? It went well?
Child:	[Nods yes.]
Father:	Come on. You did well? Very good?
Child:	[Laughs and smiles.]
Father:	Very good?
Child:	[Smiles and nods yes.]

The excerpt that follows illustrates a mother talking with her son about *exciting aspects of his school experiences*. This mother underscores the importance of peers for fun at school but, as in a previous narrative, she also turns to a discussion of the role of teachers:

Mother:	. . . What else you did at school? You like school?
Child:	Yup.
Mother:	How much you like school?

Child:	A lot.
Mother:	A lot.
Child:	Yeah.
Mother:	Why you like school?
Child:	(Be)cause they're fun.
Mother:	It's fun? . . . You like the kids?
Child:	Yeah.
Mother:	They play with you . . . ?
Child:	Yeah.
Mother:	How (a)bout your teachers?
Child:	They good.
Mother:	. . . Yeah . . . they teach you a lot of stuff?
Child:	Yeah.
Mother:	. . . And what's her name? What's the teacher's name?
Child:	Miss Samson.
Mother:	Miss Samson? And how (a)bout your friends . . . in school?

Additionally, parents suggested that academic achievements and being well behaved in the school yield *positive, tangible consequences.* Two fathers discussed the relationship between academic success and concrete rewards with their 5-year-old children. Both fathers teach their children that they are accountable for their actions in settings outside the home and that educational attainment is important to both children and their family.

For example, in the next excerpt between a father and his daughter, taken from the end of their conversation, the father instructs his daughter that proper behavior across school and home contexts is a prerequisite for holiday gifts:

Father:	So, are you gonna come over for Christmas with Daddy? . . .
Child:	Open my presents.
Father:	Yes! We have a lot of presents. Santa Claus gonna bring you a lot of presents. But, you have to behave in school, okay? And you have to listen to Mommy.

Likewise, in the following narrative, a father teaches his son that doing well at school is rewarding. The father encourages his son to reflect on his own behavior in determining whether he is deserving of a birthday gift:

Father:	So, what do you want for your birthday? You think you've been good? You think you deserve a gift?
Child:	Yeah.
Father:	Yeah. You've been doing your homework, right?
Child:	Yeah.

Summary. By selecting school as a topic of their shared narratives, both mothers and fathers expressed the value of education and that rewards come with hard work. Mothers and fathers talked about school experiences with their son and daughter at rather comparable rates. Both mothers and fathers also indirectly conveyed important messages about school being another essential community for children's social and academic development and that being successful in school brings pride back to the family.

GENERAL DISCUSSION

We presented a qualitative analysis of parent–child narratives in a sample of 37 mother–child and father–child dyads from diverse Latino backgrounds. The study addressed two main gaps in the literature – an absence of studies on father–child narratives and a lack of attention to narrative exchanges in children from low-income, ethnically diverse backgrounds. Although narratives serve many functions, we focused specifically on the role of narratives in relaying cultural lessons to children. By describing similarities and differences in the lessons that mothers and fathers elaborated in their shared narratives, our work emphasized the role of both parents in children's social-cultural development.

Both mothers and fathers (rather than children) tended to select the topic of the shared narratives, which in itself may have communicated their role as authority figures to their children (e.g., Halgunseth et al., 2006). Moreover, by selecting the topic of narratives, parents implicitly highlighted what they considered to be worthy topics of conversation. In particular, we identified three main themes in the personal narratives that Latino mothers and fathers shared with their child: (1) the role of the family (*familismo*) in children's lives, (2) gender roles, and (3) educational achievements. Overall, mothers and fathers discussed lessons on family, gender socialization, and school rather comparably, although a few differences were present in terms of parent and child gender, as revisited in the next section.

The Importance of Family

Our research indicates that mothers and fathers alike centered their narratives largely on family-oriented topics with both their son and their daughter. This predominance of stories about family (i.e., 60 of 72 parent–child narratives) corroborates research on the value of *familismo* in Latino families (e.g., Halgunseth et al., 2006). Extant research suggests that a fundamental facet of the social and identity development of Latino children and youth is the child's family and social networks (e.g., Solís, 1995), which includes both immediate relatives and extended family (e.g., Bengston, 2001). Latino families have been characterized as emphasizing an interdependent orientation (e.g., Halgunseth et al., 2006; Oyserman, Coon, & Kemmelmeier, 2002), which is typically evident in their actions and conversations (e.g., Delgado-Gaitán, 1994; Harwood, Miller, & Irizarry, 1995; Melzi, 2000). The theme of relatedness has been traditionally defined as a sense of connection to a larger group or community (Bakan, 1966; McAdams, 1988) in contrast to independence, which has typically been considered as characteristic of Western cultures (Ely et al., 1998).

Within the broader theme of *familismo,* several subthemes were elaborated, including being able to identify relatives and having fun with and expressing affection toward family members. Both parents highlighted a variety of fun activities in the context of family, yet our findings indicated a slightly greater tendency for mothers to discuss the family unit as being enjoyable. Additionally, parents rather comparably underscored the special function of the grandmother in boys' and girls' conception about familial ties. Although both mothers and fathers emphasized the importance of family when talking with their child, several fathers shared stories about maintaining ties to relatives outside of the United States (thus maintaining roots to cultural heritage), whereas mothers tended to focus on more proximal members of the family.

Furthermore, themes around family addressed proper demeanor in family settings, which aligns with the notion that Latinos value children who are *bien educados* (Melzi, 2000). The term *bien educados* goes beyond academic performance to notions of respect and socially appropriate behaviors toward family members (Melzi, 2000). In turn, this reverence reflects on parents' child-rearing goals, including gender socialization. Recent work describes the emphasis on appropriate social conduct as illustrative of the larger concept of collectivism or interdependence (Leyendecker, Lamb, Harwood, & Schölmerich, 2002; Miller & Harwood, 2001), in which children's self-concepts are integrally tied to other individuals (Leyendecker et al., 2002). In our research, although a small number, mothers and fathers similarly taught their children about being helpful and conducting themselves in socially and culturally appropriate ways, including obeying parents and other authority figures. In these stories, parents shared their belief that generous, obedient children produce happiness in the beneficiary of their kind acts, in themselves, and in their family.

Messages About Gender Roles

A second major lesson identified in the shared narratives was a focus on how boys and girls should behave, look, and feel. The growth of gender concepts is a multidimensional process occurring in a larger social-cultural context (e.g., Miller, Trautner, & Ruble, 2006). Social-cognitive theory states that children develop sex-typed behaviors and abilities as a function of cognitive developmental changes in interaction with social influences (e .g., Bussey & Bandura, 1999; Ruble, Martin, & Berenbaum, 2006). Numerous studies have highlighted the use of emotion words in mother–child conversations (e.g., Burger & Miller, 1999; Eisenberg, 1999; Flannagan & Perese, 1998; Garner, Jones, Gaddy, & Rennie, 1997), as well as gender differences in parents' and children's use of emotion in lower-income households (Eisenberg, 1999; Flannagan & Perese, 1998). A common finding is that mother–daughter dyads mention more emotion words than mother–son dyads. Moreover, numerous studies indicate that mother–daughter dyads discuss more negative emotions than mother–son dyads, and these negative emotions generally include feelings of sadness and dislike (e.g., Fivush, 1991).

Our work extends this research by noting specific gender themes that both mothers and fathers used in reminiscing with their son or daughter. Parents of boys generally stressed actions, emotional strength, and bravery; in contrast, parents of girls typically emphasized family-related experiences, social activities, companionship, and sometimes fear. Through such stories, mother–child and father–child narratives became opportunities for the transmission of specific cultural and social messages to boys and girls from both parents.

Notably, parents moved beyond action-based topics with boys and socially based topics with girls to also focus on an explicit gender role and emotions expected of their child. It is interesting that three mothers emphasized their daughter's physical appearance, whereas no fathers did. This may suggest Latino mothers' value of young girls' outward qualities in shaping their identity and, specifically, their "girlhood." Furthermore, mothers and fathers alike used their narrative as a way to talk about acceptable emotions for young children – namely, girls' fear and boys' courage. Our findings, therefore, reveal general similarities in parents' implicit and explicit messages about children's gender-prescribed behaviors and feelings. These gender-specific lessons often unfolded in the larger context of family.

EDUCATIONAL ACHIEVEMENTS IN LATINO FAMILIES

Finally, given the documented importance of scholastic attainment for Latino families, it was expected that parent–child dyads would choose to speak about school experiences, which they did. Of the 74 narratives, 16 highlighted academic achievement, and mothers and fathers talked about school experiences with their son or daughter rather comparably. Parents expressed the notion that achievement would help build the child's self-concept and lead to family pride. By engaging in school-related topics of conversation with their child, mothers and fathers illustrated how academic success helps to fulfill satisfaction both individually (child) and collectively (family). Nonetheless, unlike the mother–child narratives, a few father–child narratives suggested that perseverance in school would result in very tangible rewards, such as a gift.

This emphasis on school achievement accords with existing research and policy discussions on the role of academics in Latino families. Latino children and youth reflect increasingly high proportions of immigrants to the United States, and researchers and educators are particularly concerned about supporting the academic prospects of Latino children so that they may ultimately achieve satisfying careers (Chapa & De La Rosa, 2006). In terms of research, studies with Latino youth have demonstrated how Latinos define and construct educational experiences in their lives. For example, in an ethnographic study of the narratives of 27 Mexican and Puerto Rican adolescents, both eighth-grade and high-school students revealed three "selves" that needed to be integrated in order to attain success in school: family, student, and career (Quiroz, 2001). As a group, Latino students generally experienced many hardships in school, including the challenges of biculturalism, first- and second-language acquisition, and having positive relations with their teachers (Quiroz, 2001). Another aspect of a majority of the narratives was a student's desire "to be a somebody" (Quiroz, 2001, p.341) despite academic challenges. Studies have shown that becoming successful academically may be tied to the importance of family and, in turn, reflects back on the family in Latino groups (e.g., Gándara, 2005; Suárez-Orozco & Suárez-Orozco, 1995). Our research is focused on much earlier developmental periods and suggests that already by preschool, parent–child narratives in Latino families emphasize school values as important topics of socialization.

CONCLUSION

In conclusion, personal narratives are a vehicle for sharing cultural beliefs as well as practicing oral language skills that are important for children's transition to formal schooling. Therefore, there is potential for this research on mother–child and father–child personal narratives to inform educators, researchers, and practitioners about ways that families from diverse Latino backgrounds share memories with their children while simultaneously strengthening necessary language skills. Given the rise of Latino families in the United States, teachers and practitioners must be sensitive to the needs of these families, and parent–child reminiscing might be one way of understanding the cultural ideologies of ethnically diverse parents and children. For example, early-childhood programs may promote parent–child oral storytelling as part of children's preparedness for kindergarten entry, and such strategies have been found to be effective for children and families from other cultural backgrounds (e.g., Peterson et al., 1999). Through forums such as parent workshops, families from diverse, low-income Latino backgrounds may be encouraged to learn about how daily conversations with their children play an important role in children's overall development. Educators might also incorporate the sharing of personal stories during storytelling in their curriculum practices. These programs may encourage parent–child narratives as part of children's developing emergent literacy skills and as a way to promote social and cultural development (e.g., Gallimore & Goldenberg, 2001; Rueda, Monzo, Blacher, Shapiro, & González, 2005).

Our research also contributes theoretically to understanding the cultural practices and socialization of Latino families living in the United States. Future directions of our work include advancing an understanding of how parents and children influence the overall themes and structural elements of one another's narratives. Examination of how both mother–child and father–child relationships shape the developmental trajectories of Latino children from low-income families is also warranted.

In summary, although narrative research has described stories in diverse Spanish-speaking families both within and outside the United States (Melzi, 2000; Melzi & Caspe, 2005; Melzi & Fernández, 2004), virtually no work has compared and contrasted mother–child and father–child narratives in low-income, Latino families living in the United States. This chapter aimed to address these specific gaps. The cultural lessons that Latino mothers and fathers shared with their children during personal narratives offered children valuable opportunities to learn about their family and cultural heritage, personal identity, and the role of school relative to their community and larger society.

ACKNOWLEDGMENTS

The findings reported herein are based on research conducted as part of the national Early Head Start (EHS) Research and Evaluation Project, funded by the Administration on Children, Youth, and Families (ACYF), U.S. Department of Health and Human Services, under Contract #105–95-1936 to Mathematica Policy Research, Princeton, NJ and Columbia University's Center for Children and Families, Teachers College, in conjunction with the EHS Research Consortium. We acknowledge the continual input by Dr. Barbara A. Pan at Harvard University to the narrative work of the EHS Consortium. We offer our gratitude to Jessica Gluck and other students at New York University for their commitment and insight. Finally, we wish to thank the mothers, fathers, and children who allowed us to listen to them talk about memories they found to be meaningful reflections of their life. This work was conducted at New York University's Center for Research on Culture, Development, and Education (funded by the National Science Foundation, Grant BCS #021859, to Catherine S. Tamis-LeMonda).

REFERENCES

Adams, S., Kuebli, J., Boyle, P. A., & Fivush, R. (1995). Gender differences in parent–child conversations about past emotions: A longitudinal investigation. *Sex Roles, 33*, 309–323.

Aram, D., & Levin, I. (2001). Mother–child joint writing in low SES: Sociocultural factors, maternal mediation, and emergent literacy. *Cognitive Development, 16*, 831–852.

Astington, J. W., & Pelletier, J. (2005). Theory of mind, language, and learning in the early years: Developmental origins of school readiness. In B. D. Homer & C. S. Tamis-LeMonda (Eds.), *The development of social cognition and communication* (pp. 205–230). Mahwah, NJ: Erlbaum.

Bakan, D. (1966). *The duality of human existence: Isolation and communion in Western man.* Boston, MA: Beacon Press.

Beals, D. E., De Temple, J. M., & Dickinson, D. K. (1994). Talking and listening that support early literacy development of children from low-income families. In D. K. Dickinson (Ed.), *Bridges to literacy: Children, families, and schools* (pp. 19–40). Cambridge, MA: Basil Blackwell Ltd.

Bellinger, D. C., & Gleason, J. B. (1982). Sex differences in parental directives to young children. *Sex Roles, 8*(11), 1123–1139.

Bengtson, V. L. (2001). Beyond the nuclear family: The increasing importance of multi-generational bonds. *Journal of Marriage and the Family, 63*, 1–16.

Benson, M. S. (1997). Psychological causation and goal-based episodes: Low-income children's emerging narrative skills. *Early Childhood Research Quarterly, 12*, 439–457.

Berko Gleason, J. (1975). Fathers and other strangers: Men's speech to young children. In D. P. Dato (Ed.), *Developmental psycholinguistics: Theory and applications* (pp. 289–297). Washington, DC: Georgetown University Press.

Bornstein, M., Vibbert, M., Tal, J., & O'Donnell, K. (1992). Toddler language and play in the second year: Stability, covariation, and influences of parenting. *First Language, 12*, 323–338.

Bredekamp, S. (2004). Play and school readiness. In E. F. Zigler, D. G. Singer, & S. J. Bishop-Josef (Eds.), *Children's play: The roots of reading* (pp. 159–174). Washington, DC: Zero to Three/National Center for Infants, Toddlers and Families.

Brockmeier, J. (2001). From the end to the beginning: Retrospective teleology in auto-biography. In J. Brockmeier & D. Carbaugh (Eds.), *Narrative and identity: Studies in autobiography, self and culture*. Philadelphia, PA: John Benjamins Publishing Company.

Bruner, J. (2002). *Making stories: Law, literature, life*. New York: Farrar, Straus, and Giroux.

Burger, L. K., & Miller, P. J. (1999). Early talk about the past revisited: Affect in working-class and middle-class children's co-narrations. *Journal of Child Language, 26*, 133–162.

Burns, M. S., Griffin, P., & Snow, C. E. (1999). *Starting out right: A guide to promoting children's reading success*. Washington, DC: National Academy Press.

Bussey, K., & Bandura, A. (1999). Social cognitive theory of gender development and differentiation. *Psychological Review, 106*, 676–713.

Chapa, J., & De La Rosa, B. (2006). The problematic pipeline: Demographic trends and Latino participation in graduate science, technology, engineering, and mathematics programs. *Journal of Hispanic Higher Education, 5*(3), 203–221.

Current Population Survey (2005). Retrieved April 23, 2007, from http://www.bls.gov/cps/.

Davidson, R., & Snow, C. (1996). Five-year-olds' interactions with fathers vs. mothers. *First Language, 16*, 223–242.

Delgado-Gaitán, C. (1994). Consejos: The power of cultural narratives. *Anthropology & Education Quarterly, 25* (3), 298–316.

Dickinson, D. K. (1991). Teacher agenda and setting: Constraints on conversation in preschools. In A. McCabe & C. Peterson (Eds.), *Developing narrative structure* (pp. 255–301). Hillsdale, NJ: Lawrence Erlbaum Associates.

Dickinson, D. K., & McCabe, A. (2001). Bringing it all together: The multiple origins, skills, and environmental supports of early literacy. *Learning Disabilities Research & Practice, 16*(4), 186–202.

Dickinson, D. K., McCabe, A., Anastasopoulos, L., Peisner-Feinberg, E., & Poe, M. (2003). The comprehensive language approach to early literacy: The interrelationships among vocabulary, phonological sensitivity, and print knowledge among preschool-aged children. *The Journal of Educational Psychology, 95*, 465–481.

Dickinson, D. K., & Tabors, P. O. (2001). *Beginning literacy with language: Young children learning at home and school.* Baltimore, MD: Paul H. Brookes Publishing Co.

Dunn, J., Bretherton, I., & Munn, P. (1987). Conversations about feeling states between mothers and their young children. *Developmental Psychology, 23,* 132–139.

Eisenberg, A. (1999). Emotion talk among Mexican American and Anglo American mothers and children from two social classes. *Merrill-Palmer Quarterly, 45,* 267–284.

Ely, R., & Berko Gleason, J. (1995). Socialization across contexts. In P. Fletcher & B. MacWhinney (Eds.), *The handbook of child language* (pp. 251–270). Cambridge, MA: Blackwell Publishers.

Ely, R., Berko, Gleason, J., MacGibbon, A., & Zaretsky, E. (2001). Attention to language: Lessons learned at the dinner table. *Social Development, 10*(3), 355–373.

Ely, R., Melzi, G., Hadge, L., & McCabe, A. (1998). Being brave, being nice: Themes of agency and communion in children's narratives. *Journal of Personality, 66,* 257–284.

Fiorentino, L., & Howe, N. (2004). Language competence, narrative ability, and school readiness in low-income preschool children. *Canadian Journal of Behavioural Science, 36*(4), 280–294.

Fivush, R. (1991). The social construction of personal narratives. *Merrill-Palmer Quarterly, 37,* 59–82.

Fivush, R., & Haden, C. (Eds.) (2003). *Autobiographical memory and the construction of a narrative self* (pp. 29–48). Mahwah, NJ: Lawrence Erlbaum Associates.

Fivush, R., & Nelson, K. (2004). Culture and language in the emergence of autobiographical memory. *Psychological Science, 15*(9), 573–577.

Flannagan, D., & Perese, S. (1998). Emotional references in mother–daughter and mother–son dyads' conversations about school. *Sex Roles, 39,* 353–367.

Gallimore, R., & Goldenberg, C. (2001). Analyzing cultural models and settings to connect minority achievement and school improvement research. *Educational Psychologist, 36*(1), 45–56.

Gándara, P. (2005). Fragile futures: Risk and vulnerability among Latino high achievers. ETS Policy Information Report. Retrieved August 28, 2007, from www.ets.org/research/pic.

Garner, P. W., Jones, D. C., Gaddy, G., & Rennie, K. M. (1997). Low-income mothers' conversations about emotions and their children's emotional competence. *Social Development, 6*(1), 37–52.

Haden, C. A. (2003). Joint encoding and joint reminiscing: Implications for young children's understanding and remembering of personal experiences. In R. Fivush & C. A. Haden (Eds.), *Autobiographical memory and the construction of a narrative self* (pp. 49–69). Mahwah, NJ: Lawrence Erlbaum Associates.

Haden, C. A., Haine, R. A., & Fivush, R. (1997). Developing narrative structure in parent–child reminiscing across preschool years. *Developmental Psychology, 33,* 295–307.

Halgunseth, L. C., Ispa, J. M., & Ruddy, D. (2006). Parental control in Latino families: An integrated review of the literature. *Child Development, 77*(5), 1282–1297.

Harwood, R. L., Miller, J. G., & Irizarry, N. L. (1995). *Culture and attachment: Perceptions of the child in context.* New York: Guilford Press.

Heath, S. B. (1994). Taking a cross-cultural look at narratives. In K. G. Butler (Ed.), *Cross-cultural perspectives in language assessment and intervention* (pp. 54–64). Gaithersburg, MD: Aspen Publishers, Inc.

Hudson, J. A., & Shapiro, L. R. (1991). From knowing to telling: The development of children's scripts, stories, and personal narratives. In A. McCabe & C. Peterson (Eds.), *Developing narrative structure* (pp. 89–136). Hillsdale, NJ: Erlbaum.

Lamb, M. E. (1997). *The role of the father in child development* (3rd ed.). New York: Wiley.

Lamb, M. E. (2004). *The role of the father in child development* (4th ed.). Hoboken, NJ: Wiley.

Leadbeater, B., & Way, N. (2007). *Urban girls: Building strengths.* New York: New York University Press.

Leaper, C., Anderson, K. J., & Sanders, P. (1998). Moderators of gender effects on parents' talk to their children: A meta-analysis. *Developmental Psychology, 34,* 3–27.

Leichtman, M. D. (1999). Cultural, social, and maturational influences on childhood amnesia. In L. Balter & C. S. Tamis-LeMonda (Eds.), *Child psychology: A handbook of contemporary issues* (pp. 447–466). Philadelphia, PA: Taylor & Francis.

Leyendecker, B., Lamb, M. E., Harwood, R. L., & Schölmerich, A. (2002). Mothers' socialization goals and evaluations of desirable and undesirable everyday situations in two diverse cultural groups. *International Journal of Behavioral Development, 26*(3), 348–258.

McAdams, D. P. (1988). *Power, intimacy, and the life story: Personological inquiries into identity.* New York: Guilford Press.

McAdams, D. P. (1993). *The stories we live by: Personal myths and the making of the self.* New York: William Morrow.

McCabe, A., & Peterson, C. (1991). Getting the story: A longitudinal study of parental styles in eliciting narratives and developing narrative skill. In A. McCabe & C. Peterson (Eds.), *Developing narrative structure* (pp. 217–253). Hillsdale, NJ: Lawrence Erlbaum Associates.

Melzi, G. (2000). Cultural variations in the construction of personal narratives: Central American and European American mothers' elicitation styles. *Discourse Processes, 30*(2), 153–177.

Melzi, G., & Caspe, M. (2005). Variations in maternal narrative styles during book-reading interactions. *Narrative Inquiry, 15*(1), 101–125.

Melzi, G., & Fernández, C. (2004). Talking about past emotions: Conversations between Peruvian mothers and their preschool children. *Sex Roles, 50* (9/10), 641–657.

Merriam, S. B. (2001). *Qualitative research and case study applications in education.* California: John Wiley & Sons, Inc.

Michaels, S. (1981). "Sharing time": An oral preparation for literacy. *Language in Society, 10,* 423–442.

Miller, A. M., & Harwood, R. L. (2001). Long-term socialization goals and the construction of infants' social networks among middle-class Anglo and Puerto Rican mothers. *International Journal of Behavioral Development, 25,* 450–457.

Miller, C. F., Trautner, H. M., & Ruble, D. N. (2006). The role of gender stereotypes in children's preferences and behavior. In L. Balter & C. S. Tamis-LeMonda (Eds.), *Child psychology: A handbook of contemporary issues, Vol. 2* (pp. 293–323). New York: Psychology Press, Taylor and Francis Group.

Miller, P. J., & Sperry, L. L. (1988). Early talk about the past: The origins of conversational stories of personal experience. *Journal of Child Language, 15,* 293–315.

Nelson, K. (1996). *Language in cognitive development: Emergence of the mediated mind*. Cambridge: Cambridge University Press.

Nelson, K. (2001). Language and the self: From the "Experiencing I" to the "Continuing Me." In C. Moore & K. Lemmon (Eds.), *The self in time: Developmental perspectives* (pp. 15–33). Mahwah, NJ: Lawrence Erlbaum Associates.

Nelson, K. (2003). Narrative and self, myth and memory: Emergence of the cultural self. In R. Fivush & C. A. Haden (Eds.), *Autobiographical memory and the construction of a narrative self* (pp. 3–28). Mahwah, NJ: Lawrence Erlbaum Associates.

Nelson, K., & Fivush, R. (2004). The emergence of autobiographical memory: A social-cultural developmental theory. *Psychology Review, 111*(2), 486–511.

Newcombe, R., & Reese, E. (2004). Evaluations and orientations in mother–child narratives as a function of attachment security: A longitudinal investigation. *International Journal of Behavioral Development, 28*(3), 230–245.

Ochs, E., & Capps, L. (2001). *Living narrative: Creating lives in everyday storytelling*. Cambridge, MA: Harvard University Press.

Oller, D. K., & Pearson, B. Z. (2002). Assessing the effects of bilingualism: A background. In D. K. Oller & R. E. Eilers (Eds.), *Language and literacy in bilingual children* (pp. 3–21). Clevedon, UK: Multilingual Matters.

Oyserman, D., Coon, H. M., & Kemmelmeier, M. (2002). Rethinking individualism and collectivism: Evaluation of theoretical assumptions and meta-analyses. *Psychological Bulletin, 128*(1), 3–72.

Parke, R. D. (2004). Fathers, families, and the future: A plethora of plausible predictions. *Merrill-Palmer Quarterly, 50*(4), 456–470.

Peterson, C., Jesso, B., & McCabe, A. (1999). Encouraging narratives in preschoolers: An intervention study. *Journal of Child Language, 26*, 49–67.

Pillemer, D. B. (1998). *Momentous events, vivid memories*. Cambridge, MA: Harvard University Press.

Quiroz, P. A. (2001). The silencing of Latino student "voice": Puerto Rican and Mexican narratives in eighth grade and high school. *Anthropology & Education Quarterly, 32*(3), 326–349.

Reese, E. (1995). Predicting children's literacy from mother–child conversations. *Cognitive Development, 10*(3), 381–405.

Reese, E., & Farrant, K. (2003). Social origins of reminiscing. In R. Fivush & C. A. Haden (Eds.), *Autobiographical memory and the construction of a narrative self* (pp. 29–48). Mahwah, NJ: Lawrence Erlbaum Associates.

Reese, E., & Fivush, R. (1993). Parental styles of talking about the past. *Developmental Psychology, 29*, 596–606.

Reese, E., Haden, C. A., & Fivush, R. (1993). Mother–child conversations about the past: Relationships of style and memory over time. *Cognitive Development, 8*, 403–430.

Reese, E., Haden, C. A., & Fivush, R. (1996). Mothers, fathers, daughters, sons: Gender differences in autobiographical reminiscing. *Research on Language and Social Interaction, 29*(1), 27–56.

Rogoff, B. (1990). *Apprenticeship in thinking: Cognitive development in social context*. New York: Oxford University Press.

Roth, F. P., Speece, D. L., & Cooper, D. H. (2002). A longitudinal analysis of the connection between oral language and early reading. *Journal of Educational Research, 95*, 259–272.

Ruble, D. N., Martin, C., & Berenbaum, S. (2006). Gender development. In W. Damon & R. M. Lerner (Series Eds.) & N. Eisenberg (Vol. Ed.), *Handbook of child psychology: Vol. 3. Social, emotional, and personality development* (6th ed., pp. 858–932). New York: Wiley.

Rueda, R., Monzo, L., Blacher, J., Shapiro, J., & González, J. (2005). Cultural models and practices regarding transition: A view from Latina mothers of young adults with developmental disabilities. *Exceptional Children, 71*(4), 401–414.

Shatil, E., Share, D. C., & Levin, I. (2000). On the contribution of kindergarten writing to grade-one literacy: A longitudinal study in Hebrew. *Applied Psycholinguistics, 21*, 1–21.

Snow, C. (1983). Literacy and language: Relationships during the preschool years. *Harvard Educational Review, 53*(2), 165–189.

Snow, C. E., Burns, M. S., & Griffin, P. (Eds.) (1998). *Preventing reading difficulties in young children.* Washington, DC: National Academy Press.

Snow, C. E., & Dickinson, D. K. (1990). Social sources of narrative skills at home and at school. *First Language, 10*, 87–103.

Snow, C. E., Porche, M. V., Tabors, P. O., & Harris, S. R. (2007). *Is literacy enough? Pathways to academic success for adolescents.* Baltimore, MD: Paul H. Brookes Publishing Co.

Snow, C. E., Tabors, P. O., Nicholson, P., & Kurland, B. (1995). SHELL: Oral language and early literacy skills in kindergarten and first-grade children. *Journal of Research in Childhood Education, 10*, 37–48.

Solís, J. (1995). The status of Latino children and youth: Challenges and prospects. In R. E. Zambrana (Ed.), *Understanding Latino families: Scholarship, policy, and practice* (pp. 62–81). Thousand Oaks, CA: Sage Publications, Inc.

Suárez-Orozco, M. M., & Suárez-Orozco, C. (1995). The cultural patterning of achievement motivation: A comparison of Mexican, Mexican immigrant, Mexican American, and non-Latino American students. In R.G. Rumbaut & W. Cornelius (Eds.), *California's immigrant children: Theory, research, and implication for educational policy* (pp. 161–190). La Jolla, CA: Center for U.S.–Mexican Studies.

Tamis-LeMonda, C. S., & Cabrera, N. (2002). *Handbook of father involvement: Multidisciplinary perspectives.* Mahwah, NJ: Lawrence Erlbaum Associates.

Tamis-LeMonda, C. S., Cristofaro, T. N., & Baumwell, L. (2008). *Mother–child and father–child conversations during free play.* Manuscript under review.

Tamis-LeMonda, C. S., Shannon, J. D., Cabrera, N. J., & Lamb, M. E. (2004). Fathers and mothers at play with their 2- and 3-year-olds: Contributions to language and cognitive development. *Child Development, 75*(6), 1806–1820.

Tomasello, M., Conti-Ramsden, G., & Ewert, B. (1990). Young children's conversations with their mothers and fathers: Differences in breakdown and repair. *Journal of Child Language, 17*, 115–130.

Uccelli, P., Hemphill, L., Pan, B. A., & Snow, C. (1999). Telling two kinds of stories: Sources of narrative skill. In L. Balter & C. S. Tamis-LeMonda (Eds.), *Child psychology: A handbook of contemporary issues* (pp. 215–233). Philadelphia, PA: Taylor & Francis.

Uccelli, P., & Páez, M. M. (2007). Narrative and vocabulary development of bilingual children from kindergarten to first grade: Developmental changes and associations among English and Spanish skills. *Language, Speech, and Hearing Services in Schools, 38*, 225–236.

U.S. Department of Commerce, Bureau of the Census (2001). Retrieved April 23, 2007, from http://www.census.gov/pubinfo/www/NEWhispML1.html.

Vygotsky, L. S. (1978). *Mind in society*. Cambridge, MA: Harvard University Press.

Wahler, R. G., & Castlebury, F. D. (2002). Personal narratives as maps of the social ecosystem. *Clinical Psychology Review, 22*, 297–314.

Wang, Q. (2006). Relations of maternal style and child self-concept to autobiographical memories in Chinese, Chinese immigrant, and European American 3-year-olds. *Child Development, 77*(6), 1794–1809.

Watson, R. (2002). Literacy and oral language: Implications for early literacy acquisition. In S. B. Neuman & D. K. Dickinson (Eds.), *Handbook of early literacy research* (pp. 43–53). New York: The Guilford Press.

Way, N. (1998). *Everyday courage: The lives and stories of urban teenagers*. New York: New York University Press.

Way, N., & Chu, J. (2004). *Adolescent boys: Exploring diverse cultures of boyhood*. New York: New York University Press.

Whitehurst, G. J., & Lonigan, C. J. (2002). Emergent literacy: Development from prereaders to readers. In S. B. Neuman & D. K. Dickinson (Eds.), *Handbook of early literacy research* (pp. 11–29). New York: The Guilford Press.

Whitehurst, G. J., Zevenbergen, A. A., Crone, D. A., Schultz, M. D., Velting, O. N., & Fischel, J. E. (1999). Outcomes of an emergent literacy intervention from Head Start through second grade. *Journal of Educational Psychology, 91*, 251–272.

Wiley, A. R., Rose, A. J., Burger, L. K., & Miller, P. J. (1998). Constructing autonomous selves through narrative practices: A comparative study of working-class and middle-class families. *Child Development, 69*, 833–847.

Zevenbergen, A. A., Whitehurst, G. J., & Zevenbergen, J. A. (2003). Effects of a shared-reading intervention on the inclusion of evaluative devices in narratives of children from low-income families. *Applied Developmental Psychology, 24*, 1–15.

5

Evaluation in Spanish-Speaking Mother–Child Narratives: The Social and Sense-Making Function of Internal-State References

CAMILA FERNÁNDEZ AND GIGLIANA MELZI

Key words: narrative, evaluation, internal states, mother–child conversations, theory-of-mind, social cognition, autobiographical memory, Spanish, Latino children.

ABSTRACT

Young children's sociocognitive skills, such as their understanding of others' feelings and their ability to explain human action in terms of beliefs, emotions, and intentions, has been associated with naturally occurring talk about internal states in everyday family interactions. The frequency with which children engage in conversations about internal states is related to various aspects of sociocognitive development, including emotion recognition, affective perspective-taking, and false-belief understanding. Various individual and contextual factors influence the language used between parents and children during daily family interactions. However, most studies to date have examined the use of internal-state language in English-speaking homes; thus, results might not be generalizable to other cultural groups. The current study addressed this gap in the literature by examining the manner in which Spanish-speaking Peruvian mothers discussed internal states with their preschooler in two narrative contexts: conversations about the personal past and storybook-sharing interactions. The conversations in these two contexts between 32 middle-class mothers and their preschool-aged children (i.e., ages 3 and 5) were analyzed for the frequency and patterns of use of internal-state references. Results show gender and age differences in the use of internal-state references only in the narrative-conversation context. The chapter concludes with a discussion of the theoretical and empirical links between children's narrative competence and their sociocognitive skills.

INTRODUCTION

Narratives, whether oral or written, lie at the center of human endeavors and relationships, serving multiple functions across various domains. Narratives, especially those we share in conversations with others, give structure to and provide a framework for the interpretation of our lived experiences (Bruner, 1986). As one of the earlier socialization activities, the process of sharing narratives plays a crucial role in children's socioemotional development – for instance, in creating and maintaining social bonds and in shaping self-concept (Farrar, Fasig, & Welch-Ross, 1997; Fivush & Nelson, 2006; Nelson, 1993; Wang & Fivush, 2005; Welch-Ross, 1995). The transactional process between narrative and socioemotional development begins in the early years as young children begin to share their personal experiences through routine family inter-actions, such as conversations about ongoing events, mealtime conversations about past experiences, and sharing books. These everyday interactions pro-vide a context in which children begin to organize and interpret key personal events by integrating factual information and their subjective interpretation of the experiences (e.g., Fivush & Nelson, 2006; Nelson & Fivush, 2004). This sub-jective information of narrative discourse, known as evaluation, is at the core of the social and sense-making functions of narratives and at the same time reflects children's developing sociocognitive skills – their awareness and understanding of the human mind and behavior (Charman & Shmueli-Goetz, 1998; Curenton, 2004; Fivush, 1993). Thus, conversations between caregivers and children can be viewed as a practice in which social, cognitive, and emotional development inter-sect. In this sense, narrative analysis provides a rich source for understanding interactions among these three developmental domains.

Given its subjective and personal nature, the evaluative function of narratives reflects cultural goals, norms, values, and belief systems that vary across ethnic and cultural groups (Wang & Fivush, 2005). Although there is evidence of sig-nificant differences in the structure and the content of mother–child narrative conversations (Fivush & Wang, 2005; Minami & McCabe, 1991, 1995; Mullen & Yi, 1995; Wang, Leichtman, & Davies, 2000), few cultural studies have focused exclusively on evaluation use. The few studies available have examined cultural variations in narrative evaluation with East Asian and European American fam-ilies, and have done so mainly in the context of reminiscing. To our knowledge, there are only a few studies examining evaluation use with Spanish-speaking groups (see chapters 6 and 9, this volume, for examples) and across diverse conversational contexts.

This chapter reviews past and current research on narrative evaluation in Spanish-speaking children's discourse, focusing on the links among children's evaluative competence in narrative production, autobiographical memory, and social cognition. In particular, the main goal of this chapter is to describe how narrative evaluation (through the use of internal-state references in different narrative contexts) highlights key aspects of children's experience that aid in explaining interpersonal behavior and interpreting human intentions, beliefs, desires, and emotions. Specifically, this study addresses the following two questions: (1) What are differences in the use of internal-state references between two narrative contexts – book-sharing interactions and conversations about personal experience?; and (2) Are there age or gender differences in the use of internal-state references associated with the specific contexts of interaction?

SOCIOCOGNITIVE FUNCTIONS OF NARRATIVE EVALUATION

When individuals share past personal experiences with others, they recapitulate lived events in two ways: recapturing factual information and making subjective interpretations. Labov and Waletzky (1967) first described and coined these functions of narrative discourse as *referential* and *evaluative*, respectively. Children implicitly learn about these functions of narrative through the early conversations about their personal experiences with important others, such as parents. During these conversations, parents help children describe their key experiences, interpret them, and determine their significance (Fivush, Haden, & Reese, 2006). Little by little, a child's memories of past personal experiences, encoded and shared verbally, allow the child to construct a represented self with a past, a present, and a future. In other words, the actual process of sharing lived experiences through language is the primary steppingstone for a child's construction of an autobiographical self (Nelson, 2003).

Autobiographical memory has been defined as the collection of remembered personal experiences, judged as relevant to one's sense of self and central to one's personal life story (Welch-Ross, 1995). The verbal reinstatement of personal experience, which usually occurs in the form of social interaction as we share with others our recollection of specific events, is fundamental to consolidate autobiographical memories (Welch-Ross, 1995). In fact, it has been argued that autobiographical memory is social in nature because it originates from social interaction and is motivated by social connectedness (Nelson, 1993).

The construction of early narratives of self can be observed around the age of 2 years, when children start sharing their experiences with parents and other family members (Eisenberg, 1985; Hudson, 1990; McCabe & Peterson, 1991). Parents' linguistic input during conversations about their child's past experiences helps the child recall, organize, and interpret relevant information in the form of a coherent and cohesive personal story that eventually builds to an enduring concept of self (Fivush, 1994; Wang & Fivush, 2005; Welch-Ross, Fasig, & Farrar, 1999). Parents' reminiscing style influences children's developing narrative ability and, therefore, also shapes the emergence of autobiographical memories (e.g., Haden, Haine, & Fivush, 1997; Hudson, 1990; McCabe & Peterson, 1991; Reese & Fivush, 1993; Welch-Ross, 1997).

The individual differences in parental reminiscing style influence children's recall of personal experiences, key for the development of autobiographical memory (e.g., Hudson, 1990; McCabe & Peterson, 1991; Nelson, 1993; Nelson & Fivush, 2004; Reese & Fivush, 1993; Reese, Haden, & Fivush, 1993). Mothers who narrate experiences in more elaborative ways facilitate children's capacity to provide rich descriptions of past events and enhance their ability to represent personal experiences in detailed ways (Fivush et al., 2006; McCabe & Peterson, 1991). In fact, the link between mothers' reminiscing style and children's event memory and narrative ability has been demonstrated in controlled experimental studies (Boland, Haden, & Ornstein, 2003; Peterson, Jesso, & McCabe, 1999). For example, Peterson et al. (1999) trained mothers to talk about past events in an elaborative way with their 3-year-old children and compared them with mother–child dyads that were not trained. As the authors predicted, children from the training group showed gains in vocabulary 1 year later and provided more complex past event narratives 2 years later, compared to children in the control group. Boland et al. (2003), as another example, used a similar experimental methodology to examine the relation between maternal conversational style during an event and children's subsequent remembering of the experience; they found that training mothers on elaborative strategies had substantial effects on children's language skills, their recollection of the experience, and the quality of their subsequent narration. In addition, evidence from longitudinal research suggests that the extent to which mothers include subjective information through evaluative devices, such as emotional and mental states terms, in narrative conversations with their children predicts the quality of children's independent past narratives later on, even after controlling for earlier narrative skills (Haden et al., 1997).

Parent–child talk about the past not only provides organizational structures for memories about the self but is also a rich source of content-specific and interpretive information (Alexander, Miller, & Hengst, 2001; Fivush & Wang, 2005; Melzi, Fernández, Caspe, & Dale, under review; Miller, Sandel, Liang, & Fung, 2001). In other words, conversations about past experiences include facts about occurrences and, perhaps more important, the subjective interpretations of those events. In recounting past experiences, parents not only sequence events and describe settings but also provide information that conveys their personal interpretation of the events (Labov & Waletzky, 1967; Peterson & McCabe, 1983). Interpretations of personal experiences often appear in the form of references to emotions and mental states embedded in the narrative, and they serve to focus the attention of the listener explicitly on the aspects of events worth remembering. Furthermore, references to thoughts, opinions, beliefs, and desires provide a subjective framework for representing the past and constructing self-knowledge (Welch-Ross et al., 1999). This type of evaluative information, therefore, gives narratives a subjective quality marking the narrator's perspective and highlighting the personal significance of narrated past experiences (Fivush, 1993, 2001).

With time, through the actual verbal sharing and evaluation of past experiences, life stories are incorporated as defining aspects of self (e.g., Fivush & Buckner, 2003; Fivush & Nelson, 2006; Nelson & Fivush, 2004). Welch-Ross et al. (1999) examined the relationship between narrative evaluation – specifically, the use of references to emotions and mental-state terms – and organized self-knowledge in preschool-aged children. They found that, in fact, references to emotions were a significant predictor of self-organization scores (as measured by the Self-View Questionnaire, Eder, 1990) after controlling for linguistic skill. Similarly, Bird and Reese (2006) found that emotion talk in mother–child reminiscing was the best predictor of children's self-concept consistency. Therefore, it seems that not only the actual process of reminiscing but also the use of evaluative devices – specifically, the use of references to internal states – is crucial for the construction of a self-concept.

Narrative evaluation also has bearing on children's understanding of mind and emotion (Reese & Cleveland, 2006; Rudek & Haden, 2005). Through conversations about personal experiences, children learn to appreciate other persons' internal states and gradually become able to differentiate them from their own (Dunn, Bretherton, & Munn, 1987; Furrow, Moore, Davidge, & Chiasson, 1992). Children's exposure to and participation in discussions about mental states and emotions during early family interactions play a central role in their understanding of people as psychological beings, particularly in theory-of-mind development (Brown, Donelan-McCall, & Dunn, 1996; Guajardo & Watson, 2002; Hughes & Dunn, 1997, 1998). A wide range of studies has reported significant relations between the frequency of children's conversations about internal states with parents and siblings and their *psychological* understanding, as measured by children's performance in emotion recognition (Dunn, Brown, & Beardsall, 1991), affective perspective-taking (Dunn & Brown, 1993), and false-belief tasks (Brown et al., 1996; Dunn, Brown, Slomkowski, Tesla, & Youngblade, 1991; Hughes & Dunn, 1998). For example, Hughes and Dunn (1998) found that children who engaged in frequent references to mental-state talk with their friends at 33 months of age showed higher false-belief understanding concurrently and 1 year later.

Mental-state language embedded in mother–child conversations calls attention to the child's personal experience of an event, and the ways in which it might differ from someone else's experience of the same event. Thus, narrative evaluation in the form of explicit references to thoughts, beliefs, desires, and emotions provides the child with information about the underlying motives for human actions and shows potential differences in perspectives. In fact, children of mothers who are more elaborative during reminiscing, particularly those who use metamemory comments more frequently, have a more advanced understanding of the mind (Reese & Cleveland, 2006). Collectively, the findings of the studies reviewed thus far show that narrative evaluation – specifically, the use of internal-state language – contributes to children's understanding of others' inner worlds and represents significant advances in sociocognitive development.

Sources of Variations in Narrative Evaluation

The discourse used with children during daily interactions reflects and is dictated by individual as well as cultural communicative patterns and ideologies (Schieffelin & Ochs, 1986, Garrett & Baquedano-López, 2002). Parent–child interactions are a main socialization context and language is the primary means through which children are socialized. Differences in the socialization and child-rearing goals parents uphold are reflected in the topics they choose to discuss with their children and manner in which they choose to interact and converse with them.

Past cross-cultural work on parent-child narrative conversations has shown differences in both the content and the structure of narrative interactions. The great portion of this work has largely focused on East Asian (e.g., Chinese, Japanese and Korean) cultural groups (Miller, Wiley, Fung, & Liang, 1997; Mullen & Yi, 1995; Wang, 2001; Wang et al., 2000). (However, for a review of Spanish-speaking Latino parent-child conversations see Caspe & Melzi, chapter 2, and Wishard Guerra, chapter 7, this volume.) Findings from these studies show that East Asian mother-child conversations are more hierarchical with the mother taking a more active role in narrating, whereas European American dyads are more symmetrical and are co-constructed by both mother and child (Wang et al., 2000). Unlike Eurepean American caregivers, East Asian mothers discourage their children from producing elaborated narratives (Minami & McCabe, 1991, 1995; Mullen & Yi, 1995; Wang et al., 2000). With regard to the content of the conversation, East Asian dyads focus more on behavioral expectations and social norms, whereas European American dyads focus on the child's feelings and thoughts (Mullen & Yi, 1995). When discussing emotionally salient events in conversations about the past, East Asian parents interpret children's emotions as resulting from the child's social behavior and very often use these instances of explicit emotional references as an opportunity to teach the child proper conduct. In comparison, European American mothers often address the causes of children's feelings and discuss them in great detail (Fivush & Wang, 2005; Wang & Fivush, 2005). Thus, depending on the parents' cultural background, references to internal states might serve to help children cope with their feelings, develop a unique autobiographical self, instill cultural values, or teach moral conduct (Wang, 2001, 2003; Wang & Fivush, 2005).

Studies have also documented gender differences in the styles parents use to support boys' and girls' narrations, as well as the topics and content of the conversations (for a review see Fivush & Buckner, 2003). Both mothers and fathers, for example, ask girls to include more social events and emotional reactions to events to a greater extent than they ask boys (Buckner & Fivush, 2000; Fivush, 1991; Fivush, Brotman, Buckner, & Goodman, 2000). They also encourage girls to include a greater diversity of emotional labels and to talk about negative emotions, such as sadness and dislike, more than they encourage boys to do so (Fivush, 1991). In comparison to conversations with boys, parents place past events and emotions in the context of interpersonal relationships with their girls, and encourage girls to include more people in their narratives (Fivush & Buckner, 2003). Although most of the gender work has been conducted with European American samples, there is some indication that gender differences are present across diverse socio-cultural groups in the U.S., including African American and Mexican American groups (Eisenberg, 1999; Flannagan & Perese, 1998). However, these finding do not necessarily hold across all cultural groups (e.g., Melzi & Fernández, 2004; see also King & Gallagher, chapter 6 this volume for a lengthier discussion on differences with Spanish-speaking Latino samples).

Both gender and cultural differences in the early narrative environment lead to differences in the structure and content of children's independent narratives. Not surprisingly, girls produce longer, more coherent and descriptive narratives than boys (Buckner & Fivush, 1998). They also tend to include more people in their narratives and more emotions than do boys (Fivush & Buckner, 2003). In addition, as compared to boys, girls place their past experiences within a social context and include more themes of affiliation (Buckner & Fivush, 1998).

Variations in children's narratives are also associated with differences in parents' scaffolding style across different cultural groups (Leichtman, Wang, & Pillemer, 2003). For example, in a study comparing Korean, Chinese and European American children's narratives, Han, Leichtman, and Wang (1998) found that European American children's narratives were longer and had more descriptions, more personal judgments and opinions, as well as more personal thoughts and cognitions than both Chinese and Korean children's narratives. More recent studies corroborate these findings showing that European American children produce more descriptive narratives of self and elaborate on their internal attributes, whereas Chinese children produce shorter narratives that focus on social interaction and routines (Wang, 2004). As is apparent from this brief review, both culture and gender are two main sources of variation in the inclusion of internal-state language during narrative conversations, thereby suggesting that the social sense-making function of narrative evaluation might also differ along these person variables.

Surprisingly, a less investigated source of variation on parent-child narratives is the interaction context in which the conversation takes place. The available research suggests that maternal reminiscing style tends to be consistent across types of memories (e.g., shared versus unshared past events) (Reese & Brown, 2000), across time (Farrant & Reese, 2000; Reese et al., 1993; Rudek & Haden, 2005), and across children in the same family (Haden, 1998). Even though reminiscing style seems to be a stable characteristic of the parent, it might vary depending on specific interaction contexts (Reese, 2002). Maternal reminiscing style, for example, does not generalize to other conversational contexts, like free play (Haden & Fivush, 1996; Kleinknecht & Beike, 2004). Some conversational contexts might call for the use of evaluative devices to a greater degree, whereas other contexts might require the recollection of referential and factual information. The prevalence of explicit narrative evaluation and its impact on children's autobiographical memory and social cognition might differ depending on the conversational context in which it occurs (Fivush et al., 2006; Kleinknecht & Beike, 2004; Rudek & Haden, 2005). However, not many studies have made cross-context comparisons, so definitive conclusions regarding evaluation patterns are ill-advised at the present time.

In a seminal study that used language data from the Child Language Exchange System (CHILDES), Bartsch and Wellman (1995) examined children's understanding of persons by focusing on how children talked about the mental and psychological states that underlie overt behavior. Another line of research also has linked children's understanding of psychological states with their narrative ability, demonstrating that when children are allowed to link events in a coherent narrative, they show a better understanding of other's minds (Lewis, Freeman, Hagestadt, & Douglas, 1994). Despite these contributions to how children reason about the mind in verbal ways, we still know very little about the significance of cultural and linguistic differences in the ways that parents and their children discuss, explain, or emphasize emotions and other internal states across different contexts of interaction. The current study examined the social and sense-making function of narrative evaluation in a sample of Spanish-speaking Peruvian dyads through the use of internal-state references across two different narrative interaction contexts: a semi-naturalistic family reminiscing and a semi-structured book-sharing. Specifically, the aim of the study was twofold: (1) to describe differences in the patterns of maternal narrative evaluation, looking at mothers' and children's use of internal-state language in two contexts – past personal experience and book-sharing conversations; and (2) to describe age and gender variations in the patterns of internal-state language use.

METHODS

Participants

Thirty-two *Limeño*[1] Peruvian middle-class mothers and their preschool children participated in the study. Dyads were recruited in Lima, Peru, and were monolingual Spanish speakers. Children were from two age groups: 3-year-olds

---

[1] *Limeño* is the term used to refer to the natives of Lima, implying both coastal and urban living.

($M = 42.8$ months, $SD = 3.8$) and 5-year-olds ($M = 64.8$ months, $SD = 3.4$). Each age group was evenly divided by gender. All children, with one exception, attended a preschool or daycare center either full- or part-time. According to parental reports, all children were developing normally. As part of routine daycare/preschool services, 68% of the children had been formally assessed for cognitive or linguistic delays and none were diagnosed with developmental concerns. The mean age reported for children's first words was 10 months.

The average household consisted of six to seven members, including nuclear and extended relatives and household help. Families had a range of one to four children, with an average of two children per family. Of the dyads, 87% lived in a two-parent home and 13% lived in a single-parent home. The mothers' ages ranged from 24 to 39 years ($M = 31.81$, $SD = 3.99$). All parents had completed high school and also attended post–highschool institutions, which is representative of approximately 30% of the urban Peruvian population ranked by educational level in 2006 (Instituto Nacional de Estadística e Informática, 2007). All fathers worked outside the home either independently or employed in professional jobs (e.g., engineers, university professors, entrepreneurs, veterinarians, managers, and politicians). Of the mothers, 75% worked outside the home and held a semiprofessional or clerical position. Based on Peruvian standards of educational level and professional experience, participating families were middle to upper-middle class (see Table 5.1 for sociodemographic profiles by children's age group).

Procedure

A native Spanish-speaking Peruvian researcher visited mothers and children in their home one time; the visit lasted approximately 4 hours. The mothers were told that the researcher was interested in investigating how children talked with family members in different contexts. Each mother was asked to engage in the following two types of tasks with her child:

1. *Narrative conversation.* The first task consisted of a conversation about the child's personal experiences. Each mother was instructed to have a conversation with her child about three shared events the child had experienced recently. The mothers were asked to talk about one specific event at a time and to avoid retelling movies or storybooks. Written instructions were also provided, but no further specifications concerning this task were given.
2. *Book-sharing interaction.* The second task consisted of a book-sharing exchange. The mothers were asked to share with their child a wordless picture book, *Frog, Where Are You?* (Mayer, 1969). Also, the mothers were instructed to engage with the child's comments as they normally would and to take as much time as they needed. This wordless

Table 5.1. *Sociodemographic profiles of participants by age group*

	3-year-olds (N = 16)	5-year-olds (N = 16)
	M (Range)	*M* (Range)
CHILDREN		
Age	3;7 (3;0–4;0)	5;5 (5;0–5;11)
Age of first words	10 mo (5–18)	10 mo (6–20)
Birth order		
First-born	10	12
Second-born	2	1
Later-born	4	3
MOTHERS		
Age	29 (24–35)	32 (27–39)
Years of education	16 (12–18)	17 (13–20)
FATHERS		
Age	35 (28–41)	35 (29–40)
Years of education	16 (14–24)	17 (12–23)
HOME		
Household size	7 (3–11)	6 (4–8)
Number of children	2 (1–4)	2 (1–3)

book-sharing task has been used extensively to elicit narratives from children of different cultural and linguistic backgrounds (Berman & Slobin, 1994) and provides a variety of semistandardized language use measures suitable for comparisons across groups.

The researchers told the children that they were interested in tape-recording the child's voice and offered them the opportunity to hear their audio-recorded voice on completion of the tasks. The researcher was in the home while the dyads completed the conversation and book-sharing tasks but was not present in the room where the recordings took place. Neither the researcher nor anyone else interacted with either mother or child while they were engaged in the tasks.

Transcription and Coding

Tapes were transcribed using a standardized format, the Codes for Analysis of Human Language (CHAT), available through the CHILDES project (MacWhinney, 2000). A native Spanish speaker transcribed all Spanish audiotapes. Transcriptions were then verified by a native Peruvian Spanish speaker. Conversations about personal experience were segmented into narrative exchanges using verbal and nonverbal cues provided by mothers and children (e.g., comments such as *ahora cuéntame sobre...* [now let's talk about...], *cuéntame sobre la vez que* ... [tell me about the time ...], *ya no quiero* [I don't want to], and *¿algo más?* [anything else?]). Only narrative exchanges in which children contributed at least one novel event were coded.

Book-sharing exchanges were segmented into three types of speech events: prereading, book-sharing, and postreading discussions (Melzi & Caspe, 2005). Prereading exchanges consisted of the dialogue that occurred between mother and child from the beginning of audio-recording until initiation of the actual story line (e.g., title, author, predictions about the story). Reading exchanges consisted of all conversation about the pictures in the book, identified either through linguistic cues (e.g., "*un día*" [one day], "*había una vez*" [once upon a time], and "*vamos a ver*" [let's see]) or pictorial cues (e.g., mention of bedroom, jar, and moon). Postreading exchanges were defined as conversational exchanges that were not related to the last picture in the book and that took place after the narration of the storybook had been completed (e.g., questions about how the child liked the story, review questions to test the child's comprehension). In cases in which the mother read the book multiple times, only the first reading was coded and analyzed. Prereading and postreading discussions were not included in the final analyses because not all dyads engaged in those types of interactions.

Each reference made to an internal state or subjective (internal) characteristic of a person, animal, or object (fictional or real) was coded for the type of internal state discussed and for three specific discourse features: (1) speech context of internal state, (2) pragmatic function of the utterance in which the inner-world reference was embedded, and (3) the referent of the internal state or subjective characteristic. Intercoder reliability was estimated between the authors on 20% of all transcripts using Cohen's Kappa (Cohen, 1960). Kappa coefficients are provided in each respective section.

Types of Internal States

Six types of internal states were coded: (1) references to affective states (e.g., *estar triste* [to be sad]) and to behaviors associated with such states (e.g., *llorar* [to cry]); (2) expressions of intention, which include volition and desire (e.g., *querer algo* [want something], *tratar* [attempt]); (3) expressions of obligations (e.g., *tener que* [had to]); (4) references to cognitive mental states (e.g., *saber* [to know]); (5) references to sensory perception (e.g., *oír* [to hear]); and (6) references to physiological states (e.g., *tener sueño* [to be sleepy]). Inter-rater reliability for inner-world references was .97.

Discourse Features

Utterances that contained the internal states were then coded for three discourse features: (1) speech context, which identified the main speech event to which the utterance and thus the internal state belonged; (2) pragmatic function, which identified the manner in which the internal was discussed; and (3) referent, which identified the individual who received the action or experienced the internal state. Cohen's Kappa for all discourse features was .84, which shows almost perfect reliability.

Speech context was further subdivided into *narrative context* (i.e., belonging to the story world); *nonnarrative-related context* (i.e., any portion of the conversation that is external to the narration of the story but is relevant to the narrative, such as comments about the story made by the narrator, metanarrative comments, anecdotes directly linked to the story, and response to an event in the book); and *nonnarrative-unrelated context* (i.e., any portion of the conversation that is external to the narration of the story, such as random comments and real-world intrusions).

Pragmatic function code included two main codes: *descriptive function* (i.e., attributing an internal state or commenting about the inner world of a character or person in a single utterance without exploring the causes or consequences; for example, Mother: *El niño se molestó* [The boy was mad]); and *explanatory function* (i.e., the speaker explicitly discusses the causes and consequences of an internal state; for example, Mother: *Uy! El niño se molestó porque el perro rompió la casita de la ranita* [Oh! The boy was mad because the dog broke the froggie's jar]). For the referent of the internal state, three major codes were used: *characters of the story*, *narrator/audience* (e.g., mother and child), and *other*.

RESULTS

First, we describe how mother–child dyads used internal-state references during book-reading conversations and conversations about personal experiences. Second, we present an analysis of differences in narrative evaluation across contexts of interaction. And, finally, we address age- and gender-related differences in the use of internal-state references.

Number and Types of Internal-State References

In the personal-narrative task, most mother–child dyads produced approximately three personal narratives[2] about shared experiences per conversation ranging in length from 15 to 115 utterances for the mother ($M = 51.91$, $SD = 25.78$) and from 11 to 88 for the child ($M = 39.86$, $SD = 20.47$). The most common events that dyads discussed were trips: to the zoo, to the beach, to a restaurant, to a birthday party, to family members' homes, and other special trips (e.g., to another state).

There was great variability in the dyads' use of internal-state references in this context, ranging from 0 to 66 ($M = 30.00$, $SD = 18.61$) across all narratives. In all conversations, mothers introduced approximately 64.52% of all internal-state references, whereas children introduced 35.47%. As shown in Figure 5.1, the most frequent type of internal-state references were words denoting affective

---

[2] Although dyads were instructed to talk about three shared events and thus produce three narratives, in some cases, they produced more or less than three narratives.

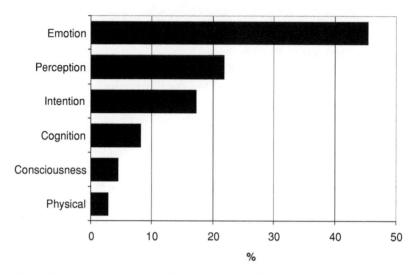

Figure 5.1. Percentage of Internal-State References by Type in Personal-Narrative Context.

states (e.g., sad), followed by words referring to sensory perceptions (e.g., heard), expressions of intention, volition, desire, and obligation (e.g., wanted, tried, had to), followed by cognitive terms (e.g., thought and knowledge), as the following excerpt between a mother and her 3-year-old son illustrates. Words in bold represent internal state references. For ease of understanding, *[<] [>]* symbols denote overlap in the conversation; + ⋯ denotes incompletion; +, denotes self-completion; and ++ denotes other completion.

	Spanish Original	English Translation
Mother:	*¿**Te acuerdas** que ayer nos fuimos a la playa y entramos a la casita?*	Do you **remember** that yesterday we went to the beach and we walked in a house?
Child:	*¿A qué casita?*	What house?
Mother:	*Que estábamos este… con Julie y con su amiga viendo una casa que no tenía muebles, ¿te acuerdas?*	We were with, um… Julie and her friend visiting a house with no furniture, do you remember?
Child:	*Sí.*	Yes.
Mother:	*¿Y que después este…nos fuimos a almorzar?*	And that afterwards, um… we went to lunch?
Child:	*[Nods]*	[Nods]
Mother:	*¿Qué comiste?*	What did you eat?
Child:	***No sé.***	**I don't know.**
Mother:	*¿Pescado?*	Fish?

Child:	*[No answer]*	[No Answer]
Mother:	*¿No te acuerdas?*	You **don't remember**?
Child:	*Pero yo no quería mi comida.*	But, **I didn't want** my food.
Mother:	*¿Tú no querías comer?*	You **didn't want** to eat?
Child:	*No.*	No.
Mother:	*¿No?*	No?
Child:	*Y te molestaste.*	And you **got mad**.
Mother:	*Sí pues, ¿por qué me molesté?*	Of course I did, **why did I get mad**?
Child:	*Porque yo no quería comer.*	Because **I didn't want** my food.
Mother:	*Y qué comiste al final?*	What did you eat at the end?
Child:	*Nada.* Chi + . . .	Nothing. Chee + . . .
Mother:	*Chi .*	Chee.
Child:	+,*zi* + . . .	+, ee + . . .
Mother:	*¿Zi?*	Ee?
Child:	+,*to!*	Tos!
Mother:	*Chizitos.*	Cheetos.
Mother:	*¿Y qué más comiste?*	And what else did you eat?
Child:	*Cho*+ . . .	Cho + . . .
Mother:	*Cho.*	Cho.
Child:	+,*co* + . . .	+,co + . . .
Mother:	*Choco.*	Choco.
Child:	+,*la* + . . .	+, l + . . .
Mother:	*la.*	l .
Child:	+,*te.*	+, late
Mother:	*¿Y qué más?*	And what else?
Child:	*¿Qué más?*	What else?
Mother:	*Sí.*	Yes.
Child:	*Y tú no me diste chocolate, mentirosa.*	And you didn't give me chocolate, you are lying!
Mother:	*¿Tú me has dicho? [laughs]*	Didn't you just say so? [laughs]
Child:	*¡Oh!*	Oh!
Mother:	*Pero alguien te compró un chupete. ¿Quién fue?*	But someone bought you a lollipop. Who was it?
Child:	*Ma [>] +* . . .	Ma [>] + . . .
Mother:	*Ma [<] +* . . .	Ma [<] + . . .
Child:	+, *nu*+ . . .	+, nu + . . .
Child:	+, *el.*	+, el.

Mother:	*Manuel.*	Manuel.
Child:	*Mario.*	Mario.
Mother:	*Mario no. No se llama Mario.*	Mario no. His name is not Mario.
Child:	*Ah ah.*	Ah ah.
Mother:	*¿Y después en la noche?*	And at night?
Child:	*¿Ma?*	Mom?
Mother:	*¿En la noche **te acuerdas** que nos fuimos a comer con el abuelo?*	At night, **remember** that we ate with grandpa?
Mother:	*¿Qué comiste ahí?*	What did you eat then?
Child:	*Anticucho.*	Anticucho.[3]
Mother:	*¿Anticucho con qué más?*	Anticucho with what?
Child:	*¿Con qué?*	With what?
Mother:	*Con pa + . . .*	With pota + . . .
Child:	*++ pa:.*	++ toes.
Mother:	*¿Y tú comiste todo?*	And did you eat everything?
Child:	*Sí.*	Yes.

The least frequent were words referring to consciousness (e.g., sleeping) and physiological states (e.g., hungry). In terms of the pragmatic function, the majority of internal-state references were used to attribute to or comment on the inner world of the mother, the child, or any person mentioned in the narrative (91.23%). Only a small number of the references were used to discuss explicitly the causes and consequences of an internal state and thus served an explanatory function (8.77%).

In the book-sharing task, the mothers were instructed to share the book with their child as they normally would. Most dyads (78%) engaged in prereading and postreading episodes, which consisted of brief introductions to the task, comments about the storybook before or after reading the wordless book, or attempts to recall the story. The episodes ranged from 1 to 86 maternal utterances ($M = 12.41$, $SD = 19.81$) and from 1 to 68 child utterances ($M = 6.97$, $SD = 13.74$). However, because not all dyads engaged in prereading and postreading discussions, analyses were conducted only on the main book-sharing narration. On average, storybook narratives consisted of 152 maternal utterances ($M = 152.06$, $SD = 47.19$) and 37 child utterances ($M = 37.03$, $SD = 43.60$). There were no significant gender- or age-related differences in the length of the narratives produced.

The dyads' use of internal-state references in this context ranged from 11 to 58 ($M = 34.37$, $SD = 13.09$); most (98.3 %), however, were introduced by the

---

[3] *Anticucho* is a traditional coastal dish (especially in the area of Lima and Ica) consisting of macerated and grilled pieces of cow heart.

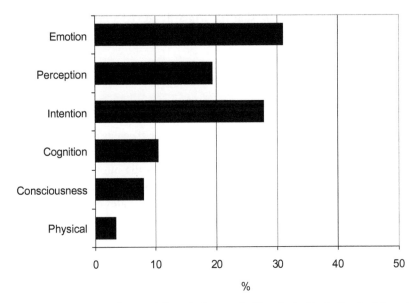

Figure 5.2. Percentage of Internal-State References by Type in the Book-Sharing Narrative Context.

mother. As shown in Figure 5.2, the types of references to internal states that dyads used during the storybook narrative were similar to those used during the personal-narrative conversations. The most frequent were references to affective states, followed by expressions of intention, volition, desire, and obligation, and words referring to sensory perceptions. To illustrate, in the following excerpt, a mother and her 3-year-old daughter talk about the point in the story when the dog falls out of the window. Bolded words represent the internal state references.

	Spanish Original	English Translation
Mother:	*Y en eso el perrito de travieso también jugando con la botella, se cayó.*	And then the doggie because he was mischievous and was playing with the bottle, fell.
Child:	*¿Y acá?*	And here?
Mother:	*Se cayó. Se golpeó. Entonces el niñito **asustado** se bajó de la ventana. Y lo agarró al perrito que es todo un travieso también.*	He fell. He hit himself. Then the little boy was **scared** and got down from the window. He grabbed the little dog who was really mischievous.
Child:	*¡Ahh!*	Ohh!

The least frequent were words referring to cognitive, consciousness, and physiological states. As was the case in the personal-narrative task, references to internal states during book-sharing primarily served a descriptive function (81.90 %) and only a small percentage (18.10%) served an explanatory function.

Differences Across Contexts

Our interest in looking at differences across the two narrative contexts – personal experience (or reminiscing) and book-sharing conversations – demanded that in the first task, dyads speak about various past shared events thereby producing at least three narratives, and in the second task, that they share a wordless book as one narrative exchange. Given the differences in the number and length of narratives inherent in each task, we used a comparable measure of internal-state use across the two contexts: the ratio of total internal states produced from the total number of utterances in the narrative exchanges for each conversational context (i.e., PNC index, BKS index). To explore differences in the patterns of mothers' and children's use of internal-state language in two contexts, we conducted a two-way, repeated-measures ANOVA on the indices of internal-state references with type of context as the within-group factor and age and gender as the between-group factors. Results showed a significant within-subjects effect (i.e., interaction context) on narrative evaluation: $F(1,28) = 71.32$, $p < .001$,[4] partial $\eta^2 = .72$. No significant effects were found for age group or gender. It is surprising that all dyads, irrespective of children's age or gender, included significantly more references to internal states in the book-sharing interaction context ($M = 0.18$, $SD = 0.08$) than in the personal-narrative conversation ($M = 0.06$, $SD = 0.03$) (Figures 5.3 and 5.4). It is also worth noting that up to 71% of the variance in the use of internal-state references was explained by the type of context, suggesting that in this case, context rather than person variables was more important in accounting for the dyad's patterns of narrative evaluation.

GENDER AND AGE DIFFERENCES

Our second research objective was to explore age and gender variations in the use of internal-state references associated with the specific contexts of interaction independently. In terms of production, mother–child dyads did not differ significantly in the total number of shared narratives produced by either gender or age group. Similarly, there were no gender- or age-related patterns in the events about which mothers and children chose to talk, nor were there significant gender- or age-related differences in length of the narratives produced. To describe age and gender variations in the patterns of internal-state language use observed in the personal-narrative context, we conducted a two-way ANOVA on the index of internal-state references for the personal-experience conversational context

---

[4] We used the Greenhouse-Geisser epsilon, which is the most conservative for a small sample size.

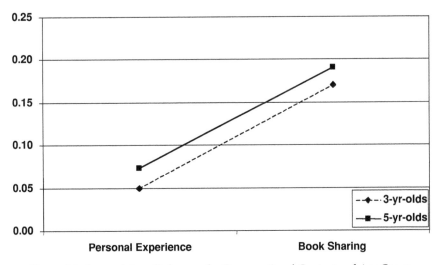

Figure 5.3. Internal-State References by Conversational Context and Age Group.

(PNC index), with age and gender as the between-group factors. Similarly, we explored age and gender variations in the patterns of internal-state language use observed in the book-sharing context through a two-way ANOVA, with age and gender as the between-group factors and the index of internal-state references for the book-sharing context as the criterion variable.

No significant age or gender differences in the use of internal-state references were found for the book-sharing context. However, significant gender effects – $F(1, 28) = 4.65, p < .05$, partial $\eta^2 = 0.14$ – and age-group effects – $F(1, 28) = 6.42$, $p < .05$, partial $\eta^2 = 0.19$ – were found for the personal-experience conversational

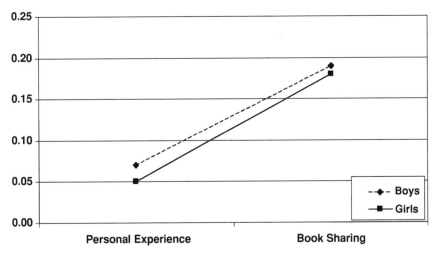

Figure 5.4. Internal-State References by Conversational Context and Gender.

context. Mother–son dyads ($M = 0.07$, $SD = 0.02$) included significantly more internal references than mother–daughter dyads ($M = 0.05$, $SD = 0.03$). By the same token, dyads with 5-year-olds ($M = 0.07$, $SD = 0.02$) included significantly more internal references than dyads with 3-year-olds ($M = 0.04$, $SD = 0.03$). These findings suggest that to a certain extent, individual differences in narrative evaluation depend on person variables like children's age and gender, but these differences do not necessarily hold across contexts. In other words, children's age and gender explain 14% and 19% of the variability in the personal-experience evaluation index, respectively, but have no significant explanatory power when looking at the variability in the book-sharing evaluation index.

DISCUSSION

The purpose of this chapter was to examine the social and sense-making function of narrative evaluation in a sample of Spanish-speaking Peruvian dyads through the use of internal-state references across two interaction contexts. First, we examined differences in the patterns of maternal narrative evaluation, looking at mothers' and children's use of internal-state language in two contexts: past personal experience and book-sharing conversations. Even though reminiscing style tends to be a consistent characteristic of the mother across time in a particular conversational context (Farrant & Reese, 2000; Reese et al., 1993; Rudek & Haden, 2005), there is some evidence that it does not necessarily generalize across other conversational contexts (Haden & Fivush, 1996; Kleinknecht & Beike, 2004). Certain narrative contexts might call for the use of evaluative devices to a greater degree, whereas others might require the recollection of referential and factual information. Our results show that, in fact, dyads included significantly more references to internal states in the book-sharing than in the personal-narrative conversational context. The higher frequency of internal states in the book-sharing task might be partly due to the type of stimulus chosen to elicit the narrative. The picture book contains several scenes in which the characters are depicted as experiencing an emotion or intending to carry on an action; therefore, all dyads, irrespective of children's age or gender, included more references to internal states during this task. The mothers' interaction style might have also contributed to creating this difference. In 84% of the dyads, mothers adopted a storytelling style (see Caspe & Melzi, chapter 2, this volume; Melzi, Schick, & Kennedy, 2007). As such, in order to be more engaging, mothers might rely on internal-state language as a way to embellish and enrich the story. The use of references to internal states in the narrative might help children understand characters' actions, thereby contributing to their comprehension of the story. Thus, conversations that emerge during book-sharing routines might be a context of dyadic interaction in which children learn about the link among human emotions, beliefs, intentions, and their overt actions.

Differences in the types of internal-state references are indicative of potential differences in the sense-making function of narrative evaluation in the two contexts we examined. For example, 45.47% of the internal-state references that dyads used in the personal-narrative conversational context were emotions or behavioral expressions of affect, whereas in the book-sharing conversational context, 31% of the references were of this type. Conversely, 17.21% of the references in the personal-experience narratives were expressions of volition or intention, compared to 27.72% in the book-reading narratives. This divergence in the types of internal-state references by conversational context might suggest that the sense-making function of narrative evaluation varies depending on the context of interaction. For example, repeated reminiscing about past experience provides mothers with an opportunity to help children make sense of their felt emotions, and to coconstruct an autobiographical memory that takes into account children's emotional life, which eventually leads them to develop an integrated concept of self (Fivush & Nelson, 2006). In contrast, narrative evaluation in book-sharing conversations might be a context in which children are more inclined to learn that actions are guided by the internal states as they maintain some distance from their own experiences. Therefore, sharing books might allow mothers and children to discuss and understand the relation between human motivation and behavior in a way that is potentially less threatening or emotionally arousing for children than discussing their actual personal experience.

The second goal of the study was to describe age and gender variations in the patterns of internal-state language use. Age and gender differences in narrative evaluation were found only in the personal-experience conversational context, in which mother–son dyads and dyads with 5-year-old children used significantly more references to internal states compared to mother–daughter dyads and dyads with 3-year-old children. The fact that significant gender and age differences were found in the personal-experience conversations but not in the book-sharing narratives supports claims made by scholars that reminiscing about one's past personal experiences is a fundamental context for the socialization of gender roles (e.g., Fivush & Buckner, 2003). Book-sharing, by comparison, appears to be a more neutral socialization context, at least in terms of children's gender, because the content of the narrative is already predetermined. As previously discussed, because the link between internal states and actions in the book-sharing context maintains a certain distance from a child's personal experience, patterns of narrative evaluation among mother–son dyads are not different from those of mother–daughter dyads, at least in terms of frequency of internal-state references. Collectively, these findings emphasize the importance of considering context of interaction when investigating the functions of narrative evaluation, with each conversational context playing a different function for children's social and sociocognitive development.

A closer look at the significant gender differences in the use of internal-state language showed that these differences are driven mostly by references to emotions (Melzi & Fernández, 2004). Our results are contrary to the more common finding that references to emotions are more frequent in mother–daughter conversations than in mother–son conversations (Fivush et al., 2000; Fivush & Wang, 2005). We must recall that language use and, by extension, narrative practices are the primary means through which children are socialized across various cultures. Therefore, language and narrative use, especially those with and around children, reflect gender- and culture-specific ideologies (Ochs & Capps, 2001; Schieffelin & Ochs, 1986). To understand the differences between our results and those of U.S. studies, we therefore need to explore the gender ideologies and socialization practices among middle-class Limeños.

The work of Fuller (1997, 1998), a Peruvian anthropologist, on femininity and masculinity is among the few studies, to our knowledge, that address the development of a gendered self in middle-class Limeño Peruvian society. The Peruvian society, as in many other Latin American communities, is characterized by a profound allegiance to the family. This ideology shapes everyday practices, including features of parent–child interaction that both reflect and encourage different views of self-definition. The self for both genders must be relational because it needs to incorporate one's role as an offspring, a sibling, a spouse, and a parent. Although Peruvian boys and girls are expected to define themselves as connected to others, they are encouraged to do so to varying degrees. Gender roles in Peru are strictly defined; thus, boys are also socialized to develop a more heightened sense of autonomy and assertiveness as compared to girls. As such, boys at some point in their development will be expected to control and refrain from openly discussing their emotions, whereas girls will be allowed to express their emotions more freely. Fuller provides compelling evidence suggesting that the duality in boys' self-definition – to be relational and autonomous – is achieved through a separation of the home[5] and public life. Male participants recall that during the preschool years, they were allowed to express openly their emotions, especially with female family members. As the boys' social world expanded beyond the home, they began to receive messages (e.g., from peers and teachers) about controlling their display of emotionality, in particular those emotions thought to show weakness such as crying and sadness. The gender differences in references to emotions in our study can be understood in light of these socialization practices. Given that the children in our study were of preschool age and were interacting with their mother, it is possible that the language used reflects the mother's attempt to encourage the development of a relational self.

---

[5] It is worth noting that participants in Fuller's studies did not talk about fathers as playing an important role in their early development. When they did, findings were contradicting, with some fathers adopting more flexible gender roles than others.

In conclusion, results of this study illustrate the intricate relationship between narrative evaluation in parent–child conversations and children's sociocognitive development. We might conceptualize two different levels of sociocognitive understanding: *close-to-the-self* and *distant-from-the-self*. Personal-narrative conversations might be a context in which mother–child interactions foster *close-to-the-self* understanding, whereas book-sharing conversations might foster *distant-from-the-self* understanding. In this sense, our findings support previous research, which suggests that the prevalence of explicit narrative evaluation and its impact on children's autobiographical memory and social cognition might differ depending on the conversational context in which it occurs (Fivush et al., 2006; Kleinknecht & Beike, 2004; Rudek & Haden, 2005). However, conclusions about the stability of narrative evaluation patterns across contexts are tentative because not many studies have made cross-context comparisons. Our findings also emphasize the need to understand gender and age variations commonly reported in the literature within the context of interaction in which these emerge. Often, group differences are observed in certain interactive contexts but might not be necessarily present in other contexts that are studied less frequently. Context differences might override group differences if taken into account; thus, the need exists to examine dyads' linguistic production across diverse narrative contexts. Finally, our findings illustrate how cultural practices, especially those related to developing gendered selves, are embedded in mother–child narrative practices.

ACKNOWLEDGMENTS

Support for the collection of the data reported herein was provided to the second author of this chapter by New York University Research Challenge Fund. The authors would like to acknowledge Cecilia Baraybar for collecting all data in Lima, Peru.

REFERENCES

Adams, S., Kuebli, J., Boyle, P. A., & Fivush, R. (1995). Gender differences in parent–child conversations about past emotions: A longitudinal investigation. *Sex Roles, 33*(5–6), 309–323.

Alexander, K. J., Miller, P. J., & Hengst, J. A. (2001). Young children's emotional attachments to stories. *Social Development, 10*(3), 374–398.

Bartsch, K., & Wellman, H. M. (1995). *Children talk about the mind*. London: Oxford University Press.

Berman, R. A., & Slobin, D. I. (1994). *Relating events in narrative: A cross-linguistic developmental study*. Hillsdale, NJ: Lawrence Erlbaum.

Bird, A., & Reese, E. (2006). Emotional reminiscing and the development of an autobiographical self. *Developmental Psychology, 42*(4), 613–626.

Boland, A. M., Haden, C. A., & Ornstein, P. A. (2003). Boosting children's memory by training mothers in the use of an elaborative conversational style as an event unfolds. *Journal of Cognition and Development, 4*(1), 39–65.

Brown, J., Donelan-McCall, N., & Dunn, J. (1996). Why talk about mental states: The significance of children's conversations with friends, siblings, and mothers. *Child Development, 67*(3), 836–849.

Bruner, J. (1986). *Actual minds, possible worlds.* Cambridge, MA: Harvard University Press.

Buckner, J. P., & Fivush, R. (1998). Gender and self in children's autobiographical narratives. *Applied Cognitive Psychology, 12*(4), 407–429.

Buckner, J. P., & Fivush, R. (2000). Gendered themes in family reminiscing. *Memory, 8*(6), 401–412.

Charman, T., & Shmueli-Goetz, Y. (1998). The relationship between theory of mind, language and narrative discourse: An experimental study. *Current Psychology of Cognition, 17*(2), 245–271.

Choi, S. H. (1992). Communicative socialization processes: Korea and Canada. In S. Iwawaki, Y. Kashima, & K. Leung (Eds.), *Innovations in cross-cultural psychology.* Lisse, Netherlands: Swets & Zeitlinger Publishers.

Cohen, J. (1960). A coefficient of agreement for nominal scales. *Educational and Psychological Measurement, 20,* 37–46.

Curenton, S. M. (2004). The association between narratives and theory of mind for low-income preschoolers. *Early Education and Development, 15*(2), 121–145.

Dunn, J., Bretherton, I., & Munn, P. (1987). Conversations about feeling states between mothers and their young children. *Developmental Psychology, 23*(1), 132–139.

Dunn, J., & Brown, J. R. (1993). Early conversations about causality: Content, pragmatics and developmental change. *British Journal of Developmental Psychology, 11*(2), 107–123.

Dunn, J., Brown, J., & Beardsall, L. (1991). Family talk about feeling states and children's later understanding of others' emotions. *Developmental Psychology, 27*(3), 448–455.

Dunn, J., Brown, J., Slomkowski, C., Tesla, C., & Youngblade, L. M. (1991). Young children's understanding of other people's feelings and beliefs: Individual differences and their antecedents. *Child Development, 62*(6), 1352–1366.

Eder, R. A. (1990). Uncovering young children's psychological selves: Individual and developmental differences. *Child Development, 61,* 849–863.

Eisenberg, A. R. (1985). Learning to describe past experiences in conversation. *Discourse Processes, 8,* 177–204.

Eisenberg, A. R. (1999). Emotion talk among Mexican American and Anglo American mothers and children from two social classes. *Merrill-Palmer Quarterly, 45*(2), 267–284.

Eisenberg, A. R. (2002). Maternal teaching talk within families of Mexican descent: Influences of task and socioeconomic status. *Hispanic Journal of Behavioral Sciences. Special Issue: Conversations within Mexican-descent families: Diverse contexts for language socialization and learning, 24*(2), 206–224.

Ely, R., & McCabe, A. (1993). Remembered voices. *Journal of Child Language, 20,* 671–696.

Farrant, K., & Reese, E. (2000). Maternal style and children's participation in reminiscing: Steppingstones in children's autobiographical memory development. *Journal of Cognition and Development, 1*(2), 193–225.

Farrar, M. J., Fasig, L. G., & Welch-Ross, M. K. (1997). Attachment and emotion in autobiographical memory development. *Journal of Experimental Child Psychology, 67*(3), 389–408.

Fivush, R. (1991). Gender and emotion in mother-child conversations about the past. *Journal of Narrative and Life History, 1*(4), 325-341.

Fivush, R. (1993). Emotional content of parent–child conversations about the past. In C. A. Nelson (Ed.), *Memory and affect in development: The Minnesota symposia on child psychology* (Vol. 26, pp. 39–77). Hillsdale, NJ: Lawrence Erlbaum.

Fivush, R. (1994). Constructing narrative, emotion, and self in parent–child conversations about the past. In U. Neisser & R. Fivush (Eds.), *The remembering self: Construction and accuracy in the self-narrative.* Emory symposia in cognition (pp. 136–157). New York: Cambridge University Press.

Fivush, R. (2001). Owning experience: Developing subjective perspective in autobiographical narratives. In C. Moore & K. Lemmon (Eds.), *The self in time: Developmental perspectives* (pp. 35–52). Mahwah, NJ: Lawrence Erlbaum.

Fivush, R., Brotman, M. A., Buckner, J. P., & Goodman, S. H. (2000). Gender differences in parent-child emotion narratives. *Sex Roles, 42*(3–4), 233–253.

Fivush, R., & Buckner, J. P. (2003). Creating gender and identity through autobiographical narratives. In R. Fivush & C. A. Haden (Eds.), *Autobiographical memory and the construction of a narrative self: Developmental and cultural perspectives* (pp. 149–167). Mahwah, NJ: Lawrence Erlbaum.

Fivush, R., Haden, C. A., & Reese, E. (2006). Elaborating on elaborations: Role of material reminiscing style in cognitive and socioemotional development. *Child Development, 77*(6), 1568–1588.

Fivush, R., & Nelson, K. (2006). Parent–child reminiscing locates the self in the past. *British Journal of Developmental Psychology, 24*(1), 235–251.

Fivush, R., & Wang, Q. (2005). Emotion talk in mother–child conversations of the shared past: The effects of culture, gender, and event valence. *Journal of Cognition and Development, 6*(4), 489–506.

Flannagan, D., & Perese, S. (1998). Emotional references in mother–daughter and mother–son dyads' conversations about school. *Sex Roles, 39*(5–6), 353–367.

Fuller, N. (1997). *Identidades masculinas.* Lima: Pontificia Universidad Católica del Perú.

Fuller, N. (1998). *Dilemas de la femineidad: Mujeres de la clase media en el Perú.* Lima: Pontificia Universidad Católica del Perú.

Fung, H., & Cheng, E. C. (2001). Across time and beyond skin: Self and transgression in the everyday socialization of shame among Taiwanese preschool children. *Social Development, 10*(3), 420–437.

Furrow, D., Moore, C., Davidge, J., & Chiasson, L. (1992). Mental terms in mothers' and children's speech: Similarities and relationships. *Journal of Child Language, 19*(3), 617–631.

Garrett, P. B., & Baquedano-López, P. (2002). Language socialization: Reproduction and continuity, transformation and change. *Annual Review of Anthropology, 31*, 339–361.

Guajardo, N. R., & Watson, A. C. (2002). Narrative discourse and theory of mind development. *Journal of Genetic Psychology, 163*(3), 305–325.

Han, J. J., Leichtman, M. D., & Wang, Q. (1998). Autobiographical memory in Korean, Chinese and American children. *Developmental Psychology, 34*(4), 701–713.

Haden, C. A. (1998). Reminiscing with different children: Relating maternal stylistic consistency and sibling similarity in talk about the past. *Developmental Psychology, 34*(1), 99–114.

Haden, C. A., & Fivush, R. (1996). Contextual variation in maternal conversational styles. *Merrill-Palmer Quarterly, 42*(2), 200–227.

Haden, C. A., Haine, R. A., & Fivush, R. (1997). Developing narrative structure in parent–child reminiscing across the preschool years. *Developmental Psychology, 33*(2), 295–307.

Hudson, J. A. (1990). The emergence of autobiographical memory in mother–child conversations. In R. Fivush & J. A. Hudson (Eds.), *Knowing and remembering in young children* (pp. 166–196). New York: Cambridge University Press.

Hughes, C., & Dunn, J. (1997). "Pretend you didn't know": Preschooler's talk about mental states in pretend play. *Cognitive Development, 12*(4), 381–403.

Hughes, C., & Dunn, J. (1998). Understanding mind and emotion: Longitudinal associations with mental-state talk between young friends. *Developmental Psychology, 34*(5), 1026–1037.

Instituto Nacional de Estadística e Informática (2007). Compendio estadístico: Logro educacional. Retrieved April 27, 2008 from http://www.inei.gob.pe.

Kleinknecht, E., & Beike, D. R. (2004). How knowing and doing inform an autobiography: Relations among preschoolers' theory of mind, narrative, and event memory skills. *Applied Cognitive Psychology, 18*(6), 745–764.

Labov, W., & Waletzky, J. (1967). Narrative analysis: Oral versions of personal experience. In J. Helm (Ed.), *Essays on the verbal and visual art*. Seattle: University of Washington Press.

Leichtman, M. D., Wang, Q., & Pillemer, D. B. (2003). Cultural variations in interdependence and autobiographical memory: Lessons from Korea, China, India and the United States. In R. Fivush & C. A. Haden (Eds.), *Autobiographical memory and the construction of a narrative self: Developmental and cultural perspectives* (pp. 73–97). Mahwah: Lawrence Erlbaum.

Lewis, C., Freeman, N. H., Hagestadt, C., & Douglas, H. (1994). Narrative access and production in preschoolers' false belief reasoning. *Cognitive Development, 9*, 397–424.

MacWhinney, B. (2000). *The CHILDES project: Tools for analyzing talk*. Mahwah, NJ: Lawrence Erlbaum.

Mayer, M. (1969). *Frog, where are you?* New York: Penguin Books.

McCabe, A., & Peterson, C. (1991). Getting the story: A longitudinal study of parental styles in eliciting narratives and developing narrative skill. In A. McCabe & C. Peterson (Eds.), *Developing narrative structure* (pp. 217–253). Hillsdale, NJ: Erlbaum.

Melzi, G., & Caspe, M. (2005). Variations in maternal narrative styles during book-reading interactions. *Narrative Inquiry, 15*(1), 101–125.

Melzi, G., & Fernández, C. (2004). Talking about past emotions: Conversations between Peruvian mothers and their preschool children. *Sex Roles, 50*(9–10), 153–177.

Melzi, G., Fernández, C., Caspe, M., & Dale, K. (2008). *Agency and communion in mother–child conversations about the past: Cultural and gender variations*. Manuscript submitted for publication.

Melzi, G., Schick, A., & Kennedy, J. (2007, April). Cultural variations in mother–child discourse strategies across narrative context. Poster presented at the Society for Research in Child Development, Boston, MA.

Miller, P., Fung, H., & Mintz, J. (1996). Self-construction through narrative practices: A Chinese and American comparison of early socialization. *Ethos, 24*(2), 237–280.

Miller, P. H., Wiley, A. R., Fung, H., & Liang, C. (1997). Personal storytelling as a medium of socialization in Chinese and American families. *Child Development, 68*(3), 557–568.

Miller, P. H., Sandel, T. L., Liang, C., & Fung, H. (2001). Narrating transgressions in Longwood: The discourses, meanings, and paradoxes of an American socializing practice. *Ethos, 29*(2), 159–186.

Minami, M., & McCabe, A. (1991). Haiku as a discourse regulation device: A stanza analysis of Japanese children's personal narratives. *Language in Society, 20*(4), 577–599.

Minami, M., & McCabe, A. (1995). Rice balls and bear hunts: Japanese and North American family narrative patterns. *Journal of Child Language, 22*(2), 423–445.

Mullen, M. K., & Yi, S. (1995). The cultural context of talk about the past: Implications for the development of autobiographical memory. *Cognitive Development, 10*(3), 407–419.

Nelson, K. (1993). The psychological and social origins of autobiographical memory. *Psychological Science, 4*(1), 7–14.

Nelson, K. (2003). Narrative and self, myth and memory: Emergence of the cultural self. In R. Fivush & C. A. Haden (Eds.), *Autobiographical memory and the construction of a narrative self: Developmental and cultural perspectives* (pp. 3–28). Mahwah, NJ: Lawrence Erlbaum.

Nelson, K., & Fivush, R. (2004). The emergence of autobiographical memory: A social-cultural developmental theory. *Psychological Review, 111*(2), 486–511.

Ochs, E., & Capps, L. (2001). *Living narrative: Creating lives in everyday storytelling.* Cambridge, MA: Harvard University Press.

Peterson, C., Jesso, B., & McCabe, A. (1999). Encouraging narratives in preschoolers: An intervention study. *Journal of Child Language, 26*(1), 49–67.

Peterson, C., & McCabe, A. (1983). *Developmental psycholinguistics: Three ways of looking at a child's narrative.* New York: Plenum.

Reese, E. (2002). Social factors in the development of autobiographical memory: The state of the art. *Social Development, 11*(1), 124–142.

Reese, E., & Brown, N. (2000). Reminiscing and recounting in the preschool years. *Applied Cognitive Psychology, 14*(1), 1–17.

Reese, E., & Cleveland, E. S. (2006). Mother–child reminiscing and children's understanding of mind. *Merrill-Palmer Quarterly. Special Issue: Parent-Child Discourse and the Early Development of Understanding, 52*(1), 17–43.

Reese, E., & Fivush, R. (1993). Parental styles of talking about the past. *Developmental Psychology, 29*(3), 596–606.

Reese, E., Haden, C. A., & Fivush, R. (1993). Mother–child conversations about the past: Relationships of style and memory over time. *Cognitive Development, 8*(4), 403–430.

Rudek, D. J., & Haden, C. A. (2005). Mothers' and preschoolers' mental-state language during reminiscing over time. *Merrill-Palmer Quarterly, 51*(4), 523–549.

Schieffelin, B., & Ochs, E. (1986). Language socialization *Annual Review of Anthropology, 15*, 163–191.

Wang, Q. (2001). "Did you have fun?" American and Chinese mother–child conversations about shared emotional experiences. *Cognitive Development, 16*(2), 693–715.

Wang, Q. (2003). Emotion situation knowledge in American and Chinese preschool children and adults. *Cognition and Emotion, 17*(5), 725–746.

Wang, Q. (2004). The emergence of cultural self-constructs: Autobiographical memory and self-description in European American and Chinese children. *Developmental Psychology, 40*(1), 3-15.

Wang, Q., & Fivush, R. (2005). Mother–child conversations of emotionally salient events: Exploring the functions of emotional reminiscing in European American and Chinese families. *Social Development, 14*(3), 473–495.

Wang, Q., Leichtman, M. D., & Davies, K. I. (2000). Sharing memories and telling stories: American and Chinese mothers and their 3-year-olds. *Memory, 8*(3), 159–177.

Welch-Ross, M. K. (1995). An integrative model of the development of autobiographical memory. *Developmental Review, 15*(3), 338–365.

Welch-Ross, M. K. (1997). Mother–child participation in conversation about the past: Relationships to preschoolers' theory of mind. *Developmental Psychology, 33*(4), 618–629.

Welch-Ross, M. K., Fasig, L. G., & Farrar, M. J. (1999). Predictors of preschoolers' self-knowledge: Reference to emotion and mental states in mother–child conversation about past events. *Cognitive Development, 14*(3), 401–422.

6

Love, Diminutives, and Gender Socialization in Andean Mother–Child Narrative Conversations

KENDALL A. KING AND COLLEEN GALLAGHER

Key Words: diminutive, evaluative morphology, emotion, narrative, evaluation, Spanish, Andes, maternal speech

ABSTRACT

This chapter investigates how emotional words and diminutives function as evaluative resources within mother–child narrative conversations. Participants included 32 Indigenous Spanish-speaking mother–child pairs from the southern Ecuadorian Andes. Mothers were asked to record interactions in which they participated in narrative conversations with their child. Findings suggest that diminutives played a salient part in the socialization of emotion in this Indigenous community. Both quantitative and qualitative analyses indicated gender differences in uses of these types of evaluation and, in particular, in how diminutives and emotional words were used together, with 5-year-old girls hearing significantly more diminutives in emotional utterances than 3-year-old girls and more than boys of both age groups. Implications for narrative evaluation and language socialization are discussed.

INTRODUCTION

Narratives are often defined as stories about actual or imaginary past events (McCabe, 1991). Early and foundational work on narrative (e.g., Labov & Waletzky, 1967) identified *evaluation* as a central narrative component. As Labov and Waletzky (1967) demonstrated, a narrative's referential functions might be carried out perfectly well; however, without evaluation, the narrative tends to be difficult to understand and lacks significance – in their words, "it has no point" (p. 33). Daiute and Nelson (1997) extended this work, pointing out that as children develop narrative discourse skills, evaluation helps them learn how to situate or position themselves within society. Through dialogic interaction, evaluation emerges as the central, social element of narration, and one that entails both "cultural and personal aspects of sense-making" (Daiute & Nelson, 1997, p. 215).

Narrative evaluation is accomplished through a variety of linguistic means, including direct statements of opinion, repetition, constructed dialogue, exclamations, prosodic devices, lexical choices, and similes and metaphors, to name a few (Labov & Waletzky, 1967; Peterson & McCabe, 1983; also see Berman, 1997). Narrative evaluation can also be embedded in references to internal emotional states or to actions such as crying, which have emotional underpinnings (Melzi & Fernández, 2004). Furthermore, as illustrated in this chapter, in some languages such as Spanish, narrative evaluation is encoded through the use of particular types of evaluative morphology – most notably through diminutives. *Diminutives*, or word endings such as *–ito* or *–ita* (e.g., *mamá* → *mamita*), connote endearment and positive affect and, as detailed herein, are powerful interactional resources in a number of ways.

This chapter explores how preschool-aged Ecuadorian Andean girls and boys are socialized into different ways of being, feeling, and behaving through narrative conversations with their mother, and it focuses in particular on the evaluative function of diminutives and emotion words within narratives in achieving this. Both diminutives – whose evaluative role in narration has often been overlooked – and references to emotion offer rich sites for analysis of how culture-specific values are transmitted, enacted, and negotiated in everyday conversations. This chapter builds on two distinct lines of research in each area and then further extends this work by considering how diminutives and emotional reference function together in mother–child evaluation of past events. Through quantitative and qualitative analysis of two types of evaluation (i.e., diminutives and emotional reference), this chapter contributes to our understanding of how children are socialized to particular gendered values, attitudes, and ways of being through participation in narrative conversations, as well as how children are socialized to use diminutives and emotion words in culturally appropriate ways as they participate in these conversations.

Emotion and Gender in Narratives

All narratives are rooted in a particular cultural context and are generally coherent with the worldview of the community to which the narrator belongs. Narratives thus encode culture-specific ways of making meaning out of experiences (Heath, 1983; Invernizzi & Abouzeid, 1995; Ochs & Capps, 2001; Polanyi, 1981; Scollon & Scollon, 1981), including emotional experiences. As adults make reference to emotion through storytelling, or guide children to do so, they provide a model for how children should talk about, express, evaluate, and interpret emotions with respect to particular events (Fivush, 1991; Melzi, 2000; Melzi & Fernández, 2004).

Although the process of interpreting emotional events through narrative might be universal, previous research on how children express emotion in conversations about past experiences largely has focused on middle-class, English-speaking, European American families (e.g., Adams, Kuebli, Boyle, & Fivush, 1995; Fivush, 1991; Fivush, Brotman, Buckner, & Goodman, 2000). This work generally reports differences in how caregivers discuss emotions with boys and with girls (Fivush, 1991; Fivush & Buckner, 2000; Flannagan & Perese, 1998). Overall, this work suggests that caregivers tend to engage girls in discussions of emotion with greater frequency; to discuss emotions of sadness and dislike more with girls; and to discuss emotions of anger more with boys (Fivush, 1991). Furthermore, whereas mother–daughter dyads have been found to discuss emotions in the context of interpersonal relationships, mother–son pairs are more likely to discuss the causes and consequences of emotions (Cervantes & Callanan, 1998; Fivush et al., 2000).

These gendered patterns of emotional expression, however, are not necessarily shared by all cultural groups. For instance, research with middle-class Peruvians paints a different picture. Melzi and Fernández report that "mothers who talked with their sons made more emotional references than did mothers who talked with their daughters" (2004, p. 652). Moreover, and in contrast to U.S. findings, Peruvian mothers of boys tended to use more positive emotion words than mothers of girls; thus, "boys have greater opportunities than girls to discuss positive emotions, but somewhat similar opportunities to discuss negative emotions" (p. 655) with their mother.

This apparent difference between U.S. and Latin American socialization patterns sheds light on possible origins of cross-cultural differences in adult emotional expression. Yet the extent to which the findings of Melzi and Fernández with middle-class Peruvian mothers can be generalized to other Latin American populations remains unclear. Although their participants were urban, educated, and middle-class native Spanish speakers, many Latin Americans live under very different circumstances with limited access to formal education or to standard Spanish and with distinct, non-European cultural heritages and identities. For instance, across the Andean nations of Peru, Ecuador, and Bolivia, roughly one third of the population identifies as Indigenous (i.e., non-European) and speaks an Indigenous language monolingually or in addition to Spanish (King & Hornberger, 2004). The question of how Indigenous Latin American parents socialize their children to different gender expectations and to what extent this parallels mainstream (i.e., non-Indigenous, Spanish-monolingual) Latin American patterns in the region remains an open and important question.

Diminutives and Emotion

Children internalize community expectations and develop expertise for using both diminutives and emotional reference in particular sociocultural contexts through conversational interactions with more competent others. This process of socialization has been described as involving "interactional display (covert or overt) to a novice of expected ways of thinking, feeling, and acting" (Ochs, 1986, p. 2). This process, perhaps more accurately described as multiple overlapping and related processes, is largely realized through language (Garret & Baquedano-López, 2002) and is uncovered through detailed analysis of naturalistic language use in particular cultural contexts.

Use of diminutives within narratives provides a prime site for the analysis of culture-specific and gendered patterns of emotion. Whereas the various linguistic means of accomplishing evaluation within narrative have been studied extensively (e.g., Peterson & McCabe, 1983), little work has examined how diminutives function in similar ways. This is very likely because most narrative work has been conducted in English, a language that has a limited and unproductive evaluative morphology system relative to other languages (see King & Melzi, 2004, for further discussion).

Within narratives, diminutives play an important role in communicating maternally expected notions of being, behaving, feeling, and relating to others. As widely noted and well documented, diminutives also carry culture-specific meanings while compactly conveying context-specific sentiments and attitudes. For instance, Wierzbicka, writing about diminutives in Australian English, connects their use (e.g., *mozzies* for mosquitoes) with aspects of Australian identity: "anti-sentimentality, jocular cynicism, a tendency to knock things down to size, 'mateship', good-natured humour, love of informality, and dislike for 'long words'" (1991, p. 56; in Dressler & Barbaresi, 1994). More generally, Wierzbicka argues that "painstaking semantic analysis of culture-specific meanings encoded in language" is the best method for identifying these cultural predispositions (2003). This approach rests on the premise that each language reflects a certain universe of meaning. Words that are particularly important to a given language community are usually untranslatable into other languages: there are simply no equivalent words or expressions in other languages. For example, in Ecuadorian Spanish, families may address their young sons or grandsons with the term of endearment *papito*, which would literally translate to "little father," but that has no direct equivalent in English.

In most varieties of Spanish, including those spoken in Indigenous Andean areas, diminutives are most often realized through the addition of the suffix *–ito* or *–ita* to a noun (e.g., *casa* → *casita* "*house*") or an adjective (e.g., *guapa* → *guapita* "*good-looking*"), and they carry a wide range of meanings. While *–ito/–ita* literally translates as *small*, it also connotes affection, endearment, or cuteness. These Spanish diminutives are prime candidates for such semantic analysis of culture-specific meanings because although there are similarities across languages in the connotations of diminutives, they often do not have equivalents in other languages. For instance, a common nickname in parts of Latin America is *gordito* (fat+DIM/MASC), which translates into English most closely as "fatty." However, this translation fails to capture the endearment and positive affect of the term, as well as its connotation of an attractive and generally pleasing appearance (whereas in much of the United States and Europe, "fatty" would hardly be complimentary). Diminutives thus provide a means for examining a specific linguistic form that links to particular sociocultural contexts and values.

From a developmental perspective, in turn, child language research points to the importance of diminutives – a long-established feature of child-directed speech (CDS) or "motherese" (Ferguson, 1977) – in creating an affectionate, supportive environment for talk (Melzi & King, 2003), as well as one that facilitates the acquisition of gender, stress, and other systems (Kempe & Brookes, 1998). King and Melzi (2004), for instance, demonstrate how mothers' and children's imitations of their interlocutors' diminutized words promoted overall diminutive use. This work highlights the acute sensitivity of both speakers to each others' language and the potential of this mutual fine-tuning for establishing an intimate context that positively influences children's language development.

Other research has pointed to the importance of diminutives in facilitating the acquisition of particular rules systems (Kempe & Brookes, 1998). As an example, Kempe, Brooks, Mironova, and Fedorova (2003) found that young children (2;9–4;8) who were shown pictures of familiar and novel animals and presented with the animal name in either simplex or diminutive form produced fewer agreement errors when presented with the diminutive form. Diminutives in languages such as Spanish (1) regularize and make transparent gender markings (e.g., *flor* becomes *florecita*), and (2) regularize stress (i.e., irregular words follow the standard pattern once diminutized). Both of these processes potentially simplify and facilitate acquisition of morphological rules.

Thus, several converging lines of research on diminutives suggest that they (1) are culturally salient and potentially rich sites for analysis; (2) help to create an affectionate, intimate site of talk; (3) facilitate children's acquisition of morphological rule systems; and (4) potentially play an underexamined evaluative role in Andean parent–child narration. However, much of what we know about diminutives is based on controlled experimental studies or analysis of written texts. With few exceptions (e.g., King & Melzi, 2004), this work has not examined naturalistic language use. Furthermore, none of this research has examined how diminutive usage might vary across different Spanish-speaking groups or cultures. This chapter begins to fill this gap and explores how these potential gender differences in emotional socialization are enacted in a context that has been relatively little studied, the southern Ecuadorian Andean highlands. Within this context, this study investigates how (1) diminutives are used by mothers of boys and mothers of girls; (2) emotion words are used by mothers of boys and by mothers of girls; and (3) diminutives are used to highlight emotions in the context of mother–child narrative conversations.

METHODS

Setting and Participants

Study participants were Indigenous mothers and children from the rural areas in and around the Andean highland town of Saraguro in southern Ecuador (see King, 2001, for more information about local context). Ecuador is a small multilingual, multicultural country of approximately 13 million people. Approximately 45% of the citizens live in poverty and, by most measures, socioeconomic inequality is pronounced (World Bank, 2007). Although Spanish has long been the official language of the country, between a quarter and a third of the population speaks an Indigenous language, the most widely spoken of which is Quichua (King & Haboud, 2002).

The Indigenous people who live in and around the town of Saraguro are known as Saraguros; they overwhelmingly self-identify as Indigenous and mark themselves as such with distinctive clothing and hairstyles. Yet, despite the surge in ethnic consciousness within both Ecuador and the Saraguro region in recent decades, Saraguros are in the process of shifting from Quichua dominance to Spanish dominance. Currently, most of the children and many of the adults are monolingual in Spanish. Even as Indigenous consciousness has grown, the use of Quichua has continued to decline in Saraguro. This lack of Quichua language competence and use has increasingly become a source of concern and even embarrassment for some Saraguros. Many Saraguro communities now openly discuss the importance of revitalizing Quichua and the need for both children and adults to acquire the language.

Concomitant with these linguistic shifts have come significant social, cultural, and economic changes. In the early 1960s, few Saraguros had more than 2 or 3 years of formal schooling and most were engaged exclusively in agricultural work, tending to small plots of land and raising small herds of animals. By the late 1990s, Saraguros were employed in a wide variety of occupations, as:

> carpenters and shoe makers, nuns, doctors, dentists, nurses, drug-store owners, veterinarians, lawyers, musicians, elected officials at the *cantón* and national levels, government bureaucrats, directors of regional NGO programs, shop owners, muleteers, gold-camp laborers, construction laborers, maids, owners of body repair shops, mechanics, welders, leaders of pan-indigenous movements, primary and high school teachers and directors of schools. (Belote & Belote, 1997, para. 13)

Increased internal movement (to Ecuador's major cities) and international migration (to Spain and the United States) for short- or long-term employment have also been a major shift. In some Saraguro communities, it is estimated that between a quarter and a third of the population is living abroad. While Saraguros have become more mobile, they have also become more politically active with, for instance, Luis Macas, a prominent Saraguro, serving as Ecuador's first Indigenous senator and, in 2006, as a presidential candidate.

Table 6.1. *Sociodemographic profiles of participants by gender*

	Boys (N = 16)	Girls (N = 16)
	M (Range)	M (Range)
CHILDREN		
Age	4;4 (3;0–5;9)	4;6 (3;2–5;11)
Age of first words	1;4 (0;8–2;0)	0;11 (0;4–1;6)
MOTHERS		
Age	32 (22–44)	28 (21–48)
Years of education	7.06 (6–12)	7.84 (1.5–13)
N employed outside the Home	0	4
FATHERS		
Age	33 (24–42)	31 (20–46)
Years of education	6.41 (1–12)	8.56 (4–16)
N employed outside the Home	7	9
HOME		
Household size	7 (4–10)	7 (4–13)
N of children	4 (1–9)	3 (1–7)

For the current study, Saraguro mothers and their preschool-aged children were recruited by two Spanish-speaking researchers who drew on the first author's previous research network in the region (King, 2001). Participants consisted of 32 mothers and their children, equally balanced between boys and girls and 3- and 5-year-olds (Table 6.1). The mothers of children from each gender and age group were of comparable socioeconomic status. Although mothers of girls reported a higher mean educational level than mothers of boys, this difference was not statistically significant. Four of the mothers of girls were employed outside the home, whereas all the remaining mothers of boys and girls alike worked at home. Stated occupations included homemaker, agricultural worker, crafts worker, public employee, and preschool teacher. All mothers reported that their children were Spanish-dominant, although 24 noted that their children were also exposed to limited amounts of Quichua in the home.

Procedures

Each of the 32 mother–child pairs was visited in their home and received the same set of instructions. Researchers asked mothers to elicit from their child six personal narratives of recent past events: three in which the mothers had participated with the child and three during which the mothers had been absent. Mothers were instructed not to ask their children to sing or recount tales from movies or storybooks. Printed directions were given to each participant in addition to a verbal explanation. Researchers removed themselves from the immediate vicinity and did not take part in the conversations. Pairs were allowed to determine the length of their conversations. Conversations between mothers and preschoolers were digitally recorded.

Coding and Analysis

The conversations were transcribed by a team of Spanish-speaking researchers in a standardized format, Codes for the Human Analysis of Language (CHAT), available through the Child Language Data Exchange System (CHILDES) (MacWhinney, 2000). A native Spanish speaker from highland Ecuador verified the accuracy of the transcriptions. Because mother–child interactions tended to include multiple, overlapping narratives, often interspersed with related "here and now" talk, narratives were not segmented and all recorded speech for each dyad was analyzed.

Using Computerized Language Analyses (CLAN) programs available through CHILDES, all diminutives and emotion words in the transcripts were identified for quantitative and qualitative analysis. Qualitative analysis involved detailed interpretive examination of the discourse patterns surrounding diminutive and emotional word use, including content and tone of parental talk. Quantitative analysis proceeded along two lines, with separate rounds of coding for emotional words and diminutized words.

Emotion Coding

Each emotion word used by mother or child was coded based on Dunn, Bretherton, and Munn (1987); see also Melzi and Fernández (2004). Emotion words included any overt references to feelings or desires and were coded as one of the following:

1. *Positive*: Reference to an emotion such as love, pleasure, surprise, sympathy, or desire, or to a physical state of being that signals an emotion (e.g., *amor* [love], *querer* [to want], *gustar* [to like/to be pleasing]).
2. *Negative*: Reference to an emotion such as anger, contempt, displeasure, fear, sadness, or shame, or to a physical state of being that signals an emotion (e.g., *llorar* [to cry], *enojado* [angered]).
3. *Other*: An unspecified feeling or a reference to a nonspecific feeling or emotion (e.g., *sentir* [to feel]).

The percentage of agreement between the two coders was greater than 90% for emotion words.

Diminutive Coding

All diminutives in the transcripts were identified and coded for both landing site and function. Values for landing site were mutually exclusive and assigned as follows:

1. *Nouns*: Words that refer to humans, the child participant, animals, objects, or abstract ideas (e.g., *casita* [HOUSE-DIM/FEM]).
2. *Adverbs*: Words that modify verbs or adjectives; words that establish time or place (e.g., *acasito* [THERE-DIM/MASC]; *demasiadito* [TOO MUCH-DIM/MASC]).
3. *Adjectives*: Words that modify nouns or pronouns (e.g., *malito* [BAD-DIM/MASC]).

Where ambiguity existed, the word class of the landing site was determined by sentential context.

In addition to landing site, mothers' diminutives were also coded for function of the utterance in which they occurred. Each diminutive received one of the following three codes:

1. *Command*: An imperative or request sequence to the child (e.g., *Cántate un cantito* [Sing a SONG-DIM/MASC]).
2. *Expansion*: An utterance that encourages the child to expand on a previous utterance. Diminutives in expansions function to keep the child on task, confirm positive or expected responses by the child, and expand the child's utterance. In the example that follows, we see a diminutive in the final expansion question.

		Spanish Original	English Translation
1	**Mother:**	*¿Mm, en el jardín qué hiciste ayer [///] en qué te hicieron ayer?*	Mm, in nursery school what did you do yesterday? [///] in what did you do yesterday?
2	**Child:**	*xxx la capita.*	xxx the cape-**DIM/FEM**
3	**Mother:**	*¿Pusieron capa?*	They put on a cape?
4	**Child:**	*Sí.*	Yes.
5	**Mother:**	*¿Por qué te pusieron la capita?*	Why did they put the cape-**DIM/FEM** on you?

3. *Other*: Utterances with maternal diminutives that do not fit either of the other two definitions.

The percentage of agreement between the two coders was greater than 89% for emotion words for all diminutive coding.

Following the coding for diminutives and emotional references at the word level, totals for all categories were tabulated. The raw frequencies were used for comparisons; in addition, to control for varied length of narrative conversations across different mother–child dyads, comparisons and analyses were also conducted based on percentages of diminutives (i.e., the number of diminutives relative to the total number of words per conversation) or percentage of emotional references (i.e., the number of emotion words relative to the total number of words per conversation). The presentation of results notes whether raw frequencies or percentages are being reported.

These frequencies and percentages were compared statistically using *t*-tests as follows: diminutives used by mothers of boys and girls and 3- and 5-year-olds; emotion words used by mothers of boys and girls and 3- and 5-year-olds; diminutives used in emotional and nonemotional references; and diminutives used in emotional references by mothers of boys and girls and 3- and 5-year-olds. Findings of statistical significance are illustrated through and expanded on by qualitative trends in the data.

RESULTS

Findings are organized in three sections: (1) how diminutives are used by mothers with their child; (2) how emotion words are used by mothers with their child; and (3) how diminutives are used to highlight emotions within the context of the narrative conversations. Our quantitative and qualitative analyses are integrated here, with each of the three sections beginning with a quantitative overview of general patterns, followed by (where relevant) qualitative analysis and excerpts from transcripts.

Overall, our analysis indicates gender and age differences in how mothers employed diminutives and emotional words with their child. Whereas mothers of boys and mothers of girls used diminutives in *quantitatively* similar ways, they tended to use them in *qualitatively* different ways. Girls also generally heard greater reference to positive emotions than did boys, and 5-year-old girls heard significantly more diminutives in emotional utterances than 3-year-old girls and boys of both age groups. Together, the data suggest that diminutives play an important role in socializing emotion and that as children get older, diminutives in emotional utterances are used in gender-specific ways.

How Are Diminutives Used by Mothers of Boys and Mothers of Girls?

Together, mother–child pairs used a total of 537 diminutives throughout the course of their narrative conversations; 338 were used by mothers and 199 by children. With respect to placement of diminutives, nouns were the form most often diminutized by mothers (82.12%), followed by adverbs (14.24%) and adjectives (3.64%). This finding contradicts previous work suggesting that nouns, followed by adjectives and then adverbs, are most common landing sites for diminutives (Bauer, 1997). This difference in our data might well be due to the fact that mothers frequently issued commands (see the following discussion) and these commands often contained adverbs (e.g., *habla clarito* [speak clearly-DIM/MASC]). The majority of mothers' diminutives functioned as expansion requests (57.88%), whereas the rest were commands (18.80%) or served some other function (23.94%). Mothers tended to use these diminutive forms and functions with similar frequencies in their narrative conversations regardless of the gender of their child.

Yet, while the landing site and function of maternal diminutives did not differ quantitatively by gender of the child, patterns of use differed qualitatively. In particular, mothers of daughters tended to use diminutives to stress love, affection, and closeness. As an example, in the following excerpt between a mother and her 3-year-old daughter, the mother used diminutives to emphasize love toward the child's grandmother and toward others:

Excerpt 1.

		Spanish Original	English Translation
1	**Mother:**	*¿Y la abuelita qué hacía? (. . .) ¿Les cuidaba?*	And grandma-**DIM/FEM**, what was she doing? (. . .) Did she take care of you?
2	**Child:**	*Sí.*	Yes.
3	**Mother:**	*¿Mm, qué más? ¿Ustedes sí le querían a la abuelita?*	Mm, what else? Did you love grandma-**DIM/FEM**?
4	**Child:**	*¿A cuál abuelita?*	Which grandma-**DIM/FEM**?
5	**Mother:**	*A abuelita Majitan.*	Grandma-**DIM/FEM** Majitan.
6	**Child:**	*Abuelita Majitan, sí.*	Grandma-**DIM/FEM** Majitan, yes.
7	**Mother:**	*Sí, ¿qué más?*	Yes, what else?
8	**Child:**	*Queremos a los toditos.*	We love everyone-**DIM/MAS**.
9	**Mother:**	*Quieren ustedes a los toditos.*	You love everyone-**DIM/MAS**.
10	**Child:**	*Sí.*	Yes.

In Excerpt 1, the mother prompted her daughter to state her love for her grandmother with a yes or no question in line 3. The mother encouraged or set the stage for a positive statement of affection both by supplying a yes-no question (effectively leaving the child with only two options) *and* pairing it with the diminutized form of "grandmother." Following her positive statement of affection for her grandmother (line 6), the girl was prompted for further emotional expression (line 7). In line 8, she stated that she loved everyone (using the diminutized form of "all"), which was reinforced and affirmed as "correct" by her mother's repetition. As exemplified here, diminutives allow the mother to teach appropriate references to affection and allow the child to display her mastery of expected attitudes with respect to others.

In the following conversation between a mother and her 5-year-old daughter, the diminutized form of "alone" was used to encourage an expression of desire for closeness with the child's mother.

Excerpt 2.

		Spanish Original	English Translation
1	**Mother:**	*¿Sí quieres estar con tu papi?*	Do you want to be with your daddy?
2	**Child:**	*Sí.*	Yes.
3	**Mother:**	*¿Y conmigo por qué no quieres estar?*	And with me, why don't you want to be (with me)?
4	**Child:**	*Un poco también con usted sí quiero estar.*	I want to be with you a little too.
5	**Mother:**	*¿No quieres estar conmigo?*	You don't want to be with me?
6	**Mother:**	*¿Y si yo me voy de aquí quedas solita?*	And if I leave here do you stay alone-**DIM/FEM**?
7	**Child:**	*No.*	No.
8	**Mother:**	*¿Quieres quedar solita?*	Do you want to stay alone-**DIM/FEM**?
9	**Child:**	*No.*	No.
10	**Mother:**	*¿No quieres quedar solita?*	You don't want to stay alone-**DIM/FEM**?
11	**Child:**	*No.*	No.
12	**Mother:**	*¿Y cuando yo [/] yo me voy xxx xxx usted se queda solita?*	And when I [/] I go xxx xxx you stay alone-**DIM/FEM**?
13	**Mother:**	*¿No quieres quedar?*	You don't want to stay?
14	**Child:**	*No.*	No.
15	**Mother:**	*¿Sí quieres estar conmigo?*	Do you want to be with me?
16	**Child:**	*Sí.*	Yes.

In Excerpt 2, we see that the mother asked her daughter why she did not like to be with her mother (line 3). When the child provided an answer that lacked in terms of the intensity of desire ("a little") (line 4), the mother pursued a line of questioning in order to elicit the expected response (lines 5–16). As in Excerpt 1, these questions guided the child toward the desired response by pairing diminutives with questions that frame or predispose the child to answering in a particular way. For example, in line 10, the mother asked her child, "You don't want to stay alone-DIM/FEM?" and the child responded that she did not. The diminutization of "alone" stressed the "aloneness" of "alone." From a framework of narrative analysis, it can also be seen as a form of evaluation because it helps "tell the reader what to think" (Peterson & McCabe, 1983, p. 32) about a situation or, in this case, strongly hints to the child the appropriate response. Through the diminutization of "alone" in this hypothetical situation, both smallness and aloneness are stressed, and empathy for the central character (the child) has been created. Here again, diminutives play a role in the socialization of the value of closeness with family members through their evaluative function in narrative conversation between mother and daughter.

Whereas mothers showed a tendency to use diminutives with girls to socialize affection, this was much less evident in narrative conversations with boys. When mothers used diminutives with their son, they tended to use diminutized forms to refer to animals and objects in the child's world and to encourage the child to offer more detail. This is exemplified in the following excerpt between a 3-year-old boy and his mother:

Excerpt 3.

		Spanish Original	English Translation
1	**Mother:**	*¿A ver, qué es esto?*	Let's see, what is this?
2	**Child:**	*xxx culleba.*	xxx snake.
3	**Mother:**	*¿Qué hace la culebrita?*	What does the snake-**DIM/FEM** do?
4	**Child:**	*xxx cho [?].*	xxx cho [?].
5	**Mother:**	*¿Qué más?*	What else?
6	**Child:**	*Conejo.*	Rabbit.
7	**Mother:**	*¿Qué hace el conejito?*	What does the rabbit-**DIM/MASC** do?
8	**Child:**	*¡Comer!*	Eat!
9	**Mother:**	*¿Qué está comiendo?*	What is he eating?
10	**Child:**	*Da chus [?].*	Da chus [?].
11	**Mother:**	*¿A ver qué es esto?*	Let's see what is this?
12	**Child:**	*Pelotita.*	Ball-**DIM/FEM**.
13	**Mother:**	*¿Quién juega con la pelotita?*	Who plays with the ball-**DIM/FEM**?
14	**Child:**	*Yo.*	Me.

In Excerpt 3, the mother encouraged her son to display his knowledge of animals and other objects. Both times (lines 2 and 6), the child introduced an animal using the simplex form and the mother followed up with a request for more information using a diminutized form of the same noun (lines 3 and 7). Finally, the child introduced the diminutized form of the word "ball" himself (line 12), and the mother again followed up with an action-oriented question using the diminutized form (line 13). Here, diminutives were not conveying closeness or love or affection toward these objects; rather, their primary function was to reinforce, encourage, and expand the child's participation in the conversation (King & Melzi, 2004).

In sum, mothers of boys and mothers of girls used diminutives in quantitatively similar ways; with boys and with girls, maternal diminutives were most

Table 6.2. *Emotion words in mothers' speech: Mean and standard deviation from raw frequency*

	Mothers of girls M (SD)	Mothers of boys M (SD)	Total M (SD)
Positive	16.94 (18.39)	7.88 (8.66)	12.41 (14.87)
Negative	3.81 (4.28)	3.63 (7.43)	3.72 (5.96)
Total	20.75 (19.88)	11.5 (14.27)	16.13 (17.66)

frequently attached to nouns and functioned as expansion requests. However, diminutive use differed qualitatively, with diminutives playing a role in the socialization of love, closeness, and affection for girls. As such, they can be seen as a resource for evaluation in narrative conversation, similar to other strategies for signaling evaluation such as reference to emotional states (Peterson & McCabe, 1983), a point we develop further in the next section.

How Are Emotion Words Used by Mothers of Girls and Mothers of Boys?

In total, 615 emotional references were made by mother–child dyads: 525 by mothers and 90 by children. Overall, children heard significantly more positive ($M = 12.41$, $SD = 14.87$) than negative ($M = 3.72$, $SD = 5.96$) emotion words ($t(31) = 3.46$, $p < .05$) (Table 6.2). In addition, girls heard significantly more positive emotion words ($M = 16.94$, $SD = 18.39$) than did boys ($M = 7.88$, $SD = 8.66$) ($t(15) = -1.85$, $p < .05$) when compared in terms of raw frequency of occurrence; however, when the length of the conversation was controlled, that difference was not statistically significant.

How Are Diminutives Used to Highlight Emotions?

Diminutives have been shown to carry connotations of intimacy and playfulness (Ettinger, 1974, cited in Dressler & Barbaresi, 1994; Jurafsky, 1996), as well as emotionality (Alonso, 1961; Inchaurralde, 1997); thus viewed within a framework of narrative analysis, they also potentially serve an evaluative function. To probe the connection between diminutives and emotionality, we also examined how diminutives and emotion words worked together to socialize children into culturally appropriate ways of referring to emotion and, in particular, we investigated whether gender differences existed in these patterns.

First, we asked whether diminutives were more likely to appear in utterances that contained at least one emotional reference as defined for purposes of this study. Analysis of maternal speech showed that the percentage of diminutives in mothers' emotional utterances ($M = 7.97$, $SD = 1.86$) was significantly higher than in nonemotional utterances ($M = 1.85$, $SD = 0.19$) ($t(25) = 3.24$,

Table 6.3. *Diminutives as a percentage of total emotion and nonemotion utterances*

	Emotional utterance		Nonemotional utterances	
	Girls *M (SD)*	Boys *M (SD)*	Girls *M (SD)*	Boys *M (SD)*
3-year-olds	8.54 (10.45)	5.25 (12.45)	1.79 (0.32)	1.96 (0.41)
5-year-olds	12.24 (5.86)	6.21 (7.87)	1.68 (0.20)	1.98 (0.55)
Total	10.25 (8.52)	5.70 (10.18)	1.74 (0.19)	1.70 (0.32)
Overall Total	7.97 (1.86)		1.85 (0.19)	

$p < .05$) (Table 6.3). In other words, maternal diminutives were more likely to occur in emotionally charged utterances than in nonemotional utterances. Thus, diminutives potentially served to intensify or, at least, to reflect the emotionality in the utterances.

Once a relationship was established between emotional utterances and diminutized words in maternal speech, our next question was whether girls were, in fact, more likely than boys to hear such diminutized emotional utterances. Results suggest age-specific gender differences in the use of diminutives within emotional utterances. Whereas 3-year-old girls and boys heard diminutized emotional utterances with similar frequencies, 5-year-old girls heard significantly more diminutives in emotional utterances ($t(5) = -2.04$, $p < .05$) than did 5-year-old boys (see Table 6.3).

Taken together, these data suggest that diminutives are more likely to occur in utterances that contain an emotional reference and, furthermore, that 5-year-old girls are more likely to hear such emotional and diminutized utterances than 5-year-old boys. This tendency is illustrated in the following excerpt of a mother and her 5-year-old daughter in conversation. The two were engaged in playful talk surrounding the word for "ladybug" (i.e., *mariquita*, not a diminutive), which they treated as if it were a girl's name:

Excerpt 4.

		Spanish Original	**English Translation**
1	**Mother:**	*¿La mariquita Pérez es tu amiga o no?*	Is ladybug Perez your friend or not?
2	**Child:**	*Sí.*	Yes.
3	**Mother:**	*¿Te gusta mucho?*	You like her a lot?
4	**Child:**	*Sí.*	Yes.
5	**Mother:**	*¿Por qué te gusta [>]?*	Why do you like her [>]?
6	**Sister:**	*Catalina [<]!*	Catalina [<]!
7	**Child:**	*Porque ella me hace cosquill**itas**.*	Because she gives me the tickles-**DIM/FEM**.

8	**Mother:**	*¿Qué hace cosquillitas?*	What gives you the tickles-**DIM/FEM**?
9	**Mother:**	*¿En qué te hace cosquillitas?*	Where does she give you tickles-**DIM/FEM**?
10	**Child:**	*En la mano.*	On my hand.
11	**Mother:**	*¿En la mano?*	On your hand?
12	**Child:**	*Sí.*	Yes.
13	**Mother:**	*¿Y después le [/] le pones allí en la flor que [///] para que viva o le matas?*	And then you put her there on the flower that so that she can live or do you kill her?
14	**Child:**	*Ahh que viva.*	Ahh so that she lives.
15	**Mother:**	*¿Que viva?*	So that she lives?
16	**Child:**	*Sí.*	Yes.
17	**Mother:**	*¿No le matas?*	You don't kill her?
18	**Mother:**	*¿No?*	No?
19	**Mother:**	*Ah.*	Ah.
20	**Mother:**	*### pues qué bien.*	### well very good.
21	**Child:**	*xxx.*	xxx.
22	**Mother:**	*Que les dejes que vivan los animalitos.*	That you let animals-**DIM/MASC** live.
23	**Mother:**	*No se les mata a los animalitos, hay que dejarles +/.*	Animals-**DIM/MASC** don't get killed you have to leave them.

The pair discussed playing with a ladybug and, in the end, allowing her to live rather than killing her. The analogy to interacting with a human friend was established through both the play on words, which accords the ladybug a human-like name, and the mother's question about whether the ladybug was a friend (line 1). In addition, the child emphasized her interaction with this "friend" by noting that the insect gave her "*cosquillitas*" (little tickles) (line 7), potentially signaling feelings of fondness toward the friend and the situation with the use of the diminutive. Finally, the mother asked about her daughter's treatment of the ladybug by providing two options: either the daughter put it on the flower so it could live or she killed it. The daughter opted for the former, and the mother approved of her treatment with the direct evaluation, "good," as well as a statement that the child allows "*animalitos*" (little animals) to live (lines 20–23). Diminutives functioned here in conjunction with other linguistic resources to promote the values of empathy, benevolence, cooperation, and compassion toward animals and, by analogy, toward friends.

As in Excerpt 1, diminutives play a role when parents are working to correct undesirable attitudes and teach the values expected within a child's family and culture. In the following excerpt, two diminutized forms served in tandem with an emotional reference as a mother guided her 5-year-old daughter to the proper stance toward a distressing event with her grandmother:

Excerpt 5.

		Spanish Original	English Translation
1	**Mother:**	*¿Y ahí fue cuando te perdiste?*	And that's where it was when you got lost?
2	**Child:**	*Sí.*	Yes.
3	**Mother:**	*¿Y cuando te fuiste con una señora y te dieron manzana y caña?*	And when you went with a lady and they gave you an apple and sugarcane?
4	**Child:**	*Sí.*	Yes.
5	**Mother:**	*¿Sí?*	Yes?
6	**Sister:**	*¿Y cómo se llama esa +/?*	And what was her name?
7	**Mother:**	*¿Pero allí [///] cuando te fuiste allí cómo te sentiste?*	But there [///] when you went there, how did you feel?
8	**Mother:**	*¿Bien o mal?*	Good or bad?
9	**Child:**	*Bien.*	Good.
10	**Mother:**	*¿Bien por haberte perdido y dejado a la abuelita solita?*	Good for having gotten lost and left your grandmother-**DIM/FEM** alone-**DIM/FEM**?
11	**Child:**	*Sí.*	Yes.
12	**Mother:**	*Ahhh.*	Ahh.
13	**Mother:**	*¿Pero te sentías bien? Tú también llorabas y ¿así te sentías bien?*	But you felt good? You were also crying and you felt good?
14	**Mother:**	*### ¿o mal?*	### or bad?
15	**Child:**	*Mal.*	Bad.
16	**Mother:**	*¿Mal?*	Bad?
17	**Child:**	*Sí.*	Yes.
18	**Mother:**	*¿Te sentías mal cuando estabas perdida?*	You felt bad when you were lost?
19	**Child:**	*Sí.*	Yes.

In Excerpt 5, the mother asked her daughter to recount how she felt when she got lost. The daughter replied that she felt good, an answer that evidently did not fit with the mother's expectations or desired emotional response. In reaction to the child's "incorrect" answer, the mother attempted to elicit the expected stance toward this upsetting event; she questioned the child about feeling good about getting lost and leaving her grandmother all alone (line 10). Diminutives played a clear role in this emotional reference; the mother juxtaposed the improper emotion (feeling good) with the unfortunate event (getting lost) and the result (grandmother all alone) by using two diminutized forms to represent the grand-mother's situation. When this did not work, the mother persisted with more questions and reference to a physical state (crying) that generally contradicts feeling good until her daughter finally displayed the stance the mother desired and expected. Diminutives served to intensify the emotionality of the mother's utterances and, together, these two forms of evaluation helped signal to the child an important lesson to be taken from this series of events: getting lost was an unpleasant event that had made her feel bad. This excerpt provides a clear example of how diminutives function in children's socialization to emotionality.

DISCUSSION AND CONCLUSION

This study of diminutives and emotional reference in maternal speech has addressed three related questions: (1) How are diminutives used by mothers of boys and mothers of girls to evaluate narrative action?; (2) How are emotion words used by mothers of boys and mothers of girls to evaluate narrative action?; and (3) How are diminutives used to highlight emotional reference within nar-ratives? The main results and the significance of each question are addressed in turn.

First, in terms of overall diminutive use by mothers, quantitative results indicate that all mothers most frequently diminutized nouns, often with the apparent purpose of encouraging the child to expand on a prior utterance. Quantitative analysis revealed no statistically significant gender differences in diminutive use, a finding that is consistent with prior research on diminutive use among Latin American mothers in conversational narrative contexts (Melzi & King, 2003).

Although there were no significant *quantitative* gender differences in maternal use of diminutives, mothers of boys and mothers of girls tended to use this form of evaluative morphology in *qualitatively* different ways. Mothers of daughters were more likely to use diminutives to emphasize love, closeness, and affection in narrative conversation, whereas mothers of boys tended to use diminutized forms to refer to animals and objects in the child's world and to encourage the child to offer more detail. Differing patterns of diminutive use between mothers of boys and mothers of girls suggest gender-specific socialization processes in this Indigenous Ecuadorian community. From a young age, girls are exposed to – and encouraged to participate in – narrative conversations that highlight relationships and positive affect through use of particular types of evaluative morphology.

Second, in terms of emotional reference in mothers' speech, all children were significantly more likely to hear references to positive rather than negative emo-tion. Mothers of girls tended to discuss positive emotion more frequently than mothers of boys, although this difference was not statistically significant when length of conversation was controlled. This tendency toward greater discussion of positive emotion with girls is consistent with overall trends in data reported by Fivush (1991) but contradictory to that reported by Melzi and Fernández (2004). The Fivush (1991) study was conducted with White, middle-class mother–child dyads in the United States, whereas Melzi and Fernández (2004) analyzed conversations between middle-class Peruvian mothers and their children. Such contradictory findings from studies conducted in three separate contexts may point to the role of individual differences in interaction or locally situated practices with respect to the discussion of positive and negative emotions with boys and girls. It is possible that rather than any universal standard, discussion of emotion may depend on the dynamics within a given conversation, family, or community. These differing findings suggest the need for more research in this area.

Data relating to the third question – the use of diminutives in emotional references – were more conclusive. Diminutives were significantly more likely to occur in emotional rather than nonemotional utterances overall; furthermore, 5-year-old girls were significantly more likely to hear diminutized forms in emotional references than their 3-year-old counterparts as well as *both* 3- and 5-year-old boys. These quantitative results reinforce the notion that diminutives carry an emotional connotation and, therefore, that they can perform evaluative roles in narration; furthermore, results suggest that diminutives play a function in gender-specific emotional socialization. This important role of diminutives in narrative evaluation in languages such as Spanish has perhaps been overlooked because many studies have focused exclusively on narratives in English and other languages that have weak systems of evaluative morphology.

The qualitative analysis illustrates how diminutives function to intensify emotional reference and to serve an evaluative function within narrative exchanges. Diminutives in emotional utterances highlight and reinforce the mothers' emotional evaluation of the event and demonstrate for children the appropriate way to interpret and talk about past events in a particular manner. With 5-year-old girls in particular, these two resources for evaluation – diminutives and reference to emotion – highlight values of love, closeness, and kindness. This observation supports the results of prior work (Fivush et al., 2000), which found that mothers tend to use emotions to emphasize interpersonal relationships with girls.

The finding that 5-year-old girls hear more diminutives in utterances containing an emotional reference than 3-year-old girls runs counter to prior research on the developmental aspect of diminutives; on the whole, children hear fewer diminutives as they get older (Berko Gleason, Perlmann, Ely, & Evans, 1994; Melzi & King, 2003). The greater presence of diminutized emotional utterances in speech directed at older preschool-aged girls could be due to increasingly differentiated gender role expectations for girls and boys who have reached the age of five. Although 3-year-old boys and girls may not yet be expected to display different attitudes with respect to interpersonal relationships, perhaps by age five, girls are expected to display a value of intimacy with and affection toward others. Saraguro mothers, therefore, increase their own modeling of the language of love, intimacy, friendship, and kindness in interaction with their daughters. This possible gender- and culture-specific expectation for behavior highlights the importance of attention to culture-specific linguistic constructions and ways of making meaning out of experience in future research into cross-cultural narration and language socialization.

In summary, both quantitative and qualitative evidence suggests that diminutives play an important evaluative function in mother–child narration. This finding supports prior work that emphasizes the role of narration in child language socialization (Ochs & Capps, 2001); the aspects of narration investigated in this study play a part in socializing children to talk about and display particular attitudes toward emotional events. Boys and girls tended to hear more references to positive than negative emotion, a fact that might be linked to one of this study's other findings: namely, that diminutives occurred more frequently in emotional than nonemotional references. If diminutive use in narrative connotes positive feelings of love, closeness, and intimacy (King & Melzi, 2004), then they will naturally encourage a positive orientation in the emotional utterances in which they are used. One future line of research might investigate the relative use of diminutives in reference to specific positive and negative emotions, such as happiness, fear, and anger. Such a study could help define nuances in the situational usage of diminutives in the discussion of emotional events. Nevertheless, the more frequent occurrence of diminutives in emotional than nonemotional references suggests a salient role for this type of evaluative morphology in the establishment of affect in narrative conversation. Diminutives tend to support mothers' efforts to teach, model, and elicit the culturally appropriate stance toward emotional events and to highlight positive values of empathy, love, benevolence, and friendship. This study provides evidence that Indigenous mothers in the rural Ecuadorian Andes undertake such efforts in different ways when speaking with daughters and with sons.

More broadly, this chapter has illustrated how diminutives and emotional reference together perform an evaluative function in narrative conversations in gender-specific ways within this particular community. As children develop competence with these and other evaluative resources through repeated interactions with their mother or other caretakers, they become more fully competent members of their particular community. In this sense, as Daiute and Nelson (1997) point out, rather than simply constituting *linguistic* development, mastery of the complex evaluative function is a central component of *human* development as well.

Appendix A: *CHAT-format transcription conventions (MacWhinney, 2000) used in this paper*

Symbol	Explanation
Mother:	denotes speaker (mother)
Child:	denotes speaker (child)
Sister:	denotes speaker (sister)
.	end of declarative utterance
?	end of a question
+/.	interruption by another speaker
<text enclosed>	following symbol applies to entire string of enclosed words
[>]	overlap follows
[<]	overlap precedes
[/]	retracing without correction
[//]	retracing with correction
#	short pause
xxx	unintelligible speech
[?]	prior word or phrase unclear; transcriber's best guess

REFERENCES

Adams, S., Kuebli, J., Boyle, P. A., & Fivush, R. (1995). Gender differences in parent–child conversations about past emotions: A longitudinal investigation. *Sex Roles, 33*, 309–323.

Alonso, A. (1961). La base lingüística del español Americano. *Estudios lingüísticos. Temas hispanoamericanos*. Madrid: Gredos.

Bauer, L. (1997). Evaluative morphology: In search of universals. *Studies in Language, 21*, 533–575.

Belote, J., & Belote, L. (1997). The Saraguros, 1962–1997: A very brief overview. Retrieved June 21, 2007, from http://www.saraguro.org/overview.htm.

Berko Gleason, J., Perlmann, R. U., Ely, R., & Evans, D. W. (1994). The babytalk register: Parents' use of diminutives. In J. L. Sokolov & C. A. Snow (Eds.), *Handbook of research in language development using CHILDES*. Hillsdale, NJ: Erlbaum.

Berman, R. (1997). Narrative theory and narrative development: The Labovian impact. *Journal of Narrative and Life History, 7*(1–4), 235–244.

Cervantes, C. A., & Callanan, M. A. (1998). Labels and explanations in mother–child emotion talk: Age and gender differentiation. *Developmental Psychology, 34*, 88–98.

Daiute, C., & Nelson, K. (1997). Making sense of the sense-making function of narrative evaluation. *Journal of Narrative and Life History, 7*, 207–215.

Dressler, W. U., & Barbaresi, L. M. (1994). *Morphopragmatics: Diminutives and intensifiers in Italian, German, and other languages*. New York: Mouton de Gruyter.

Dunn, J., Bretherton, I., & Munn, P. (1987). Conversations about feeling states between mothers and their young children. *Developmental Psychology, 23*, 448–455.

Ferguson, C. A. (1977). Babytalk as a simplified register. In C. E. Snow and C. A. Ferguson (Eds.), *Talking to children: Language input and acquisition* (pp. 209–235). New York: Cambridge University Press.

Fivush, R. (1991). Gender and emotion in mother–child conversations about the past. *Journal of Narrative and Life History, 1*, 325–341.

Fivush, R., Brotman, M. A., Buckner, J. P., & Goodman, S. H. (2000). Gender differences in parent–child emotion narratives. *Sex Roles, 42*, 233–253.

Fivush, R., & Buckner, J. P. (2000). Gender, sadness, and depression: The development of emotional focus through gendered discourse. In A. H. Fischer (Ed.), *Gender and emotion: Social psychological perspectives* (pp. 232–253). Cambridge: Cambridge University Press.

Flannagan, D., & Perese, S. (1998). Emotional references in mother–daughter and mother–son dyads' conversations about school. *Sex Roles, 39*(5–6), 353–367.

Garrett, P., & Baquedano-López, P. (2002). Language socialization: Reproduction and continuity, transformation and change. *Annual Review of Anthropology, 31*, 339–361.

Heath, S. B. (1983). *Ways with words: Language, life, and work in communities and classrooms.* Cambridge: Cambridge University Press.

Inchaurralde, C. (1997). Space, reference, and emotional involvement. In S. Niemeier & R. Dirven (Eds.), *The language of emotions: Conceptualization, expression, and theoretical foundation* (pp.135–154). Amsterdam: John Benjamins.

Invernizzi, M. A., & Abouzeid, M. P. (1995). One story map does not fit all: A cross-cultural analysis of children's written story retellings. *Journal of Narrative and Life History, 5*, 1–19.

Jurafsky, D. (1996). Universal tendencies in the semantics of the diminutive. *Language, 72*, 533–578.

Kempe, V., & Brooks, P. J. (1998). Do diminutives facilitate the learning of Russian gender? In M. Gernsbacher & S. J. Derry (Eds.), *Proceedings of the Twentieth Annual Meeting of the Cognitive Science Society* (1231). Mahwah, NJ: Lawrence Erlbaum.

Kempe, V., Brooks, P. J., Mironova, N., & Fedorova, O. (2003). Diminutivisation supports gender acquisition in Russian children. *Journal of Child Language, 30*, 471–485.

King, K. A. (2001). *Language revitalization processes and prospects: Quichua in the Ecuadorian Andes.* Clevedon, UK: Multilingual Matters.

King, K., & Haboud, M. (2002). Language planning and policy in Ecuador. *Current Issues in Language Planning, 3*, 359–424.

King, K. A., & Hornberger, N. H. (2004). Introduction. Why a special issue on Quechua? *International Journal of the Sociology of Language, 167*, 1–8.

King, K. A., & Melzi, G. (2004). Intimacy, imitation and language learning: Spanish diminutives in mother–child conversations. *First Language, 24*, 241–261.

Labov, W., & Waletzky, J. (1967). Narrative analysis: Oral versions of personal experience. In J. Helm (Ed.), *Essays on the verbal and visual arts* (pp. 12–44). Seattle: University of Washington Press.

MacWhinney, B. (2000). *The CHILDES project: Tools for analyzing talk.* Mahwah, NJ: Erlbaum.

McCabe, A. (1991). Preface: Structure as a way of understanding. In A. McCabe & C. Peterson (Eds.), *Developing narrative structure* (pp. ix–xvii). Hillsdale, NJ: Lawrence Erlbaum Associates.

Melzi, G. (2000). Cultural variations in the construction of personal narratives: Central American and European American mothers' elicitation styles. *Discourse Processes, 30*, 153–177.

Melzi, G., & Fernández, C. (2004). Talking about past emotions: Conversations between Peruvian mothers and their preschool children. *Sex Roles, 50,* 641–656.

Melzi, G., & King, K. A. (2003). Spanish diminutives in mother–child conversations. *Journal of Child Language, 30,* 280–304.

Ochs, E. (1986). Introduction. In B. B. Schieffelin & E. Ochs (Eds.), *Language socialization across cultures* (pp. 1–13). Cambridge, England: Cambridge University Press.

Ochs, E., & Capps, L. (2001). *Living narrative: Creating lives in everyday storytelling.* Cambridge, MA: Harvard University Press.

Peterson, C., and McCabe, A. (1983). *Developmental psycholinguistics: Three ways of looking at a child's narrative.* New York: Plenum Press.

Polanyi, L. (1981). What stories can tell us about their teller's world. *Poetics Today, 2,* 97–112.

Scollon, R., & Scollon, S. (1981). *Narrative, literacy and face in interethnic communication.* Norwood, NJ: Ablex.

Wierzbicka, A. (2003). *Cross-cultural pragmatics: The semantics of human interaction.* Berlin: Mouton de Gruyter.

World Bank (2007). *Ecuador poverty assessment.* Washington, DC: The World Bank Group.

PART TWO

DEVELOPING INDEPENDENT NARRATION

ALLYSSA McCABE

The second part of this book picks up where the first leaves off and looks at the more monologic narrative accomplishments of diverse Spanish-speaking children. This part consists of four chapters that examine relatively unscaffolded narration in 3- through 11-year-old children from Mexico, Andean Peru, Venezuela, Costa Rica, and the Dominican Republic, some of whom now reside in the United States. After years of conversation with parents, how do Spanish-speaking children narrate more or less on their own? The answer to this question leads us quite naturally to the consequences of cultural differences in narrative structure for literacy acquisition, the topic of the third and final part of our book. The primary goal here is to sensitize readers to unique features of Spanish narrative structure in order to prevent misdiagnosis of cultural differences as deficits. As will be shown, all four chapters document some important differences between Latino and various types of Anglo American storytelling.

Wishard Guerra's chapter 7 makes a number of important contributions. First, she looks at early scaffolding by mothers and relates that scaffolding to older children's stand-alone narratives, which makes this chapter an excellent bridge from Part One to Part Two. Second, she documents a developmental sequence for Mexican-heritage American children that is remarkably similar to that shown previously for Anglo children (Peterson & McCabe, 1983): moving from a primarily maternal online description of actions at 3 years of age and ending at the high-point form (19%) at 4 years; 6 months to predominantly (77%) classic narrative structure in conversations with the researcher at age 6. This finding should caution us not to exaggerate differences between all Latino groups and Anglo American children's narration. Furthermore, such documentation of the developmental sequence has proven useful to speech-language pathologists attempting to determine whether a child is progressing adequately in the oral language skills prerequisite for literacy acquisition (McCabe & Rollins, 1994; Tabors, Snow, & Dickinson, 2001) and might inspire others to document such a sequence for other ethnic groups.

Throughout this book, we repeatedly stress the remarkable diversity among Latino groups, and it is worthwhile to note the contrast between the full structural high-point analyses of chapter 7 and those for other Latino groups in chapter 10. Although the Mexican American children come to resemble their Anglo peers in narration at age six, the same cannot be said for the Dominican nor Costa Rican children.

Diversity within each Latino group is another common theme. Shiro's chapter 9 focuses on diversity in narration due to socioeconomic differences and notes that such differences are particularly apparent in the production of fictional – as opposed to personal factual – narratives. The origins of this socioeconomic difference are documented in Part One, in Stansbery's chapter 3, which shows that such differences begin in socialization patterns present almost at birth. The consequences of this socioeconomic difference should give practitioners pause. For example, Janes and Kermani (2001) discovered that Latino families found that reading fictional books to their children was often seen as a chore, leading to a 70% dropout rate in a program designed to encourage parental involvement with preschool children's emergent literacy. However, when that program shifted to using a set of stories told by the Latino parents themselves – stories that were fact-based and had a high moral purpose – the parents found reading them to their children pleasurable and resulted in a 100% retention rate. Teachers, speech-language pathologists, and researchers may very well want to think carefully about the genre of narrative they emphasize (McCabe, Bliss, Bennett, & Barra, 2008).

All four chapters in this part employ some form of high-point analysis (Labov, 1972; Peterson & McCabe, 1983) to elucidate important aspects of Latino narration. Chapters 8 and 9 focus on the evaluative component of narration, whereas chapters 7 and 10 look at evaluation, complicating actions, and orientation, as well as the overall form of narratives. This finding is valuable in and of itself because there are many alternative ways to analyze narrative (Hughes, McGillivray, & Schmidek, 1997; Peterson & McCabe, 1983), and it is useful to find consensus that such a method is applicable to various Latino cultural groups. At the same time, Uccelli's chapter 8 points to the need to adapt high-point analysis to do justice to the narration of some Latino children.

Chapter 10 seeks to relate distinctive aspects of Latino narration to aesthetic values of various Latino cultures, noting the Indigenous, European, African, and Afro-Caribbean traditions that contribute to the rich mix that in various combinations is Latino culture. Latino children internalize a great deal in the conversations with their parents that were the focus of Part One, a fact that they proceed to demonstrate to relative strangers even in their preschool years – the focus of Part Two. To carefully listen or read Latino children's narratives is to discover much about their life, their relationship with their family, and what they find important (i.e., worthy of evaluation).

REFERENCES

Hughes, D., McGillivray, L., & Schmidek, M. (1997). Eau Claire, WI: Thinking Publications.

Janes, H., & Kermani, H. (2001). Caregivers' story reading to young children in family literacy programs: Pleasure or punishment? *Journal of Adolescent & Adult Literacy, 44*(5), 458–466.

Labov, W. (1972). *Language in the inner city.* Philadelphia: University of Pennsylvania Press.

McCabe, A., Bliss, L., Bennett, M. B., & Barra, G. (2008). Comparison of personal versus fictional narratives of children with language impairment. *American Journal of Speech-Language Pathology, 17,* 1–13.

McCabe, A., & Rollins, P. R. (1994). Assessment of preschool narrative skills: Prerequisite for literacy. *American Journal of Speech-Language Pathology: A Journal of Clinical Practice, 3,* 45–56.

Peterson, C., & McCabe, A. (1983). *Developmental psycholinguistics.* NY: Plenum.

Tabors, P. O., Snow, C. E., & Dickinson, D. K. (2001). Homes and schools together: Supporting language and literacy development. In D. K. Dickinson & P. O. Tabors (Eds.), *Beginning literacy with language* (pp. 313–334). Baltimore, MD: Brookes.

7

The Intersection of Language and Culture Among Mexican-Heritage Children 3 to 7 Years Old

ALISON WISHARD GUERRA

Key Words: cultural communities, narrative development, language practices, Mexican, bilingual

ABSTRACT

The primary goal of this chapter is to describe the development of narrative interactions from highly scaffolded to relatively independent narrative productions among a group of low-income Mexican-heritage children growing up in a major city in the southwestern United States. The results from this study simultaneously emphasize the cultural nature of narrative and language development coupled with the evident heterogeneity in cultural practices and developmental trajectories within a particular ethnic and linguistic group. Cultural practices are defined by the language practices enacted and endorsed by families. Variations in children's narrative development are discussed within the context of language practices, providing a platform to highlight the importance of taking a within-culture and longitudinal approach to understanding normative development among minority groups. By looking at patterns of narrative and language development within a cultural context, it is evident that these Mexican-heritage children experience a similar overall developmental trajectory as their European North American (ENA) peers and that there are important variations in narrative structure and adult scaffolding within a group often considered homogeneous. Thinking about cultural language practices appears to be necessary yet not sufficient in our understanding of an individual's development of narrative and language. The chapter ends with a discussion of the implications both for future research and applications with children and families in educational settings.

INTRODUCTION

Although Mexican-heritage children are one of the fastest growing minority populations in the United States (U.S. Census Bureau, 2001), little is known about the variations in developmental competencies among young children within this group. Latinos in the United States are a heterogeneous group in terms of country of origin, income, educational experience, and acculturation experience (Contreras, Kerns, & Neal-Barnett, 2002; García & Cuéllar, 2006), yet they are typically grouped together and compared to other ethnic groups, often masking developmental differences related to cultural variations (Contreras et al., 2002; García Coll, Contran, Jenkins, McAdoo, Crinic, Wasik, & García, 1996). The intent of this chapter is to develop an understanding of the different ways that low-income Mexican-heritage families engage in everyday language and narrative practices and how this relates to the progression from highly scaffolded protonarrative interactions, to coconstructed narratives, to relatively independent narratives. Coconstructed narratives are analyzed at three time points: in naturalistic mother–child conversations when children are 36 months, in semi-elicited mother–child narrative interactions when children are 54 months, and in elicited child–researcher narratives when children are approximately 78 months (6.5 years).

The development of complex oral narrative skills is important for children's readiness for school and is an important precursor to the acquisition of literacy (Bishop & Edmundson, 1987; Imbens-Bailey & Snow, 1997; Snow, 1983). This is especially critical for Spanish-speaking Latino children who are at higher risk for academic difficulties and continue to receive lower scores on tests of reading achievement than other groups (National Center for Education, 2003). Narrative development begins at a very early age through coconstructed protonarrative interactions between young children and other family members. Despite its potential importance to Mexican-heritage and other Latino children, there is little extant literature on variations in their language practices and the subsequent impact on narrative development.

This study was guided by a theoretical framework that highlights the importance of placing development within the context of cultural communities and everyday cultural practices, including language practices. This framework calls for within-group longitudinal observations to understand heterogeneity in normative development before engaging in comparisons across cultures. Heterogeneity is investigated through examining the influence of language practices on children's narrative development. When applying this theoretical approach to the study of narratives among Mexican-heritage children, it becomes evident that although the research base demonstrates a general developmental continuum for narrative skills (McCabe, 1997; Ochs & Capps, 2001; Peterson & McCabe, 1983; Snow, 1983) and that the development of narrative skills varies across cultural communities (Heath, 1983; McCabe, 1997; Melzi, 2000; Minami & McCabe, 1995), we know relatively little about the heterogeneity of development within Latino Spanish-speaking cultures.

Language socialization theory assumes that although language development is influenced by advances in perception and cognition, language always develops within a social context that consists of daily routines and relationships with primary caregivers (Garret & Baquedano-López, 2002; Ochs & Schieffelin, 1995; Vygotsky, 1978). This includes the study of how children are socialized *through* the use of language as well as how children are socialized to *use* language, and it focuses explicit attention on the ways in which culture influences human development by looking at how and why narratives are constructed and used in a given cultural community. Although it is generally accepted that there is a wide variety of language practices across cultures, current scholars focusing on issues of culture and development argue that there is also notable diversity in normative development within cultural groups (García Coll et al., 1996). Specifically, among immigrant Latino families, variations in language practices are subsequently related to variations in language development experienced by individual children (Schecter & Bayley, 2002).

Cultural Community Participation and Language Practices

Participants in cultural communities have a common set of everyday practices that serve to organize the care of and interaction with children (Rogoff, 2003). Within this framework, a cultural community is defined as a grouping of people who share goals, beliefs, and everyday practices and often a racial or ethnic identity. This approach has proven useful in current ongoing analyses within the larger Early Head Start (EHS) study when looking at other developmental domains (Howes, Wishard Guerra, & Zucker, 2007; Howes, Wishard Guerra, & Zucker, 2008). For the current analysis of children's narrative development, the notions of cultural communities (Harwood, Scholmeric, & Schulze, 2000; Rogoff, 2003) and language practices (Heath, 1983; Schecter & Bayley, 2002) help explain the different ways that families interact around language and how these interactions prepare children to engage in independent narrative interactions by early elementary school.

Children become socialized into the language practices of their culture beginning in infancy (Goodwin, 1990; Heath, 1983; Schecter & Bayley, 2002). Language choices and patterns of language use, then, are simultaneously one of the most basic and complex ways that adults and children navigate the multiple worlds that comprise their everyday life. Within every context that individuals find themselves in, including the home, school, neighborhood, or extended family, there are distinct adaptive and valued language practices that children and adults draw from, creating a combination of practices used to successfully navigate through each set of interactions (see this volume, chapters 2, 6, and 11). Language socialization research examines the process through which children learn the knowledge and practices necessary for them to become competent members of their community (Garret & Baquedano-López, 2002). How, when, and why people engage in various language practices is related to cultural values, societal values, political shifts, and geographical influences. Whereas many immigrant Latino families are concerned with ensuring that their children maintain command of their native language, fearing the depletive effect of English-only public education, other families may live in communities operating almost entirely in Spanish, creating little concern over Spanish maintenance. Despite this difference, all families continue to expose their children to the language practices that enable them to become competent members of the community (Schecter & Bayley, 2002), and these language practices are directly related to children's language development. For example, a child in a family that highly values biliteracy will likely have more opportunities for reading and writing in both languages and will thus have more developed biliteracy skills than a child whose family values oral fluency in both languages but not necessarily written fluency.

Understanding the development of language practices from a sociocultural perspective includes the notion of language practices as consisting of both cognitive-linguistic and sociocultural factors (Ochs & Schieffelin, 1995; Rogoff, Mistry, Göncü, & Mosier, 1993). As such, language practices are adaptive patterns of daily use strategies – such as language choices, language-use rules, and mixing languages – that families organize and maintain to accomplish specific tasks deemed necessary and valuable in the family, ethnic, or geographic community. Like all cultural practices, language practices vary widely because they are constituted by individuals to address specific needs and cultural values of the family niche and are indirectly influenced by both distal and proximal features of the environment (Gallimore & Goldenberg, 1993; Heath, 1982; Reese, Garnier, Gallimore, & Goldenberg, 2000).

In this perspective, language practices occur on two levels: (1) those practices that are *enacted* by parents and families as part of normal everyday routine interactions; and (2) those practices that are *articulated* as specific cultural values held by parents for their family. Enacted language practices include the ordinary way that language is used to organize and mediate social interactions, as well as the types of language and literacy activities that children and families engage in on a regular basis. Enacted language practices might include daily book-reading as part of the bedtime routine or regular participation in translating speech and written texts. Through enacted language practices, children learn how to become competent members of their community by repeated engagement in everyday language interactions. Articulated language practices include spoken values and goals around appropriate use of language, including which language is used where and with whom as well as language goals that parents hold for their children in the future. Articulated language practices might include the parental belief that Spanish should be the dominant language inside the home or the expressed goal for the children to be biliterate in both Spanish and English. Through articulated language practices, children learn about expressed rules and guidelines that help them navigate through different kinds of language interactions. Both sets of language practices that children are exposed to and engage in shape the patterns of language and narrative development and the ultimate acquisition of literacy.

Narrative Development in Latino Families

Research on Latino children's narrative development suggests that they may have different experiences with narrative interactions and a different understanding of the form and function of narratives than children from other ethnic and cultural backgrounds (Melzi, 2000; Silva & McCabe, 1996). In a study looking at working-class European American and Latino mothers' narratives with their children, Gleason & Melzi (1997) found that although narrative interactions about a shared experience appeared quite similar, narrative interactions about an unshared experience were quite different. The Anglo mothers took an active role, directing the child toward the more academic goals of creating a classically structured narrative. The Latino mothers, in contrast, took a more passive role, allowing the child to direct the conversation and supporting the child's efforts to engage in social talk with the mother.

These cross-cultural differences might be explained by the mothers' interpretation of the purpose of the narrative task, reflecting parental values evident elsewhere in the culture (Melzi, 2000). Cross-cultural research on socialization and child-rearing practices has shown that whereas Latino parents place high value on social behavior and interpersonal relationships, Anglo parents tend to be more didactic and place higher value on independence and development of academic skills (Azmitia, Cooper, García, & Dunbar, 1996; Silva & McCabe, 1996). These differences in socialization practices potentially have an important impact on the organization and production of narratives where narrative interactions among Latino children and their mother may be more of a shared social experience, whereas narrative interactions among middle-class White children and their mothers may be more of an academic production.

Results from comparative studies of Latino and European American narrative production suggest that there are important differences in narrative organization, structure, and content (Eisenberg, 1985; Gutiérrez-Clellen & Hienrichs-Ramos, 1993; Gutiérrez-Clellen & Iglesias, 1992; Melzi, 2000). Yet, such comparisons, typically looking at static points in time, often minimize both within-group and cross-group variations in developmental trajectories. García Coll et al. (1996) suggested that minority children may experience different developmental trajectories than their majority peers, yet few studies have used similar narrative assessments over time to investigate whether Latino dual-language-learning children experience similar general trajectories in the development of narrative skills.

In summary, the primary objective of this study is to examine – in a longitudinal fashion – narrative development from highly scaffolded to relatively independent narrative productions from 3 to $6\frac{1}{2}$ years in Mexican-heritage children using a standard assessment of narrative complexity that has been used with majority children. I expected variations in patterns of development to be associated with engagement in language practices. Specifically, the goals of this analysis are threefold: (1) to describe the development of narrative coherence and complexity among a group of low-income Mexican-heritage children aged 3 to 6½ years old; (2) to describe the range of cultural language practices enacted and articulated by those families; and (3) to discuss variations in children's narrative development within the context of language practices, providing a platform to highlight the importance of taking a within-culture and longitudinal approach to understanding normative development among minority groups.

METHODOLOGY

Participants

Sixty-five children and their mothers participated in this research. The sample in this analysis is limited to mothers who self-identified as Mexican-heritage women and who were randomly assigned to the intervention group of the National EHS Research Project. At the onset of the project, families with infants under 8 months old were randomly assigned to the intervention or control group within one local EHS site of the national longitudinal evaluation of EHS. This site intervention included home visits from EHS staff to assist with parenting practices and did not include enrollment in center-based EHS services. All families received referrals and EHS support to find local child-care programs. Although families were not enrolled in an EHS center-based child-care program as part of their participation, a few children were enrolled in Head Start center-based programs once they turned 3 years old. The research visits were independent of the intervention-program home visits.

Half (50.8%) of the children were girls. Of the mothers, 93% spoke Spanish as their primary language and in all of these cases, Spanish was the language used in the household and in our research; 89% of the mothers were not born in the United States. Most Mexican migrating mothers had come from rural areas around Oaxaca and Jalisco as young women, on average 3.1 years prior to the birth of the target child. The mothers ranged in age from 14 to 35 years old when their child was born, with a modal mother age of 25 years ($M = 26.2$, $SD = 13$). The average maternal education in years was 8.7 ($SD = 3.72$); 47% had received all of their schooling in rural areas of Mexico.

Procedures

As part of the EHS data-collection protocol, all mothers and children were visited in their home when the child was 36 and 54 months old. Mothers and children were again visited when the child was in first grade, at approximately 78 months old, as part of a local follow-up visit. The 36- and 54-month home visits included an audio-recorded maternal interview, naturalistic observations, and video recordings of mother–child interactions. The 78-month home visit included individual audio-recorded interviews with the mother and child. To maintain the sample, the same research staff member remained in contact with the family during the course of the project, whenever possible. All of the interviewers and participant observers were bicultural and bilingual in Spanish and English.

Language Practices

Enacted Language Practices

Enacted language practices were captured through a combination of home observations and parent reports of the types and frequency of language and literacy activities available to children during the 36- and 54-month visits. The Language and Cognitive Stimulation Subscale of the HOME, preschool version (Caldwell & Bradley, 1984), was used to assess the overall language and literacy environment of the home. The scale scores are slightly different at each time point because there are changes in the measure to adapt to developmental changes. At 36 months, the maximum score is 13, whereas at 54 months, the maximum score is 16. To adjust for this difference, scores were created to capture the proportion of total possible points received. Mothers were also asked to report on the frequency of reading that they engaged in with their child at both 36 and 54 months.

Articulated Language Practices

Articulated language practices were captured through ethnographic maternal interviews at both 36 and 78 months, in which mothers talked about personal and family beliefs and practices around language usage inside and outside of the home for herself, her child, and the family in general. Dichotomous codes of articulated language practices at 36 months were gleaned from the Cultural Change Interview (Rosenblatt, Garza-Mourino, & Howes, 2004) at 36 months. The codes included whether the mother was bilingual, whether she articulated learning English as a major personal or family goal in life, whether she articulated that language is an obstacle in her daily life (i.e., in her job, doing daily chores such as grocery shopping, interacting with her child's school, or other daily routines), that she sees her child as an avenue to help her learn English, whether she plans to enroll in English classes, that she sees language as an important cultural value for the family or as a vehicle for cultural maintenance in the family, and that language skills (English, Spanish, or bilingual) are a great advantage for any member of the family.

During the 78-month home visit, mothers were asked again to think about beliefs and practices around language usage inside and outside of the home for herself, her child, and the family in general. This interview included specific questions about the mother's goals for language practices in the future. Guided by ethnographic studies of recent Mexican American immigrants (Bayley & Schecter, 2003; Schecter & Bayley, 2002), a series of articulated language practice codes were created first on a random 10% of the interviews and then revised on an additional random 10%. Reliability was established with a second Spanish–English bilingual researcher on 15% of all interviews using Cohen's Kappa. Kappa values ranged from 0.92 to 1.0.

Narrative Samples

At each visit, narrative interaction language samples were collected using different methods that were developmentally appropriate for the age under investigation (as described herein). Narratives were identified using the following definition (Sperry & Sperry, 1996): "Any topic-centered discourse asserted *by the child* and containing at least one verb about a displaced event and one other utterance relevant to the topic" (p. 446). All interactions were audiotaped and videotaped and later transcribed in the original language using the Codes for the Human Analysis of Transcripts (CHAT) of the CHILDES system (MacWhinney, 2000). All transcriptions were then verified by a second Spanish–English bilingual researcher.

Early Protonarrative Task (36 Months)
During the home visit, each mother was given a puppet and asked to engage her child in play with it. Verbal interactions and language play between mother and child were video-recorded as they played with the puppet.

Semi-Elicited Narrative Task (54 Months)
During the home visit, mothers were prompted to ask their child to tell them a story about something exciting that had happened in the last 2 weeks. Mother–child dyads were video-recorded for 2 minutes while they coconstructed a narrative. At the end of 2 minutes, the child was presented with a toy to play with for a different task. One narrative per dyad was collected.

Child-Elicited Narratives (78 Months)
During the home visit, during a 10- to 15-minute period, children were asked by the researcher to tell at least three stories about things that had happened to them recently in whichever language they felt most comfortable speaking. Following Peterson & McCabe's (1983) conversational-prompt technique, the researcher engaged in conversation with the child by first sharing a personal experience of her own and then, with minimal prompts and scaffolds, asking the child to tell a story of his or her own.

Coding Categories

Basic Language Characteristics
Narrative interactions at each time point were compared on the dominant language(s) used in the narrative and the number of narratives produced at 78

months when children had the option to tell more than one story. To code the dominant language in each sample, when the use of the second language was greater than 30%, the narrative interaction was considered bilingual in nature. Number of words and mean length of utterance (MLU) were also calculated but were not included in these analyses due to the use of Spanish and English and the concern about accurately comparing MLU across languages (Bedore, 2004; Bland-Stewart & Fitzgerald, 2001).

Highpoint Analysis
Narrative coherence increases with age and language development and is a good measure of overall narrative development (Peterson & McCabe, 1983). At all three time points, narrative productions were coded for overall coherence of the narrative using a coding scheme adapted from Peterson and McCabe's (1983) highpoint analysis (based on Labov, 1972). For coconstructed narratives, the highpoint analysis was applied to the narrative as a whole, with each narrative receiving one code. Intercoder reliability was established with two additional Spanish–English bilingual researchers on 20% of all transcripts using Cohen's (1960) Kappa. The Kappa statistic for agreement on the one highpoint score per narrative was 0.99.

1. *Unsuccessful attempt*: Child refused to engage in narrative interaction.
2. *Present-tense description*: Child and mother engaged in a present-tense description of an immediate activity.
3. *One-event*: Narrative includes only one past-tense event.
4. *Two-event*: Narrative includes only two past-tense events.
5. *Leapfrog*: Narrative includes more than two past-tense events, but the order of events does not mirror the sequence in which the events occurred.
6. *Chronological*: Narrative includes more than two past-tense events and events are in chronological sequence, but there is no concentration of evaluative comments or highpoint.
7. *End at highpoint*: Narrative includes more than two past-tense events and a highpoint, but there is no resolution.
8. *Classic*: Narrative includes more than two past-tense events, a highpoint, and a resolution.

Narrative Elements Provided by Child and Adult
Beyond the overall coherence of the narrative, additional elements of the coconstructed and independent narratives at 54 and 78 months were coded to capture developmental changes in the quality and quantity of the child's contribution to the narrative interaction, as well as changes in the frequency of adult scaffolding strategies across the two time points. A coding scheme created by the national EHS team was adapted for use with the 54- and 78-month narrative interactions

and includes the following elements: child's participation, narrative features provided by the child, child's use of connectives in narrative, and frequency of adult scaffolding strategies. Intercoder reliability was established with two additional Spanish–English bilingual researchers on 20% of all transcript schemes using Cohen's (1960) Kappa. The Kappa statistic for agreement on the global coding scheme ranged from 0.85 to 1.0 on each item.

CHILD'S PARTICIPATION. The child's participation was coded at 54 and 78 months for both whether the child's utterances were primarily prompted or independent and the overall level of participation in the narrative interaction, ranging from refusing to participate, to minimally participating, to taking control of the narrative.

1. *No response*: Child does not produce any utterances after being prompted to engage.
2. *Refuses to participate*: Child actively refuses to participate by stating that he or she does not want to tell a story or to talk with the mother.
3. *Minimally participates*: Child minimally participates by responding with few utterances in response to adult bids.
4. *Initial refusal*: Child initially refuses to participate and then agrees and begins to engage with adult.
5. *Imitates mother/researcher*: Child follows adult lead without adding any additional information.
6. *Follows mother/researcher's lead*: Child follows adult lead and contributes new information.
7. *Takes control of telling*: Child leads narrative interaction, providing most of the relevant information.

NARRATIVE FEATURES PROVIDED BY THE CHILD. Each narrative was coded for whether the child contributed the following features to the narrative interaction: event, description, evaluation, setting (time and place), participants, and appendages.

CHILDREN'S USE OF CONNECTIVES IN NARRATIVE. Each narrative was coded for the child's overall use of connectives. The following three categories were included:

1. *No connectives:* Child did not use any connectives in narrative.
2. *Basic connectives:* All connectives were basic connective words including *and, so, then, and so,* or *and then.*
3. *Sophisticated connectives:* Use of at least one more sophisticated connective word including *but, only, before, after, when,* or *finally.*

Table 7.1. *Language of narratives over time*

	% Spanish	% English	% Bilingual
36 months	88.1	11.9	0
54 months	74.7	19.8	5.5
78 months	31.3	67.2	1.6

ADULT SCAFFOLDING STRATEGIES. Adult scaffolding at 54 and 78 months was coded for overall frequency of support/scaffolding provided (i.e., rarely, sometimes, or frequently).

RESULTS AND DISCUSSION

Becoming Independent Narrators: Narrative Development From 3 to 6 Years Old

One of the primary goals of this study is to describe variations in the narrative development of a group of low-income Mexican-heritage children growing up in bilingual environments. The data presented herein show that the overall complexity in children's narratives became more complex over time and that children used more English in their narratives by 78 months. At 36 months, children engaged in protonarrative interactions with their mother, with the mother taking more control of the interaction. At 54 months, children coconstructed narratives of past events with their mother, whereas at 78 months, children told relatively independent narratives to the researcher.

Basic Language Characteristics of Narratives

Language Used in Narratives
As expected, the exclusive use of Spanish in narrative interactions decreased with the child's age from 88% of narrative interactions at 36 months, to 75% at 54 months, to 31.3% at 78 months. Although Spanish remained the dominant language used by the mother–child dyads in narrative interactions at 36 and 54 months, by 78 months most children preferred to tell their narratives in English and only one child engaged in a bilingual narrative. It is important that during the 36- and 54-month visits, children generally followed the lead of the mother in terms of the language used in the narrative. Considering that most mothers were monolingual Spanish speakers, it is not surprising that most coconstructed narratives were also in Spanish. At 78 months, despite being approached by the researcher in both Spanish and English and encouraged to speak in whichever language the child felt more comfortable using, 31% of children still preferred to speak in Spanish. Table 7.1 presents the proportion of narrative interactions in each language over time. To assess whether the complexity of children's

Table 7.2. *Highpoint story structures over time compared with McCabe & Peterson's European North American English-speaking children*

Story structure	36 Months	54 Months	78 Months
Unsuccessful attempt	7.8	11	0
Present-tense description	82.4[†]	1.1	0
1. One event	5.9	4.4	0
2. Two event	3.9	2.2	0
3. Leapfrog	0	15.4	0
4. Chronological	0	30.8[†]	5.2
5. End at highpoint	0	19.8	17.2
6. Classic	0	15.4	77.6[†]

Note: Numbers indicate the percentage of each structural type at each age.
[†]Most common structure produced by children at each age.

narratives differed by the language used, all narrative elements were tested for differences in language usage in the narrative interaction. Significant differences are reported in the next section within each set of findings.

Highpoint Analysis Assessing Overall Narrative Story Structure
The overall complexity in children's narratives in Spanish and English became increasingly more complex over time and by 78 months was on a par with a previous study looking at narrative development in a sample of ENA, English-speaking children (McCabe, 1997; Peterson & McCabe, 1983). From $3\frac{1}{2}$ to 6 years old, McCabe and Peterson (1983, cited in McCabe, 1997) found that the most common narrative structures produced by children were the two-event ($3\frac{1}{2}$ years), leapfrog (4 years), end at highpoint (5 years), and classic narrative (6 years). Although demonstrating a slightly different developmental trajectory, by the 78-month visit ($6\frac{1}{2}$ years), 77.6% of the Mexican-heritage children in the sample told at least one narrative with a classic story structure. Table 7.2 presents percentages of story-structure types at each age.

36 Months: Mother Demonstrates
As expected due to the instructions of the activity, at 36 months most mother–child dyads did not successfully engage in a narrative interaction depicting a personal experience; instead, 82.4% of all interactions were characterized as present-tense descriptions of present interactions. Of the mother-child dyads, 8% of mothers were unable to get their child to engage with them at all and 6% coproduced a one-event personal narrative. In the following excerpt, Juan[1] aged 36 months, and his mother engage in a present-tense description about what the pig-puppet they are playing with does and what noises a pig makes:

[1] All names used in narrative examples are pseudonyms

	Spanish Original	English Translation
Mother:	*¿Cómo le hace?*	How does it go?
Mother:	*Oink, oink.*	Oink, oink.
Mother:	*Mira qué bonito.*	Look how pretty.
Child:	*xxx.*	xxx.
Mother:	*No, le hace oink, oink.*	No, it goes oink, oink.
Child:	*Oink, oink. . .*	Oink, oink. . .
Mother:	*Métele la mano.*	Put your hand in.
Mother:	*Mira cómo le hace mira.*	Look what it does.
Mother:	*Oye lo que dice.*	Listen to what it says.
Mother:	*¿Oíste?*	Did you hear?
Child:	*Ajá. . .*	Ah.
Mother:	*¿Cómo le hace?*	How does it do it?
Mother:	*Oink, oink.*	Oink, oink.
Child:	*Oink, oink.*	Oink, oink.
Mother:	*Oink, onk.*	Oink, oink.

54 Months: Mother Scaffolds

By 54 months, however, there is much more variability in highpoint scores of coherence, ranging from present-tense description to classic narrative, with the most common type of narrative classified as the chronological narrative. In contrast to Juan, who remains in a present-tense description of the normal sound that a pig makes, Carla recounts to her mother all of the things she saw at the park. Although Carla's narrative is about a past-tense personal event, there is no highpoint, no culmination of evaluations, and no resolution.

	Spanish Original	English Translation
Mother:	*Dime, ¿cómo te fue en el parque?*	Tell me how it was at the park.
Child:	*Um, fue bien.*	Um, it was good.
Mother:	*¿Qué te gustó más de la, del parque?*	What did you like most about the, about the park?
Child:	*Jugar.*	Playing.
Mother:	*Ah huh.*	Ah huh.
Mother:	*¿Con quién jugaste?*	Who did you play with?
Child:	*Con Carina.*	With Carina.
Mother:	*Sí, ¿quién más?*	Yes, who else?
Child:	*Jugué con ella.*	I played with her.
Mother:	*¿Oh sí?*	Oh yes?
Mother:	*¿Qué otra cosas miraron aparte de los juegos?*	What other thing did you see besides the games?

Child:	*Vimos dogs.*	We saw dogs.
Mother:	*¿Ah huh?*	Ah huh?
Child:	*Vimos patos.*	We saw ducks.
Mother:	*Patos, ¿ah huh?*	Ducks, ah huh?
Child:	*Y, mi xxx a. . .*	And, my xxx to. . .
Mother:	*¿Qué otra cosa?*	What other thing?
Child:	*xxx de eso.*	xxx of this.
Mother:	*¿Sí?*	Yes?
Mother:	*¿Y qué comieron?*	And what did you eat?
Child:	*Comida.*	Food.
Mother:	*Necesitas hablar un poco más fuerte.*	You need to speak a little more loudly.
Child:	*¿Qué?*	What?
Mother:	*¿Tú qué comiste?*	What did you eat?
Child	*Este. . . comida.*	That. . . food.
Mother:	*Pero ¿qué comida?*	But what food?
Mother:	*¿Huh?*	Huh?
Child:	*xxx.*	xxx.
Mother:	*Ah huh.*	Ah huh.

78 Months: Child Demonstrates Narrative Independence

By 78 months, just over 77% of the children told narratives classified as a classic story structure. Similar to Carla's narrative, Paula's narrative is a past-tense personal event and includes a chronological explanation of the events that occurred; however, Paula's narrative also includes a climax or highpoint in her story as well as a resolution or conclusion of that problem:

English Original

Child:	Umm, one day.
Researcher:	Uh huh.
Child:	That we were playing, umm.
Child:	We were playing the playground then that.
Researcher:	Uh huh.
Child:	That we umm.
Researcher:	Uh huh.
Child:	xxx and three friends went over there.
Child:	But I said don't go over there.
Researcher:	Ah huh.
Child:	But then.
Child:	But then I was alone.
Child:	So I went to play in the, in the, in the correct area.
Child:	But then they just went on the in the monkey bars and the slide.
Child:	And all of that stuff and the swings.

Child:	But then I said don't go over there.
Child:	But they still went.
Researcher:	They still went?
Child:	Yeah.
Researcher:	And then?
Child:	And then I said I'm going tell the teacher.
Researcher:	And then?
Researcher:	What happened?
Child:	Uh, then I told the teacher that they're not in the right area.
Child:	Then the teacher said . . .
Child:	Umm, I'm going to, they're going to be in the umm, in another classroom.
Researcher:	In another classroom?
Researcher:	And then?
Child:	And then I was sad.
Researcher:	And then you were sad?
Child:	Yeah.
Child:	Cause those were my best friends.

Table 7.3. *78-month narratives*

	Minimum	Maximum	$M\,(SD)$
Average number of narratives	1	10	4.16 (1.90)
Mean highpoint score across all narratives	2.67	6	4.99 (0.87)
78 months (highest highpoint score)	4.00	6.00	5.72 (0.56)
Proportion of classic narratives	0	1	0.44 (0.36)

In the 78-month narrative interaction, the researcher attempted to elicit at least three narratives, and often received more, in a 10- to 15-minute period. Children told an average of 4.16 narratives, ranging from 1 to 10. In the 6-point highpoint story-structure scale, the average highpoint score across all narratives at 78 months was 4.99, just about an end-at-highpoint structure. When selecting the highest scored narrative of all the narratives told by each child, the mean score was 5.72, just about a classic narrative structure, ranging from a chronological to a classic narrative. Looking across all narrative productions, an average of 44% of each child's narratives were coded as classic. Again, we see significant variability in the proportion of narratives scored as a classic narrative. The most complex narrative, defined by the highpoint score, was selected for subsequent analyses. Table 7.3 presents mean scores for the 78-month narrative interactions.

DIFFERENCES IN STORY STRUCTURE BY LANGUAGE USED. The only significant group differences in highpoint score by language used was in the narrative interaction at 54 months, with children producing a bilingual narrative ($M = 3.4$; $N = 5$) having lower scores than children speaking in Spanish ($M = 4.19$; $N = 57$) or English alone ($M = 4.41$; $N = 17$), $F(2,64) = 2.35$, $p < .01$.

Table 7.4. *Child's participation in narrative interaction*

	54 Months	78 Months
Types of Child Talk		
Mostly prompted	61.6[†]	25.3
Mostly independent	38.4	74.7[†]
Child's Participation		
No response	2.3	0
Refuses to participate	6.9	0
Minimally participates	8.0	0
Initial refusal	5.7	10.5
Imitates mother/researcher	5.7	0
Follows mother/ researcher's lead	39.1[†]	26.3
Takes control of telling	26.4	68.4[†]

Note: Numbers in table represent percentage of children in each participation category.
[†]Most common participation structure by children at each age.

NARRATIVE ELEMENTS PROVIDED BY CHILD AND ADULT

By looking at the narrative elements provided by the child and the adult, we see that children demonstrated more control over the narrative interaction from the 54- to 78-month narrative interactions. At 78 months, children needed less prompting, took more control of the narrative, provided more of the narrative features such as event and description, used more connectives, and received less adult scaffolding. Although this is possibly related to the changes in the nature of the protocol, it is also likely to be an indication of developmental change in overall narrative skills.

Child Participation

As expected, given the changes in narrative scenarios, there was a shift toward more independent and autonomous interactions from 54 to 78 months. At 54 months, when a mother was prompted to ask her child to tell her a story, the majority of the child's utterances were "mostly prompted" by the mother and the child primarily followed the mother's lead. At 78 months, when the children were encouraged to tell the researcher a story on their own, the majority of children told independent narratives with infrequent prompting and tended to take control of the telling (Table 7.4). There were no group differences in child participation by the language of the narrative interaction.

Narrative Features Provided by Child

There was a general increase in the percentage of children who provided each narrative feature from 54 to 78 months. At 54 months, children provided all

Table 7.5. *Narrative features provided by child*

	54 Months	78 Months
Event	88.5	100
Description	77.0	94.7
Evaluation	52.9	65.8
Setting (time & place)	73.6	92.1
Participants	66.7	89.5
Appendages	10.3	52.6

Note: Numbers represent percentage of children who included each narrative feature.

possible narrative features at least half of the time, except for providing an appendage, whereas by 78 months, most children provided most of the narrative features (Table 7.5).

Child's Use of Connectives in Narrative

A child's use of connectives in narratives was included as an additional way to look at the complexity of narratives at 54 and 78 months. The data indicate that at 78 months, children had an overall more advanced command of the use of connectives. At 54 months, children either did not use any connectives (42.5%) or used basic connectives such as *and* (55.2%) in their narratives. At 78 months, 98% of all children used basic connectives. There were no group differences in children's use of connectives by language.

Adult Scaffolding Strategies

Frequency of maternal and researcher scaffolding strategies were coded at 54 and 78 months. It was most common for mothers at 54 months and researchers at 78 months to give "some" scaffolding to children, with the overall frequency of scaffolding decreasing at 78 months. Using a mean score for the frequency of adult scaffolding strategies at 54 and 78 months (rarely = 1; frequent = 3), multivariate tests of group difference on language used in narrative showed there were significant differences in the frequency of adult scaffolding at both 54 and 78 months based on the primary language of the narrative interaction (Table 7.6). At 54 months, mothers participating in an English narrative gave less frequent scaffolding ($M = 1.86$) than mothers participating in a Spanish narrative ($M = 2.32$), $F(2,62) = 2.21$, $p < .05$. It is interesting that at 78 months, the pattern is reversed, with researchers participating in English-narrative interactions giving more frequent scaffolding strategies ($M = 2.17$) than those in Spanish-narrative interactions ($M = 1.5$), $F(2,33) = 7.48$, $p < .01$. The overall number of children speaking in English increased substantially at 78 months, indicating that more

Table 7.6. *Adult scaffolding strategies*

	54 Months	78 Months
Frequency		
Rarely	10.3	24.3
Sometimes	56.3	56.8
Frequently	33.3	18.9

Note: Numbers in table represent percentage of narratives at each age.

children were choosing to speak in their second language at 78 months. This difference in language choice is important when considering the significance of the increase in scaffolding in English-language narratives at 78 months.

UNDERSTANDING HETEROGENEITY IN LANGUAGE PRACTICES

Heterogeneity was first assessed by investigating the different language practices that families engage in, including reading activities, language-usage preferences, and maternal beliefs about language. Heterogeneity was then assessed by looking at how children's narrative engagement varied relative to family language practices.

Language Practices

Enacted Language Practices

Enacted language practices include a global assessment of the home language and literacy environment and maternal responses to the frequency of adult–child reading at 36 and 54 months. Both assessments demonstrate a wide range in the enacted language practices of families in this sample, with some families engaging in daily reading and providing a complex language and literacy environment, whereas other families engaged in little to no reading and provided a very basic language and literacy environment. Decreasing mean proportion scores on the Home Observation for Measurement of the Environment (HOME) (Caldwell & Bradley, 1984) language and literacy subscales from 36 to 54 months ($M = 0.83$ and 0.63, respectively) indicate that parents appear to be providing a more stimulating language and literacy environment when their children are 36 months old than when they are 54 months old; $t(64) = 6.06$, $p < .001$. It appears that whereas parents are doing a relatively good job of providing a stimulating language and literacy environment at 36 months, by 54 months when children's language and cognitive abilities have become more advanced, they are not doing as well.

Although the overall language and literacy environment may be less stimulating for a 54-month-old child, mothers tended to read more to their

Table 7.7. *Enacted language practice*

	36 Months			54 Months		
HOME Language & Cognitive Stimulation Scale: Proportion of Total Possible Points						
	Minimum	*Maximum*	*M (SD)*	*Minimum*	*Maximum*	*M (SD)*
	0.38	1.00	0.83 (0.15)	0.14	0.88	0.63 (0.15)
Reading Frequency	%			%		
1. Rarely or never	4.9			6.5		
2. Once a week	46.9			18.3		
3. Few times a week	29.6			38.7		
4. Every day	18.5			36.6		

54-month-old child than to their 36-month-old. Mothers were significantly more likely to report daily reading to their child at 54 months (36% of mothers) than at 36 months (18% of mothers); $t(64) = 2.93$, p < .01. At 54 months old children are beginning to identify letters and words and to understand concepts of print. These developmental changes may lead mothers to feel that reading to their child is more appropriate given their child's increasing awareness of print. Table 7.7 presents HOME proportion scores and percentages of reading frequency at 36 and 54 months. Despite an overall trend in increasing frequency of book-reading, there remains quite a bit of variability in this sample. It is especially noteworthy that almost half (47%) of the mothers at 36 months and 18% of the mothers at 54 months report only reading to their children once a week. Frequent book-reading experiences during the preschool years can be essential to the development of literacy skills (Raikes et al., 2006).

Articulated Language Practices
Articulated language practices, captured through parent interviews at 36 and 78 months, indicate variability in the mother's primary concerns and beliefs around language use for herself and her family. At 36 months, dichotomous codes of articulated language practices indicate that about a quarter of the mothers consider themselves bilingual, whereas another 20% report that learning English is either a major goal for the future, is a major obstacle in daily life, and/or that they plan to enroll in English classes in the future. Table 7.8 lists the frequencies of each code within the sample.

At 78 months, parents were again asked about language usage as well as beliefs and goals about language practices. Most mothers reported that Spanish was the primary language in the home and the primary language they used with their child. However, 45% of mothers reported that their child spoke with them primarily in Spanish and 67% reported that their child spoke with other children in the home primarily in English, with only 5.7% speaking primarily in Spanish with other children in the home. Mothers were also asked about whether they

Table 7.8. *36-Month articulated language practices*

Language practices	%
Mother is bilingual	23.5
Learning English is a major goal	19.6
Language is an obstacle in daily life	21.6
Child is an avenue to learn English	11.8
Plans to enroll in English classes	19.6
Language maintenance is seen as an important cultural value	14.9
Language is a great advantage	17.8

had a strong preference for which language should be spoken in the home and whether they had "rules" about language usage. Just about half (47%) of the mothers reported a "strong preference" for Spanish to be the only language spoken in the home, whereas 27% reported a "strong preference" for both languages to be spoken in the home. Another 14% of mothers had no preference about which language was used in the home. Mothers were also asked about the primary language their child used to speak with their father and siblings. Table 7.9 shows that 33% of mothers reported that their children speak in a different language with their father, with fewer children using a combination of Spanish and English and more children speaking either entirely in Spanish or English; 58% of mothers reported that their children speak in a different language when speaking with their siblings, with most (67%) using only English, followed by a combination of English and Spanish.

Table 7.9. *78-Month reports on language spoken in the home*

	Spanish	English	Bilingual	No Preference
Maternal Reports on Language Use In and Out of the Home				
Primary home language	77.1	15.7	7.1	
Mother's primary language with child	71	11.6	15.9	
Child's primary language with mother	45.3	20.3	34.4	
Child's primary language with father	48.5	30.3	21.1	
Child's primary language with siblings	5.7	67.7	27.1	
	Yes	*No*		
Child uses a different language with father than with mother	33	68		
Child uses a different language with siblings than with mother	58	42		
Maternal Desires on Language Use in the Home				
Mother's preferred language in home	47.1	13.3	27.1	14.3

Note: Numbers in table represent percentage of families endorsing each practice.

Table 7.10. *Associations between narrative elements and language enacted practices*

	36 month reading frequency	36 month daily reading	54 month reading frequency	54 month daily reading	36 month HOME	54 month HOME
Highpoint score						
36 months	−.07	.10	−.11	−.07	−.02	.00
54 months	.12	.04	−.16	−.04	.17	.04
Highest 78-m	.14	.16	.20	.10	**.68****	−.13
Mean 78-m	.25	.15	.12	.05	**.48***	−.17
Child's participation						
54 months	**.33***	**.26***	−.07	−.07	.08	−.20
78 months	.16	−.02	.20	.24	.21	.04
Frequency of scaffolding						
54 months	−.10	**−.26***	.11	.14	−.13	.04
78-monhts	−.03	.04	−.04	−.19	.17	−.03

Note: Pearson Product Moment Correlation Coefficients. $^*p < .05$, $^{**}p < .01$.

Understanding Variations in Narrative Development Across Language Practices

Language Practices and Narrative Elements

Narrative elements were analyzed relative to the enacted and articulated language practices. Time-lagged correlation analyses revealed several significant associations between enacted language practices at 36 months and narrative elements at 54 and 78 months (Table 7.10 lists correlation coefficients). Children living in a home characterized by more complex language environments at 36 months as measured by the HOME had more complex narratives at 78 months. Children who were read to daily at 36 months had higher rates of participation in the narrative interaction at 54 months and had less frequent maternal scaffolding at 54 months. Only the time-lagged correlations reached statistical significance, suggesting that early language and cognitive stimulation has a stronger impact on later narrative outcomes than current language and cognitive stimulation.

Children's narrative skills develop from early playful language interactions that over time become complex narratives coconstructed with adult primary caregivers and then independent narrative productions with the child taking control of the telling (McCabe, 1997; McCabe & Peterson, 1991; Ochs & Capps, 2001; Snow, 1983; Sperry & Sperry, 1996). Yet, research focusing on cultural variations in narrative development demonstrates considerable variability in adult scaffolding strategies, content, and structure of narrative development among Latino children and families. By describing the narrative interactions of a group of Mexican-heritage children across three time points, we see that these children demonstrate both a similar overall pattern of narrative development by

6 years old to their ENA peers and considerable variability in the complexity of earlier narrative interactions. Furthermore, these low-income Mexican-heritage families were found to engage in a wide variety of everyday language practices, in which early language practices were found to have an impact on the later development of narrative skills. These findings are significant in that they demonstrate that not only are these children relatively on a par with English-speaking ENA children by first grade, but also that there are important differences in everyday language practices that are significant in the long-term narrative development of a group of children typically treated as a homogeneous group.

As researchers and practitioners interested in the development of minority children in general and Latino children in particular, it is imperative that we continue to strive to understand how heterogeneity in everyday cultural practices impacts normative developmental trajectories. This requires not only a focus on longitudinal research but also a theoretical framework that provides an alternative way to define cultural communities beyond ethnic, linguistic, and socioeconomic markers. The theoretical framework of cultural communities and everyday language practices presented in this chapter is perhaps of equal importance to the findings presented herein. By using shared cultural practices as the mechanism to define cultural communities, we are moving away from the limiting practices of comparing one cultural group to another and toward a methodology that allows us to understand heterogeneity among Latino families and its impact on children's developmental outcomes.

Normative Narrative Development

Cultural variations in mother–child communication patterns have been found to impact the structure and content of narrative interactions (Heath, 1983; Melzi, 2000; Schieffelin & Ochs, 1986). Specifically, when looking at narrative interactions of mother–child dyads at any given age, noteworthy differences have been found between Latino and ENA mother–child dyads (Gleason & Melzi, 1997; Gutiérrez-Clellen, 2002; Melzi, 2000; Silva & McCabe, 1996). Although these age-specific variations in maternal scaffolding strategies and subsequent child narrative outcomes provide important insight into the intersection of language development and cultural practices, for dual-language-learning children, it is especially important to take a broader look at the overall developmental patterns of language and narrative development. In thinking about the connection between narrative competency and later development of literacy skills for Latino children, what matters most may not be what is happening at an individual time point but rather the overall trajectory of narrative development.

The current data are unique among extant research on cultural variations in narrative development in general and among Latino children specifically in that the pattern of individual narrative development was tracked for a specific group of Mexican-heritage children from 3 to $6^{1}/_{2}$ years old. Although developmental theorists interested in minority-child development have suggested that minority children may experience different normative developmental trajectories than their majority peers (García Coll et al., 1996; Rogoff, 2003), the current data demonstrate that this group of Mexican-heritage children experienced a similar pattern in their overall development of narrative structure as the ENA children presented by McCabe (1997). Peterson and McCabe (1983) documented that by 4 years old, the most common type of narrative has a leapfrog structure and by 5 years old has the end-at-highpoint pattern. In the current sample, at 54 months we see significant variability, with most narratives ranging from leapfrog to a classic narrative structure. The biggest difference between this sample of Mexican-heritage children and McCabe and Peterson's sample is seen at 3 years old. In the current sample, just fewer than 10% of the 36-month-old children engaged in any past-tense narrative interaction at all during the puppet task, whereas the majority (63%) presented by McCabe engaged in at least a two-event narrative by $3\frac{1}{2}$ years old in the narrative elicitation task. While this is likely related to methodological differences in elicitation strategies, it remains interesting that although the highpoint scale was developed to use with a group of working-class ENA families, the children in this sample appear to be falling within similar developmental patterns.

Whereas differences in methodological approaches in the collection of narrative interactions between these two samples likely has an impact on the structural complexity of the narrative interaction, it is also likely that cultural variations in parental beliefs around the function and value of narrative interactions among 3-year-olds has an impact. As the previous literature on differences between narrative interactions of Latino and ENA mother–child dyads suggests (Melzi, 2000; Silva & McCabe, 1996), these Mexican-heritage children may be more likely to experience conversational interactions with adults as a playful time to develop social and interpersonal skills, whereas McCabe's ENA children may be more likely to experience conversational interactions as a time to communicate facts and information and to develop cognitive skills. Still, whereas some differences in the most frequent stage of narrative structure continue to exist in the 4- to 5-year-old period, by the 6- to 7-year-old period, the majority of children in both samples told narratives with a classic narrative structure. In fact, by 78 months, the majority (78%) of these Mexican-heritage children told narratives with a classic structure, whereas only 35% and 48% of McCabe's 6- and 7-year-olds, respectively, told a narrative with a classic structure.

By 78 months (i.e., first grade), the majority of these children had experienced between 1 and 3 years of public schooling in English (most children attended English-only, state-funded preschool programs located on the elementary school campus beginning at $4\frac{1}{2}$ years). During the first two periods, these young children were beginning to navigate through not only two languages but also different sets of language practices at home and at school that likely included different adult expectations and scaffolding strategies around narrative interactions. Children who successfully managed to transition from primarily

Spanish-language narratives at 54 months to English-language narratives at 78 months may have gained more experience simultaneously attending to content, structure, and language choice – resulting in more developed narrative productions – than their monolingual peers. During the bilingual or code-switching phase, however, it appears that the combined task of organizing two languages as well as the structural coherence of the narrative creates a greater cognitive challenge resulting in a less well-organized and less coherent story, explaining the lower highpoint story structure scores for 54-month-old children engaging in dual-language narrative interactions. It is interesting that by 78 months, there is no difference in highpoint structure based on the language of the interaction, suggesting that perhaps by 78 months, children have acquired sufficient mastery or sufficient experience in simultaneously attending to the use of two languages together with overall coherence of their story.

Heterogeneity in Language Practices
In this project, we found significant variations in children's individual development of narrative skills and in everyday language practices of the Mexican-heritage families. This finding is important in understanding the role that culture plays in children's development by allowing us to take a closer look at developmental patterns within cultural communities, supporting the argument that low-income Mexican-heritage children and families are a heterogeneous group whose developmental patterns need to be investigated within cultural communities. The theoretical and methodological approach to defining cultural communities by assessing cultural practices has allowed a more detailed investigation of the variations in everyday cultural practices and how they influence narrative development.

Assessing both enacted and articulated language practices is in line with language-socialization theories, suggesting that what parents do around language as well as what they believe around language practices makes an impact on language development. The enacted language practices, including the language and literacy environment of the home and the frequency of adult–child reading, demonstrate that within this sample, families range from having a home described as very basic to more advanced in the quality of the language and literacy environment and from reading daily to rarely or never at both 36 and 54 months.

Narrative Development Related to Variations in Language Practices
In line with language-socialization theory, variations in the ways that families act around language practices were related to children's overall development of narrative coherence, with the time-lagged correlations presented in Table 7.10 suggesting that early language practices are important indicators of later narrative development. Families who focused on providing a literacy-rich environment early in the child's life (i.e., at 36 months) appear to have set the foundation

for the child becoming a competent and independent narrator by first grade. Perhaps due to the overall decrease in the language and literacy environment for 54-month-olds, the later language and literacy environment did not appear to have a continued impact on narrative development. In the case of reading frequency, recall that the overall trend was for parents to engage in less frequent reading at 36 months than at 54 months, with roughly half of the children in the sample being read to once a week or less. Those children who were read to more frequently at 36 months took more control of the telling and required less maternal scaffolding during the 54-month coconstructed narratives. Both sets of findings emphasize the importance of the quality and quantity of early language and literacy experiences on later developmental outcomes.

CONCLUSIONS

These Mexican-heritage families differ in how they use and think about language practices as ways to organize their daily life. This notion is important in understanding the role that culture plays in children's development by allowing us to take a closer look at developmental patterns within cultural communities. Thinking about cultural practices is necessary but perhaps not sufficient to fully understand narrative and language development among dual-language-learning Latino children. Clearly, the way families are thinking about language, the types of environment they create in their family, and the way they speak and interact with their children around language makes a difference in narrative development. Specifically, providing rich language and literacy experiences early on is important for later narrative development.

This study has provided an important description of narrative development over a critical period of language development in a group that has not yet been followed in such a longitudinal fashion. Whereas there do appear to be important differences in parent scaffolding strategies and content orientation among this group of Mexican-heritage children, they appear to experience a similar overall pattern of narrative development when reviewing the preschool to early elementary school period. This in itself is an important contribution to our knowledge about Mexican-heritage dual-language-learning children's narrative development. Likewise, the fact that families engage in a wide variety of language practices gives testimony to the argument that we must think carefully about what defines one's cultural community. At the very least, the definition of culture or community goes far beyond a simple social address defined by ethnicity, language, or income.

This study focused exclusively on the practices within the family and, as such, addressed just one small part of the cultural context in which families are participating. Although it provides an important part, by its nature it cannot complete the picture. This is particularly true when thinking about children's language development and changes in language practices enacted in the family. Participation in the public school system creates rapid changes in the language practices enacted by children that may or may not be in line with parents' goals for their children or with the practices that parents enact with their children. This is an essential component to consider in future studies. Particularly when considering the specific nature of narrative development and the role of narratives as a tool for supporting both social and cognitive development, future studies might explicitly ask parents about why they tell stories with their children: What is the function of storytelling? Is it only a way to communicate unshared events or does it have a broader social function, such as to enable children to understand family relationships or an academic function? Moreover, we might ask teachers of different ethnic backgrounds what they think the purpose of storytelling is: How is storytelling supported in the classroom? Why would they recommend that parents engage in storytelling with children? In summary, the results from this study create a baseline of data from which to continue investigating the intersection of culture and language and its ultimate impact on children's development.

Implications for Researchers and Educators

Research on normal narrative development among minority children has important implications for researchers and educators. Understanding patterns of language development relative to cultural beliefs and practices is essential for teachers to both develop reasonable expectations of children's early narrative interactions in the classroom and to design effective learning environments for young children. The data presented herein suggest that there may be important differences in Mexican-heritage children's early narrative interactions in preschool but that by first grade, most children will be on a par with ENA English-speaking children. This is by no means a message to educators that after first grade, cultural differences do not need to be attended to but rather a message that Mexican-heritage children can produce coherent and complex narratives and that teachers should maintain high expectations for all children.

Home-language practices shape language and literacy development. Children whose practices more closely resemble those of the school community may experience less difficulty in literacy development than children with other kinds of home-language experiences. Because demographics are changing, we need more research on language socialization and the connection to the development of academic language skills. Given the link between narratives and social and linguistic development, narrative assessments should be included in evaluations and intervention programs for children at risk for language or literacy difficulties.

REFERENCES

Azmitia, M., Cooper, C. R., García, E. E., & Dunbar, N. N. (1996). The ecology of family guidance in low-income Mexican American and European American families. *Social Development, 5*(1), 1–23.

Bayley, R., & Schecter, S. R. (2003). Introduction: Toward a dynamic model of language socialization. In R. Bayley & S. R. Schecter (Eds.), *Language socialization in bilingual and multilingual societies*. Great Britain: Cromwell Press.

Bedore, L. (2004). Bilingual language development and disorders in Spanish–English speakers. In B. A. Goldstein (Ed.), *Bilingual language development and disorders in Spanish-English speakers* (pp. 163–185). Baltimore, MD: Paul H. Brookes Publishing.

Bishop, D., & Edmundson, A. (1987). Language-impaired 4-year-olds: Distinguishing transient from persistent impairment. *Journal of Speech and Hearing Disorders, 52*, 156–173.

Bland-Stewart, L. M., & Fitzgerald, Z. M. (2001). Use of Brown's 14 grammatical morphemes by bilingual Hispanic preschoolers: A pilot study. *Communication Disorders Quarterly, 22*(4), 171–186.

Caldwell, B., & Bradley, R. (1984). *Home Observation for Measurement of the Environment*. Little Rock, AR: University of Arkansas at Little Rock.

Cohen, J. (1960). A coefficient of agreement for nominal scales. *Educational and Psychological Measurement, 20*, 37–46.

Contreras, J. M., Kerns, K., & Neal-Barnett, A. M. (Eds.) (2002). *Latino children and families in the United States: Current research and future directions*. Westport, CT: Praeger.

Eisenberg, A. (1985). Learning to describe past experiences in conversation. *Discourse processes, 8*, 177–204.

Gallimore, R., & Goldenberg, C. (1993). Activity settings of early literacy: Home and school factors in children's emergent literacy. In E. Forman, N. Minick, & C.A. Stone (Eds.), *Contexts for learning: Sociocultural dynamics in children's development* (pp. 315–335). Oxford: Oxford University Press.

García, E., & Cuéllar, D. (2006). Who are these linguistically and culturally diverse students? *Teachers College Record, 108*(11), 2220–2246.

García Coll, C., Contran, L., Jenkins, R., McAdoo, H. P., Crinic, K., Wasik, B. H., & García, H. V. (1996). An integrative model for the study of developmental competencies in minority children. *Child Development, 67*, 1891–1941.

Garret, P. B., & Baquedano-López, P. (2002). Language socialization: Reproduction and continuity, transformation and change. *Annual Review of Anthropology, 31*, 339–361.

Gleason, J. B., & Melzi, G. (1997). The mutual construction of narrative by mothers and children: Cross-cultural observations. *Journal of Narrative and Life History. Special Issue: Oral Versions of Personal Experiences: Three Decades of Narrative Analysis, 7*(1–4), 217–222.

Goodwin, M. H. (1990). Tactical uses of stories: Participation frameworks within girls' and boys' disputes. In D. Tannen (Ed.) *Gender and Conversational Interaction*. New York: Oxford University Press.

Gutiérrez-Clellen, V. F., & Hienrichs-Ramos, L. (1993). Referential cohesion in the narratives of Spanish-speaking children: A developmental study. *Journal of Speech and Hearing Research, 36*, 559–568.

Gutiérrez-Clellen, V. F. 2002. Narratives in two languages. Assessing performance of bilingual children. *Linguistics and Education, 13*, 175–197.

Gutiérrez-Clellen, V. F., & Iglesias, A. (1992). Causal coherence in the oral narratives of Spanish-speaking children. *Journal of Speech and Hearing Research, 35*, 363–372.

Harwood, R., Scholmeric, A., & Schulze, P. A. (2000). Homogeneity and heterogeneity in cultural belief systems. In S. Harkness, C. Raeff, & C. M. Super (Eds.), *New directions for child and adolescent development: Variability in the social construction of the child* (pp. 41–57). San Francisco: Jossey-Bass Publications.

Heath, S. B. (1982). What no bedtime story means: Narrative skills at home and school. *Language in Society, 11,* 49–76.

Heath, S. B. (1983). *Ways with words.* Cambridge: Oxford University Press.

Howes, C., Wishard Guerra, A. G., & Zucker, E. (2007). Cultural communities and parenting practices in Mexican-heritage families. *Parenting: Science and Practice, 7,* 1–36.

Howes, C., Wishard Guerra, A. G., & Zucker, E. (2008). Migrating from Mexico and sharing pretend with peers in the United States. *Merrill-Palmer Quarterly, 54,* 256–288.

Imbens-Bailey, A. L., & Snow, C. E. (1997). Making meaning in parent–child interaction: A pragmatic approach. In A. McCabe & C. Mandell, *The problem of meaning: Behavioral and cognitive perspectives* (pp. 261–295). A volume of *Advances in Psychology,* Amsterdam: North-Holland Elsevier Science B.V.

Labov, W. (1972). *Language in the inner city: Studies in the Black English vernacular.* Philadelphia: University of Pennsylvania Press.

MacWhinney, B. (2000). *The CHILDES project: Tools for analyzing talk.* Mahwah, NJ: Lawrence Erlbaum Associates.

McCabe, A. (1997). Developmental and cross-cultural aspects of children's narration. In Michael Bamberg (Ed.), *Narrative development: Six approaches.* Mahwah, NJ: Lawrence Erlbaum Associates.

McCabe, A. & Peterson, C. (Eds.). (1991). *Developing Narrative Structure.* Hillsdale, NJ: Lawrence Erlbaum Associates.

Melzi, G. (2000). Cultural variations in the construction of personal narratives: Central American and European American mothers' elicitation styles. *Discourse Processes, 30,* 2, 153–177.

Minami, M., & McCabe, A. (1995). Rice balls and bear hunts: Japanese and North American family narrative patterns. *Journal of Child Language, 22*(2), 423–445.

Muñoz, M. L., Gillam, R. B., Peña, E. D., & Gulley-Faehnle, A. (2003). Measures of language development in fictional narratives of Latino children. *Language, Speech, and Hearing Services in Schools, 34,* 332–342.

National Center for Education (2003). *The condition of education for Hispanic Americans.*

Ochs, E., & Capps, L. (2001). *The living narrative: Creating lives in everyday storytelling.* Cambridge, MA: Harvard University Press.

Ochs, E., & Schieffelin, B. (1995) The impact of language socialization on grammatical development. In P. Fletcher and B. MacWhinney (Eds.), *The handbook of child language* (pp. 73–94). Oxford: Blackwell.

Peterson, C., & McCabe, A. (1983). *Developmental psycholinguistics: Three ways of looking at a child's narrative.* New York, NY: Plenum.

Raikes, H., Pan, B. A., Luze, G., Tamis-LeMonda, C. S., Brooks-Gunn, J., Constantine, J., Tarullo, L., Raikes, A., & Rodriguez, E. (2006). Mother–child book-reading in low-income families: Correlates and outcomes during the first three years of life. *Child Development, 77*(4), 924–953.

Reese, L., Garnier, H., Gallimore, R., & Goldenberg, C. (2000). A longitudinal analysis of the ecocultural antecedents of emergent Spanish literacy and subsequent English reading achievement of Spanish-speaking students. *American Educational Research Journal, 37*(3), 633–662.

Rogoff, B. (2003). *The cultural nature of human development.* New York: Oxford University Press.

Rogoff, B., Mistry, J., Gönçü, A., & Mosier, C. (1993). *Guided participation in cultural activity by toddlers and caregivers. Monographs of the Society for Research in Child Development, 58* (7, Serial No. 236).

Rosenblatt, S., Garza-Mourino, R., & Howes, C. (2004). How did you end up here? Collaborative ways of listening to Mexican immigrant mothers as they contemplate their lives there/then and here/now: The story of the Cultural Change Interview (CCI). Los Angeles: University of California, Unpublished manuscript.

Schecter, S. R., & Bayley, B. (2002). *Language as cultural practices:* Mexicanos el en Norte. Hillsdale, NJ: Lawrence Erlbaum Associates.

Schieffelin, B., & Ochs, E. (1986). Language socialization. *Annual Review of Anthropology, 15,* 163–191.

Silva, M. J., & McCabe, A. (1996). Vignettes of the continuous and family ties: Some Latino American traditions. In A. McCabe (Ed.), *Chameleon readers: Teaching children to appreciate all kinds of good stories.* New York: McGraw-Hill.

Snow, C. (1983). Literacy and language: Relationships during the preschool years. *Harvard Educational Review* (53), 165–189.

Sperry, L., & Sperry, D. (1996). Early development of narrative skills. *Cognitive Development, 11,* 443–465.

U.S. Census Bureau (2001). *The Hispanic Population: Census 2000 Brief.*

Vygotsky, L. S. (1978). *Mind in society: The development of higher psychological processes.* Cambridge, MA: Harvard University Press.

8

Beyond Chronicity: Evaluation and Temporality in Spanish-Speaking Children's Personal Narratives

PAOLA UCCELLI

Key Words: narrative, language development, Andean, Spanish-speaking children, temporality, evaluation

ABSTRACT

This chapter focuses on Spanish-speaking children's evaluation and temporality in the construction of personal narratives. The study analyzes 32 personal narratives produced by 8 Andean Spanish-speaking children from the Andean city of Cusco in Peru. All children were monolingual speakers of the Andean Spanish variety and came from lower-middle-class families. Half the children were preschoolers (4;9 to 5;5 years) and the other half were first-graders (6;6 to 7;8 years). Both age groups were balanced in terms of gender. Children were interviewed and tape-recorded by the author using the *Conversational Map of Narratives of Real Experiences* (McCabe & Rollins, 1994) as the elicitation procedure. Narratives were transcribed using CHAT conventions (MacWhinney, 2000) and were subsequently coded for narrative components (Peterson & McCabe, 1983) and temporal organization (Genette, 1980). Results indicated that contrary to the sequentiality and single-story structure reported as characteristic of U.S. European American English-speaking children, these Andean Spanish-speaking children's narratives present a distinctive feature labeled herein as *structural evaluation*. Structural evaluation takes two forms, either (1) a functional deviation from the timeline of real events; or (2) a chain of independent stories connected within the boundaries of a single narrative. These young narrators used these strategies to evaluate a specific point in the narrative, consequently affecting both the temporal organization of events and the episodic complexity of the narratives. Deviations from the timeline are usually identified as indicators of language pathology or immaturity for U.S. European American English-speaking children. In these Andean children's narratives, conversely, departures from the timeline served a rhetorical function that reflected a sophisticated discourse skill. Results highlight the need of data-driven interpretative approaches of

Spanish-speakers' narratives in a field increasingly focused on cultural/linguistic diversity but still dominated by Anglo-centric views of development.

Narrative Development and Sequentiality

Meaning resides not only in *what* we say but also in *how* we say it. In narratives of real experience, we convey messages through both reference to real-world events and the way in which we structure those events into a whole. The narrativization of personal experiences is one of the earliest discourse forms acquired (Nelson, 1986) and a primary means by which children make sense not only of their world but also of *themselves in* the world (Bruner, 1990). These narrative structures vary across cultures, and children learn them gradually as they become competent members of their specific cultural group. In this study, the focus is on how Andean Spanish-speaking children from Cusco, Peru, structure and evaluate their personal narratives.

The study of cultural and linguistic variation in children's narrative performance has shed light on crucial differences in developmental paths. On the one hand, cross-linguistic studies attending to typological differences suggest an influence of language-specific grammatical features on children's narrative development (Slobin, 1996). On the other hand, cross-cultural studies, which focus on culture as the source of variation, have documented the impact of culturally valued patterns of communication on children's narrative development. These studies highlight the importance of interactional and sociocultural factors in development and warn us against universal standards for assessing narrative performance. These studies have documented, for example, that the topic-chaining discourse style (Michaels, 1981) and parallelism (Cazden, Michaels, & Tabors, 1985; Gee, 1996) of African American children's narratives and the multiepisodic quality of Japanese children's narratives (Minami, 2001; Minami & McCabe, 1991) are appropriate and desirable patterns in these children's speech community.

There is, however, a pervasive notion regarding narrative structure that is hardly ever contested and is usually assumed to be a requisite for appropriate narrative performance. This notion is *sequentiality* or *linearity* (Ochs & Capps, 2001) – that is, a chronological representation of events.

The study of children's narratives, in general, has assumed sequentiality as a telos toward which discourse structures progress, and it has focused on the study of chronologically organized narratives (Ochs & Capps, 2001). In fact, the classic work of Labov and Waletzky (1967), from which the majority of current studies on personal narratives stems, defines narratives precisely "by the fact that they recapitulate experience in the *same* order as the original events" (p. 21). The sequential organization of narratives has been identified as a crucial achievement in U.S. European American English-speaking children. Peterson and McCabe's (1983) research has highlighted sequentiality and focus on a single experience as goals that drive the narrative development of these children. These authors and colleagues have identified deviations from a sequential timeline as indicators of still being in an early stage of development for U.S. European American English-speaking children (McCabe & Rollins, 1994; Peterson & McCabe, 1983). In their model for assessing narrative skills, for instance, McCabe and Rollins (1994) identified seven hierarchical stages for U.S. European American English-speaking children's narrative development. Among these seven stages, "leapfrog narratives" (i.e., nonsequential) characterize the still immature performance of 4-year-olds, whereas the "classic pattern" (i.e., sequential) is reached at 6 years of age. The authors themselves define these stages as follows (McCabe & Rollins, 1994, p. 46) (brackets and emphasis are mine):

"LEAPFROG NARRATIVE: By 4, children's narratives tend to consist of more than two events that occurred on one occasion, but they narrate the **events out of sequence** in what is called Leapfrog Narrative (. . .)

CLASSIC NARRATIVE: Six-year-olds tell a well-formed story [that occurred on one occasion] that orients a listener to who, what, and where something happened, narrates a **sequence of events** that builds to some sort of climax or high point and then goes on to resolve itself . . . "

These authors found that U.S. European American English-speaking children's deviations from the timeline after 6 years of age are signs of language immaturity or language pathology. In addition, they have reported that these children convey narratives that focus on one single experience from an early age. McCabe and her colleagues have been very careful not to overgeneralize their findings to other populations. Indeed, as discussed previously, they have advanced our understanding of how narrative development varies across different cultural/linguistic groups (McCabe, 1997a). Ochs and Capps (2001) are among the few who have conceptualized the dimension of *linearity* as "a span of possibilities" (p. 83) in which events can be linked linearly or nonlinearly. They document four ways of children's nonlinear narrative practices: (1) *emotional outbursts*, when a narrative event triggers a child's emotional reaction in the present time; (2) *incoherent narratives*, which are the result of a child's cognitive limitations; (3) *narrative as problem solving*, in which the child is uncertain about a facet of the narrated experience and is trying to figure it out; and (4) *parallelism*, as the artful repetition of themes and forms characteristic of African American narratives. In their framework, the first three scenarios still constitute some disruption either in development or in the narration process. Only the fourth type, parallelism, is the result of a cultural aesthetic of a specific narrative tradition. Given that parallelism is not the dominant narrative aesthetic in U.S. schools, however, researchers have documented the difficulties these children face when at school they are confronted with narrative expectations that focus on sequentiality (Gee, 1996; Michaels, 1981; Ochs & Capps, 2001). The central role of sequentiality of discourse as well as the focus on a single experience, identified as dominant expectations both in developmental research and in U.S. schools call for further investigation of this dimension in different populations. Whereas the narrative aesthetics of African American children in the United States have received considerable attention, it is still necessary to study the narrative structures of other cultural groups, exploring in particular the possibility that discourse deviations from sequentiality and focus on a single experience could be linguistically and culturally appropriate for some children. It could even be the case that for some European American English-speaking children, narrative performances that go beyond chronicity and single experience represent higher levels of achievement, just not visible in the developmental range so far studied.

In contrast to the emphasis on sequentiality characteristic of the study of children's narratives, in the field of contemporary poetics, departures from the timeline are conceived of as crucial in textual analysis (Genette, 1980; Rimmon-Kenan, 1983). Widely known narrative theories advanced by Genette and Rimmon-Kenan highlight that literary narratives rarely follow a chronological pattern and most often deviate from it. In their studies of literary works, these authors demonstrate how moves out of chronicity are important strategies through which the narrator signals different meanings. In Rimmon-Kenan's words (1983, p. 17):

> "Strict linear chronology is neither natural nor an actual characteristic of most stories. It is a conventional 'norm' which has become so widespread as to [...] acquire a pseudo-natural status."

The analysis offered herein focuses on the form-and-meaning relations that emerge from exploring two dimensions that lie in the interplay between representation of experience and discourse macrostructure in children's narratives: *temporality* and *scope*. Borrowing concepts from contemporary poetics, this study explores *temporal representations* – chronicity and beyond-chronicity relations – in the oral personal narratives of Peruvian Andean Spanish-speaking children as contrasted to those of U.S. Midwestern English-speaking children. A complementary structural analysis examines these narratives' *scope* – that is, the narrativization of single versus multiple experiences. Although the main goal of the study is to focus on the yet unknown narrative patterns of Andean Spanish-speaking children, it was designed as comparative so that the patterns described for the extensively studied U.S. Midwestern group could be taken as a point of reference in the temporal and structural analysis of Andean narratives.

Andean Spanish-speaking children are a particularly appealing group for studying narrative temporal organization because the anthropological literature has repeatedly highlighted that the Andean concept of time cannot be described through a linear representation, as in Western philosophies, but rather as a cyclical or spiral one, where recursive circularity is the driving force that constantly combines past, present, and future (Manga Qespi, 1994; Ortiz, 1992; Randall, 1982). As Randall synthesizes it (1982, pp. 48–49):

> The Andean mind (. . .) views history as a series of cycles (. . .) in which linear time has little meaning (. . .) This concept of world cycles continues to be the vision of contemporary Andean indigenous peoples.

Along these lines, Ortiz (1992) highlights that Andean myths captured in oral tradition could be better described as a mosaic of short narratives linked together by thematic bonds, repetitions, or aesthetic principles. Even though making a connection between orally transmitted myths and children's narratives is neither a goal nor an assumption of this chapter, this body of research suggests a possible enculturation and socialization context in which sequentiality and single focus are not especially emphasized.

In no way does this study attempt to generalize the patterns described herein as distinct and exclusive characteristics of these two cultural/linguistic groups. The data of this study simply suggest an alternative narrative model that could prove relevant for children in other cultures and languages, which is offered here as an optional framework for interpreting children's narrative performances and not as a strict definition of a specific cultural/linguistic group.

Sociocultural Context

While narrative studies of varied cultural and linguistic groups are rapidly expanding, the global structure of diverse Spanish-speaking children's narratives still needs further research. The increasing available data suggest that Spanish-speaking children tend to produce narratives that differ from other cultural/linguistic groups (Bocaz, 1989; Gutiérrez-Clellen & Heinrichs-Ramos, 1993; Gutiérrez-Clellen & Quinn, 1995; Sebastián & Slobin, 1994; Shiro, 2003). In a comparative study of narratives produced by low-income African American and Latino children (from Central America and the Caribbean), Rodino, Gimbert, Pérez, and McCabe (1991) found that Latino children did not generally narrate using sequences of events but instead favored description and evaluation. These authors claim that sequencing events is not an important characteristic of Latino narrative discourse. Although some common narrative features across diverse populations of Latino children might exist, we cannot assume that this is necessarily the case. Spanish is a widely spoken language, and the description of Spanish-speaking children from diverse communities may shed light on varied ways to portray experience in discourse.

Andean means herein that the participating children, as well as their parents and siblings, were born, raised, and have lived all their life in the highlands of Peru. The Andean regions are home to a little less than a third of the Peruvian population in a country with about 27 million inhabitants (INEI, 2005). The children in this study are specifically from Cusco, one of the most important urban centers located in the Southern Andes.

The "Andean Spanish variety properly speaking" (Escobar, 1978) is a native Spanish variety spoken in the Northern and Southern Andes and is the product of the coexistence of Spanish and Quechua in this particular Andean region.[1] Its lexicon is predominantly Spanish, but many phonological and grammatical features reflect a Quechua influence (Cerrón Palomino, 1972; Escobar, 1978; Pozzi-Escot, 1972).

Although important research has focused on the study of Andean bilingual children and bilingual education (e.g., Hornberger, 1988; Montoya, 1990; Pozzi-Escot & Zúñiga, 1989), still little is known about language development in monolingual speakers of Andean Spanish. Furthermore, even though extensive research has documented the grammatical and phonological features of adult Andean Spanish (e.g., Camacho, Paredes, & Sánchez, 1995; Escobar, 1978; Godenzzi, 1995), the discourse level has received scarce attention (Zavala, 2001; see also chapter 6, this volume). Some research has looked at the discourse of women in the Andes (Seligmann, 2004); however, gender has not yet been explored in Peruvian Andean children's discourse. Different gender-based patterns of socialization (Uccelli, F. 1999) and school practices (Ames, 2005) have been reported for *rural* Andean children, suggesting that gender might be also a relevant dimension to consider for *urban* Andean children. Previous research on gender and narrative has reported, for instance, that English-speaking girls use evaluative devices in narratives earlier than boys (Peterson, 2001); that Mexican American mothers talk more about emotions with their daughters (Flannagan & Perese, 1998); and that urban mothers from Lima, Peru, discuss more positive emotions with their sons than with their daughters in conversations about the past (Melzi & Fernández, 2004). This line of research points to evaluation as the narrative component that might display the most salient differences across genders.

In summary, by studying the discourse of urban monolingual Andean Spanish-speaking girls and boys, this exploration seeks to shed initial light on the ways in which these children construct their personal narratives.

METHODS

Participants and Procedures

A total of 16 children participated in this study: 8 Peruvian Andean Spanish-speaking children and 8 U.S. Midwestern English-speaking children from

[1] Escobar (1978) identified two other Andean Spanish varieties: the "Altiplano Spanish variety," highly influenced by Aymara, and the "Coastal and Southwestern Andean Spanish variety."

Peterson and McCabe's (1983) dataset, whose transcribed narratives were made available thanks to the generosity of Allyssa McCabe. The children's ages ranged from 4;9 to 7;8 years and were equally divided, within each cultural/linguistic group, into preschoolers (4;9 to 5;5 years) and first-graders (6;6 to 7;8 years). Both age groups were also balanced in terms of gender.

All Andean children were monolingual speakers of Spanish whose parents were bilingual in Quechua and Spanish, and they came from lower-middle-class families. Children were from Cusco, a city located in the highlands of Peru, and all attended the same urban school. According to teacher reports and school records, none of the children had repeated a grade or had any sensory, intellectual, language, or learning difficulty. I interviewed each of the children in their school setting with a Spanish translation of the same elicitation procedure used by Peterson and McCabe (1983), the *Conversational Map of Narratives of Real Experiences* (McCabe & Rollins, 1994). After interviews were tape-recorded and completely transcribed, the four longest narratives of each child were selected for analysis (following McCabe & Rollins, 1994) for a total of 32 narratives.

The total U.S. Midwestern group from which this subsample was drawn consisted of 96 Caucasian, working-class, monolingual English-speaking children between the ages of 3;6 and 9;6 years from a nursery school and an elementary school in a small town in Ohio. Of these, eight children were randomly selected after matching them by age and gender with the Andean Spanish-speaking participants. Because Peterson and McCabe selected the 3 longest narratives per child, a total of 24 narratives were analyzed for this group.

In summary, a total of 56 narratives, all transcribed in CHILDES format (MacWhinney, 2000), comprised the corpus analyzed in this chapter.

Dimensions of Analysis

Defining a Narrative

Labov and Waletzky (1967, p. 28) defined a minimal narrative as "a sequence of two restricted [independent] clauses which are temporally ordered." They further highlighted the role of temporality in narratives by adding that "any sequence of clauses which contains at least one temporal juncture is a narrative." This classic definition was adopted by Peterson and McCabe (1983) in their influential highpoint analysis of children's narrative development and has guided several other linguistic approaches to the study of child narratives (Bamberg, 1997). As Bamberg (1997) pointed out, this definition implies a minimum requirement of two individual events sequentially ordered and assumes predicates marked by tensed verbs.

More recently, other researchers have used expanded versions of the Labov and Waletzky definition. McCabe (1997b), for instance, in reporting 2-year-olds' productions of one-event narratives, states that "had we not adopted a broad definition of narrative; that is, had we defined a minimal narrative as consisting of two past events in sequence . . . these early productions would have been excluded" (McCabe, 1997b, p. 144). Minami (2001) takes this point further, highlighting that older children and even adults produce appropriate narratives that contain only one event – for example, some Japanese haiku narratives follow a minimalist tradition of storytelling (Minami & McCabe, 1991). Because this is an initial approach toward understanding the narrative performance of a cultural/linguistic group that has not been previously studied, I also opted for a broad definition of personal narrative: a type of connected discourse that provides an account of related events that have been personally experienced (Hudson & Shapiro, 1991).

Analytical Instruments
Contemporary poetics (Genette, 1980; Rimmon-Kenan, 1983), episodic analysis (Peterson & McCabe, 1983), and highpoint analysis (Peterson & McCabe, 1983) are the three sources used in this chapter to analyze the following dimensions of narrative:

1. *Temporal representation.* This dimension can be best described by Genette's (1980) notion of "order." Following Genette, "order" concerns the relations between the succession of events and their linear disposition in the narrative text. In his framework, anachronies are a crucial aspect of textual analysis; thus, these analytical instruments aim to identify the following narrative temporal departures:
   • *Temporal graph.* To display the relationship between the timeline of events and the narrative timeline, a simple graph was designed. First, the clauses classified as events (i.e., temporally anchored actions of the characters or natural occurrences, such as *I fell down*) were selected. Background actions, such as *My grandmother was living in the country/ she had a lot of harvest* or *I was taking the can to my room*, offered descriptive information that functions as setting. Therefore, they were not included in the selection. The second step involved plotting the sequence of these selected clauses against the sequence of real events to which they refer. (Figure 8.1 displays a temporal graph that represents a chronological sequence.)
   • *Temporal categories.* The two possible deviations from sequentiality are:
     – *Analepsis* (i.e., retrospection or flashback) is the narration of an event at a point in the text after later events have been told.
     – *Prolepsis* (i.e., foreshadowing or anticipation) is the narration of an event at a point in the text before earlier events have been told (Rimmon-Kenan, 1983).
2. *Scope.* Scope refers to the narrativization of single versus multiple experiences. In the field of children's narratives, two main structural analyses dominate the scene. The first is *episodic analysis* or *story grammar*, which describes narratives as composed of problem-solving episodes

that contain causal components, such as *events, attempts,* or *consequences* (Mandler & Johnson, 1977; Stein & Glenn, 1979. The second, *highpoint analysis,* which is Peterson and McCabe's (1983) adaptation of the Labovian method (Labov & Waletzky, 1967), conceives of narrative as recapitulation of events structured around a climax – that is, a highly evaluated point. Narrative components are defined, in this framework, based on the contrast between referential (i.e., actions and background information) and evaluative elements (i.e., devices that signal the narrator's perspective). Whereas story grammar has been traditionally applied to fictional narratives and highpoint analysis to personal narratives, these two methods can be integrated into an analytical instrument that provides insights from both. In this study, I applied an integrated analytical instrument that included the following codes[2]:

- *Clause-level codes*: Clauses were coded according to Peterson and McCabe's (1983) adaptation of episodic categories, but *evaluation* was added. Any unit that was present in the narrative because of causal requirement was coded as an *event,* a *motivating state,* an *attempt,* or a *consequence.* Additional units were coded as *setting, reactions, appendages,* or *evaluation.*

- *Structural patterns*: At a higher level, clauses were organized into larger units, labeled *structural patterns* (Peterson & McCabe, 1983). These structural patterns were defined on the basis of connectedness and causal relationships among clauses.

3. *Evaluative dimension*: Evaluation refers to the individual meanings emphasized through storytelling. As defined by Labov and Waletzky (1967, p. 37), evaluation is "the part of the narrative which reveals the attitude of the narrator towards the narrative by emphasizing the relative importance of some units as compared to others." This dimension affects the structuring of narratives because the most salient events are highlighted through varied linguistic strategies that do not advance the narrative plot: by repeating them, explicitly telling how important they are, raising intonation, adding a series of adjectives, or accompanying them with onomatopoeias and/or elongations (Peterson & McCabe, 1983). By capturing linguistic devices that express the narrators' attitude, the analysis enters the realm of interpretation. Through this dimension, it is possible to understand how meaning and structure affect each other in the construction of narratives.

Inter-rater reliability for coding categories was assessed using Cohen's Kappa (Cohen, 1960). Of the randomly selected narratives, 15% were coded by another

---

[2] It is important to clarify here that my analyses do not carry over the assumption of universals held by episodic analysts but rather simply attempt to identify the specific characteristics of the predominant narrative patterns for this specific group of children.

Temporal Analysis of Narrative 1

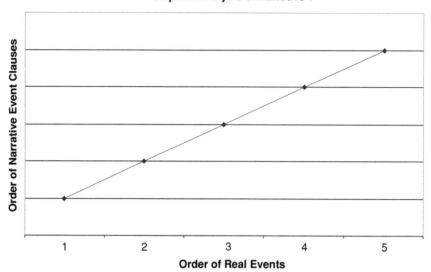

Figure 8.1. Temporal analysis of Narrative 1, told by Gonzalo, a 7;9-year-old boy.

Peruvian researcher who was bilingual in Spanish and English. A coefficient of 0.71 was computed, which is regarded as good agreement by Bakeman and Gottman (1986). Afterwards, all remaining disagreements were resolved.

RESULTS

Temporal Representation

As introduced previously, "order" (Genette, 1980) concerns the relations between the succession of real events and their linear disposition in the text. The following temporal graph used to visually display this relation is offered here with an example:

Order of Real Events [Real Timeline]	Clause Number [Narrative Timeline]
1 approached the bee}	5 *I approached {it = the bee}*
2 I got stung by it	6 *I got stung*
3 someone took the sting out	8 *and {they} took its sting out of me*
4 it itched	9 *but it itched*
5 it still itches	10 *it still itches*
(Narrative 1: Gonzalo, 7;9 years)	

As Figure 8.1 shows, the narrative produced by Gonzalo, an Andean 7;9-year-old boy, displays a temporal organization that mirrors the order of real events.

Table 8.1. *Narratives divided by temporal organization and number of children*
producing each type

	Andean Spanish-speaking children		U.S. midwestern English-speaking children	
	Sequential	Nonsequential	Sequential	Non-sequential
Narratives	14 (44%)	18 (56%)	11 (46%)	13 (54%)
Children	7 (88%)	8 (100%)	6 (75%)	7 (88%)

The Y axis displays the narrative timeline – that is, the order in which narrative event clauses were presented by the child. For example, *I approached {it}* was the first event clause in this child's narrative. The X axis displays the real timeline of events – that is, the order in which the actual events (those reported by narrative event clauses) occurred in the real experience. For example, the narrative event clause *I approached {it}* referred to the real event I approached the bee.[3] In the graph, each *narrative event clause* is matched with the corresponding real event it reports. Figure 8.1 shows that the first *narrative event clause* told by the child referred to the real event that happened first in his experience (see bottom left of graph); the second *narrative event clause* referred to the second real event; and so on, displaying a narrative timeline that corresponded to the real timeline of the experience. Therefore, this narrative displays a sequential pattern.

Pure sequentiality, however, is not the predominant pattern for the narratives analyzed in this study. Table 8.1 indicates the number of sequential versus nonsequential narratives found for each group.

As shown in Table 8.1, 18 of 32 (56%) of the narratives told by Andean children are nonsequential. It is interesting that for the U.S. Midwestern children, the distribution of sequential (46%) versus nonsequential (54%) narratives is almost identical, in proportional terms.

Group differences emerged, however, when a closer examination of the nonsequential category was undertaken. The sequential category contains only narratives that mirror the timeline of events; however, within the nonsequential category, two kinds of departures were identified during the analysis: partial and full departures.

Partial Departures
Partial departures from sequentiality are nonsequential events that are expressed either through reported speech or in the form of an abstract (i.e., a brief summary of what is to come). As Rimmon-Kenan (1983) states, instead of being directly attributed to the narrator, these analepses and prolepses are filtered. An example

---

[3] In all examples, narrative event clauses are written in italics and the real events that those clauses report are underlined.

Table 8.2. *Narratives classified by type of temporal representation*

	Sequential	Partial	Full
32 Andean Narratives	14 (44%)	10 (31%)	8 (25%)
24 U.S. Midwestern Narratives	11 (46%)	11 (46%)	2 (8%)

of a partial departure is the following fragment by an Andean 5-year-old boy: *"I got sick on Sunday and my father called the doctor and the nurse said that the doctor went on a trip"* (Alonso, 5;1 years). Even though the trip of the doctor in this narrative was the first event that happened in the timeline of real events, this does not constitute a real analepsis because it is part of a chronological and reportorial speech act.

An interesting finding is that abstracts and reported speech departures are inversely distributed in the two cultural/linguistic groups: more than half of the partial departures in English narratives occur in the form of an abstract (7/11), but only 3 of 10 of the Spanish narratives with partial departures include abstracts, whereas all the others contain departures through reported speech.

Abstracts and reported speech clauses serve very different functions within narratives. Thus, these findings could justify two independent hypotheses. First, the narratives of U.S. Midwestern children in this group seem to reflect that a brief summary of the narrative to come is a highly valued feature, whereas for Andean Spanish-speaking children, that narrative feature does not seem to be particularly relevant. Previous research on Peruvian Spanish-speaking children also highlights the absence of abstracts in those children's narratives (Minaya-Portella, 1980). Second, in contrast to the English narratives, Andean Spanish narratives contain many reports of characters' actual words. These narrative preferences could signal cultural values associated with different skills and varied forms of parsing and selecting what is worth talking about in each society.

In summary, partial departures are not real analepses attributable to the narrator (Rimmon-Kenan, 1983) and, because the boundaries of chronicity have not really been surpassed, narratives with partial departures can still be described as following a sequential organization. Therefore, the core of the comparison along the temporal dimension entails the exploration of full departures.

Full Departures

These departures are the narrator's moves that deviate from the timeline by referring directly to nonsequential events. As Table 8.2 indicates, of the 18 nonsequential Andean narratives, 8 (equivalent to 25% of that group) contain full departures. On the contrary, there were just 2 English narratives with full departures of 13 nonsequential English narratives.

Moreover, when narratives were divided into age groups (i.e., preschoolers and first-graders), the differences became even more striking. As shown in Table 8.3,

Table 8.3. *Andean Spanish-speaking children's narratives classified by type of temporal representation and divided into age groups*

	Sequential	Partial	Full
16 Preschoolers' narratives	9 (56%)	6 (38%)	1 (6%)
16 First-graders' narratives	5 (31%)	4 (25%)	7 (44%)

the number of sequential narratives and narratives with partial departures decreases in older Andean children, whereas the number of narratives with full departures increases considerably. In contrast to the English group, where only one first-grader produced one narrative with full departures, almost all Andean first-graders produced one or more narratives with full departures (the seven narratives were produced by three of the four Andean first-graders). This more salient difference in the older age groups suggests movement toward different cultural/linguistic models of narrative performance.

In summary, at the temporal representation level, one fourth of the Spanish narratives exhibited full departures, whereas fewer than one tenth of the English narratives displayed this temporal deviation. Moreover, *all* Andean children in this sample produced at least one narrative with some kind of departure from the timeline of real events. In addition, almost all of them (i.e., seven of the eight) produced at least one sequential narrative as well; in other words, these children can also narrate chronologically organized structures. These findings suggest that in contrast to the U.S. Midwestern children, as Andean children grow older, the predominant pattern is *not* to remain within the boundaries of sequentiality but rather to move beyond chronicity.

Scope: Narrativization of One Versus Multiple Experiences
Beyond the level of the clause, at the level of structural patterns, the scope of what gets narrativized within the boundaries of one narrative was compared across the groups.

First, the number of *sequences* and *episodes* – the major types of structural patterns – contained in a single narrative were used as an index of how many structural patterns the child was integrating within a single narrative.[4] *Episodes* or *sequences* identify the connected parts of the main action of *one* happening (e.g., approaching a flower; being stung by a bee; going home and being cured by mother). A *happening* refers to the connected events that occurred at one

[4] Notice that a higher number of structures does not necessarily index a higher degree of narrative sophistication because a one-episode narrative that involves elaborated causal and temporal connections could be "more complex" than a "simple" account that contains a series of action sequences. In any case, how to define "complexity" is in itself a controversial issue and one that does not directly concern us here. Thus, the term *structural multiplicity* does not contain any assumptions regarding complexity.

Table 8.4. *Multistructural narratives divided by number of anecdotes and by number of different children producing each type*

	Andean Spanish-speaking children		U.S. midwestern English-speaking children	
	Unianecdotal narratives	Multianecdotal narratives	Unianecdotal narratives	Multianecdotal narratives
Narratives	9/32 (28%)	8/32 (25%)	6/24 (25%)	2/24 (8%)
Children	4 (50%)	5 (63%)	4 (50%)	2 (25%)

This table contains only the narratives identified as multistructural (i.e., 17 Andean and 8 Midwestern narratives) because only those structures allow for a multianecdotal pattern.

occasion. Some narratives in this dataset referred not only to one happening but also to many connected happenings within the boundaries of one narrative (e.g., vaccination as a baby; surgery at 3 years of age; recent visit to the doctor). The term *anecdote* is used from now on to refer to one happening within a longer narrative.[5]

First, narratives were classified into two kinds: *unistructural* (i.e., those with one sequence or one episode) and *multistructural* (i.e., those with more than one episode or a combination of sequences and episodes). Whereas 53% of the Spanish narratives display a multistructural organization, more than half of the English narratives (63%) present a unistructural one.

Then, narratives were further classified as *unianecdotal* (i.e., those with only one anecdote) and *multianecdotal* narratives (i.e., those that link different anecdotes within the boundaries of one narrative). Frequencies of unianecdotal and multianecdotal narratives are reported in Table 8.4.

The most interesting finding regarding overall structure is that 25% – a quarter of the narratives produced by the Andean children – are not only multistructural but also multianecdotal. In contrast, only two U.S. children's narratives (less than 10%) contain more than one anecdote.

UNDERSTANDING THE RESULTS

As Tables 8.5 through 8.7 summarize, the previous sections reported the proportional differences in the two cultural/linguistic groups, highlighting the

---

[5] The criteria for specifying the boundaries between anecdotes were inductively derived from the data analysis. These boundaries were established on the basis of shifts in a combination of some of the following narrative elements:

- narrator: from protagonist narrator to witness narrator
- characters: from set of characters A to set of characters B
- time and setting: non-contiguous change of setting and time of action
- conflict definition: a shift in the specificity of the conflict (e.g., from a happening about a stomachache to an independent one about a very high fever)

Table 8.5. *Narratives with full departures*

Full departures – All children	
Andean Spanish narratives	Midwestern English narratives
8/32 (25%)	2/24 (8%)

Table 8.6. *Narratives with full departures among first-graders*

Full departures – First-graders	
Andean Spanish Narratives	Midwestern English Narratives
7/16 (44%)	1/12 (8%)

Table 8.7. *Narratives with multiple anecdotes*

Multianecdotal narratives – All children	
Andean spanish narratives	Midwestern english narratives
8/32 (25%)	2/24 (8%)

Andean children's tendencies toward temporal departures and multianecdotal narratives.

In contrast to the conclusions from U.S. research, the departures from temporality in the Andean Spanish narratives do not appear as problematic or as evidence of language deficiencies. On the contrary, narratives with full departures were some of the most sophisticated and effective texts in this dataset. Why do Andean narratives seem coherent and effective despite these "deviations" and "lack of single focus"? In line with Ochs and Capps' (2001) conceptualization of *linearity* as a range of possibilities, the narrative structures described herein seem to constitute yet another possibility of a nonlinear narrative aesthetic. The following section offers an interpretative framework in which temporal departures and multianecdotal structures are understood as *functional* within the global structure of these texts.

Andean Spanish Narratives: Beyond Chronicity

One of Labov and Waletzky's (1967) main contributions was the description of evaluation as occurring by *suspending* the recapitulation of events. In the case of these Andean Spanish-speaking children, however, evaluation is conveyed not through suspension of the timeline but rather through the alteration of the order of the real timeline. This evaluative strategy is not located within the boundaries of the clause but rather affects the whole structure of the narratives; therefore, I call it *structural evaluation*.

Following Genette's (1980) terminology, *analepses* are "flashbacks" or "retrospection" and *prolepses* are "foreshadowing" or "anticipation." Andean Spanish narratives displayed both analepses and prolepses as *functional departures* from the timeline – that is, as strategies serving the purpose of signaling the narrator's perspective toward the narrated experience.

Narratives with Analeptic Evaluation
In this narrative, Lara, a 7;6-year-old girl, brought an embedded story from the past to emphasize one specific point, as follows:

		Spanish Original	English Translation
	Interviewer:	*¿Y aquí en tu labio qué te pasó?*	And what happened here on your lip?
1	Child:	*Es que me cayó una lata.*	A can hit me.
	Interviewer:	*¿Cómo fue? Cuéntame.*	How did it happen? Tell me about it.
2	Child:	*Es que yo estaba llevando a mi cuarto una lata*	I was taking a can to my room
3		*después mi hermano me estaba haciendo*	and then my brother was showing me
4		*para jugar como volley*	[that he wanted] to play volleyball [with the can]
5		*y mi hermano me lo tiró*	and my brother threw it to me
6		*y me cayó en acá*	and {it} hit me here [pointing to her lip]
7		*y mi mami me lo quería coser*	and my mom wanted to stitch it
8		*pero mi papi no me lo quería hacer coser*	but my daddy didn't want to stitch it
9		**porque a mi hermano lo cosieron esto**	**because my brother was stitched**
10		**y quedó feo**	**And {his scar} became awful**
11		*y mi papi me puso huevo.*	And my daddy put egg [on my lip].[6]
			(Narrative 2, by Lara 7;6 years)

Figure 8.2 displays the relationship between the narrative timeline and the order of real events:

---

[6] To use egg for curing wounds is a common practice in some Andean regions.

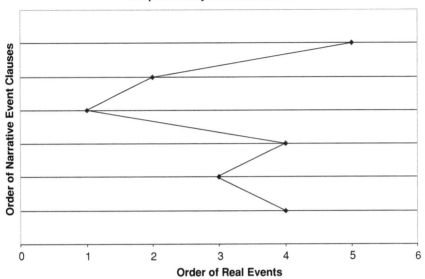

Figure 8.2. Temporal analysis of Narrative 2, told by Lara, a 7;6-year-old girl.

Order of Real Events	Order of Narrative Event Clauses
[Real Timeline]	[Narrative Timeline]
	1 *a can hit me*
1 my brother was stitched	5 ***and*** *my brother threw it to me*
2 and his scar became awful	6 *and {it} hit me here* [pointing to her lip]
3 my brother threw a can to me	9 because *my brother was stitched*
4 the can hit me on my lip	10 *and {his scar} became awful*
5 my daddy put egg on it	11 *and my daddy put egg {on it}*

As the temporal graph shows, Lara starts by expressing the main event of the narrative as an abstract: *a can hit me.* Then she goes back to the previous events that caused that to happen and narrates them in sequence. After that, she makes the most interesting temporal move: she introduces a second anecdote, about her brother, from a past that antedates the starting point of the first anecdote. Why does this girl "violate" chronicity? To understand this narrative, the dimensions of evaluation and causality need to be included in the analysis. The meaning this girl is constructing resides not only in the content of her clauses but also in the way in which she has organized them. By introducing this second anecdote at this point of the narrative, Lara is both explaining and evaluating the fact that she was not given stitches – like her brother had been – but rather was cured with an egg, as her father wanted. This temporal deviation is far from being the result of a language delay or of any other linguistic difficulty. On the contrary, it reflects a complex ability to associate experiences that occurred at different times and integrate them into a single narrative frame by establishing relationships of causality and evaluation. In this case of structural evaluation, the second anecdote is reported after later events have already been told; therefore, I call it a *narrative with analeptic evaluation* (Rimmon-Kenan, 1983).

Another example that displays a functional deviation from the real timeline is the narrative told by Ana, a 6;9-year-old girl. In the following narrative, Ana tells us about one time when she got injured and needed to be cured by a doctor in the hospital:

		Spanish Original	English Translation
1	**Child:**	*Un día en el hospital Antonio Lorena, no venía el panadero*	One day in the Antonio Lorena hospital the baker wasn't coming
2		*para que yo desayune*	so that I could have breakfast
3		*es que no había desayunado en mi casa*	because I hadn't had breakfast at home
4		*porque mi mami como trabaja en el hospital Antonio Lorena*	because my mom works at the Antonio Lorena hospital
5		*nos apuramos rápido*	{we} hurried up quickly
6		*y no venía el panadero*	and the baker wasn't coming
7		*entonces al fin que llegó*	then finally {he} arrived
8		*y estaban arreglando el piso*	and {some people} were fixing the floor
9		*porque mi mami antes trabajaba*	because in the past my mom used to work
10		*para cocinar*	{so she could} cook
11		*y entonces estaban arreglando el piso*	and so {they} were fixing the floor
12		*y yo me he desbarrancado*	and I ran
13		*y me he caído*	and {I} fell down
14		*y toda mi cara sangre había*	and there was blood all over my face
	Interviewer:	*¡Oh! ¡Toda tu cara de sangre! ¿Y entonces?*	Oh! All your face with blood and then?
15	**Child:**	*Me han curado*	{They} cured me
16		*me han llevado donde la jefa de mi mamá*	{they} brought me to my mother's boss
17		*para que me quede*	so that {I} could stay there
18		*después me han curado*	after that {they} cured me

		Spanish Original	English Translation
19		*hasta me ha salido de mi nariz sangre chajjí así*	even my nose bled chajj! like this
20		*y mi mami pensaba*	and my mom thought
21		*que me la había <roto> [?]*	that it was <broken> [?]
22		*y nada, no había ninguna heridita*	and nothing, there was no wound
23		*y la doctora nos dijo*	and the doctor told us
24		*que había sido como caí*	that {it} was since {I} fell down {it}
25		*reventó así y así*	{it} burst like this and this [enacting the bleeding of her nose with her hands]
	Interviewer:	*Cayó un chorro*	Lots {of blood} came out
26	**Child:**	*Chass! cayó así*	Splash! {it = the blood} came out like this
27		*y entonces después me curó pues*	and then later {she} cured me
28		*en esa edad mi hermano tenía cuatro cinco*	at that age my brother was four years old
29		*ya estaba en colegio*	{he} was already in school
30		*y entonces desde ese día no me ha gustado correr mucho.*	and then since that day I don't like to run very much.
			(Narrative 3, by Ana, 6;9 years)

Order of Real Events	**Order of Narrative Event Clauses**
[Real Timeline]	[Narrative Timeline]
1 we hurried up	5
2 the baker arrived	7
3 I ran	12
4 I fell down	13, 24
5 my nose "exploded"	25
6 my nose bled	19, 26
7 they brought me to my mother's boss	16
8 they cured me	15, 18, 27
9 the doctor said	23

As displayed by Figure 8.3, as Ana's narrative unfolds, the anachronies become more frequent. The first proleptic event is clause 15, which is offered as a label,

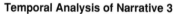

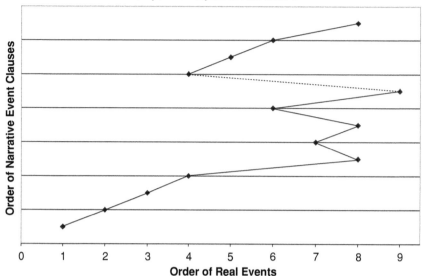

Figure 8.3. Temporal analysis of Narrative 3, told by Ana; a 6;9 year-old girl.

or generalization, for the episode to follow. Ana says "I got cured" and then starts specifying the details in which that happened. Then, the first analeptic move is clause 19, where she refers to the fact that her nose bled – information that she had already conveyed in a descriptive form in clause 14. This event is repeated once more in clause 26. It is interesting that this girl is not introducing an external anecdote, as Lara did in the previous example. In this narrative, Ana is altering the chronicity within the events of one single anecdote. As strange as this narrative might appear to foreign eyes and ears, it was perceived by me as perfectly acceptable and highly entertaining at the time of the interview.[7] Here, as with the previous example, the temporal analysis combined with the evaluative dimension offers an illuminating perspective for interpreting how meaning and structure are intertwined in Ana's performance. First, if we observe the analeptic events of this narrative (i.e., clauses 19 and 26),[8] it becomes evident that both refer to the most emotionally charged moment of Ana's narrativized experience: the moment her nose bled. Both clauses include, in addition, evaluative onomatopoeias, and the second one (i.e., clause 26) is even accompanied by the physical enactment of the scene. Thus, these analeptic events are both functioning as evaluative devices to emphasize how awful her accident was.

---

[7] In fact, I was not even aware of anything happening at the temporal level.
[8] Clauses 24 and 25 are "reported-speech clauses" of what the doctor said; therefore, they are just partial departures.

Temporal Analysis of Narrative 4

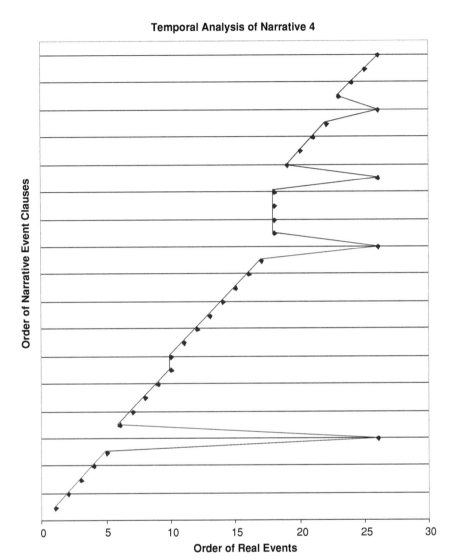

Figure 8.4. Temporal analysis of Narrative 4, told by Ana; a 6;9 year-old girl.

Then, if we go further to analyze the events that Ana chooses to repeat throughout the narrative, they are the cause of the most emotionally loaded point (13, 24); the most emotionally charged point, itself (19, 26); and the final resolution (15, 18, 27). Contrary to telling a temporally disorganized narrative, what this girl is doing is rhetorically evaluating the most salient events of this particular experience through the narrative structure. Instead of arbitrarily telling nonsequential events in a disorganized fashion, she discriminates and selects the events that "deserve" to be highlighted through retrospection and repetition, and she achieves a dramatic performance that is highly effective.

Narratives With Proleptic Evaluation

Narrative 4 presents a series of continuing episodes about the life of Samanta, Ana's (6;9 years) cat. This especially long narrative consists of 95 clauses grouped in 6 episodes, which could be labeled as follows: (1) the arrival of the cat at Ana's home; (2) Ana's mother's acceptance of the cat; (3) the process of naming the cat; (4) and (5) the process of Samanta becoming a spoiled cat; (6) an evaluative episode; and (7) finally, a reference to Samanta's descendants (see Appendix A for the complete version of this narrative). Throughout this extended "life history," a proleptic event is constantly stated: the fact that Samanta turned into a spoiled and lazy pet when she grew up. Ana moves beyond chronicity several times in her telling: she highlights the final end of her narrative and goes back to continue with the cat's story. This interesting narrative connects episodes of the lifetime of a cat with the function of showing how the narrator herself and her family caused the transformation of Samanta into a spoiled pet. The episodes themselves are thus evaluative, but the point is further emphasized by repeated reference to the proleptic event: Samanta's spoiling. Figure 8.4 displays the temporal graph of this narrative.

In summary, these three narratives illustrate not only that these children express departures from the timeline but also that such departures function to evaluate a specific point in the story.

MIDWESTERN ENGLISH NARRATIVES: CHRONICITY AS THE GOAL

In the English dataset, the two full departures – in addition to representing a minimal proportion of the group – exhibit very different characteristics from those observed in the Spanish group. One narrative with full departure was produced by a 5-year-old girl, Lucy, and the other by a 7-year-old girl, Rose. The relevant fragments of both narratives are reproduced herein.

PART 1

Child:	My friend Gary Shovel, he's in first grade
	and I went over there
	and they were eating supper
	(…)
	And I was waiting on the bed
	and, um, Gary, well, he, his mother gave him a jelly glass
	and he broke it
Interviewer:	And he broke it.

PART 2

Child:	**After it was, um, after it,** whatever was in there **well** he drank it out after, after a while he was playing around with Cindy (. . .)
Child:	**Uh, yeah, and, um, well,** they got, when they played then he musta knocked his elbow, but it musta . . .
Interviewer:	He must have knocked his elbow? Uh huh?
Child:	And, and, then, um, jelly glass musta slipped offa the table and it broke.

The next narrative is about a trip to Rose's Grandpa, Jamie, and Elsie's house. After an elaborated orientation, Rose continues as follows[9]:

Child:		(. . .)
	15	so, we ate breakfast
	16	we got dressed
	17	packed our suitcases (. . .)
	20	so we went
	21	and we got there (. . .)
	29	and we called Jamie for surprise
	30	and, so we went there
	31	and Ricky told us
	32	where she (= Elsie) was, at Margaret's, at the party
	33	Ricky didn't want to go
	34	See, he's lazy
	35	*He flunked a lot of times*
	36	*He just graduated*
Interviewer	Oh.	
Child	**And, so** [pause] we went over to Margaret's and knocked on the door	

(Rose, 7-year-old girl)

The highlighted portions of the examples in both narratives indicate that the moves out of chronicity are signaled by discourse markers (Schiffrin, 1994), which function both as flashing lights and as transitional bridges between the chronological sequence and the deviation. This is an illuminating finding

---

[9] Given the length of this narrative, I have selected just the clauses containing temporally anchored events, which are the relevant ones for the analysis.

that retrospectively enriches the analysis of Andean Spanish narratives by fore-grounding the natural way in which these children move in and out of chronic-ity without any need for special markers. Lucy's and Rose's discourse markers are expressed in the form of repetitions, hesitations, and pauses; it is enor-mously interesting that children of this young age are already recognizing the need to mark the deviation. This expressed need seems to confirm Peterson and McCabe's (1983) finding of the importance of sequentiality for this cul-tural/linguistic group. Another illustrative example of this tendency toward sequentiality is the following narrative fragment by Paul, a 5-year-old boy:

> (...) And then I went to the Amherst hospital
> **no, which before I went to the Amherst hospital**
> it was bleeding real bad (...)

This repair made by Paul suggests that he is learning to follow the order of real events in his narrative. When he suddenly jumps ahead, he then goes back, corrects himself, and then continues with the narrative. This example suggests that for this child, departures from sequentiality constitute nonacceptable moves. Not only is the form of introducing these two full departures markedly different from the Andean ones but also their function. In Lucy's narrative, she tells first – in perfect chronological sequence – the events she witnessed at her friend's house. After finishing ("and he broke it"), there is no real analeptic move because all of what she tells afterwards are not actual events but rather her conjectures about what had happened. Thus, this narrative offers a peculiar pattern in which the "pseudo-analeptic" move corresponds to the transition between narrated events and narrated conjectures. Lucy's narrative could be described as *a sequential narrative plus an addendum.*

The departure in the second example (i.e., *He flunked a lot of times. He just graduated*) matches perfectly the description of full departure. It does not, however, classify as structural evaluation. This girl is clearly deviating from the real timeline by referring directly to nonsequential events (full departure), but this analeptic move is not serving the purpose of emphasizing the main point of her story. Here, Rose is introducing a new character in her narrative and giving contextual information that serves as evidence for her assertion: *He's lazy.* No further point is emphasized by this analeptic move. In fact, the narrative is best characterized as a chain of events with no real highpoint (Peterson & McCabe, 1983).

In summary, not only are structural evaluations absent from the English dataset but, moreover, full temporal departures are rare; in the atypical cases in which they occur, they are heavily marked as deviations from the preferred sequential pattern in this cultural/linguistic group. The absence of structural evaluation in these English narratives contrasts with the increasing presence of this phenomenon in the older group of Andean Spanish-speaking children.

ANDEAN SPANISH NARRATIVES: MULTIPLE ANECDOTES

The Andean children also used supplementary anecdotes to mark important events and emphasize particular points in their narrative. Alonso's narrative is offered here as an example.

Narrative With Multianecdotal Evaluation

In narrative 5, Alonso (5;1-year-old boy) tells us, first, that his uncle got stung by a mosquito (anecdote 1); then, that his sister got stung in a different city also by a mosquito (anecdote 2); then, that he, Alonso, also got stung once (anecdote 3); and finally, he starts with a longer anecdote (4) in which he got stung at night by a mosquito and then was cured by his mother. This narrative ends with an embedded episode in which his mother gets stung while throwing away the mosquitoes that had first stung Alonso. In this case, all these anecdotes emphasize that not only he but also other people get stung. This issue is further highlighted when he says, close to the end, *my mother did not know that there were some things to sting children and mothers and fathers*. Thus, even though the evaluated point of the narrative is not clearly stated at any point, it is easily inferred from the whole structure. These stories might be seen as simply associations of related topics but, in fact, they are evaluative (see Appendix B for the complete version of this narrative).

The English multianecdotal narratives were produced by a 6-year-old girl, Karen, and by a 7-year-old boy, Brian. In the latter case, the boy told two independent anecdotes, but both happened the same day during a visit to the zoo. Thus, this narrative offers a chain of two incidents that were sequentially and closely experienced. Karen's narrative, on the other hand, connects two drowning experiences: the first one very briefly, almost in the form of an abstract, and the second one in a detailed style. It is interesting, as was also seen in the case of full departures, that Karen marks the transition to a new anecdote. She actually does it very explicitly by saying, after the first summarized anecdote, *and the next time it happened,* and continues with the second incident. However, Karen's first anecdote was so briefly developed that it is difficult to see how it could be evaluative rather than just orientative.

Again, within the narrative-components dimension, the different frequencies and characterizations of the phenomenon for the two groups suggest diverse cultural/linguistic narrative tendencies, which the differential presence of discourse markers seems to confirm.

To summarize, the main distinctive feature found in these Andean Spanish-speaking children's narratives is the use of structural evaluation. This evaluative strategy is not located at the clause level but rather affects the entire structuring of a narrative. Structural evaluation takes one of two forms, either (1) a functional deviation from the timeline of real events – which can include analepses or

Table 8.8. *Andean Spanish-speaking children's narratives with*
structural evaluation

	Sequential	Analeptic	Proleptic	Total
# of Narratives	3	4	2	9 (28%)
# of Children	3	3	2	5 (63%)

Narrative #3 presents both analeptic and proleptic moves, whereas narrative #4 presents both sequence of stories and proleptic moves. However, in this table, I classified them according to their most salient feature. Narrative #3 is included in the analeptic category and narrative #4 in the proleptic category.

prolepses; or (2) an inclusion of a sequence of anecdotes within a single narrative for emphasizing a not-always-explicit point.

Table 8.8 displays the number of narratives and children that presented structural evaluation. In summary, the table indicates that 9 of the 32 (approximately 28%) Andean narratives show what I call structural evaluation. An interesting point is that narratives with analepsis and prolepsis were told only by girls and mostly by the older girls. This finding suggests that structural evaluation that goes beyond chronicity might be a developmental phenomenon in process in the age range from 6 to 8 years and might unfold differently across genders.

GENERAL DISCUSSION AND CONCLUSION

Structural evaluation displayed by Andean Spanish-speaking children included the following three forms:

1. *Analeptic evaluation: "a return to the past."* Analeptic evaluation consists of a return to past events or anecdotes to highlight something important in the narrative (e.g., narratives 2 and 3).
2. *Proleptic evaluation: "an excursion into the future."* This strategy consists of narrating an event at a point in the text before earlier events have been told with the purpose of emphasizing the point for telling the narrative (e.g., narrative 4).
3. *Multianecdotal evaluation: "a complex sequence."* Structural multianecdotal evaluation occurs when anecdotes chronologically organized are used to emphasize the point of the story (e.g., narrative 5).

Whereas deviations from the timeline have been described as indicators of language pathology or immaturity for U.S. White English-speaking children, in these Andean children's narratives, departures from the timeline serve a rhetorical function that reflects a complex narrative ability. In narratives with analeptic and proleptic evaluation, the real sequence of events was clearly reconstructable. In addition, these children produced sequential narratives at other points in the conversation, which further confirms their ability to report experiences in a chronologically organized manner. The sequencing of events, instead of being a neglected aspect, reflects a sophisticated rhetorical ability and represents a key to understanding why narratives are being told.

Gender differences suggest that Andean boys and girls might follow distinct developmental paths in their acquisition of personal-narrative discourse. All instances of full departures were produced by girls, resulting in narratives that highlight the emotional aspect of narratives more intensely as compared to those of boys, who mostly displayed multiple anecdotes. This might respond to girls being allowed to express their vulnerable emotions more fully than boys, a finding demonstrated for English-speaking children (Jansz, 2000). As research suggests, children's participation in language exchanges provides them with cultural understandings and cultural norms for expressing emotions, which include gender-appropriate forms of expression (Fivush & Buckner, 2000; Rogoff, 1990). Within this framework, we could hypothesize that narratives offer a context in which the expression of evaluation – and emotion – follows different norms across genders. This finding is still puzzling, however, and can only suggest a line of further inquiry, given that no research is yet available on the language socialization of emotions in Andean children.

An interpretation of the contrastive findings of this study points toward a hierarchy of dimensions – temporality and evaluation – that functions distinctively in the two cultural/linguistic groups. In the Andean children's narratives, the temporal organization was subordinated to the evaluative purposes. In other words, the timeline of the narrative followed the organization of events imposed by the need of these children to evaluate certain points of their story. In the U.S. Midwestern children's narratives, on the contrary, evaluation seemed to be subordinated to temporality. The narrative timeline for these children always followed the order of real events, and evaluation was conveyed only within the limits of chronicity: the action could be suspended but not altered. It is important to highlight that the two characterizations are not presented herein as exclusive paradigms. In fact, in the English examples, *pseudo-departures* and *pseudo-multiplicities* were identified, and sequential and unistructural narratives were also produced by Andean children. These characterizations are presented as tendencies that seem to represent culturally valued and prevalent narrative forms, but they do not necessarily exhaust all or exclude other possibilities.

Indeed, an immediate question that emerges from this study is: Are the patterns described herein typical of or exclusive to young monolingual speakers of Andean Spanish as compared to those of older speakers, to other Spanish varieties, or to other languages or cultural groups? On the one hand, due to the small numbers of children in this study, the findings are not generalizable to all monolingual Andean Spanish-speaking communities. On the other hand, although this study has revealed not previously described narrative patterns and has suggested an interpretative framework in which to understand them, the question of how those tendencies might relate to different cultural/linguistic factors remains unanswered. Linguistic features present in each language, styles of socialization and enculturation, and different parental beliefs and values regarding storytelling are among the most salient hypotheses that need to be assessed in further investigations.

However, a few insights from my own research might help to partially contextualize the current results. Research has extensively documented that children are socialized into the particular ways of sharing narratives in their family and culture. This line of research points to a homotypic developmental continuity in which early narrative practices are associated with later narrative skills. Moreover, a heterotypic continuity also seems to be part of the developmental progression because not only direct narrative experiences but also even more general talk about the nonpresent that starts very early on (i.e., between 2 and 3 years of age) has been shown to be predictive of later narrative performance in English-speaking children (Uccelli, Hemphill, Pan, & Snow, 2005). Following this line of inquiry with Spanish-speaking children, I explored the early coconstruction of narratives and nonpresent talk between parents and young children. Specifically, I focused on the emergence of temporality via grammatical and discourse skills in two Spanish-speaking girls followed from 2 to 3 years of age (Uccelli, 2003). That study revealed that the two girls achieved comparable grammatical skills (Uccelli, submitted); however, each one presented different ways of organizing discourse. Whereas one girl focused on sequentiality, the other frequently altered the chronicity of events to highlight what was meaningful to her in interactions that supported these flashbacks and anticipations. It is interesting that this latter girl grew up in a Latin American family (i.e., father from Puerto Rico; mother from Lima, Peru), whereas the former girl grew up in Madrid, Spain. This study is relevant to the current findings in two ways. First, functional moves out of chronicity might not be exclusive to Andean children. Second, these nonsequential patterns of narration might evolve from initial earlier forms of nonpresent talk coconstructed with adults who support flashbacks and anticipations.

Thus, even though cyclical conceptualization of time in the Andean cosmovision might be related in some way to discourse patterns prevalent today in Andean society (Uccelli, 1999), it might not be the crucial factor behind this narrative esthetic. My subsequent research suggests that moves beyond chronicity might be present at least in other populations of Spanish speakers.

It is interesting that flashbacks and anticipations are characteristic of many famous Latin American writers, such as Vargas Llosa and García Márquez (de Toro, 1992). Those authors' moves out of chronicity are interpreted as artful strategies through which the narrator signals different meanings. Tools from contemporary narratology (Genette, 1980) have proven useful for revealing that those children's departures from chronicity constitute meaningful discourse moves. The children in this study seem to be developing toward a cultural narrative aesthetic that emphasizes storytelling as a collection of stories and includes a structural use of evaluation that functionally affects the temporal construction of narratives. The question that remains is whether *beyond-chronicity* narratives might also be prevalent in other cultural/linguistic groups.

Caution should be exerted, however, to not generalize the current findings to other Spanish-speaking populations without further research. Indeed, when compared to Rodino et al.'s (1991) findings on Caribbean and Central American children, these results offer a warning against generalizing patterns for the pan-Latino population and motivate a quest for detailed description of specific Spanish-speaking groups, so that common as well as particular discourse features can be identified. This claim also applies to Latino bilingual children from the United States. Findings on monolingual Spanish speakers' narratives might prove relevant for bilingual children, particularly given research that suggests transfer of narrative structure skills across languages (Pearson, 2002; Uccelli & Páez, 2007). However, Latino children in the United States come from different countries, from families with various characteristics, and from different language-socialization patterns. Although findings on monolingual Spanish speakers might be informative for research and practice, researchers, teachers, and clinicians need to acknowledge the wide variety entailed by the term *Latino* or *Spanish speaker*.

In this world of increasing cultural/linguistic heterogeneity, the role of researchers in developing alternative models of narrative performance helps teachers and language clinicians to have alternative criteria for interpreting and assessing the performance of any child. It is becoming increasingly inaccurate to identify ethnicity, place of origin, or even language with one specific culture. Consequently, on the one hand, broad guidelines for understanding the narrative development of children from different cultural/linguistic backgrounds are extremely helpful. On the other hand, it is necessary to remember that each child is unique and reflects diverse experiences not always easily classifiable as those of one discrete cultural group. Children vary enormously even within the same cultural group. Therefore, alternative cultural/linguistic models of narrative ability should be applied as options for interpreting the performance of any child with the purpose of achieving a more realistic assessment and a deeper understanding of children's skills.

ACKNOWLEDGMENTS

I want to express my gratitude to Catherine Snow, Sheldon White, Ruth Berman, and Allyssa McCabe for their comments, support, and encouragement throughout this project. Allyssa's generosity deserves special thanks because she made her data available to me for comparative purposes. I also want to thank the Spencer Foundation for a grant that supported the writing of this study. Thanks also go to Nani Pease and Gigliana Melzi for their help with transcription and reliability, respectively. Finally, my deepest thanks go to the children who cheerfully shared their stories with me and to the Pukllasunchis School in Cusco, which trustingly and generously opened its doors to me.

APPENDIX A: NARRATIVE 4 BY ANA (6;9 YEAR-OLD GIRL)

INV:	INV:
¿Quieres contarme algo más o no?	Do you want to tell me something else or not?

CHILD:	CHILD:
De cuando ha venido mi gata Samanta a mi casa.	About when my cat Samanta came home.

INV:	INV:
Ah, cuéntame.	OK, tell me about it.

CHILD:

Mi mamá tenía una amiga	My mother had a friend
y su amiga tenía una gata bien hermosita	and her friend had a really beautiful cat
así de este porte	{it was} like this big
	[shows size with her hands]
bien hermosita tenía	{she} had a really beautiful {one}
pero yo no sé	but I don't know
cómo es su mama de la Samanta.	what Samanta's mother looks like.
Así que ese día Fabricio y yo estábamos durmiendo con Marlene ahí en la cama	So that day Fabricio [her brother] and me were sleeping with Marlene on the bed
estábamos durmiendo	{we} were sleeping
y Fabri abrió la puerta	and Fabri opened the door
todavía nosotros estábamos durmiendo	{we} were still sleeping
y yo tenía una herida acá	and I had an injury here
	[points to her arm]
y fui a la sala	and {I} went to the living room
y vi a la gatita pues	and {I} saw the little cat
¡miau miau miau! me hizo	meow, meow, meow the cat did to me
me quería mucho	{she = the cat} loved me very much
¡mua! le di un beso	mua! {I} gave her a kiss
entonces como la estaba apretando tanto	then since {I} was hugging her so much
no me arañó nada	{she} didn't scratch me or anything
era media mansita	{she} was a little tame
cuando era bebita.	when {she} was a baby.
Ahora se ha vuelto una peleonera	Now {she} has become a spoiled fighter

INV:	INV:
Así... una peleonera.	So... a spoiled fighter

CHILD:

Ajá.

Y entonces cuando mi mamá vino
yo la escondí en una silla
"Como me quieres
me vas a aceptar"

"¡Vete!"
"¡Vete!"
Y no le hacía ver a mi mamá
y no le había tapado nada

así nomás le estaba haciendo

y el gato se había escapado
y mi mami "¡Ay, qué bonito!"
y entonces se fue la Florida.
porque su amiga se llama Florida
y entonces ella, mi mami, le pusieron Malú

INV:

¿A quién?

CHILD:

A mi gata Samanta.

INV:

Ahí le cambiaron el nombre.

CHILD:

No.

Primero le pusieron Malú.
y entonces no le gustaba
¡Malú, Malú, Malú Madera!

Nada no venía.
¡Malú, Malú, Malú Madera!
Nada.
¡Malú, Malú, Malú Madera!
Nada.

CHILD:

Mhm.

And then when my mom came
I hid it under a chair
"Since you love me
you will obey me"
[as if talking to her cat]

"Go away!"
"Go away!"
And {I} did not let my mom see her
and {I} had not even covered her or anything

just like that {I} was doing
[moving her arms]

and the cat had escaped
and my mom: "Oh, how pretty!"
and then Florida left
because her friend is called Florida
and then she, my mom, named her Malú

INV:

Whom {did they name}?

CHILD:

My cat Samanta.

INV:

Then {you} changed her name.

CHILD:

No.

First {they = impersonal} named her Malú
and then she did not like {it}
Malú, Malú, Malú Madera!
[name of a Brazilian actress]

nothing, {she} would not come
Malú, Malú, Malú Madera!
Nothing.
Malú, Malú, Malú Madera!
Nothing.

Entonces el Fabri dijo:	Then Fabri said:
"Frazada"	"Blanket"
	[meaning: Let's call her Blanket]
Entonces mi mami dijo:	Then my mommy said:
"Ya sé,	"I know,
que se llame Samanta."	{she} should be called Samanta."
y le pusieron el nombre pues Samantita.	and then {they = impersonal} named her Samantita.
Y un día la Samantita había estado mal con tos	And one day Samantita was sick with a cough
y la estaban curando	and {they = impersonal} were healing her
y una mañana a la Samanta <cada> le compraban su atún	and one morning for Samanta <every>, {they = impersonal} would buy her tuna
ahora ya no le compran	now they = impersonal don't buy that anymore.
INV:	**INV:**
Ya no . . .	Not anymore . . .
CHILD:	**CHILD:**
Ya no.	Not anymore.
Es que se ha vuelto una majadera.	Because {she} has become spoiled.
Entonces ese día yo le enseñé	Then that day I taught her
y tenía una cunita, una cajita pues	and {she} had a little cradle, a box
para que duerma.	to sleep in.
Entonces yo le digo,	Then I say,
yo le enseñé así	I taught her like that
ahora se ha vuelto una vaga por eso	now {she} has become lazy because of that
porque yo le he enseñado eso	because I have taught her that.
INV:	**INV:**
¿Qué le has enseñado?	What have you taught her?
CHILD:	**CHILD:**
"Métete."	"Go in"
	[as if talking to her cat]
"Métete en tu cama."	"Go in bed"
Los enfermitos nomás se ponen a la cama	Only sick {people/animals} go to bed
y la tape así y nada la gatita no quería	and {I} covered her, and nothing the cat did not want to
"Métete."	"Go in."

Así y me fui rápido.	Like that and {I} left quickly.
yo me he ido rápido.	I left quickly.
y la gatita estaba ahí	and the cat was there
aburrida estaba.	{she} was bored.
Es que sé	I know
que tenía hambre	{she} was hungry
por eso iba a traerle atún.	that's why {I} was going to bring her tuna.
Pero no tenía hambre,	But {she} was not hungry,
Nada.	Nothing.
Así que desde ese día ya se ha vuelto una vaga.	So since that day she has become lazy.

INV:

Desde ese día se volvió una vaga . . .

CHILD:

Y pronto va creciendo

va creciendo

y ahora es bonita

pero es una rascamiche

INV:

Since that day she became lazy . . .

CHILD:

And soon {she} is growing

and growing

and now {she} is pretty

but {she} is too spoiled

[**CHILD** uses particularly funny word for "lazy" here]

y además de eso te quita la carne de tu boca,	and besides that, {she} takes the meat away from your mouth.

INV:

¡Qué cosa!

CHILD:

Es una medio raterita la Samanta ahora

Ahora si la Samanta está llorando,

no como antes que siempre le comprábamos su atún diario

ahora ya no le compramos su atún

"Oye, ya estás grande."

INV:

What!

CHILD:

Samanta is like a little thief now

Now if Samanta is crying,

not like before when {we} used to buy her tuna daily

now {we} don't buy her tuna any longer

"Hey, you are old now"

[as if **CHILD** is talking to cat]

y su hijito pues se quedó	and her son stayed [with us]
En la primera cría todos se murieron	In the first litter, all of them died
pero en la segunda sigue vivo uno, el negro	but in the second {litter} one is alive, the black one
y sus hermanitos más están en otras casas.	and his little siblings are in other houses.

APPENDIX B: NARRATIVE 5 BY ALONSO (5;1-YEAR-OLD BOY)

INV:

¿Y algún otro bicho?

CHILD:

Le vi a mi tío.

a mi tío, a mi tío que le había picado quí

también a mi hermana

y aquí le picó un mosco en Quillabamba

INV:

Le picó un mosco en Quillabamba.
¿Y de ahí?

CHILD:

De ahí, de ahí, también a mí me picó.

INV:

¿Cómo fue?

CHILD:

Me picó aquí en xx unas veces en Moyopata.

INV:

¿Y te dolió?

CHILD:

Sí.

INV:

¿Y qué pasó después?

CHILD:

Después pasió [=pasó] una cosa
que cuando dormí en la cama
en la cama no sabía mi mama
que había unas cosas
unas cosas para picar a los niños y a las mamás y a los papás
me había picado.

INV:

Otro te picó en la noche. ¿Y después?

INV:

And by any other insect?

CHILD:

{I} saw my uncle.

my uncle, my uncle had gotten stung here
[**CHILD** points to shoulder]

{I} also {saw} my sister

and here she got stung by a mosquito in Quillabamba [a Peruvian city]
[**CHILD** points to his arm]

INV:

She got stung by a mosquito in Quillabamba. And then?

CHILD:

Then, then, I got stung too.

INV:

What happened?

CHILD:

I got stung here in xx sometimes in Moyopata [a Peruvian city]

INV:

And did it hurt?

CHILD:

Yes.

INV:

And what happened next?

CHILD:

Then one thing happened
that when {I} slept on the bed
on the bed, my mother did not know
that there were some things
some things that sting children, mothers, and fathers
{it} stung me.

INV:

You were stung by another one at night
And then?

CHILD:	CHILD:
Después me dolió.	Then it hurt.
Mi mamá me curó eso.	My mom cured me of that.
y ya botó esas cosas.	and {she} threw these things away
y un bicho a su mano le cogió	and a bug caught her hand
y le hizo eso	and did it to her
y el bicho se escapó.	and the bug escaped.

REFERENCES

Ames, P. (2005). When access is not enough: Educational exclusion of rural girls in Peru. In S. Aikman & E. Unterhalter (Eds.), *Beyond access*. London: Oxfam Publishing.

Bakeman, R., & Gottman, J. (1986). *Observing interaction: An introduction to sequential analysis*. New York, NY: Cambridge University Press.

Bamberg, M. (1997). *Narrative development: Six approaches*. Mahwah, NJ: Lawrence Erlbaum Associates.

Bocaz, A. (1989). Desarrollo de la referencia temporal adverbial. *Lenguas Modernas, 16*, 23–40.

Bruner, J. (1990). *Acts of meaning*. Cambridge, MA: Harvard University Press.

Camacho, J., Paredes, L., & Sánchez, L. (1995). The genitive clitic and the genitive construction in Andean Spanish. *Probus, 7*(2), 133–146.

Cazden, C., Michaels, S., & Tabors, P. (1985). Spontaneous repairs in sharing time narratives: The intersection of metalinguistic awareness, speech event, and narrative style. In S. Freedman (Ed.), *The acquisition of written language* (pp. 51–64). Norwood, NJ: Ablex.

Cerrón Palomino, R. (1972). Enseñanza del castellano: Deslindes y perspectivas. In A. Escobar (Ed.), *El reto del multilingüismo en el Perú*. Lima: Instituto de Estudios Peruanos.

Cohen, J. (1960). A coefficient of agreement for nominal scales. *Educational and Psychological Measurement, 20*, 37–46.

de Toro, A. (1992). Los laberintos del tiempo: Temporalidad y narración como estrategia textual y lectoral en la novela contemporánea. G. García Márquez, M. Vargas Llosa, J. Rulfo, A. Robbe-Grillet. Frankfurt am Main: Vervuert Verlag.

Escobar, A. (1978). *Variaciones sociolingüísticas del castellano en el Perú*. Lima: Instituto de Estudios Peruanos.

Fivush, R., & Buckner, J. P. (2000). Gender, sadness, and depression: The development of emotional focus through gendered discourse. In A. H. Fischer (Ed.), *Gender and emotion: Social psychological perspectives* (pp. 232–253). Cambridge, UK: Cambridge University Press.

Flannagan, D., & Perese, S. (1998). Emotional references in mother–daughter and mother–son dyads' conversations about school. *Sex Roles, 39*, 353–367.

Gee, J. (1996). *Social linguistics and literacies: Ideology in discourses*. London: Taylor and Francis.

Genette, G. (1980). *Narrative discourse*. Ithaca, NY: Cornell University Press.

Godenzzi, J. C. (1995). The Spanish language in contact with Quechua and Aymara: The use of the article. In C. Silva Corvalán (Ed.), *Spanish in four continents: Studies in language contact and bilingualism* (pp. 101–116). Washington, DC: Georgetown University Press.

Gutiérrez-Clellen, V., & Heinrichs-Ramos, L. (1993). Referential cohesion in the narratives of Spanish-speaking children: A developmental study. *Journal of Speech and Hearing Research, 36*(3), 559–567.

Gutiérrez-Clellen, V., & Quinn, R. (1995). Accommodating cultural differences in narrative style: A multicultural perspective. *Topics in Language Disorders, 15*(4), 54–67.

Hornberger, N. (1988). *Bilingual education and language maintenance: A Southern Peruvian Quechua case.* Providence, RI: Foris Publications.

Hudson, J. A. (1993). Reminiscing with mothers and others: Autobiographical memory in young two-year-olds. *Journal of Narrative and Life History, 3*(1), 1–32.

Hudson, J. A., & Shapiro, L. R. (1991). From knowing to telling: The development of children's scripts, stories and personal narratives. In A. McCabe & C. Peterson (Eds.), *Developing narrative structure* (pp. 89–136). Hillsdale, NJ: Lawrence Erlbaum Associates.

INEI (2005). *X Censo de Población y V de Vivienda.* Lima: Instituto Nacional de Estadística e Información.

Jansz, J. (2000). Masculine identity and restrictive emotionality. In A. H. Fischer (Ed.), *Gender and emotion: Social psychological perspectives* (pp. 166–186). Cambridge, UK: Cambridge University Press.

Labov, W., & Waletzky, C. (1967). Narrative analysis: Oral versions of personal experience. In J. Helm (Ed.), *Essays on the verbal and visual arts.* Washington, DC: American Ethnological Society.

MacWhinney, B. (2000). *The CHILDES Project: Computational tools for analyzing talk.* Hillsdale, NJ: Lawrence Erlbaum.

Mandler, J. M., & Johnson, N. S. (1977). Remembrance of things parsed: Story structure and recall. *Cognitive Psychology, 9,* 111–151.

Manga Qespi, A. E. (1994). Pacha: Un concepto andino de espacio y tiempo. *Revista Española de Antropología Americana, 24,* 155–189.

McCabe, A. (1997a). Cultural background and storytelling: A review and implications for schooling. *The Elementary School Journal, 97*(5), 453–473.

McCabe, A. (1997b). Developmental and cross-cultural aspects of children's narration. In M. G. W. Bamberg (Ed.), *Narrative development: Six approaches* (pp. 137–174). Mahwah, NJ: Lawrence Erlbaum.

McCabe, A., & Rollins, P. R. (1994). Assessment of preschool narrative skills: Prerequisite for literacy. *American Journal of Speech-Language Pathology: A Journal of Clinical Practice, 4,* 45–56.

Melzi, G., & Fernández, C. (2004). Talking about past emotions: Conversations between Peruvian mothers and their preschool children. *Sex Roles, 50*(9/10), 641–657.

Michaels, S. (1981). "Sharing time": Children's narrative styles and differential access to literacy. *Language in Society, 10,* 423–442.

Minami, M. (2001). Maternal styles of narrative elicitation and the development of children's narrative skill: A study on parental scaffolding. *Narrative Inquiry, 11*(1), 55–80.

Minami, M., & McCabe, A. (1991). Haiku as a discourse regulation device: A stanza analysis of Japanese children's personal narratives. *Language in Society, 20*(4), 577–599.

Minaya-Portella, L. (1980). *Analysis of children's Peruvian Spanish narratives: Implications for the preparation of basic readers.* Unpublished doctoral disseration. University of Texas at Austin.

Montoya, R. (1990). *Por una educación bilingüe en el Perú: Reflexiones sobre cultura y socialismo.* Lima: Mosca Azul Editories.

Nelson, K. (1989). Monologue as the linguistic construction of self in time. In K. Nelson (Ed.), *Narratives from the crib.* Cambridge, MA: Harvard University Press.

Ochs, E., & Capps, L. (2001). Living narratives: Creating lives in everyday storytelling. Cambridge, MA: Harvard University Press.

Ortiz, A. (1992). El tratamiento del tiempo en los mitos andinos. *Debates en antropología, 8,* 66–76. Lima: Pontificia Universidad Católica del Perú.

Pearson, B. Z. (2002). Narrative competence among monolingual and bilingual school children in Miami. In D. K. Oller & R. E. Eilers (Eds.), *Language and literacy in bilingual children* (pp. 135–174). Clevedon, UK: Multilingual Matters.

Peterson, C. (2001). "I was really, really, really mad!" Children's use of evaluative devices in narratives about emotional events. *Sex Roles, 45,* 801–825.

Peterson, C., & McCabe, A. (1983). *Developmental psycholinguistics: Three ways of looking at a child's narrative.* New York, NY: Plenum Press.

Pozzi-Escot, I. (1972). El castellano en el Perú: Norma culta nacional vs. norma culta regional. In A. Escobar (Ed.), *El reto del multilingüismo en el Perú.* Lima: Instituto de Estudios Peruanos.

Pozzi-Escot, I., & Zúñiga, M. (1989). *Temas de lingüística aplicada.* Lima: CONCYTEC.

Randall, R. (1982). Qoyllur Rit'i, an Inca fiesta of the Pleiades: A reflection of time and space in the Andean world. *Institut Français d'Études Andines, 11,* 37–81.

Rimmon-Kenan, S. (1983). *Narrative fiction: Contemporary poetics.* New York, NY: Routledge.

Rodino, A., Gimbert, C., Pérez, C., & McCabe, A. (1991). *Getting your point across: Contrastive sequencing in low-income African American and Latino children's personal narratives.* Paper presented at the 16th Annual Conference on Language Development, Boston University.

Rogoff, B. (1990). *Apprenticeship in thinking: Cognitive development in social context.* Oxford: Oxford University Press.

Schiffrin, D. (1994). *Approaches to discourse.* Cambridge, MA: Blackwell.

Sebastián, E., & Slobin, D. (1994). Development of linguistic forms: Spanish. In R. Berman & D. Slobin (Eds.), *Relating events in narrative: A cross-linguistic developmental study* (pp. 239–284). Hillsdale, NJ: Lawrence Erlbaum.

Seligmann, L. (2004). Peruvian street lives: Culture, power, and economy among market women of Cusco. Urbana: University of Illinois Press.

Shiro, M. (2003). Genre and evaluation in narrative development. *Journal of Child Language, 30*(1), 165–195.

Slobin, D. (1996). Two ways to travel: Verbs of motion in English and Spanish. In M. Shibatani & S. Thompson (Eds.), *Grammatical constructions: Their form and meaning.* New York: Oxford University Press.

Stein, N. L. & Glenn, C. G. (1979). An analysis of story comprehension in elementary school children. In R. O. Freedle (Ed.), *New directions in discourse processing* (pp. 255–282). Norwood, NJ: Ablex, Hillsdale.

Uccelli, F. (1999). Democracia en el sur andino: Posibilidades y esfuerzos de las familias campesinas para educar a sus hijos. In M. Tanaka (Ed.), *El poder visto desde abajo.* Lima: Instituto de Estudios Peruanos.

Uccelli, P. (1999). *Temporality and evaluation in Andean Spanish-speaking children's narratives.* Paper presented as an invited speaker at Developmental Colloquium, New York University.

Uccelli, P. (2003). *Time and narratives: The development of temporality in young Spanish-speaking children.* Unpublished doctoral dissertation. Harvard Graduate School of Education.

Uccelli, P., Hemphill, L., Pan, B., & Snow, C. (2005). Conversing with toddlers about the nonpresent: Precursors to narrative development in two genres. In L. Balter & C. Tamis-LeMonda (Eds.), *Child psychology: A handbook of contemporary issues.* New York: Psychology Press.

Uccelli, P., & Páez, M. (2007). Narrative and vocabulary development of bilingual children from kindergarten to first grade: Developmental changes and associations among English and Spanish skills. *Language, Speech, and Hearing Services in Schools, 38*(3), 225–236.

Uccelli, P. (in press). Emerging temporality: Past-tense and temporal/aspectual markers in Spanish-speaking children's intra-conversational narratives. *Journal of Child Language.*

Zavala, V. (2001). Borrowing evidential functions from Quechua: The role of *pues* as a discourse marker in Andean Spanish. *Journal of Pragmatics: An Interdisciplinary Journal of Language Studies, 2001 July, 3*(7), 999–1023.

9

Narrative Stance in Venezuelan Children's Stories

MARTHA SHIRO

Key words: narrative genre, evaluative language, discourse perspective

ABSTRACT

This chapter focuses on Venezuelan children's use of evaluative language in the construction of narrative stance. Two types of stories, personal and fictional, are compared in terms of the strategies used in narrative perspective building. Certain aspects of evaluative language (e.g., use of modal expressions and reported speech) are examined in detail to determine how children combine the voice of *self* and *other* in narrative production. The main purpose is to determine the ways in which narrative type, children's age, gender, and social class affect narrative production.

For this study, 444 (personal and fictional) stories were elicited in semistructured interviews conducted in 6 (public and private) schools with 113 monolingual native speakers of Venezuelan Spanish between the ages of 6 and 11. Of these children, 52 were girls and 61 were boys; 54 were from a low-socio-economic status (SES) and 59 were from a high-SES background. The results show that children adjust to genre requirements because the same child can use different strategies in personal and fictional narratives. The findings also suggest that certain grammatical forms (e.g., modal expressions) are still developing in this age group. Moreover, children's sociocultural background has a considerable effect in fictional storytelling, but the effect of SES is negligible in the production of personal narratives. This in-depth analysis of school-age children's oral narrative abilities can shed light on the difficulties they may face when they start acquiring productive and receptive skills related to written narratives.

INTRODUCTION

"To breathe is to judge" – an observation attributed to the British poet, John Dryden, in the 17th century and cited by Sarangi (2003, p. 165) – highlights

213

the idea that evaluating is an inescapable, omnipresent human activity. Relative to evaluation in language, Sarangi (2003, p. 165) offers Voloshinov's statement (1973, p. 105):

> No utterance can be put together without value judgment. Every utterance is above all an evaluative orientation. Therefore, each element in a living utterance not only has a meaning but also has a value.

Functional approaches to language use (Halliday, 1985; Jakobson, 1975) have emphasized that conveying information is not always the main or the only purpose of communication. Evaluating is just as important, if not more so, depending on the communicative event in which the interaction is taking place. Halliday (2004) suggests that the ideational function explains how speakers and writers use linguistic resources to inform and to convey experience, whereas the interpersonal function encompasses the options for evaluating through linguistic means.

In this chapter, I examine the ways in which Venezuelan children use evaluative language in the construction of narrative perspective. For the purposes of this study, evaluative language in narrative production is understood as linguistic expressions referring to emotions, attitudes, beliefs, and affect –that is, nonfactual, perspective-building elements contributing to the expressive function of the story (Labov, 1972; Shiro, 2003, 2004). Because all language use is inserted in a contextual framework, language functions are combined in different ways depending on the discourse genre being constructed and on the speaker's communicative purposes within a particular situational context (e.g., Bakhtin, 1986; Shiro, 2003). In this study, the uses of evaluative language are examined in two different types of narrative discourse: personal experience and fictional storytelling. Studies on narrative-discourse production (Labov, 1972; Shiro, 1999–2000, 2001) agree on the importance of evaluative language in "getting the story across" – in other words, in ensuring that the story is a meaningful contribution to the ongoing interaction. Labov (1972) explained that each narrative should carry implicitly the answers to the listener's question: "Why are you telling me this now?" To fulfill this requirement, the narrative is organized around a highpoint and is told from a certain point of view (just like a painting is drawn from a certain angle).

The main purpose of this chapter is to examine how children construct a narrative perspective in different storytelling activities. The questions that guided this research are as follows:

1. How is evaluative language used in narrative perspective building?
2. In what ways do a child's age, SES, and gender affect the representation of *self* and *other* in narrative discourse?
3. What effect, if any, does narrative genre have on how a child builds discourse perspective?

This chapter is organized in two sections. First, I focus on the use of evaluative language in general and its contribution to narrative perspective building in personal and fictional stories, thus highlighting the development of children's ability to adjust to the contextual requirements of the interaction (Shiro, 2003). Second, I take a closer look at a specific type of evaluative language – speech representation – through which the combination of narrative voices is explicitly displayed.

CONCEPTUAL FRAMEWORK

Narrating is a fundamental activity in all contexts of language use: it is frequent in everyday language, in spoken and written forms, and in academic and literary uses of discourse. It is considered the means by which experience is conveyed to others and, as such, it serves to express subjectivity. Because children are surrounded with narrative discourse, they start developing storytelling abilities from the early age of 2 years, but it takes many more years for them to master all aspects and types of narrative discourse (Hudson & Shapiro, 1991; Peterson & McCabe, 1983).

Most studies on narratives emphasize the dual characteristic of this genre. Labov (1972) maintains that narratives have two basic functions (i.e., the referential and the expressive); Bruner (1990) describes a dual narrative landscape (i.e., the landscape of action and the landscape of consciousness). By expressing subjectivity, narratives contribute greatly to the construction and representation of a sense of self (Polkinghorne, 1991). Children go through phases in the process of self-construction through narratives (Engel, 1995). In the early phases, narratives are coconstructed by a parent and the child (Snow, 1990). Children gradually increase their participation in the narrative production by taking longer turns and taking the initiative more often. In this process, children acquire the ability to portray self and other in discourse (Astington, 1990; Lucariello, 1995). As a result, children can construct multiple perspectives in a story.

Undoubtedly, in the process of storytelling, it is the child, as a narrator, who filters all expressions of evaluation. However, when a child says, "The rat felt lost in the woods," he or she is clearly indicating that two distinct perspectives are at play: one is the narrator telling the story and the other is the character whose fear is being reported. Thus, evaluative language, which serves to express subjectivity, can be attributed to a first person (who is either a character in the story and/or a narrator) or to a third person (generally, a character in the story). Note that evaluation in narratives can only be grouped in first- and third-person perspectives, if comments to the addressee are excluded from the narrative text. I excluded these forms of address because they do not belong to the story-world that the child is representing, despite the fact that these comments might play an important evaluative role in the narrative at a discourse level. Here again, we come across the multifunctional aspect of evaluative expressions in narrative discourse. Discussion of this aspect, however, is beyond the scope of this study, which focuses on children's representation of thought, emotion, and speech as evaluative devices in narratives. Therefore, evaluative expressions assigned to the interlocutor (i.e., *imagínate* ["imagine"], *ves* ["(you) see"], *sabes* ["you know"]) are excluded from this analysis.

EVALUATIVE LANGUAGE AND NARRATIVE STANCE

Speakers necessarily adopt a certain point of view when using evaluative language because it expresses (the speaker's or others') subjectivity by reflecting emotion, thought, and speech. First- and third-person evaluations are defined as the agents to whom the evaluative assessment is attributed. Thus, when a child says, "I think they didn't notice that the little rat fell," the expression of cognition in the first clause is attributed to the speaker (i.e., first-person evaluation) and the expression of cognition in the second clause is attributed to someone else (i.e., third-person evaluation). A narrative in which first-person evaluation predominates is told from the narrator's perspective. In contrast, a narrative in which third-person evaluation is abundant, voices different from the narrator's take the lead. We can hypothesize that in fictional stories, third-person evaluation is more frequent (e.g., "Lion King was sad," "Samba got scared"), whereas in personal anecdotes, first-person evaluation is more abundant (e.g., "I was sad," "I got scared").

First-person evaluation may be singular or plural. When singular, it refers to the individual narrator/character. When plural, the evaluative expression is attributed to a group that should include the speaker/narrator. Third-person evaluation may also be singular or plural, but neither includes the speaker/narrator. Mühlhäusler and Harré (1990) explain that pronouns in discourse have primarily two functions: deictic and anaphorical. Although most studies focus on the anaphorical function (i.e., reference to some antecedent in discourse), the authors suggest that the deictic function of pronouns is more prevalent. Within the deictic function, pronouns are indexical; that is, they point to an extralinguistic referent. Mühlhäusler and Harré observed that first-person pronouns are doubly indexical. On the one hand, they situate the speaker in space and time; on the other, they indicate the speaker's degree of commitment or who takes moral responsibility for the speech act being performed. An example of who takes moral responsibility for an utterance is when an epistemic verb introduces a statement (e.g., "I think it will be finished soon"). Here, the speaker's commitment to the statement is qualified, and his or her moral responsibility for "it will be finished soon" is limited. More detachment on the speaker's part is possible if the utterance were, "He thinks it will be finished soon," given that the speaker explicitly leaves the moral responsibility for the statement to someone else and allows himself or herself the freedom to disagree. These distinctions can be grouped on a continuum of displacement, in Chafe's terms (1994), between spatiotemporal displacement and displacement of the self in representation of consciousness. According to Chafe's analysis, in spatiotemporal displacement, *represented* consciousness (i.e., the story-world) is displaced from the *representing* consciousness (i.e., the narrator's world) because the former is remote in space and time, whereas the latter operates in the speaker's immediate context. Displacement of self adds another dimension of remoteness because the representing consciousness (i.e., the story-world perspective) and the represented consciousness (i.e., the narrator's stance) belong to different persons.

A major difficulty, then, that a child faces in a narrative performance is the issue of displacement of self – namely, whether the narrative voice is attributed to a narrator or a character in the story, or whether certain attitudes are assigned to a character different from the self. In this chapter, I examine how children combine voices in narrative production, focusing on their representation of self and other by means of their use of evaluative language.

Because the most evident form of displacement of self is attributing the words one is uttering to another speaker (i.e., reporting somebody else's speech), a closer look at the different ways speech is reported can shed light on children's abilities regarding narrative perspective building. Therefore, in the second part of this chapter, I include an in-depth analysis of how children represent the story characters' speech by the use of reported speech.

METHOD

Participants

For this study, 113 first- and fourth-grade children were selected from three public and three private schools in Caracas. The children were monolingual native speakers of Venezuelan Spanish.

In the Venezuelan context, the rift between social classes is reflected in the educational system. Public education is considered inefficient, and a number of low-income families who care about their children's education make an effort to send them to private schools despite the economic burden that this may represent. As a result, public schools serve a low-SES population: children whose families cannot afford to pay for tuition. The three public schools selected for this study were situated in *barrios* ("neighborhoods") of extreme poverty. Thus, all the children interviewed in these schools come from a very low-SES background.

The social stratification of private schools is more varied for the reasons given previously. All SES groups strive for access to a private school because it promises an easier road to higher education. (A university degree is still a symbol for social mobility in Venezuela; however, in real life, a university graduate may earn less than a plumber or an electrician.) The three private schools selected for

Table 9.1. *Distribution of the sample (N = 113)*

	Low SES	High SES	Total
First-graders	27 children	29 children	56 children
Fourth-graders	27 children	30 children	57 children
TOTALS	54 children	59 children	113 children

this study served a high-SES population. Admission to these schools was very difficult and tuition fees extremely high. Therefore, the children interviewed in these schools belonged to very affluent families. The distribution in terms of age groups and SES is shown in Table 9.1.

The group consisted of 61 boys and 52 girls. The higher number of boys was due to the fact that one of the private schools was funded by a Catholic congregation (i.e., *La Compañía de Jesús*) and became coed only in the last 10 years. Even now, boys outnumber girls in every class.

As shown in Table 9.2, the children belonged to two separate age groups: the first-graders' mean was 7;2 years and the fourth-graders' mean was 10;1 years.

Procedures

The children selected for this study produced 444 stories in interviews in which they participated in four tasks. In two tasks, they produced fictional stories; in the other two tasks, they recounted personal narratives. In both fictional and personal narratives, each child responded to two types of elicitation. For the first, called *structured*, the child was given a model narrative to follow. In the case of the fictional-narrative task, the structured prompt was a wordless film, *Picnic*, which the child recounted.

In the personal-narrative task, the interviewer produced a short personal narrative and asked the children if something similar had happened to them. The interviewer produced three structured prompts in the personal-narrative task, given that children were not easily motivated to answer those prompts. If a child produced more than one narrative in response to the prompts, only the

Table 9.2. *Children's ages (N = 113)*

	Mean	SD	Range
First-graders	7;2*	0;5	6;5–7;11
Fourth-graders	10;1	0;5	9;1–10;9
The sample	8;8	1;7	6;5–10;9

*7 years and 2 months

Table 9.3. *Distribution of the narratives (N = 444)*

	Personal structured stories	Personal open-ended stories	Fictional structured stories	Fictional open-ended stories	Total
High-SES First-graders	29	29	29	29	116
Low-SES First-graders	25	26	27	26	104
High-SES Fourth-graders	29	29	30	30	118
Low-SES Fourth-graders	27	25	27	27	106
TOTALS	110	109	113	112	444

longest narrative (i.e., containing the highest number of clauses) was selected for the analysis.

For the second prompt, called *open*, children were asked an open question: in the fictional task, "Tell me your favorite film"; and in the personal-narrative activity, "Tell me something scary that happened to you." As shown in Table 9.3, not all children responded to all four prompts. The most "successful" prompt, the one to which every child responded, was the wordless video, *Picnic*.

All interviews were recorded and transcribed in Codes for the Human Analysis of Transcriptions (CHAT) (MacWhinney, 2000). The coding of the data reflected the use of evaluative language. The categories (described in Shiro, 2003) represented expressions of emotion, cognition, intention, relation, perception, and reported speech. For each category, perspective was indicated by signaling whether the evaluative expression was used from a first- or third-person viewpoint (see the appendix for examples of each analytic category). Cases of reported speech were analyzed in depth, focusing on whose voice was being reported; in what way was the reported language expressed (i.e., direct, indirect, free, or onomatopoeia); and the ways in which the report was framed by a reporting verb, clause, or expression.

To examine how narrative evaluation varies in terms of the entity to which it is assigned, I divided all evaluative expressions into those that refer to the first person (i.e., the child when it appears in singular or the child included in a group when it is plural) and those that refer to a third person, singular, or plural (i.e., incorporating the "voices" of other characters to that of the narrator). Thus, I have constructed two variables – a first-person and a third-person evaluation for each evaluative category (i.e., cognition = COG1, COG3; perception = PER1, PER 3) – to determine whose voice is present in the evaluative expressions. Each measure is calculated by multiplying the number of occurrences by 100 and then dividing by the number of clauses in the narratives. Thus, these measures express the percentages of evaluative clauses in the four narrative tasks combined for which the length of the narrative is controlled. The overall tendency of whose voice predominates in the narrative is reflected in the composite variables (i.e., evaluation = EVA1, EVA3), which measure for each child the percentage in the four narratives of all evaluative devices in the first and third person, respectively. Examination of evaluative expressions attributed to the self (i.e., first person) or to others (i.e., third person) enables us to observe how children shift perspectives in their narrative performance. It sheds light on whether children prefer to use certain evaluative devices in the first person (or third person) as well as children's tendencies to tell stories from the perspective of the self or the other.

For the more qualitative analysis of reported speech, in addition to labeling first- and third-person perspective, I registered which story character's voice was being reported and which type of reporting verb was used to introduce the reported utterances.

All transcripts were coded by the researcher. Two independent raters coded 20% of the narratives for all evaluative categories. Inter-rater reliability using Cohen's Kappa was estimated at 0.86, corrected for chance agreement.

THE RESULTS

Use of Evaluative Language in Narrative Perspective Building

As an initial approach, I examined the use of all types of evaluations to determine whether these expressions contributed equally to the representation of self and other in Venezuelan children's narrative production (Table 9.4).

The values for overall evaluation show that children tend to take a third-person stance in their narratives. However, the most frequent evaluative category, perception, was used mostly in first person, whereas all other categories appear

Table 9.4 *Descriptive statistics for evaluation type by evaluative stance*

Evaluation type	First person		Third person	
	M (SD)	Range	M (SD)	Range
Overall evaluation	17.75 (7.43)	1.85–41.05	27.82 (7.91)	5.08–46.40
Relation	0.97 (1.36)	0–6.93	9.18 (5.12)	0–28.57
Intention	0.98 (1.66)	0–10.77	4.76 (2.66)	0–13.86
Cognition	0.84 (1.20)	0–7.69	2.82 (1.87)	0–6.90
Perception	11.74 (6.99)	0–34.74	2.73 (2.28)	0–10.08
Emotion	1.11 (1.27)	0–6.45	2.35 (2.11)	0–9.76
Reported speech	0.79 (2.20)	0–16	2.27 (6.31)	0–29.03

to be predominantly presented in third person (exceeding by far their frequency in first person).

As a whole, third-person evaluation was more frequent than first-person evaluation. Comparing the overall mean of third-person evaluation, 27.82, to the overall mean of first-person evaluation, 17.75, a two-tailed T-test ($t_{2,105} = -7.67$, $p < .000$) showed a statistically significant difference, implying that school-age children's narratives are not essentially self-centered.

The delicate weaving of first- and third-person perspectives can be seen in the following extract of a 7-year-old's narrative (Alexis, male, 7;1 years, low-SES):

Spanish Original	English Translation
Mi mamá me contó un día que cuando yo estaba aprendiendo a caminar, que [...] en mi [...] mi tío dejó una taza de café, dejó que la sacaran de la cocina, y yo me la [...] y yo la agarré.	My mom told me one day that when I was learning to walk, that [...] my uncle left a cup of coffee, [he] let them take it out from the kitchen, and I [...] took it.

In just a few utterances, the child refers to a personal experience he had heard from his mother, an incident in which he got burned as a result of his uncle's carelessness. In this narrative, three perspectives are intertwined. First, the responsibility of the narrative's truth lies with the mother, who told the story in the first place. Second, the protagonist is the speaker who becomes the victim of the uncle's carelessness. Third, the motivating factor for the chain of events is the uncle's negligence, which was blamed for the accident.

The relationships among these kinds of evaluative expressions confirm the hypothesis that the use of first- and third-person evaluation is not necessarily an individual preference that children use at random. Rather, the analysis of the narratives suggests that the developmental trends of first- and third-person evaluation are different. Children increase their use of third-person evaluation with age ($F_{(2, 104)} = 1.48$, $p < .08$) (although the statistical analysis only approaches the significance level, we can detect a tendency in children's use of evaluation). As I examine the effect of age and SES on the development of evaluative language, I find that even though it only approaches significance ($F_{(3, 103)} = 2.4$, $p < .10$), first-person evaluation decreases with age in working-class children's narratives and increases slightly in middle-class children's narratives, whereas third-person evaluation increases slightly in both SES groups.

Thus, the tentative conclusion that can be drawn from this analysis is that there is a systematic pattern that children follow to express perspective in narratives. Previous findings (Shiro, 1999–2000, 2001) have already shown that children's development and SES shape the ways they use evaluative expressions. Older high-SES children use more evaluative expressions in their narratives. They also concentrate more evaluative expressions at the highpoint and, in general, tend to use a larger number of different evaluative categories than younger children (Shiro, 2003).

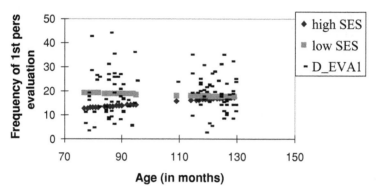

Figure 9.1. Fitted interaction effect of first-person evaluation (D_EVA1) on age and SES.

The analysis of the data in this study also shows that first- and third-person evaluations follow different developmental paths, as shown in Figure 9.1. Although third-person evaluation increases with age in both SES groups, high-SES children make more use, on average, of third-person evaluation than low-SES children. On the other hand, first- person evaluation has a tendency to decrease with age in low-SES children, whereas it increases with age in high-SES children's narratives. The implication of these conclusions is that there is a certain pattern in how children use evaluative expressions in oral narratives. To gain a better understanding of this pattern, it is necessary to determine to what extent genre affects the use of first- and third-person evaluative language.

NARRATIVE VOICE AND NARRATIVE GENRE

In narrative production, speakers must adopt a perspective from which they represent the self and others. Examination of the agent to whom the evaluation is attributed may shed light on how children's narrative skills develop. As discussed previously, a major distinction exists between evaluation attributed to the narrator and evaluation attributed to a character in the narrative. Therefore, I compared the use of first- and third-person evaluation in fictional and personal narratives.[1]

It is possible to assume that in fictional narratives, third-person evaluation is more frequent than in personal narratives, given the required additional displacement of self that characterizes fiction (Chafe, 1994; Ehrlich, 1990; Hyon & Sulzby, 1992; Scollon & Scollon, 1981).

---

[1] It is important to mention that the evaluative expressions in fiction (EVAF) reflect the use of evaluative expressions in two narrative tasks – open and structured – combined. Similarly, evaluative expressions in personal narratives (EVAP) combine the uses of evaluation in two personal-narrative tasks – open and structured – as described in the section about methods.

Table 9.5 *Mean, standard deviation, and range for evaluative stance in fictional and personal narratives (N = 107)*

Evaluative stance	Mean	Standard deviation	Range
Third-person stance in fiction	37.43	11.70	10.81–72.04
First-person stance in fiction	11.42	6.66	0–26.56
First-person stance in personal experience	30.09	17.64	0–93.33
Third-person stance in personal experience	12.54	11.36	0–47.37

The analysis reflected in Table 9.5 suggests that third-person evaluation in fictional narratives is the most frequently used, whereas first-person evaluation in personal narratives is second in rank, just as genre requirements would predict. However, the presence of first-person evaluation in fictional narratives and third-person evaluation in personal narratives cannot be ignored because it implies that fictional stories are not told solely from a third-person perspective, nor are personal narratives recounted from a first-person outlook alone.

Analysis of Pearson's bivariate correlation coefficients (as shown in Table 9.6) indicates that older children are likely to use more third-person evaluative expressions in fictional stories and tend to use fewer third-person expressions in personal narratives, following the constraints of the genre. However, the correlations also suggest that first-person evaluations in fictional narratives are more frequent in the high-SES group, implying that different "voices" are combined in their fictional stories. In personal narratives, no similar SES effect is found. This analysis shows that high-SES children are developing a narrative skill, which implies the combination of voices in fictional stories by making the

Table 9.6. *Correlation matrix of first- and third-person evaluation in fictional and personal narratives with age, SES (N = 107)*

	First-person evaluation, in fiction	Third-person evaluation in fiction	First-person evaluation, personal narrative	Third-person evaluation, personal narrative	Age	SES
First-person, fiction	1.00	−0.30**	0.18	−0.03	0.07	0.20*
Third-person, fiction		1.00	0.07	0.09	0.28**	0.06
First-person, personal narrative			1.00	−0.06	0.13	0.06
Third-person, personal narrative				1.00	−0.17~	0.15
Age					1.00	0.11
SES						1.00

~ $p < 0.1$ * $p < 0.05$ ** $p < 0.01$ *** $p < 0.001$

narrator's viewpoint more explicit. The following excerpt illustrates how the narrator's voice (underlined) is expressed in fictional stories (Chris, male, 10;9 years, high-SES):

Spanish Original	English Translation
Bueno, que dos [. . .] dos chamos enterrarron en [. . .] en mil ¿qué?, en 1869 un juego que [. . .] que <u>era de terror</u>. era [. . .] entonces este [. . .] en 1969 ya, un chamo lo encontró. y lo empezó a jugar. Entonces [. . .] entonces si [. . .] como sacó cinco. Sacó un cinco en los dados. Y él estaba jugando con una amiga. Sacó un cinco. y entonces el juego le dijo que [. . .] este [. . .] se me [. . .] tenía que meterse en el juego. Y cuando sacaban un cinco y un ocho volvía a poder salir. Entonces pasaron veintiseis años, <u>creo yo, no sé</u>. Este [. . .] un chamo sacó este [. . .] un cinco. Entonces apareció un león y <u>apareció él</u>, pero después. Y entonces [. . .] <u>bueno</u>, y entonces como la [. . .] la chama que estaba jugando con él, ya la edad, ya <u>tenía como cuarenta treinta y pico de años</u>. Este [. . .] tenía que seguir jugando. Porque si no lo te [. . .] si seguía jugando le podía suceder algo. Entonces los chamitos [. . .] dos [. . .] una chamita y un chamito que fueron los que sacaron el cinco también tenían que seguir jugando hasta que terminaran el juego. Hasta que lo terminaron. Y volvieron a retroceder veintiséis años, <u>creo</u>. Y volvie [..] volvió a dar resul [..] volvieron a subir hasta 1969, hasta 1996. Sí, pero <u>salían</u> monstruos, eh [. . .] rinocerontes, elefantes, <u>bueno</u> muchas cosas.	Well, that two kids, in one thousand something, in 1869, buried a terrifying game. Then, in a thousand <u>what?</u> In 1969, a kid found it and started to play. Then, then, as he threw 5, the dice said 5 and he was playing with a friend. He threw 5. And then the game told him that he had to get into the game. And when they threw 5 and 8, he could come out again. Then, 26 years went by, <u>I think, I don't know</u>. A kid threw 5, then a <u>lion appeared and he appeared</u>, but after that, then, <u>well</u>, then as the girl who was playing with him was <u>already forty, thirty something years old</u>, he had to play on because otherwise something [wrong] could happen. Then, the little boy and the little girl who had thrown 5 had to go on playing too till the game would be over. Till the game was over and they went back 26 years, <u>I believe</u>, they were again in 1969, till 1969. Yeah, but lots of <u>monsters were coming out</u>, rhinoceros, elephants, <u>well</u>, lots of things.

This is a passage of a 10-year-old's summary of *Jumanji* (1995, Columbia Pictures). Chris starts out by qualifying the game *un juego de terror* ("a terrifying game"), where he expresses his opinion of the game. Other traces of Chris's "voice" in this passage are as follows:

1. The use of epistemic modality: *creo, no sé, tenía como treinta y pico años, bueno* ("[I] believe," "[I] don't know," "[she] was about thirty something," "well").
2. The use of verbs like *apareció* ("appeared") and *salían* ("came out"), in which the narrator's visual perspective is clearly expressed. When the child describes that a lion appeared or that the monsters were coming

out, he is clearly taking his own visual focus. The proof can be found in the sequence, *apareció el león y apareció él* ("the lion appeared and he [= the protagonist] appeared"), where the narrator's perspective on the lion's appearance may coincide with the characters' perspective, but it cannot be the same as the narrator's perspective on the protagonist's own appearance in *apareció él.*

These first-person evaluative devices are intertwined with third-person evaluation – for example, the indirect reported speech, *el juego le dijo que tenía que meterse* ("the game told him that [he] had to get in [the game]"), where the game is personified and tells the boy what to do.

In summary, third-person evaluation in fictional stories increases with age, following genre requirements, for both SES groups. However, third-person evaluation in personal narratives decreases in low-SES groups (also following – as stated in the hypothesis – genre requirements), but it increases in high-SES children's narratives, in which a different narrative skill seems to be developing.

In personal narratives, the results suggest that the situation is the inverse. No main effect ($F_{(2,104)} = 0.99$, $p < .38$) or interaction effect ($F_{(3,103)} = 0.69$, $p < .56$) of age and SES combined is found in first-person evaluation, but there is an interaction effect of age and SES on the frequency of third-person evaluation ($F_{(3,103)} = 4.57, p < .005$). It seems to be the case that low-SES children in the early school years are adjusting their use of evaluative expressions to the requirements of prototypical personal narratives (i.e., first-person narratives), whereas high-SES children tend to introduce new perspectives in their accounts of personal experience. We find, yet again, that high-SES children tend to introduce more than one point of view in their narratives, thus combining their own and other story characters' perspectives in personal anecdotes.

These findings reinforce the idea that frequency of evaluative expressions alone cannot accurately explain children's developing narrative skills. Uses of evaluative language and its contribution to narrative perspective vary with the type of narrative that is being produced.

Combining Voices: Representing Speech in Narratives

This second part of this study is devoted to the detailed analysis of speech representation in narratives because it sheds light on how children introduce voices explicitly in their stories. Reporting speech in discourse is an important resource when signaling whose perspective is adopted by the speaker. In children's narratives, reported speech reflects a child's degree of commitment with the information contained in the reported utterances (Shiro, 2004). As discussed previously, the coding of data included four types of reporting: direct, indirect, free, and onomatopoeia.

1. Direct speech is defined as any instance of "textual" quote, as in the following excerpt (César, male, 10;4 years, high-SES):

Spanish Original	English Translation
Entonces estaban los dos vigilantes con las armas afuera diciendo y que: "No salgas ahorita, César, porque el que está ahí es un ladrón."	Then, there were two guards, with their weapons ready, saying like: "Don't leave now Cesar, because the guy there is a thief."

2. Indirect reported speech represents the instances when the content of the spoken utterances, not the actual wording, is inserted in the speaker's utterances, as in the following excerpt (Alexis, male, 7;1 years, low-SES):

Spanish Original	English Translation
Mi mamá me contó un día que cuando yo estaba aprendiendo a caminar, que mi tío dejó una taza de café, dejó que la sacaran en la cocina y yo me la agarré.	My mother told me that one day when I was learning to walk, that my uncle left a cup of coffee, left it in the kitchen (to be taken out), and I grabbed it.

3. Free reporting consists of an utterance in which the speaker reports the communicative purpose of the reported speech without making reference to its content, as in the following excerpt (María, female, 10;9 years, high-SES):

Spanish Original	English Translation
Entonces empezamos a jugar a la ouija y una amiguita de nosotros nos cuenta una cosa que a su hermana le pasó jugando a la ouija.	Then we started playing the ouija and a friend of ours recounted a thing that happened while playing ouija.

4. Onomatopoeia represents the reporting of a sound imitating some noise, animal cries, or human emission of sounds (other than words), as in the following excerpt (Ricardo, male, 7;2 years, low-SES):

Spanish Original	English Translation
Entonces el papá y todos se fueron en el carro y el pequeñito estaba sentado atrás con su peluche y el papá hizo "po" y entonces dio la vuelta así en el aire "gua" y se cayó "pum."	Then the father and all of them left in the car and the little one was sitting in the back with his teddy bear and the father did "plop" and then (the little one) jumped in the air like this "gua" and (he) fell "pum."

In addition to the type of reporting, I have coded for the voice that was being reported (i.e., whether it belonged to the narrator or to some other character in

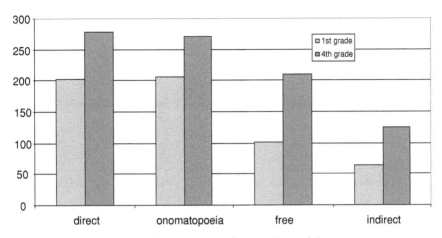

Figure 9.2. The categories of reported speech by age.

the story), as well as for the reporting verb that introduced the utterances that represented speech.

Of almost 1500 cases of reported speech found in the data, 577 were produced by first-graders and 885 by fourth-graders, showing a robust developing trend ($F_{1,111}= 4,59$, $p < .034$): older children represent speech more frequently in narratives than younger children. However, because we could hypothesize that certain kinds of reporting, such as onomatopoeia, are used as compensating resources for younger children when they could not find the linguistic expression that corresponded more closely to what they wanted to convey (Pandolfi & Herrera, 1991; Sánchez, 1987), we examined the development of each type of reporting, as represented in Figure 9.2.

The results indicate that fourth-graders increase the use of all categories of reported speech. Direct reporting and onomatopoeia (which can be considered a special case of direct reporting) remain the most frequent in both age groups. Free and indirect reporting are less frequent, but their increase with age is considerably larger than the increase reflected in direct reporting and onomatopoeia (compare 102 cases of free reporting in first-graders' narrative to 210 in fourth-graders' narrative).[2]

Another interesting result related to the children's use of reported speech in narratives is that boys use it more than girls, particularly onomatopoeia and direct speech (see Figure 9.3). It is worth mentioning that in my research on Venezuelan children's narrative abilities (Shiro, 2000a, 2000b, 2003, 2004), this is the only aspect in which I have found gender-related differences. In fact, this finding is reinforced by parents' intuitive impressions on how boys and girls differ when telling stories. I discuss these results further when I examine the variation in the use of reported speech in different narrative genres.

[2] No statistical test was carried out for these comparisons.

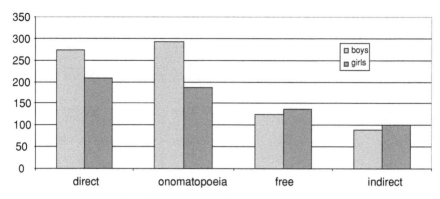

Figure 9.3. The categories of reported speech by gender.

The analysis of the data also suggests that there are SES-related differences in the use of reported speech in children's narratives.

As Figure 9.4 clearly indicates, high-SES fourth-graders almost double their use of reported speech with respect to first-graders, whereas low-SES fourth-graders do not show any increase with respect to their younger peers.

These results suggest that it is not possible to generalize about developmental trends in Venezuelan children's use of reported speech in narratives without considering factors such as gender and SES. If we admit that the production of high-SES children approximates the prestigious forms of speech, it is possible to conclude that the more frequent use of reported speech in narratives is an indication of higher narrative competence. It is surprising that this holds for the presence of onomatopoeic expressions, which, at first glance, could be taken as only fillers compensating for a child's inability to access the right word or expression (Pandolfi & Herrera, 1991).

VOICES IN FICTIONAL AND PERSONAL NARRATIVES

In this section, the narrative function of reported speech is addressed. As discussed previously, the hypothesis that reported speech (particularly the most

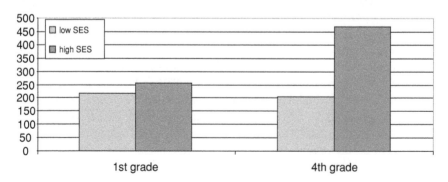

Figure 9.4. Frequency of use of reported speech by SES.

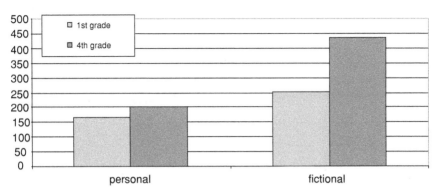

Figure 9.5. Frequency of reported speech per genre and age.

frequent types – direct reporting and onomatopoeia) is used to compensate for the lack of more sophisticated resources (Pandolfi & Herrera, 1991; Sánchez, 1987) cannot be valid. Consequently, representing the characters' speech in narratives should fulfill some other discursive functions. To find out what they are, I compared the use of reported speech in the two types of narratives, personal and fictional, analyzed in this study.

Figure 9.5 shows that first-graders report slightly more in fictional than in personal narratives, but this difference increases considerably with age. Whereas the age-related increase in personal narratives is very small, in fictional narratives, fourth-graders use almost twice as much reporting as first-graders. This tendency shows that narrative abilities depend on contextual factors (Shiro, 2003, 2004). The same child uses different skills in personal and in fictional narratives. These findings lead to the conclusion that developmental trends in narrative abilities cannot be examined in only one type of production. Children are aware of and follow genre requirements as they produce different types of discourse.

Because it was found that the use of reported speech differs according to children's SES and gender, I examined whether these factors affect equally the production of reported speech in personal and fictional narratives.

Figure 9.6 indicates that SES groups increase the use of reporting in both narrative types. The age-related increase in high-SES children is robust in personal and fictional narratives. However, SES differences in the use of reported speech seem to be less marked in personal narratives. A similar finding with respect to the use of evaluative language (Shiro, 2003) reinforces the idea that SES differences in Venezuelan children's competence in the production of personal narratives are smaller than in the production of fictional stories. Educators should be aware of these differences in narrative abilities when they need to overcome SES differences in classroom activities.

The pattern shown in Figure 9.7 implies that developmental trends differ in boys' and girls' use of reported speech when producing personal and fictional narratives. In personal narratives, only girls show an age-related increase,

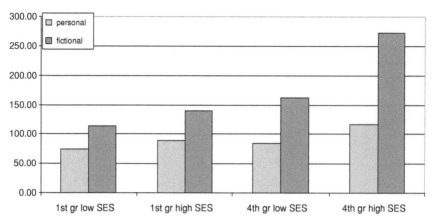

Figure 9.6. Age- and SES-related tendencies of reported speech in fictional and personal narratives.

whereas in fictional narratives, boys display a remarkably large increase with age, as compared to the more modest increase in girls' use of reporting in fiction. This result reflects again that Venezuelan boys tend to use more reported speech, particularly in fictional storytelling.

Gender differences found in the use of reported speech in English-speaking children (Ely, Gleason, & McCabe, 1996; Ely & McCabe, 1993; Goodwin, 1990) apparently contradict this finding. Studies on American and Canadian children suggest that girls tend to report speech more than boys. However, the contradiction is an illusion because the findings on English speakers' use of reported speech are limited to personal narratives produced by children between the ages of 2 and 5 years. Furthermore, it seems that none of these studies included onomatopoeic expressions in the analysis of reported speech. The trend found in Venezuelan children's narratives refers basically to fictional narrative production and children between the ages of 6 and 11 years.

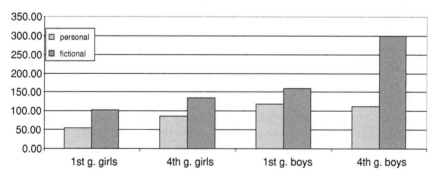

Figure 9.7. Age- and gender-related tendencies of reported speech in fictional and personal narratives.

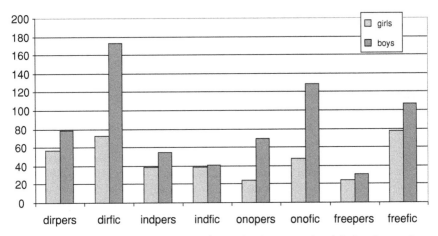

Figure 9.8. Gender differences in types of reporting in personal and fictional narratives.

As shown in Figure 9.8, in personal narratives, the differences between boys and girls using reported speech are less marked than in fictional narrative, except in the frequency of indirect speech and onomatopoeic expressions. The most remarkable gender differences are found in the use of onomatopoeic expression and direct speech in fictional storytelling. This finding suggests that Venezuelan boys tend to dramatize more than girls when producing fictional narratives.

One of the genre requirements that we expect to find in children's narratives is that they would report the voice of others more often in fictional narratives compared to their own voices in personal narratives.

As Figure 9.9 indicates, in fictional stories, children report other people's voices much more frequently than their own. In personal narratives, they also report the voices of others rather than their own, although the difference is

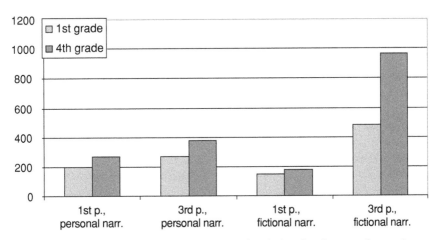

Figure 9.9. Age-related trends in voices reported in fictional and personal narratives.

smaller than in fictional stories. Let us compare how children's presentation of self is expressed in the following example (Juan, male, 10;8 years, high-SES):

Spanish Original

Bueno, una vez en casa de mi abuelo estábamos todos, y mi primo y yo, que yo tenía como cuatro años [c], mi primo tenía como ocho, subimos a [. . .] al cuarto de mi abuelo. Entonces mi abuelo tenía una pistola debajo de la cama y mi primo la agarró y [. . .] y disparó, pero se fue por la ventana el disparo y esa [. . .] estaba todo blanco y yo salí corriendo, corriendo pa' abajo y mi [. . .] y mi primo también. Entonces mi primo decía que fui yo el que disparé. Entonces mi abuelo le quitó las balas y me la dio para que yo tratara de disparar y no [. . .] y no tenía fuerzas. Entonces ahí sabía [. . .] supieron que fue mi primo.

English Translation

Well, once in my grandfather's house, we were all, my cousin and I, when I was four and my cousin was eight, we went into my grandfather's bedroom. Then my grandfather had a pistol underneath the bed and my cousin took it and and [he] fired, but the shot went through the window. [He] was all white and I left running, running down. My cousin did too. Then my cousin said that it was me who fired the shot. Then, grandfather took out the bullets and gave me the pistol to shoot. I wasn't strong enough. Then, they knew right away that it was my cousin.

In this autobiographical episode, Juan chooses not to adopt a first-person singular perspective, although he appears as a protagonist (or coprotagonist) in the incident. However, he places his cousin (*mi primo*) in the active protagonist's role. Thus, the story starts out with an orientation, where the place (*casa de mi abuelo*), the characters, and their age are described from a first-person-plural perspective. But when he gets to the complicating action, *mi primo* becomes the agent and subject in most clauses. This third-person perspective of a personal experience allows the child to present himself in a nonactive role, which makes him a helpless observer and almost a victim.[3] This position is reinforced by the child's account of the resolution, in which the grandfather exposed the cousin's lie by demonstrating that Juan was not strong enough to pull the trigger.

Juan's anecdote contrasts with Douglas's in which the prevalent perspective is that of the narrator/speaker (Douglas, male, 6;6 years, low-SES):

Spanish Original

Ah, no, un día yo me perdí en [. . .] en una playa no, yo [. . .] yo solo me perdí mi mamá me decía <ahí está Maikel> ["] y yo lo ví y cuando yo pasé, a mí se me olvidó el camino y pasé por una broma, y un señor estaba hablando así, y [. . .] y yo [. . .] y yo [. . .] y yo le pregunté su nombre y [. . .] y así me vinieron a buscar.

English Translation

Oh, no, one day I got lost at the beach. I alone got lost. Mom was telling me <there is Michael> ["] and I saw him and when I passed by, I lost my way and I passed by a thing, and a man talking like this, and I asked him his name and that's how they came to fetch me.

[3] Note that even in the clause, *salí corriendo* ("I left running"), in which the narrator is the subject and the agent, the action expressed is not exactly a part of the chain of events but rather the result of fear, an emotion that forces the child to escape.

In this episode, Douglas appears as an active agent. Using mostly first-person evaluation, he narrates how he got lost. As a result, he alone carries the blame for what happened. In fact, the evaluative device attributed to the mother (i.e., direct reported speech) clears her of any responsibility (because she had given Douglas a point of reference to find his way).

The main conclusion that can be drawn from this analysis is that the development of narrative-perspective abilities is not a linear process. Venezuelan children in this age group do not start telling self-centered narrative and then continue with narratives from the perspective of others. The displacement of self is context-dependent. Children at this age are aware of genre requirements and adjust discourse perspective to the different type of narratives they produce.

CONCLUSIONS

Several conclusions can be drawn from this analysis. First, in both fictional and personal narratives, although third-person perspective is more frequent than first-person perspective, presentation of self is an important issue. There are certain genre-specific characteristics that children learn to follow. One of these is the prototypicality of third-person evaluation in fictional stories. In personal narratives, first-person evaluation is likely to be combined with third-person evaluation. This ability seems to develop earlier in personal narratives than in fictional storytelling, a trend that can be explained by the presence in the data of both vicarious and nonvicarious personal narratives. Given that in all these narratives, the child participates as a character in the (personal narrative) story-world, the difference consists in the role that is assigned to the story characters: in the nonvicarious narrative, the child/narrator takes a protagonist role (adopting mainly a first-person perspective), whereas in the vicarious narrative, the character is assigned the role of a witness of the recounted incidents. However, as observed in Juan's story, the line between these two types of personal narratives is not easily drawn.

The results suggest that children's age, gender, and SES have an effect on how they build narrative perspective. It seems that children master first the more prototypical genre skills (e.g., the use of third-person evaluation in fictional stories). Subsequently, they learn other skills, which at first glance may reverse the genre-specific skills, but, in fact, if combined appropriately, contribute to more artful storytelling. As far as this ability is concerned, different developmental paths are followed, depending on children's SES. Low-SES children tend to increase the presence of third-person perspective in fictional stories, but high-SES children include first-person perspective in fictional narratives told from a predominantly third-person perspective.

Similarly, gender and genre differences have been found in the use of reported speech in Venezuelan children's narrative production. Fictional stories tend to present more cases of speech reporting than personal anecdotes in general, but boys use considerably more direct speech and onomatopoeic expressions in fiction than girls. Boys also use more onomatopoeic expressions in personal narratives than girls.

In summary, this study reinforces previous findings (Shiro, 2001, 2003) that refer to children's context-dependent discourse competence. The results of this study confirm that the same child can display different language skills in different narrative tasks. For example, a child may have used very few cases of reported speech in personal narratives, but his or her fictional stories display many more reporting expressions. Thus, discourse constraints, in addition to children's developmental stage, play an important role in how specific language constructions are being used.

APPENDIX

The Analytic Categories Used for Coding Evaluative Language

1. *Emotion,* expressing affect, emotion (e.g., *Se puso contenta.* "[She] was happy.").
2. *Cognition,* representing thought, beliefs (e.g., *Pensó que era un pajarito.* "[He] thought that it was a little bird.").
3. *Perception,* referring to anything that is perceived through the senses (e.g., *Vio al policía.* "[She] saw the policeman.").
4. *Physical state,* referring to a character's internal state that is physical rather than emotional (e.g., *Estaba muy cansada.* "[She] was very tired.").
5. *Intention,* referring to a character's intentions of carrying out some action (e.g., *Trató de escapar.* "[She] tried to escape.").
6. *Relation,* referring to an action that is interpreted as a relation between characters or a character and an object, rather than the action itself (e.g., *Encontraron al ratoncito.* "[They] found the rat.").
7. *Reported speech,* referring to language representing speech:
   a. *Direct:* The character's words are recorded verbatim (e.g., *Le dijo: "Por aquí señor, por favor."* "[She] told him: "Here, sir, please.").
   b. *Indirect:* The character's words are indirectly reported (e.g., *Mi mamá le dijo que yo estaba ahí.* "My mother told him that I was there.").
   c. *Free:* The lexical choices imply that speech is represented without explicitly reporting the words spoken (e.g., *Mi mamá me regañó.* "My mom nagged at me.").

REFERENCES

Astington, A. (1990). Narrative and the child's theory of mind. In B. Britton & A. Pellegrini (Eds.), *Narrative thought and narrative language* (pp. 151–172). Hillsdale, NJ: Lawrence Erlbaum Associates.

Bakhtin, M. (1986). *Speech genres and other essays*. Austin, TX: Austin University Press.

Bruner, J. (1990). *Acts of meaning*. Cambridge, MA: Harvard University Press.

Chafe, W. (1994). *Discourse, consciousness and time*. Chicago: The University of Chicago Press.

Ely, R., Gleason, B. J., & McCabe, A. (1996). "Why didn't you talk to your Mommy, honey?": Parents' and children's talk about talk. *Research on Language and Social Interaction, 29*, 7–25.

Ely, R., & McCabe, A. (1993). Remembered voices. *Journal of Child Language, 20*, 671–696.

Engel, S. (1995). *The stories children tell. Making sense of the narratives of childhood*. New York: W. H. Freeman and Company.

Ehrlich, S. (1990). *Point of view*. London: Routledge.

Goodwin, M. H. (1990). *He-said-she-said: Talk as social organization among Black children*. Bloomington: Indiana University Press.

Halliday, M. A. K. (1985). *An introduction to functional grammar*. London: Edward Arnold.

Halliday, M. A. K. (revised by Mathiessen, C.). (2004). *An introduction to functional grammar*. London: Edward Arnold.

Hudson, J., and Shapiro, L. (1991). From knowing to telling: The development of children's scripts, stories and personal narratives. In A. McCabe & C. Peterson (Eds.), *Developing narrative structure* (pp. 89–136). Hillsdale, NJ: Lawrence Erlbaum Associates.

Hyon, S. & Sulzby, E. (1992). *Black kindergartners' spoken narratives. Style, structure and task*. Paper presented at the 72nd Annual Meeting of American Research Association, San Francisco, CA, April 20–24, 1992.

Jakobson, R. (1975). *Ensayos de lingüística general*. Barcelona, España: Seix Barral.

Labov, W. (1972). The transformation of experience in narrative syntax. In W. Labov (Ed.), *Language in the inner city: Studies in the Black English vernacular* (pp. 354–405). Philadelphia: University of Pennsylvania.

Lucariello, J. 1995. Mind, culture, person: Elements in cultural psychology. *Human Development, 38*, 2–18.

MacWhinney, B. 2000. *The Childes project: Tools for analyzing talk*. Hillsdale, NJ: Lawrence Erlbaum Associates.

Mühlhäusler, P., & Harré, R. (1990). *Pronouns and people*. Oxford: Blackwell.

Pandolfi, A. M., & Herrera, M. O. (1991). La onomatopeya como recurso infantil. *Revista de Lingüística Teórica y Aplicada, 29*, 63–76.

Peterson, C. & McCabe, A. (1983). *Developmental psycholinguistics*. New York: Plenum Press.

Polkinghorne, D. (1991). Narrative and self-concept. *Journal of Narrative and Life History, 1*, 135–153.

Sánchez, J. (1987). *Dramatization devices in children's oral narratives*. Unpublished doctoral dissertation. Philadelphia: University of Pennsylvania.

Sarangi, S. (2003). Editorial: Evaluating evaluative language. *Text: An Interdisciplinary Journal for the Study of Discourse, 20*, 165–170.

Scollon, R. & Scollon, S. (1981). *Narrative, literacy and face in interethnic communication*. Norwood, NJ: Ablex Publishing Corporation.

Shiro, M. (1999–2000). Echar el cuento: Hacia un perfil de las destrezas narrativas orales en niños caraqueños. *Lenguas Modernas, 26–27,* 135–167.

Shiro, M. (2000a). Diferencias sociales en la construcción del *yo* y del *otro*: Expresiones evaluativas en la narrativa de niños caraqueños en edad escolar. In J. J. Bustos Tovar, P. Charaudeau, J. L. Girón, S. Iglesias, & C. López (Eds.), *Lengua, Discurso, Texto* (pp. 1303–1318). Madrid: Universidad Complutense and Visor Libros.

Shiro, M. (2000b). Los pequeños cuentacuentos caraqueños. *Cuadernos de Lengua y Habla, 2,* 319–337.

Shiro, M. (2001). Las habilidades evaluativas en dos tipos de discurso narrativo infantil. *Lingüística, 13,* 217–248.

Shiro, M. (2003). Genre and evaluation in narrative development. *Journal of Child Language, 30,* 165–194.

Shiro, M. (2004). Expressions of epistemic modality and construction of narrative stance in Venezuelan children's narratives. *Psychology of Language and Communication, 8,* 35–56.

Snow, C. (1990). Building memories: The ontogeny of autobiography. In D. Cicchetti & M. Beeghly (Eds.), *The self in transition: Infancy in childhood* (pp. 213–242). Chicago: The University of Chicago Press.

Voloshinov, V. (1973). *Marxism and the philosophy of language.* Cambridge, MA: Harvard University Press.

10

Mestizaje: Afro-Caribbean and Indigenous Costa Rican Children's Narratives and Links with Other Traditions

C. NICHOLAS CUNEO, ALLYSSA McCABE, AND GIGLIANA MELZI

"Just tell them who we are and that we are not all alike."
– Quote from Margarita Ávila in *Latinos*, by Earl Shorris (1992)

Key Words: narratives, children, Costa Rica, Dominican Republic, Indigenous, Afro-Caribbean

ABSTRACT

This study examined the relationship between children's narratives and a number of diverse social and cultural influences in one Dominican American and four Costa Rican Indigenous communities to explore Spanish narration in areas of linguistic and social contact. Of the total number of narratives collected, 30 were from 17 Costa Rican children (7 girls, 10 boys) of Indigenous or Afro-Caribbean descent and 36 were from 12 children (6 girls, 6 boys) from the Dominican Republic living in the United States. All children interviewed were native speakers of Spanish between the ages of 6 and 9 years (M age $= 7;1$). Personal narratives were isolated from recorded conversations, transcribed, and scored using both highpoint and story grammar analyses. When compared to a number of other ethnic groups both inside and outside of Latin America, the Indigenous and Afro-Caribbean narratives gathered in this study differed considerably and suggest that – whereas many distinct ethnic minority groups are absorbing national languages and traditions – vestigial cultural elements are being retained in children's narrative structure and content. Results are discussed relative to the narrative practices emerging from cultural and linguistic contact.

INTRODUCTION

Language-socialization studies began in the early 1980s and continue today (Garrett & Baquedano-López, 2002), focusing on how children are socialized through and in the use of language, especially in multilingual settings involving power disparities. These imbalances in power associated with languages are epitomized all across Latin America and are the focus of this chapter. The language-socialization research paradigm yields insight into language use in everyday life, including individual variation in communicative competence in language(s), changing language-socialization practices that may lead to the "loss" or transformation of existing codes, and the relevance of all these factors for socializing children into literacy (Garrett & Baquedano-López, 2002). In the language socialization paradigm, "narrative is [seen as] a primordial tool of socialization" (Garrett & Baquedano-López, 2002, p. 353) and thus should be central to any examination of relationships involving language and power. In this chapter, we seek to examine the factors contributing to narration in a few of the many language-contact situations involving Latino children in the Americas as well as to provide some insight into resulting patterns of their narration.

In our work, we view narrative as the linguistic meeting ground of culture, cognition, and emotion (McCabe, 1997). As defined by Labov (1972), a *narrative* is "at least two sequential independent clauses describing a single past event." Children use narratives to make sense of past experiences, to practice self-presentation and role-playing, and to make past events and abstractions vibrant and memorable (McCabe, 1996). On a cognitive level, the ability to produce a complete narrative is considered an indication of an expanded worldview and a budding capacity to communicate beyond the level of immediate events (e.g., Snow, Tabors, Nicholson, & Kurland, 1995). Narrative skills have been found to be predictive of later literacy and academic success, specifically in second- (Griffin, Hemphill, Camp, & Wolf, 2004), fourth-, seventh- (Tabors, Snow, & Dickinson, 2001) and tenth-grade reading comprehension (Snow, Porche, Tabors, & Harris, 2007).

Study of the form of narratives can also be instrumental in both appreciating different cultures and elucidating cultural differences. Children acquire the ability to tell a complete narrative in the structure valued by their culture by the age of 6 years, but they start telling lengthy and increasingly idiosyncratic narratives just 3 years later due to numerous factors such as gender, personality, and family conversational practices. Thus, the period between the ages of 6 and 9 years represents a time during which children's narratives are most canonical – or culturally typical (McCabe, 1996).

Latino and Amerindian/Indigenous children's narratives are among the least studied and most poorly understood. In contrast to the wealth of research that has been done on English-speaking children (especially those of European ancestry and middle- to upper-socioeconomic status), very little has been published on the development and diversity of narrative structures among Spanish-speaking Latino children either inside or outside of the United States (García, 2000; Hammer, Miccio, & Wagstaff, 2003).

What we do know about Spanish narration is that it differs from English narration in a number of ways. Frequent reference to family members provides cohesion within narratives in order to orient the narrator and listener (Rodino, Gimbert, Pérez, Craddock-Willis, & McCabe, 1991; Silva & McCabe, 1996; Uccelli, 2008, chapter 8, this volume). Melzi (2000) found that Spanish-speaking Central American mothers focus more on the conversational aspects of narrative when reminiscing with their children, whereas English-speaking European American mothers were more attentive to structure and organization of narrative. In telling stories prompted by a wordless picture book, Spanish-speaking children (from Spain, Chile, and Argentina) primarily use the present tense, whereas English speakers primarily use the past tense (Berman & Slobin, 1994; Sebastián & Slobin, 1994). Similarly, Puerto Rican adults living in New York use the historical present tense in personal narratives to dramatize key aspects (Torres, 1997). Furthermore, because Spanish privileges verbs of inherent directionality and uses a relatively small set of verbs of motion and caused motion (unlike English), Spanish narrators eschew encoding every segment of the path itself in favor of greater attention to setting the stage for the story. In a study of personal narration, adult Puerto Rican Spanish speakers narrated fewer formal openings and closings compared to English speakers (Pérez, 1998). Furthermore, Spanish speakers narrated half of the time in a classic fashion, which was the dominant form used by English speakers, but half of the time they told narratives that combined multiple experiences (Pérez, 1998). In an early study (John & Berney, 1968) of Head Start children retelling stories in response to pictures from a sequential narrative book read to them, Puerto Rican preschoolers produced stories of a similar length to those of African American children, but the Puerto Rican children produced significantly fewer action phrases. Highlighting the diversity among Latino children, however, Puerto Rican children also produced significantly fewer action phrases than did Mexican American children.

Despite indications that monolingual Spanish-speaking children narrate differently than their English-speaking peers, a few studies have found that when children are bilingual in Spanish and English, the particular language they speak does not seem to affect their discourse style, although this finding would need to be confirmed across far more bilingual groups. That is, bilingual Spanish-English Mexican American children have been found to narrate very similarly regardless of the language they use. One study (Jiménez-Silva, 1996) of 20 6- to 8-year-old Mexican American children living in California – half determined to be Spanish-dominant, half English-dominant – found that both groups of children produced personal narratives that were remarkably similar despite the fact that the former told theirs in Spanish, whereas the latter chose English. In another study of Texan Spanish-English bilingual children ages 8 to 11 years (18 with language impairment, 21 with typical language development), there were significant correlations among all key narrative variables produced by each child in both languages. That is, there were significant correlations between English and Spanish total propositions, numbers of orientative comments, use of progressive tense, productions of actions, evaluations, and codas (McCabe & Bliss, 2004–2005). Fiestas and Peña (2004) found that 4- to 7-year-old Spanish-English bilingual children told stories of equal complexity in both Spanish and English in a wordless-picture-book task. In a case study of a bilingual child narrating a wordless picture book from about 7 to 11 years in both languages, Álvarez (2003) found that the style of introducing characters in each language was not as differentiated as is typical of comparisons of monolingual speakers, indicating that there are certain aspects of a bilingual child's language that develop interdependently.

Even sparser than research on Spanish-speaking children is research on narrative development among the great majority of Indigenous groups in the Americas. Although some work has been done on local, regional, and national levels with regard to the preservation and documentation of traditional Indigenous stories (which are usually transcribed from the recorded oral narratives of tribal elders), little has been done within the realm of Amerindian children's narration. Apart from a few studies done with specific indigenous groups, such as Crago's (Crago, 1992, Pesco, Crago, & McCabe, 1996) work with the Inuit and Algonquin of Canada or Scollon and Scollon's (1981) analysis of Athabaskan narratives, comprehensive or comparative research on Indigenous children's narrative structure is slim and inconclusive (Allen, Crago, & Pesco, 2006). (For other examples of work that has been done with older Indigenous people, see Hymes, 1982, 1987; and Manuel-Dupont, Strong, & Fields, 1990.)

Afro-Caribbean children's narratives have been similarly neglected. The only work that has been done among Afro-Caribbean children involving narrative (Champion, McCabe, & Colinet, 2002–2003) focuses on the structure of Haitian American children's narratives. However, Francophonic Haiti differs vastly in language, culture, and history from the two Afro-Caribbean groups considered in this study. At the time this chapter was written, no other studies documenting the personal narrative structure and content of Afro-Caribbean children of non-Francophonic ancestry had been published.

Latin America – with its thorny history of conquest, colonialism, and contact – is full of compound situations involving language, culture, and power. Indeed, an examination of Latino narration would be conspicuously deficient without discussion of the factors contributing to narration in language-contact situations as well as some insight into resulting patterns.

The Communities

The Costa Rican and Dominican communities involved in this study are prime examples of the unique combination of parallelism and heterogeneity characterizing the many Latin American communities existing in language-contact situations today. Together, the communities' stories, as detailed herein, are illustrative of the rich complexity underlying analysis of Latino narration that derives from long and unique histories of power-infused interactions among differing cultures, languages, and peoples.

The Brunka (Boruca Territory)

The Brunka are an Indigenous people currently spread out between two small territories – Boruca and Térraba – in the southwest of Costa Rica. Research for this study was conducted in the town of Boruca, which measures 12,470 hectares in area and has a population of 2,952, of whom 47% identify as Indigenous. For hundreds of years leading up to the 16th century, the Brunka occupied a large and fertile tract of land bordering the Pacific coast of southern Costa Rica (ADIRC, 2001).

However, everything changed for the group in 1563, the year that the Brunka were first contacted by Europeans. This "contact" came in the form of *conquistador* Juan Vázquez del Coronado who, along with his troops, arrived on the Pacific coast of Costa Rica with the intention of (violently) displacing the Brunka and any other Indigenous groups encountered during his governorship of Costa Rica (Graef, 2005). With White settlement, of course, came the notorious combination of White brutality and diseases; within a matter of decades, the Brunkan population was virtually decimated. In the following centuries, the Brunka continued to endure hardship after hardship in the form of smallpox outbreaks, environmental degradation, and territorial encroachment and displacement by non-Indigenous (so-called White or *ladino*) farmers.

Deplorably, this pattern of exploitation and abuse at the hands of non-Indigenous settlers as well as the Costa Rican government has not subsided in the last half-century. In some respects, it has actually been amplified in both impact and scale. For example, in contrast to 1964, when non-Indigenous farmers owned a (relatively) moderate 34.8% of Brunkan territorial land, as of 1994, non-Indigenous farmers owned a substantial *majority* of land on the reserve, from a low of 62.8% in Boruca to a high of 86.5% in Térraba (ITCO, 1964; Calderón & Alfredo, 2003, cited in Graef, 2005). The Costa Rican government itself has contributed to the degradation of Brunkan autonomy, starting with construction of the Inter-American Highway between 1955 and 1960 directly through Brunkan land, and continuing today in the form of the state-funded Boruca Hydroelectric Project, the aim of which is to construct a giant dam right at the border of the Boruca–Térraba territory.

The Brunka's constant struggle since 1563 to exist in confrontation and contact with a dominant culture and language has acted as an insidious and corrosive force against the preservation of their own language and culture. Labeled "the most Europeanized of southern Costa Rican tribes" half a century ago by Stone (1949), the Brunka have had to assimilate in many ways to survive, losing a good deal of their original culture as a result. Cultural traditions, like mask-making, that are still in practice today are for the most part being preserved for economic value as a commodity rather than as a sacred or spiritually meaningful activity.

Although efforts are now being made to reintroduce traditional knowledge and vocabulary into the classroom and to reinvigorate past cultural traditions, without the support of community parents – many of whom barely speak a word of Brunkan, are not proud of their Indigenous background, and are indifferent about seeing their children become Westernized – such endeavors can go only so far. There are now only a few Brunkan speakers left, and in a few years it is feared the language will become extinct.

The Maleku (Margarita and Tonjibe Communities)

The Maleku Territory is home to 1,115 people, of whom only 460 (41.2% of the population) classify themselves as Indigenous (MIDEPLAN, 2002; quoted in Graef, 2005). Like the Brunka (as well as virtually every other Indigenous group in the Americas), the Maleku have been subjected to a history of exploitation, most violently and continuously at the hands of *ladino* rubber farmers from Nicaragua (a neighboring country) throughout the 19th century. According to Maleku accounts, Nicaraguan farmers were responsible for the usurpation of huge tracts of Maleku land, the environmental degradation of Maleku territory, and even the trafficking of Maleku children back to Nicaragua to work as forced laborers (Edith, Marín, & Blanco, 1996). After suffering years of such abuse, the Maleku came into contact with the Catholic bishop and evangelizer, Bernard Augusto Thiel (Cartín, 2003), who established a long-term relationship with the Maleku and helped negotiate a more peaceful existence for them while also working to incorporate his religion and language into their existence.

Unlike the Brunka, the Maleku today are in a state of cultural and economic development. The Maleku have capitalized on the appeal to Western travelers of their traditions regarding everything from medicinal plants and *artesanía* (i.e., artisanship) to house construction, and they are becoming very involved in the growing ecotourism industry. Western tourists can now, for a fee, spend a day in the community and get a glimpse of the traditional sustainable practices, medicinal plants, and artisanship techniques used by the Maleku in the past and present. In contrast to the Brunka, the Maleku language is still very much alive, with fluent speakers of all ages and a rich oral-storytelling tradition. The Maleku are proud of and interested in their ethnic background and are thus better equipped for retaining and transmitting valuable traditional knowledge and stories of all kinds in the future.

The Bribri (Shiroles Community)

The Bribri, Costa Rica's largest active indigenous group, live in the southwestern part of the country bordering Panama and number 11,174, of whom 9,636 (86.2%) identify themselves as Indigenous (MIDEPLAN, 2002, as cited in Graef, 2005). Traditionally structured in matrilineal clans, the Bribri are now spread out among 23 different and culturally distinct communities (L. D. Gómez, personal communication, August 4, 2006), each at a different stage regarding the maintenance of tradition, language, and culture. Although much evangelical work has been and continues to be done in the territory by Christian missionaries, many Bribri have held onto traditional spiritual beliefs and practices, such as shamanism (Stone, 1962). Bribri is the primary language of a number of children within the territory, for whom Spanish is first introduced in primary school. However, in the community of Shiroles, in which research for this study was conducted, Bribri was not well spoken, and all children interviewed were native speakers of Spanish with only limited exposure – through school, for example – to Bribri vocabulary and culture.

Los Afro-Caribeños (Town of Cahuita)
Cahuita is a coastal Caribbean town located in southern Costa Rica in the province of Limón, an area with a reputation not only for its extraordinary biodiversity (e.g., Cahuita National Park) but also for its celebrated cultural diversity, as reflected in the myriad types of people, music, and languages that can be heard in the town every night (Girot, Weitzner, & Fonseca, 1998). Uninhabited by permanent settlers before this past century (Indigenous Miskito hunters were said to frequent the area in the 19th century but not live there), Cahuita has already built up a rich cultural history. Cahuita was initially settled at the beginning of the 20th century by a group of Jamaican immigrants who came to Costa Rica to help construct the new railroad to Limón, which was being built for the transport of coffee (Chomsky, 1995). Once established in the area, Afro-Caribbean workers were then recruited by the United Fruit Company to work on its many banana plantations in the region. The existence of such economic opportunities – coupled with the growing visibility of Cahuita as an Afro-Caribbean cultural center – encouraged the immigration of a number of Jamaicans (i.e., 20,000 from 1900 to 1913), including many young, single men who were second-generation ex-slaves (Chomsky, 1995).

Cahuita retained its uniform Jamaican influence throughout most of the 20th century until the 1970s, when a decision by the Costa Rican government to designate much of the area as protected – in the form of a national park – dramatically changed the subsistence activities of local residents and precipitated the transformation of Cahuita into a destination for tourists (Girot et al., 1998), a move that greatly increased the size of the community and its composition. To cope with growing from a small, almost exclusively Afro-Caribbean community to a bustling international tourist attraction, Cahuita had to undergo a dramatic change in culture. Today, many Afro-Caribbean children in the community are being raised and talked to exclusively in Spanish at home, even when their parents are native English-Mekatelyu speakers. A number of Latin Americans from other countries, as well as many Chinese and Italian immigrants, have moved into the area, bringing with them their own cultural traditions. A growing population of European and Canadian expatriates has recently taken over the management of many Cahuitan businesses.

Dominican American Children's Community
Children in this community have parents who emigrated from the Dominican Republic to a large city in the Northeastern United States. They primarily speak Spanish at home but English at school ever since Massachusetts voted against the Transitional Bilingual Education program it had formerly offered. All but one child in the current study preferred to address the bilingual interviewer using English; they were asked to use the language in which they felt most comfortable talking. The children attend a school that has been identified as performing in the low to very low range in performance assessed under the federal No Child Left Behind Act. The school's population is 85% Hispanic, 83% low-income (i.e., qualifying for free or reduced-cost lunch and/or food stamps and/or Transitional Aid to Families benefits), with approximately 17% of students classified as Limited English Proficiency. Most of the children are at high risk for academic achievement; in grade four, for example, 48% of children in this school received a "needs improvement" and 27% received a "warning" on the most recent grade-four high-stakes test of reading. It is not surprising that the city in which the children live is worse than the national average for violent crimes, including murder, robbery, and aggravated assault. These statistics were recovered from public information on the Internet. However, because we wish to take every precaution to preserve the anonymity of participants, the references are not provided. They are available from the authors upon request.

Language Loss

Discussion of cultural differences in the context of mentioning possible language loss is a risky endeavor because the history of linguistics is littered with mistaken understanding of cultural differences as deficits. Nonetheless, we would be remiss if we did not raise first-language loss as a potential factor affecting all children studied in this chapter. Specifically, three of the Costa Rican communities involved in this project (i.e., Boruca, Shiroles, and Cahuita) face collective language loss, possibly leading to eventual extinction of the Indigenous language in the not-too-distant future. Although in the Dominican community in the United States, Spanish is widely spoken, the overall language pattern in the United States is for the grandchildren of non-English–speaking immigrants to develop little or none of the native language (see Zentella, 1985, 1997, for Puerto Ricans in East Harlem). In the larger communities from which our children were sampled, we saw that a collective loss of the primary language and children's individual attrition of the language spoken at home seemed to accompany the acquisition of the child's second language (i.e., Spanish in Costa Rican samples, English in the U.S. samples). However, these are impressions based on field notes because language proficiency could not be formally documented due to a variety of factors (e.g., no standardized tests are available in the indigenous languages of the Costa Rican children). Moreover, language loss varies across communities, families within communities, and children within the same family (Guardado, 2002). In the case of the Costa Ricans, for instance, Indigenous languages (i.e., Brunkan, Bribri, Maleku, and Mekatelyu) are being lost while Spanish is the dominant and second (transitioning into being the first) language acquired. In the case of the Dominican children living in the United States, Spanish is the language being lost while English is being acquired. Pan and Gleason (1986) noted that loss of ability in a child's native language often occurs when that language is used only as the home language. As children go to school, they acquire greater proficiency and literacy in the societal language, resulting in the stagnation of the primary home language. Children in these circumstances eventually perceive the home language as inadequate to express the finer points of their messages. Fillmore (1991) argued that such language loss is characteristic of societies such as the United States and Canada, where cultural and linguistic diversity is not officially valued; for example, as of November 17, 2006, 28 states had voted to establish English as the state's official language (http://www.us-english.org/inc/official/states.asp). Remarkably, in the November 2006 election in Arizona, 48% of Latinos supported such a law (Dorell, 2006). Fillmore argued that when children lose their native language, they lose the ability to communicate effectively with their parents regarding values and beliefs, among other subjective information. In turn, children's respect for their parents diminishes along with parental authority. Unfortunately, we see that language loss is not limited to the U.S. setting; Indigenous language loss has been happening across the Americas since the time of the conquest by the Spaniards. In this chapter, we give particular attention to three communities in Costa Rica (see King & Callagher, chapter 6, this volume for Ecuadorian Quichua).

In addition to powerful social reasons to rue language loss, there are literacy-related reasons. Cummins (1979, 1991) built a strong case for the transfer of metalinguistic, academic, literacy-related skills across languages – an observation that has received considerable confirmation. For example, phonological awareness in low-income Spanish and English bilingual preschool-aged children strongly transfers across languages (Dickinson, McCabe, Clark-Chiarelli, & Wolf, 2004). Spanish and English oral language skills contribute to reading within and across languages (Miller, Heilmann, Nockerts, Iglesias, Fabiano, & Francis, 2006). Cummins (1991, p. 75) noted that the California State Department of Education showed high correlations between English and Spanish reading skills.

In this chapter, we consider the possible impact of language loss on the ability to narrate. Other work on language loss has addressed various linguistic aspects. For example, the impact of first-language loss on grammar in a young bilingual Puerto Rican Spanish-English–speaking child during a 2-year period was documented (Anderson, 1999), notably including a progressive reduction of morphological and syntactical complexity in Spanish (the child's first language). However, some argue that vocabulary elements appear to suffer loss before grammatical forms in first-language loss (e.g., Moorcroft & Gardner, 1987). Such a contrast between relative loss of vocabulary and grammar might well be overstated because the two aspects of language have sometimes been found to correlate; in a careful study of 20- to 30-month-old Spanish-English bilingual children (Conboy & Thal, 2006), increases in English and Spanish sentence complexity were related to growth in same-language vocabulary but not to growth in conceptual vocabulary. The notion of language loss on the level of narrative structure has received some (although not extensive) attention. The influence of Spanish in Náhuatl discourse is complex, with evidence of lower frequency of Spanish content-word insertions accompanied by increased use of Spanish discourse connectives and insertions into Náhuatl grammatical structures (Francis & Gómez, 2003). Both functional interference and convergence has been documented in the case of cross-linguistic interference among Indigenous Quechua-Spanish bilingual children living in a language-contact situation (Sánchez, 2006). A decrease in use of the Niuean language in personal narratives from people living in New Zealand has been documented for younger versus older generations (Starks, 2006). Finally, results of language stagnation or decline in Inuktitut were inconclusive when relative exposure to English was considered (Allen et al., 2006).

Not only are most of the children interviewed for this chapter facing potential language loss, they also are all growing up in circumstances of poverty. The impact of poverty on language acquisition has long been known and is well documented in the case of English-speaking American children (e.g., Hart & Risley, 1995), with children from low-income backgrounds receiving substantially less and less positive linguistic input from their parents. Unfortunately, the issues of diminished input due to poverty and language loss due to schooling in a language other than their home language could not be teased apart with the current study participants.

This study examined the narrative structure, content, and context of production by Indigenous and Afro-Caribbean Costa Rican children from the Brunka, Maleku, Cahuita, and Bribri communities, as well as those produced by children from a U.S. immigrant community from the Dominican Republic. All participating children are members of a culture that is currently in a struggle between the dominant cultural and linguistic influence (i.e., mainstream Hispanic-European for the Costa Rican communities and mainstream Anglo-European for the U.S. community) and its own distinct ethnic identity, historical language, and traditions. The study primarily relies on qualitative and descriptive methods because the children included are diverse in age, gender, ethnicity, and abilities in both of their languages. Through our examination of children's narratives, we hope to elucidate the linguistic, cultural, and psychological development of ethnic minority children. In summary, we seek to examine the language socialization revealed in narratives told by children in several sociolinguistically and culturally heterogeneous settings characterized by bilingualism involving Spanish as the first or second language, language shift, and other phenomena associated with contact between two or more languages and cultures.

METHODS

Participants

Costa Rican
For this study, 17 Costa Rican children (7 girls, 10 boys) between the ages of 6 and 9 years were selected (*M* age = 7.1). All children spoke Spanish but many also had limited exposure to either their respective Indigenous language or English. Participants were drawn from the Indigenous communities of Boruca in the Boruca Territory (N = 7, *M* age = 6.6), Margarita in the Maleku Territory (N = 1, age = 8), Shiroles in the Talamanca-Bribri Territory (N = 4, *M* age = 6.8), and the Afro-Caribbean town of Cahuita in the province of Limón (N = 5, *M* age = 7.4). All children involved in the study were enrolled in public school systems in which instruction was primarily conducted in Spanish. However, children in each community were also exposed to a supplementary language and culture class taught in the community's historical language (i.e., Brunkan in Boruca, Maleku [Guatuso] in Margarita, English in Cahuita, and Bribri in Shiroles). All participants involved in the study came from families with limited financial means and had parents with little or no secondary education.

Dominican American
For this study, 12 children (6 boys, 6 girls) between the ages of 7 and 8 years were selected. All spoke Spanish at home and were being educated in English in a large urban city in the Northeastern United States. All Dominican participants in the study also came from families with limited financial means. Children who emigrate from the Dominican Republic have a rich cultural heritage. They speak Spanish at home and English at school and have African, European, and perhaps Taíno (i.e., Indigenous) roots.

Procedure

Narratives were elicited using a modification of a paradigm developed by Peterson and McCabe (1983) in which the examiner would tell a number of personal stories (e.g., about such events as being in an accident, getting stung by a bee, or going to the doctor) as prompts and then would ask the child, "Has anything like this ever happened to you?" Leading questions, such as (in the context of narrative elicitation) "Where were you?" or "How did you feel?" were avoided to determine what children were capable of on their own; the examiner would respond simply by repeating the last few words of the child or by asking, "And then what happened?"

True personal narratives were chosen as a genre because these children were from low socioeconomic backgrounds and there is some evidence that this is a more appropriate genre for such children; that is, Shiro (2003) studied personal and fictional (i.e., film-retelling) narratives for first- and fourth-graders in Venezuela and found that low-SES children are at a greater disadvantage when telling fictional versus personal narratives. Despite the fact that we attempted to elicit only true, personal narratives, 7 of the 30 Costa Rican narratives recorded were at least in part fictional.

Costa Rica
Interviews were conducted in a number of settings and usually entailed the examiner talking to the child while he or she was drawing a picture. Although many conversations took place in a home or classroom with only an instructor or parent watching, the presence of peers and/or siblings during interviews was not uncommon and could have had an effect on the narratives recorded (Gutiérrez-Clellen & Quinn, 1993). Similarly, conversations were not conducted in an auditory or visual vacuum. Distractions such as roosters crowing, televisions blaring, and dogs fighting in the background were relatively common with the Costa Rican children, as they certainly are a ubiquitous and daily presence in all the communities in which research was conducted. These distractions could possibly also have influenced narrative delivery (e.g., a narrative may have been cut short due to a loud noise distracting the child).

Interviews were conducted in Spanish by the first author of this chapter – a native English-speaking male of European North American descent with moderate to advanced fluency in Spanish. Although every effort was made to communicate effectively with each child and to resolve any miscommunications as they occurred, there undoubtedly was some degree of disparity between the dialect used by the examiner and that used by each child. Therefore, potential linguistic bias – which can occur when there is a "mismatch between the child's dialect and the dialect of the testing tool" – should be acknowledged and considered (Laing & Kamhi, 2003). All conversations were audiotaped, reviewed, transcribed, and scored in Spanish by the first author of this chapter. Tapes were reviewed with a native Spanish-speaking Costa Rican female who is also fluent in English. Interlistener reliability was informally and randomly evaluated; when disagreements surfaced, they were discussed until consensus was reached or a third opinion was elicited.

Dominican Republic
Dominican children were interviewed by a Dominican American interviewer fluent in both her native Spanish and English. Children chose the language that they felt most comfortable speaking; 11 chose English, 1 chose Spanish. In their choice of language, these children revealed the common tendency among immigrant American children to prefer English and to lose facility in their

native language; all but 1 of the 12 children preferred to narrate in English. Their three longest narratives were chosen for analysis because length has long been used as a rough index of complexity (Peterson & McCabe, 1983). (However, note that Muñoz, Gillam, Peña, & Gulley-Faehnle [2003] report that measures of language productivity such as total number of words may be problematic indexes of development in the fictional narratives of Latino children.)

Transcription and Coding

Two systems of analysis were used. Highpoint analysis, originally developed by Labov (1972), was selected because this approach captures the overall form of a narrative and has been used with children from a number of other ethnicities with whom the current study's children can be compared. Although prompts were for true, personal narratives, a number of Costa Rican children nonetheless gave fictional or partially fictional narratives. Therefore, we used a second analysis – story grammar analysis – developed for use with fictional narratives but which has also been used with personal narratives (e.g., Peterson & McCabe, 1983).

Highpoint Analysis
Narratives were coded using Peterson and McCabe's (1983) developmental scheme based on Labov (1972). Labov's system was developed for analysis of narration by African American children and adolescents (Labov, 1972) and subsequently applied to other groups of African American (e.g., Champion, 2003) and European North American children (e.g., Peterson & McCabe, 1983). The approach looks at the extent to which a narrative is organized sequentially around an emotional climax. Each narrative was scored as exemplifying one of the following highpoint developmental structures:

- *Classic pattern:* The narrative builds up to a highpoint, evaluatively dwells on it, and then resolves it.
- *Ending-at-the-highpoint pattern:* The narrative builds up to a highpoint and then ends; there is no resolution.
- *Leapfrogging pattern:* The narrative jumps from one event to another within an integrated experience, leaving out major events that must be inferred by the listener.
- *Chronological pattern:* The narrative is a simple description of successive events, not linked causally, and without a concentration of evaluation or highpoint.
- *Minimal-events pattern:* The narrative extensively reiterates and evaluates a couple of events, but there is no buildup to a climax.
- *General-case pattern:* There are no specific past-tense events; the discourse is essentially a script of a typical kind of event.

- *Miscellaneous pattern*: Any narrative that did not fit into one of the other categories.

Costa Rican narratives were scored in Spanish by the first author of this chapter; 40% were independently coded using highpoint analysis by a second person, and agreement between those two coders was estimated to be 92%. Agreement on 50% of the Dominican narratives coded independently by two individuals was 80%. All disagreements were discussed to consensus.

Story Grammar Analysis
The fictional narratives were also coded using story grammar analysis (Champion, Seymour, & Camarata, 1995; Peterson & McCabe, 1983; Stein & Glenn, 1979). This approach examines the extent to which a narrative conforms to European folktale structure, involving precipitation and articulation of a goal and whether that goal was achieved. Each narrative was coded as one of the following developmental structures:

- *Complete episode*: Describes aims of a protagonist and explicitly refers to plans to achieve those aims. Such an episode must contain at least three of the following: events, motivating states, attempts, and consequences – and, in any case, must include a consequence.
- *Abbreviated episode*: Describes aims of a protagonist, but planning must generally be inferred. Some motive for action must exist and lead to a specified consequence that achieves or fails to achieve the protagonist's goal, which may be inferred.
- *Reactive episode*: A set of changes or events that automatically cause other changes or events with no planning involved.
- *Action sequence*: A list of actions that are chronologically rather than causally ordered.
- *Descriptive sequence*: Describes character(s), surroundings, and habitual actions with no causal relationships.

Costa Rican narratives were scored in Spanish by the first author of this chapter; 23% were independently coded using story grammar analysis by a second person, and agreement between those two coders was estimated to be 78%. Agreement on 50% of the Dominican narratives coded independently by two individuals was 76%. Disagreements were discussed to consensus.

After all transcripts were scored, results of both analyses were tabulated (see Table 10.1. Highpoint-analysis results were categorized to show what percentage of the narratives fit in each category. Results from the story grammar analysis were also categorized; note that all seven fictional narratives were coded as the same structure – action sequence. Published findings for three cultural groups studied previously – European North Americans, African Americans, and Haitian Americans – are presented as well for comparison.

RESULTS AND DISCUSSION

Mestizaje is a term that refers to "the fusion of European and Indigenous cultures in Latin America [and] is a hallmark of colonial-era painting, architecture, and ritual objects" (Campbell, 2003). Here, we apply it to describe the structure of the Spanish-speaking Latino children's narratives that we collected. In these narratives, we truly see a rich fusion of diverse traditions and apply the concept of *mestizaje* to children's narrative practices, as well as expand its traditional meaning to include a mix of African and Jamaican traditions with the European and Indigenous cultures of Latin America.

Narrative Topics

Costa Rican children in all four ethnic minority groups are educated similarly and share Spanish as their primary native language. However, their narratives are quite different from each other and certainly from the classic European North American form (Peterson & McCabe, 1983). These narratives reflect many aspects of the children's lives. To begin with, although asked to produce memories – factual personal narratives – in some cases, children produced traditional fictional stories. In fact, the boundary between these two genres was quite blurred as factual and fictional stories were interwoven in one narrative. Consider the following narrative about a contemporary fabled figure, la Llorona, a woman who lost her baby and frightens children. Parents invoke la Llorona to exert social control on their children – for instance, as a way to keep children away from dangers such as bodies of water in which they might drown (see http://www.literacynet.org/lp/hperspectives/llorona.html). In the following unprompted narrative, a 7-year-old Brunka (Indigenous) boy begins with what was in all likelihood the commission of an actual, unsafe, forbidden act – crossing the brook – and then relates to us his fantastic encounter with la Llorona, ending with his safe return home:

Narrative 1

Spanish Original	English Translation
Es que un día yo iba pasando la quebrada. Y la mata se movía y, y yo fui a ver. Y, y era una mujer con huecos. Con un clavo y tenía una clavo así. Pegado aquí. Y era fea y andaba sangrando. Y yo corrí y había, y apareció un montón iguales. Y entonces, después yo hice los ojos así. Y después aparecí en otro lugar. Y entonces yo entré por un camino. Y llegué hasta la casa de la Llorona. Y después salí en mi casa.	It's that one day I was crossing the brook. And a plant was moving and I went to see. And, and there was a woman with holes. With a nail, and she had a nail like this. Stuck here [pointing at face]. And she was ugly and is, was bleeding. And I ran and there was, and she appeared in numbers. And then, then my eyes rolled up. And later I appeared somewhere else. And then I took a path. And I arrived at the Llorona's house. And later I appeared in my house.

In all, 7 of 30 personal narratives elicited from Costa Rican children were in some way fictional accounts such as this one. Most of these children are not read fictional stories by their parents, but this is evidence of the influence of oral fictional storytelling tradition, which is still practiced today. Further evidence of this oral tradition was a direct allusion to it by one 6-year-old Bribri boy: " . . . *y nosotros comemos, y nosotros nos acostamos, apagamos la luz, y nos cuentan un cuento*" ("and we eat, and we go to bed, turn off the lights, and they tell us a story"). Following is another story from the oral tradition, one that begins as a factual account and ends in traditional fiction, told by another 7-year-old Brunka (Indigenous) boy:

Narrative 2

Spanish Original	English Translation
Yo estaba en la pulpería. Y que mi mamá estaba llamando. Y una culebra hablaba y me correteó. Y yo no podía salir porque había culebrota, bien gorda. Y era muy grande. Y yo corrí. Y habían más, más culebras. Y que, y que yo estaba corriendo. Y que habían más y yo no podía salir. Y que todos, todos se fueron. Y que había culebra que se convirtió en persona. Pero era mala la mujer. Porque era una culebra que se convirtió en persona. Y entonces a la mujer, los hombres la llevaron al fuego y la quemaron. Pero cuando la quemaron, las culebras ¡POOM! salían por todo lado, por la panza. Era un montón de culebras que tenía en la panza. Y entonces, y entonces una culebra vivió, pero salió corriendo. Y las demás murieron. Pero la que vivió siguió, y siguió a convertirse a mujer. Y entonces quemaron otra vez la mujer. Y la quemaron con el fuego. Y le pegaron con hachas. Y después todas las culebras murieron. Y una salió. Nada más.	I was in the little store. And my mom was calling. And a snake was talking and it ran after me. I couldn't get away because there was a big snake, very fat. And it was huge. And I ran. And there were more, more snakes. And, and I was running. And there were more and I couldn't get away. And they all, they all left. And there was a snake that changed into a person. But she was bad, the woman. Because she was a snake that changed into a person. And then to the woman the men brought her to the fire and burned her. But when they burned her, the snakes POOM! came out from everywhere, from her belly. There were a ton of snakes that had been in her belly. And then, and then a snake survived but escaped running. And the others died. But the one that lived continued and continued to change into a woman. And then they burned the woman again. And she burned with the fire. And they threw axes at her. And later all the snakes died. And one escaped. That's it.

Although many details of the story have been changed or omitted by the boy, this narrative is without doubt heavily influenced by the traditional Brunkan story "La mujer que se enamoró de la culebra" (ADIRC, 2001), about a woman who gets impregnated by a serpent and is then burned at the stake. What is significant about this retelling of the traditional legend is the boy's incorporation of story into a creative narrative of personal experience, a practice rarely found among English-speaking North American children (Peterson & McCabe, 1983). This narrative offers hope in confirming the continued presence of both oral tradition and non-European interaction with these tales. As a whole, Indigenous Costa Rican children produced proportionally more fictional narratives than have been reported for European North American children (Preece, 1987). It is interesting that a similar practice has been found for urban Spanish-speaking Peruvian families, where mothers report regularly telling their children fictional stories in which the children and their friends are the main characters (Melzi & Caspe, 2005). In the case of the Dominican American children, no child interwove oral fiction into personal narratives.

The second notable aspect of narrative content was the frequent mention of deaths – of snakes, strangers, even close family members; 6 of the 23 Costa Rican personal narratives involved death and 2 fictional narratives involved killings (for a total of 26.7%). Like their European North American counterparts (Menig-Peterson & McCabe, 1977), the Costa Rican children interviewed in this study did not reveal their feelings about death directly through overt evaluation; perhaps they counted on their listener's empathy. In the following narrative, an 8-year-old Bribri (Indigenous) boy simply states at the end of his narrative that the little boy who died was his cousin (therefore, someone with whom he must have spent much time and had been close):

Narrative 3

Spanish Original

El sábado pasado se murió una persona. Después lo vinieron a enterrar. El chiquito se enfermó. Y no lo llevaron rápido a la clínica. Y después lo llevaron, cuando el chiquito estaba casi casi muerto. Entonces cuando llegó a San José, el chiquito ya iba muriendo. Y le pusieron esos sueros así ¡Sueros! ¡Sueros! ¡Sueros! Y la mamá andaba al chiquito. Y lo trajeron en ambulancia. Y lo enterraron y ya – en el cementerio. El hijo de mi tío. El chiquito era mi primo. El papá del chiquito era mi tío.

English Translation

Last Saturday a person died. Later they brought him to be buried. The little boy got sick. And they didn't take him to the clinic in time. And later they took him, when he was almost almost dead. Then when he arrived in San José, the little boy was already dying. And they put these IVs like this! IVs! IVs! IVs! And the mom was carrying the little boy. And they brought him back in an ambulance. And they buried him – in the cemetery. The son of my uncle. The little boy was my cousin. The father of the little boy was my uncle.

From talking to children and adults in all four Costa Rican communities, it is clear that accidents and death are a common occurrence in their community's existence. Yet, grief for such experiences is an emotion that children have yet to be able to express directly, and this was evident in many of the narratives. In this respect, the Costa Rican children resemble English-speaking North American children (Menig-Peterson & McCabe, 1977); however, unlike English-speaking narrators, it must be noted that a lack of evaluation was not exclusive to the Costa Rican narratives involving death, as we discuss herein.

The Dominican children also told about deaths in four narratives; however, in one case, a 7-year-old Dominican girl was quite expressive of her grief about many such experiences (italics indicate evaluation):

Narrative 4

First narrative:	When I was with my friend in my backyard one day. Ummm, her grandmother was *almost dying*. That they were gonna miss her a lot. That they were crying. *But not my little friend. No she was just scared she'd die right now. She already died. When we were, we weren't there when she died. She only died. I was so sad to see her die. I didn't see her. But they told me that she died.* On the phone, my, her, but they told me. And they told them. That was umm saying. *So I'm I'm sad. She's in the sky with God. With God.*
Second linked narrative:	*And I'm so sad about the people that died in the twin towers. Even one person that I knew.* He was a friend of my mother and father. *And he was my friend too. And he was big.* And he always was wearing a hat. *He's always different. But he sometimes he doesn't wear a hat. But now he died in the crash.* When he was going umm to Dominican Republic. *And he crashed. The plane crashed into a house. And I'm sad.*
Third linked narrative:	*Sometimes bad people go in the plane.* Sometimes they take away the pilot on the plane. And they start driving it. *Crash! That's what the bad people wanna do. They want their own town. That's what they want. Yeah, the bad people want their own town. That no one else in it. But we want to survive.* But I heard this on the computer. That they needed to find out a way to *clearness. One time I went to the twin towers. Only one time. Never again. But now that the twin towers are not here anymore, I can't go. That's so sad. It was so nice in there. Now it's destroyed* [on the verge of tears]. *I never want one other one!*

Other aspects of the children's lives are very much reflected in the content of their narratives, which included references to injuries, threats to safety, and the context of their life as revealed in their play with other children. Snakes, for example, are ubiquitous in Costa Rica, found in symbols, in living form, and hence also present in four (13.3%) of the children's narratives. One 8-year-old girl told about a time she played with another girl in such a manner as to reveal indirectly that she and her friend were aware of the poverty of their circumstances: "And then we started to play that somebody was the maid and we were rich girls." A 7-year-old Dominican boy talks about his difficult family situation in a very poignant way:

> [I have been in a car accident] with my EX-father [child stressed EX]. He stinks... My EX-dad was driving, and then he crashed into something, and I don't know what is it anyways. So a truck came and pick it up – a truck.

The children discussed their experiences at school in these narratives. For example, the following 8-year-old Dominican boy clearly articulates his view of his school:

> And sometimes I think that my school is the worst school in the world 'cause it's boring. Ummm, in school I got in trouble a thousand times for saying that um this school was the worst school in the world. Mmmhumm, I walked on the ice, and I got in trouble for doing that. And that's it.

In Narrative 3, and often throughout these children's narratives, references to many extended family members were found: "The son of my uncle. The little boy was my cousin. The father of the little boy was my uncle." In this respect, the Latino narratives considered herein resemble those of Mexican American children living in California (Cano, 1993) and Pan-Latino children living in the northeastern United States (Cristofaro & Tamis-LeMonda, chapter 4, this volume; Rodino et al., 1991; Silva & McCabe, 1996).

NARRATIVE STRUCTURE: RESULTS OF HIGHPOINT ANALYSIS

Classic narrative format in European and North American stories involves beginning a story with a description of a setting (i.e., orientation) followed by a sequence of events that build up to an emotional climax, which is heavily evaluated (e.g., "And this is the most important part" or "I was screaming and crying and screaming and crying and screaming and crying"; Peterson & McCabe, 1983). The narrator then resolves the climactic action in some way. As shown in Table 10.1, Costa Rican ethnic minority children's narratives took classic European form much less frequently than those of European North American (Peterson & McCabe, 1983), African American (Champion, 2003), and Haitian American (Champion, McCabe, & Colinet, 2002–2003) children

Table 10.1. *Comparison of Dominican and Costa Rican narratives to three other cultural groups*

	European American 6–8 years	African American 7–8 years	Haitian American 7–8 years	Dominican American 7–8 years %(N)	Costa Rican 6–9 years: %(N)
Highpoint Analysis					
Classic	48.3%	59.0%	33.0%	27.7% (10)	26.7% (8)
End at Highpoint	19%	6.5%	26.5%	25.0% (9)	13.3% (4)
Leapfrog	2%	13.0%	0%	0%	23.3% (7)
Minimal events (1–3)	4%	2.0%	33.0%	22.2% (8)	16.7% (5)
Miscellaneous (general case) or Chronological	25%	19.5%	6.7%	25.0% (9)	20.0% (6)
Story Grammar					
Multiepisodic	9.0%	Not reported	0%	0%	3.3% (1)
Complex episode	5.6%	43.5%	0%	2.7% (1)	0%
Complete episode	45.7%	34.8%	10%	8.3% (3)	3.3% (1)
Abbreviated episode	8%	0%	7%	16.7% (6)	33.3% (10)
Reactive sequences	24%	15.2%	43%	25.0% (9)	10.0% (3)
Action sequences	5.6%	2.1%	30%	30.5% (11)	33.01% (10)
Descriptive sequences	2.3%	0%	10%	16.7% (6)	16.6% (5)

Note that the European North American sample came from Peterson & McCabe (1983); average percentage from 6-, 7-, and 8-year-olds was tabulated. Children often produced narratives with more than one story grammar structure per narrative and different numbers of story grammar structures were produced at each age; thus, percentages do not add up to 100. The African American sample is from Champion, Seymour, & Camarata (1995), and the Haitian American sample is from Champion, McCabe, & Colinet (2002–2003).

in other studies, as well as the Dominican children studied herein. Because the African American, Haitian, and Dominican children to whom the Costa Rican children are compared were also living in poverty (as were some of the European North American children), the discrepant results cannot be attributed to low socioeconomic status per se, despite the fact that diminished language skills are found among low-socioeconomic-status (i.e., low SES) English-speaking children (Hart & Risley, 1995).

The Costa Rican narratives were notable for a pervasive lack of evaluation. Specifically, only 32% of the Costa Rican narrative comments were fully (20%) or partially (12%) evaluative. In contrast, 39.9% of the Dominican comments were fully (23%) or partially (16.8%) evaluative. Both groups examined herein evaluate less than European North American children, 50% of whose comments were fully (15%) or partially (35%) evaluative (Peterson & McCabe, 1983). The conspicuous lack of much evaluation when relating their experiences means that Costa Rican ethic minority children have relatively few means to state what they are feeling and thinking, as well as little opportunity to do so. Costa Rican children's ability to make sense of their experiences through narrating them is compromised by failure to develop or loss of facility in their Indigenous language –possibly eventual loss of that language itself in some cases – combined with inadequate instruction in Spanish. Yet, as discussed previously, they had striking topics to talk about: mothers who could no longer move around, yellow heart memorials for people run over, operations for heart failure, snakes, and la Llorona.

Perhaps the lack of evaluation in Costa Rican children's narrative is evidence of a cultural preference for stoicism. However, in the European North American culture, diminished evaluation is due to a relative lack of adult linguistic input. In a review of much research conducted during the past 15 or so years, Fivush, Reese, & Haden (2006) establish that children narrate longer when their mothers ask them extensive questions about their experiences. In fact, the impact of maternal elaboration on narrative skill has been demonstrated to be causal: a group of mothers who were randomly assigned to a condition in which they were asked to extend their 3-year-old child's personal narration did in fact do so; their children told longer, more complex narratives 2 years later (Peterson, Jesso, & McCabe, 1999) – therefore, such elaboration can actually be said to cause narrative development. In contrast, peers – even siblings – are far less likely to have a positive impact on language acquisition (Evans, Maxwell, & Hart, 1999; Jones & Adamson, 1987). The dominance of peer–peer interaction in the Costa Rican children's lives was evident in each community in which research was conducted. In all four communities, children were surrounded by their peers most of each day – and most of the time without adult guidance or supervision. Therefore, these Costa Rican children were not receiving much of the kind of parental linguistic input that has been shown to facilitate narrative structural development (Peterson, Jesso, & McCabe, 1999).

One notable exception to this diminished evaluation is Narrative 4; the length and extent of evaluation in the Dominican girl's narrative undoubtedly stems from having engaged in much conversation with her mother and other adults, quite possibly specifically about September 11, 2001. This child is remarkably able to express her grief, in a way that will help her continue to make sense of difficult experiences. In fact, evaluation dominated Narrative 4, which contained few actual past-tense events and was therefore considered to fall in the minimal-event category.

Following is the only classic narrative produced by any of the Costa Rican children interviewed, and even it has quite muted evaluation (bolded), which is a key macrostructural component and hallmark of classic narratives (Labov,

1972; Peterson & McCabe, 1983). This narrative was told by a 7-year-old Brunkan (Indigenous) girl:

Narrative 5

Spanish Original

*Estaba en parada de corazón. Y pasé yo no sé cuántos días en el hospital. **Tenía que ir** en una ambulancia. Y **tenían que** operarme aquí. Y cortaron aquí [muestra la cicatriz]. **Porque estaba en parada de corazón**, en el hospital de San José. Había muchos niños operados. Los daban de comer . . . las frutas. Yo estaba en una cama. Entonces me dejaron la salida. Y nada más . . .*

English Translation

I had a heart failure. And I spent I don't know how many days in the hospital. I **had** to go in an ambulance. And they **had** to operate on me here. And they cut here (showing scar). **Because my heart was failing**, in the hospital in San José. There were many kids being operated on. They gave us food to eat . . . fruit. I was in a bed. And then they allowed me to leave. And that's it . . .

Thus, highpoint analysis does not seem to be a good fit for the narratives of the Latino children studied herein. As discussed previously, Narrative 4 about September 11 was highly evaluated, although not classic in form; in fact, however, that narrative was much better developed than those that were actually classified as such (i.e., Narrative 5). The following is another classic narrative – but a very succinct one – told in English by a 7-year-old Dominican boy:

I remember what happened to my little brother. They took his teeth out right there (points) *because it hurted so much*. A doctor from New York came, take his tooth off and *made* him go to sleep, and then shot him 4 times, right? And then they gave him a toy and ice cream.

Narrative Structure: Results of Story Grammar Analysis

Story grammar analysis is a way of examining narrative originally based on analysis of Russian folktales (McCabe, 1996). This approach assesses the extent to which a narrator articulates the precipitation of a goal and whether that goal is achieved. In contrast to European North American children aged 6 through 8 years (see Table 10.1), who rarely produced descriptive and action sequences in their personal narratives (Peterson & McCabe, 1983), half of the Costa Rican children's narratives are in these relatively undeveloped story grammar categories (Stein & Glenn, 1979). Four of the narratives largely devoted to fiction were action sequences, as were approximately a fifth (i.e., six) of the personal narratives. Five of the narratives were even simpler descriptive sequences. Only a few goals were ever mentioned (e.g., "Have you seen jets that go looking for bad guys to get them and lock them up"; "I killed it because it was venomous." Dominican children show much the same pattern in this respect. Despite the fact that 10 of the 12 children mentioned accidents and/or trips to doctors, which are replete with many opportunities to talk about goals, only 3 explicitly articulated goals in this context: A 7-year-old boy said that he "needed to go to a doctor" for his broken leg and an 8-year-old girl mentioned that she had been to the hospital "to get my appendix" presumably out, but she follows this with "in Halloween I ate a lot of candy," so even that goal is less than clear. The most elaborate mention of goals is in the September 11 narrative: "That's what the bad people wanna do. They want their own town . . . But we want to survive." Again, this unusual mention of goals reflects the extensive public and, more important, familial discussion of the events surrounding that catastrophe. Children need to be engaged in a discussion of goals in order to articulate them in their own narratives. At the age of 6 to 8 years, goals pervade the narratives of European North American children (Peterson & McCabe, 1983) and African American children (Champion, 2003; Champion et al., 1995). In the world of these Costa Rican and Dominican children, however, events tend merely to happen to them, one after another, for little or no particular reason.

The impact of a tendency to produce narratives that are not organized around the precipitation and accomplishment of goals, which are key to complete episodes in story grammar, can be seen in the following recounting of "Little Red Riding Hood" by an 8-year-old Maleku girl, classified as a highly complex, multiepisodic narrative – the only one in this corpus:

Narrative 6

Spanish Original

Que cuando anda por el bosque, el lobo se la quiere comer a Caperucita. Y el lobo le dice a Caperucita, "Tú te vas al camino más largo y yo me voy por el cerca". Y el lobo llegó y asustó [a la] abuelita de Caperucita. Y después, después el lobo se vistió de la abuela. Y dijo la Caperucita, "¡Qué orejas tan grandes, tan grande!" "Es para oírte mejor." "¡Y qué narices!" "Es para olerte." "¡Qué boca tan grande!" "Es para . . . para ¡comerte!" Y después era para comer a Caperucita y a [la] abuela. Y vino un leñador y mató al lobo.

English Translation

When she walks in the forest, the wolf wants to eat Little Red Riding Hood [LRRH]. And the wolf says to LRRH. "You take the long way, I'll take the short one." And the wolf came and scared LRRH's grandma. And later, later the wolf dressed as the grandma. And LRRH said, "What huge ears you have, huge ears." "It's to hear you better." "And what a big nose!" "It's to smell you." "And such a huge mouth!" "It's to . . . to eat you!" But really, the mouth was to eat LRRH and the grandma. And a lumberjack came and killed the wolf.

Because we know the story, we can infer that the lumberjack killed the wolf to save Little Red Riding Hood, but that is not expressly stated as story grammar (along with many European North American teachers) requires. Members of numerous cultures have long been known to recall stories from cultures not their own in ways that conform more to their usual sense of story (see McCabe, 1996), and this child exemplifies that phenomenon in her version of the classic European fairy tale.

GENERAL DISCUSSION

In general, then, we have seen that the Latino children's narratives examined in this chapter are often structured in a non-European way (as captured in highpoint and story grammar analysis), suggesting vestigial elements of past oral traditions in the case of the Costa Rican children. As stated in Okpewho (1992), stories told in an oral tradition often differ considerably in structure from those told in a tradition with a long history of literacy.

In view of the poor fit between the Latino children's narratives and both highpoint and story grammar analyses, would another form of analysis function more adequately? Confronted with such an outcome in work with narratives from other ethnic groups, alternative analyses have, in fact, been successful. For example, in the case of Haitian children's narratives, an Africanist analysis of repetition, parallelism, and detailing proved more successful than highpoint or story grammar at capturing the richness of how those children recalled their experiences (Champion, McCabe, & Colinet, 2002–2003). In the case of Japanese children's narratives, a poetic analysis of lines grouped in stanzas fit well (Minami & McCabe, 1991). Those alternatives were considered and found not to be useful in the current study. That is, preliminary analysis did not reveal any considerable inclination to elaborate by means of repetition, nor any regular grouping of lines into stanzas of structurally and substantively related lines. Perhaps an analysis might be developed that would be more appropriate than any of these alternatives. However, more likely, the remarkable linguistic diversity among Latino children would make any attempt to show broad commonalities of narrative form impossible. Perhaps narrative structures available to Latino children are varied and reflect the predominant *mestizaje* of cultures that together comprise the Latin American culture. That is, among Latin American cultures, there is no one predominant narrative structure; rather, there are many, reflecting the fusion of various storytelling traditions.

Cultures develop a kind of aesthetic taste that pertains to all senses (McCabe, 1996, p. 45). To better capture the form of narration in a culture, it is advisable to look at other art forms pervasive in those cultures, bringing us at this point to the literary narratives from Latin America. For instance, we can examine novels that include magical realism (Latin American par excellence), which has been defined as "an amalgamation of realism and fantasy" (Flores, 1955). In his 1982 Nobel Prize lecture, Gabriel García Márquez narrated numerous grotesque, purportedly real events in the history of Latin America to explain the origins of magical realism (1993):

> I dare to think that it is this outsized reality, and not just its literary expression, that has deserved the attention of the Swedish Academy of Letters. A reality not of paper, but one that lives within us and determines each instant of our countless daily deaths, and that nourishes a source of insatiable creativity, full of sorrow and beauty, of which this roving and nostalgic Colombian is but one cipher more, singled out by fortune. Poets and beggars, musicians and prophets, warriors and

scoundrels, all creatures of that unbridled reality, we have had to ask but little of imagination, for our crucial problem has been a lack of conventional means to render our lives believable. This, my friends, is the crux of our solitude.

Literary fiction both echoes and shapes the ways individuals in a culture narrate. In the blending of fiction and fact in the Costa Rican children's narration, magical realism is alive and well. A child tells us a story of crossing a brook and encountering la Llorona, a mythical scary figure, seamlessly moving from what Anglo listeners hear as fact to a figure from oral fiction. Magical realism can be found in books written for children (e.g., García's [1987] *My Aunt Otilia's Spirits* or Álvarez's [2000] *The Secret Footprints*). Furthermore, the deaths that García Márquez noted and that can be found in Latino children's books like those mentioned previously pervade the narratives of the Latino children studied herein.

Musical forms also often relate to literary forms and afford insight into the diverse forms taken by these Latino children's narratives. The Dominican Republic's national music is *merengue* (Steward & Harvey, 2000), which contains lyrics teeming with magical realism, as well as African rhythms, European contra dance forms, and accordions imported from Germany – quite a rich example of *mestizaje*. *Salsa* is also relevant (Steward, 2000, p. 488):

> *Salsa* is a word with vivid associations but no absolute definitions, a tag that encompasses a rainbow assortment of Latin rhythms and styles, taking on a different hue wherever you stand in the Spanish-speaking world. In her own definition, the acknowledged Queen of Salsa, Afro-Cuban singer Celia Cruz, says, 'Salsa is Cuban music with another name. It's mambo, chachachá, rumba, son ... all the Cuban rhythms under one name.' To which a Puerto Rican might add plena and jíbaro, a Colombian cumbia, a Dominican merengue, and so it goes. Literally the word salsa means 'sauce' and in Latin American musical circles it takes its origins from a cry of appreciation for a particularly piquant or flashy solo. ... Like so much Latin music, salsa has dual roots in the Spanish music of the colonisers and in the African traditions of slave communities. The balance between these influences varies considerably from one territory to another in Latin America and the Caribbean, and salsa reflects that.

Salsa rhythms are complex (see http://www.its.caltech.edu/~daven/Notation. htm) and vary from village to village (Sweeney & Rosenberg, 2000). With such rhythmic diversity as the hallmark of salsa, which is heard ubiquitously throughout Latin America, perhaps we should not be surprised to find such diversity in the form that Latino children's narratives take.

Implications for Assessment of Latino Children's Narration

The fact that Latino children's narratives are so diverse and so distinct from European North American children's narratives means that educators and speech-language pathologists who work with Latino children run the risk of misdiagnosing cultural differences as deficits; in fact, both over- and under-diagnosis of language and literacy problems are common with low-socio-economic and ethnically diverse children (Laing & Kamhi, 2003). Guidelines to prevent such misdiagnosis have been developed (Bliss, McCabe, & Mahecha, 2001; McCabe & Bliss, 2003) and include the following: First, clinicians should try to identify the narrative styles that are used in the home, consulting with families and/or other full participants in the child's culture to determine whether the clinician's assessments of narrative difficulties are at odds with elements of narrative stressed as important by the child's community (e.g., mention of extended family members who would be seen as irrelevant by European American listeners; Rollins, McCabe, & Bliss, 2000). Second, clinicians should understand that in Latino narratives, sequencing of actions is not necessarily valued the way it is by monolingual English speakers (McCabe & Silva, 1996). Third, clinicians should assess narration apart from scores on standardized tests because narration may be intact even if those standard scores are low, or vice versa. Fourth, clinicians should understand that nonspecific vocabulary found in narratives (e.g., unidentified pronouns or vague terms) may be a function of the fact that bilingual children are mastering two languages and may not have the specific vocabulary in one or another of those languages that a mono-lingual child would be expected to have. Fifth, bilingual speakers might show pauses and hesitations in narration at a higher rate than monolingual children due to their efforts at formulating the narrative in their second language rather than to any language impairment per se (McCabe & Bliss, 2003; Pérez, 1998).

Clinicians should also be aware that use of fictional narratives, as opposed to primarily factual personal narratives, is a particular liability in the assessment of Latino children. For example, a study in which Puerto Rican preschoolers were asked to retell the film, *Frog Goes to Dinner,* found that these children were unfamiliar with the script for going to a restaurant and substituted more familiar words such as "store" for restaurant, "handkerchief" for napkin, and "policemen" for waiters (Gutiérrez-Clellen, 1990, as cited in Gutiérrez-Clellen & Quinn, 1993). Shiro (2003) found that low-SES and younger Venezuelan children are at a greater disadvantage when performing fictional narratives than when performing personal narratives, and that they evaluate the former significantly less than do their middle-class peers.

Implications for Narrative Intervention With Latino Children

Once a teacher or (preferably bilingual) clinician, in consultation with parents and/or other adult members of a Latino child's community, has determined that a particular child does indeed display language delay that involves a compromised ability to narrate, appropriate intervention procedures should be implemented. Gutiérrez-Clellen (1996) recommended that a broad range of techniques be used to facilitate narrative development in interventions with Hispanic children. Here again, guidelines have been developed (Bliss et al., 2001; McCabe & Bliss, 2003): (1) stories and materials relevant to the child's particular culture should be involved whenever possible; (2) clinicians should ask a child to describe family vignettes (e.g., preparing food, going to a festival) or engage in conversation-focused stories (Melzi, 2000), as well as to produce the kind of classic narratives (see previous discussion) valued in school; (3) contingent queries should be directed to the child, enabling the child to expand and/or clarify what he or she said; (4) parents should be encouraged to extend their children's narratives on a regular basis, which has been shown to improve narrative structure and receptive vocabulary with low-income English-speaking children (Peterson et al., 1999); and (5) school-age Latino children should be encouraged to watch certain educational shows, such as *Arthur*, which have been shown to improve narrative skills (Uchikoshi, 2005).

In one impressive study, Costantino, Malgady, and Rogler (1984, 1986) developed what they called *Cuento Therapy* (i.e., Story Therapy), which used original or modified Puerto Rican folktales or randomly assigned kindergarten through third-grade children to either a traditional or a no-therapy condition. In the *Cuento* Therapy condition, therapists and mothers read two *cuentos* bilingually as four or five children followed the narration. Therapists then led a group discussion about the characters' behavior and the moral of the *cuento* (e.g., stealing is wrong). The gist of the stories was dramatized by mothers and children and videotaped and summarized again by the therapists. After 20 weeks of therapy, children in both the original and the adapted *cuento* groups were rated less anxious than those in the control group. Both *cuento* therapies enhanced WISC-Revised Comprehension subtest scores relative to traditional art/play therapy or the control group. Furthermore, both *cuento* groups displayed less aggression than the traditional therapy group. Finally, the authors noted that the direct involvement of mothers in therapeutic intervention plus the use of culturally relevant *cuentos* were features that made this form of therapeutic intervention particularly attractive to members of that Puerto Rican community in New York City.

Such promising results related to narrative-level intervention are, unfortunately, not widely known. For example, in a review of reading studies that were conducted with bilingual, at-risk students who were in kindergarten through third grade, Vaughn, Linan-Thompson, Pollard-Durodola, Mathes, and Hagan (2006, p. 188) found evidence that bilingual Latino students "can improve their word reading, fluency, and comprehension when provided systematic and explicit interventions that focus on the critical elements of reading (phonics, spelling, fluency, and comprehension) and also provide many opportunities to read text and interpret what they are reading. Interventions that had a more structured, systematic approach that included phonics fared better than those without these elements." In other words, those authors neglected even to mention the need for – let alone the promise of – culturally relevant, narrative-level interventions.

This omission of attention to the need for intervention at the narrative level is critical, given what we have documented regarding the often un-European structure of Latino children's narratives. Ever since Bartlett (1932) asked British people to recall a North American Indian folktale and found that they tended to distort that tale to make it conform more to their own sense of what a story should be, abundant research has demonstrated that this is not a unique phenomenon (see McCabe, 1996, for a review). Children comprehend and remember more of the stories that conform to the structure of the kind of stories they have heard at home – stories that make sense to them for that reason. This finding means that children who are not exposed to the largely classical European form of stories used in American schools will need instruction that draws their attention to the importance placed on sequencing events, evaluating in narration, and focusing on problem-solving and resolution. These measures will facilitate such children's comprehension of stories they hear and read in the classroom and have both direct and indirect effects on their overall academic engagement and achievement. Similarly, to read and fully appreciate the rich literature of Latin America, students from dominant cultures may need to understand diverse narrative forms, such as the personal narratives told by their Latino peers.

To conclude, this chapter examined narratives in several groups of children, all of whom are growing up exposed to at least two languages in daily contact with each other. In Costa Rica, Spanish is the language of power and vies with Indigenous languages in the communication patterns of children. With the Dominican children, English is the language of power and vies with Spanish in the repertoire of those children. We have argued that such language socialization is common among Latino children in the Americas, and that variation both within groups and of the groups in contrast to dominant culture is one predictable result, as other researchers have noted (Garrett & Baquedano-López, 2002). In fact, variation is a hallmark of the remarkable fusion of European, Indigenous, and African cultures – the *mestizaje* that is Latin America and its people.

ACKNOWLEDGMENTS

The authors would like to thank Maga Gei, whose help with the transcription and translation of hours of Costa Rican narratives was invaluable, Shirly Vásquez for collecting the Dominican narratives, Dr. Luis D. Gómez and the Organization for Tropical Studies, who enabled the collection of the Costa Rican narratives, and, most of all, the many children, elders, and other adults from the Boruca, Margarita, Cahuita, and Shiroles communities who were kind enough to take time out of their busy schedules and genuinely engage in conversation with the first author so that we were able to gain important insight into the life, culture, and dynamics of their communities. Lastly, we would all like to thank our supportive families.

REFERENCES

Allen, S. E. M., Crago, M., & Pesco, D. (2006). The effect of majority language exposure on minority language skills: The case of Inuktitut. *The International Journal of Bilingual Education and Bilingualism, 9*(5), 578–596.

Álvarez, E. (2003). Character introduction in two languages: Its development in the stories of a Spanish-English bilingual child age 6;11–10;11. *Bilingualism: Language and Cognition, 6*(3), 227–243.

Álvarez, J. (2000). *The secret footprints.* New York: Knopf.

Anderson, R. (1999). Impact of first-language loss on grammar in a bilingual child. *Communication Disorders Quarterly, 21*(1), 4–16.

Asociación de Desarrollo Integral de Rey Curré (ADIRC) (2001). *Narraciones Brunkas.* San José, CR: Instituto De Estudios De Las Tradiciones Sagradas De Abia Yala.

Bartlett, F. C. (1932). *Remembering.* Cambridge: Cambridge University Press.

Berman, R. A., & Slobin, D. I. (1994). *Relating events in narrative: A cross-linguistic developmental study.* Hillsdale, NJ: Erlbaum.

Bliss, L. S., McCabe, A., & Mahecha, N. R. (2001). Analyses of narratives from Spanish-speaking bilingual children. *Contemporary Issues in Communication Science and Disorders, 28,* 133–139.

Bozzoli, de W., & Ching, W. (1979). *Encuesta socioeconómica en la zona de P. H. Boruca.* San José, CR: Universidad de Costa Rica e Instituto Costarricense de Eléctricidad.

Bozzoli, de W., Vegas, M. E., & Venegas, C. M. C. (1982). *Tradición Oral Indígena Costarricense.* San José, CR: Universidad De Costa Rica.

Calderón, G., & Alfredo, J. (2003). *Desarrollo hidroeléctrico y mecanismos de interacción con sociedades y territorios indígenas: El caso del P. H. Boruca de Costa Rica. Tésis de posgrado en Geografía.* Costa Rica: Ciudad Universitaria Rodrigo Facio, Universidad de Costa Rica.

Campbell, P. (2003). The art of *mestizaje:* Fusion in Latin America. *Humanities, 24*(6). Retrieved from http://www.neh.gov/news/humanities/2003-11/mestizaje.html.

Cano, L. (1993). *Analysis of Chicano children's narratives.* Unpublished course paper. Cambridge, MA: Harvard University.

Cartín, E. Z. (2003). *Crónicas de los viajes a Guatuso y Talamanca del Obispo Bernardo Augusto Thiel.* San José, CR: Editorial de la Universidad de Costa Rica.

Champion, T. B. (2003). *Understanding storytelling among African American children.* Hillsdale, NJ: Erlbaum.

Champion, T., McCabe, A., & Colinet, Y. (2002–2003). The whole world could hear: The structure of Haitian American children's narratives. *Imagination, Cognition and Personality, 22,* 381–400.

Champion, T., Seymore, H., & Camarata, A. (1995). Narrative discourse among African American children. *Journal of Narrative and Life History, 5*(4), 333–352.

Chomsky, A. (1995). Afro-Jamaican traditions and labor organizing on United Fruit Company plantations in Costa Rica, 1910. *Journal of Social History, 28*(14), 837–856.

Conboy, B. T., & Thal, D. (2006). Ties between the lexicon and grammar: Cross-sectional and longitudinal studies of bilingual toddlers. *Child Development, 77*(3), 712–735.

Constantino, G., Malgady, R. G., & Rogler, L. H. (1984). *Cuentos folklricos* as a therapeutic modality with Puerto Rican children. *Hispanic Journal of Behavioral Sciences, 6*(2), 169–178.

Constantino, G., Malgady, R. G., & Rogler, L. H. (1986). *Cuento* therapy: A cultur-ally sensitive modality for Puerto Rican children. *Journal of Consulting and Clinical Psychology, 54,* 639–645.

Crago, M. B. (1992). Communicative interaction and second-language acquisition: An Inuit example. *TESOL Quarterly, 26*(3), 487–505.

Pesco, D., Crago, M. D., & McCabe, A. (1996). Context and structure: Some North American Indian and Aboriginal Traditions. In A. McCabe (Ed.), *Chameleon readers: Teaching children to appreciate all kinds of good stories* (pp. 137–154). New York: McGraw-Hill.

Cruz, O. H. (1998). Culturas y Dinámica Regional en el Caribe Costarricense. *Anuario de Estudios Centroamericanos, 24*(2), 129–162.

Cummins, J. (1979). Linguistic interdependence and the educational development of bilingual children. *Review of Educational Research, 49,* 222–251.

Cummins, J. (1991). Interdependence of first- and second-language proficiency in bi-lingual children. In E. Bialystok (Ed.), *Language processing in bilingual children* (pp. 70–89). Cambridge: Cambridge University Press.

Dickinson, D. K., McCabe, A., Clark-Chiarelli, N., & Wolf, A. (2004). Cross-language transfer of phonological awareness in low-income Spanish and English bilingual preschool children. *Applied Psycholinguistics, 25,* 323–347.

Dorell, O. (2006, November 17). English as official language gains support at local levels. *U.S.A. Today,* p. A4.

Edith, M., Marín, N. M., & Blanco, F. M. (1996). Historias Maleku II: Vida y costumbres del indio Maleku. Heredia, Costa Rica: EFUNA.

Evans, G. W., Maxwell, L. E., & Hart, B. (1999). Parental language and verbal responsive-ness to children in crowded homes. *Developmental Psychology, 35*(4), 1020–1023.

Fiestas, C. E., & Peña, E. D. (2004). Narrative discourse in bilingual children: Language and task effects. *Language, Speech, and Hearing Services in Schools, 35,* 155–168.

Fillmore, L. W. (1991). When learning a second language means losing the first. *Early Childhood Research Quarterly, 6,* 323–346.

Fivush, R., Reese, E., & Haden, C. (2006). Elaborating on elaborations: The role of mater-nal reminiscing style in cognitive and socioemotional development. *Child Develop-ment, 77*(6), 1568–1588.

Flores, A. (1955). Magical realism in Spanish American fiction. *Hispania, XXXVIII, 2,* 187–192.

Francis, N., & Gómez, P. R. N. (2003). Language interaction in Náhuatl discourse: The influence of Spanish in child and adult narratives. *Language, Culture and Curriculum, 16*(1), 1–17.

García, G. (2000). Bilingual children's reading. In M. Kamil, P. Mosenthal, P. Pearson, & R. Barr (Eds.), *Handbook of reading research, Vol. III* (pp. 813–834). Mahwah, NJ: Lawrence Erlbaum.

García, R. (1987). *My Aunt Otilia's spirits.* San Francisco, CA: Children's Book Press.

Garrett, P. B., & Baquedano-López, P. (2002). Language socialization: Reproduction and continuity, transformation and change. *Annual Review of Anthropology, 31,* 339–361.

Girot, P. O., Weitzner, V., & Fonseca, M. B. (1998). From conflict to collaboration: The case of Cahuita National Park, Límon, Costa Rica, pp. 1–5: http://www.iascp.org/Drafts/fonseca.pdf. Accessed August 8, 2006.

Gómez, L. D. Personal communication, August 4, 2006.

Graef, D. (2005). The life of the forgotten: The impact of development on environment and tradition in the Boruca Indigenous community of Costa Rica. Honors Thesis. Princeton, NJ: Princeton University.

Griffin, T. M., Hemphill, L., Camp, L., & Wolf, D. P. (2004). Oral discourse in the preschool years and later literacy skills. *First Language, 24*(2), 123–147.

Guardado, M. (2002). Loss and maintenance of first-language skills: Case studies of Hispanic families in Vancouver. *Canadian Modern Language Review, 58*(3), 341–363.

Gutiérrez-Clellen, V. F. (1996). Narrative development and disorders in Spanish-speaking children: Implications for the bilingual interventionist. In H. Kayser (Ed.), *Bilingual speech-language pathology: An Hispanic focus* (pp. 97–127). Florence, KY: Thomson Learning.

Gutiérrez-Clellen, V. F., & Peña, E. (2001). Dynamic assessment of diverse children: A tutorial. *Language, Speech, and Hearing Services in Schools, 32*, 212–224.

Gutiérrez-Clellen, V. F., & Quinn, R. (1993). Assessing narratives of children from diverse cultural/liniguistic groups. *Language, Speech, and Hearing Services in Schools, 24*, 2–9.

Hammer, C. S., Miccio, A. W., & Wagstaff, D. A. (2003). Home literacy experiences and their relationship to bilingual preschoolers' developing English literacy abilities: An initial investigation. *Language, Speech, and Hearing Services in Schools, 34*, 20–30.

Hart, B., & Risley, T. R. (1995). *Meaningful differences in the everyday experience of young American children*. Baltimore, MD: Brookes.

Heath, S. B. (1982). What no bedtime story means. *Language in Society, 11*, 49–76.

Hymes, D. (1982). Narrative form as a "grammar" of experience: Native Americans and a glimpse of English. *Journal of Education, 2*, 121–142.

Hymes, D. (1987). Warm Springs Sahaptin narrative analysis. In J. Sherzer & A. Woodbury (Eds.), *Native American discourse: Poetics and rhetoric* (pp. 62–102). Cambridge: Cambridge University Press.

Instituto de Tierras y Colonización (ITCO) (1964). Estudio de comunidades indígenas zonas: Boruca-Térraba y China Kichá. Costa Rica: ITCO.

Instituto Nacional de Estadística y Censos (2000). Censo de Costa Rica del 2000. San José, CR: INEC.

Jiménez-Silva, M. (1996). *"Princesses, cousins, and other good things": A look at the oral narrative structures of Mexican-American children*. Unpublished qualifying paper. Cambridge, MA: Harvard University.

John, V. P., & Berney, T. D. (1968). Analysis of story retelling as a measure of the effects of ethnic content in stories. In J. Hellmuth (Ed.), *The disadvantaged child: Head Start and early intervention, Vol. 2* (pp. 257–288). New York: Brunner/Mazel Publishers.

Jones, C. P., and Adamson, L. B. (1987). Language use in mother–child and mother–child–sibling interactions. *Child Development, 58*, 356–366.

Kirtley, B. F. (1960). La Llorona and related themes. *Western Folklore, 19*(3), 155–168.

Labov, W. (1972). *Language in the inner city: Studies in the Black English vernacular.* Philadelphia: University of Pennsylvania Press.

Laing, S. P., & Kamhi, A. (2003). Alternative assessment of language and literacy in culturally and linguistically diverse populations. *Language, Speech, and Hearing Services in Schools, 34*, 44–55.

Manuel-Dupont, S., Strong, C., & Fields, T. (1990). Spoken narrative assessment: Language-impaired and Native American school-aged children. Paper presented at the American Speech-Language and Hearing Association conference. Seattle, WA.

Maroto, E. S., de González, I. P., Morales, E. G., & Umaña, A. C. (1990). *Leyendas y tradiciones Borucas*. San José, CR: Editorial De La Universidad De Costa Rica.

Márquez, G. G. (1993). The solitude of Latin America. In T. Frangsmyr (Ed.), *Nobel Lectures: Literature 1981–1990*. Singapore: World Scientific Publishing Company.

McCabe, A. (1996). *Chameleon readers: Teaching children to appreciate all kinds of good stories*. New York: McGraw-Hill.

McCabe, A. (1997). Developmental and cross-cultural aspects of children's narration. In M. Bamberg (Ed.), *Narrative development: Six approaches* (pp. 137–174). Mahwah, NJ: Erlbaum.

McCabe, A., & Bliss, L. S. (2003). *Patterns of narrative discourse*. Boston: Allyn & Bacon.

McCabe, A., & Bliss, L. S. (2004–2005). Narratives from Spanish-speaking children with impaired and typical language development. *Imagination, Cognition and Personality, 24*(4), 331–346.

McCabe, A., & Rollins, P. R. (1994). Assessment of preschool narrative skills: Prerequisite for literacy. *American Journal of Speech-Language Pathology: A Journal of Clinical Practice, 3*, 45–56.

McCabe, A., & Silva, M. J. (1996). Vignettes of the continuous and family ties: Some Latino American traditions. In A. McCabe (Ed.), *Chameleon readers: Teaching children to appreciate all kinds of good stories* (pp. 116–136). New York: McGraw-Hill.

Melzi, G. (2000). Cultural variations in the construction of personal narrative: Central American and European American mothers' elicitation style. *Discourse Processes, 30*(2), 153–177.

Melzi, G., & Caspe, M. (2005). Variations in maternal narrative styles during book-reading interactions. *Narrative Inquiry, 15*(1), 101–125.

Menig-Peterson, C., & McCabe, A. (1977). Children talk about death. *Omega, 8*, 305–317.

Miller, J. F., Heilmann, J., Nockerts, A., Iglesias, A., Fabiano, L., & Francis, D. J. (2006). Oral language and reading in bilingual children. *Learning Disabilities Research & Practice, 21*(1), 30–43.

Minami, M., & McCabe, A. (1991). Haiku as a discourse regulation device: A stanza analysis of Japanese children's personal narratives. *Language in Society, 20*, 577–600.

Ministerio de Planificación y Política Económica (MIDEPLAN) (2002). Plan Nacional de Desarrollo de los Pueblos Indígenas de Costa Rica.

Moorcroft, R., & Gardner, R. C. (1987). Linguistic factors in second-language loss. *Language Learning, 37*(3), 327–340.

Muñoz, M. L., Gillam, R. B., Peña, E. D., & Gulley-Faehnle, A. (2003). Measures of language development in fictional narratives of Latino children. *Language, Speech, and Hearing Services in Schools, 34*, 332–342.

Okpewho, I. (1992). *African oral literature*. Bloomington: Indiana University Press.

Pan, B. A., & Gleason, J. B. (1986). The study of language loss: Models and hypotheses for an emerging discipline. *Applied Psycholinguistics, 7*(3), 193–206.

Peña, E., Bedore, L. M., & Rappazzo, C. (2003). Comparison of Spanish, English, and bilingual children's performance across semantic tasks. *Language, Speech, and Hearing Services in Schools, 34*, 5–16.

Pérez, C. (1998). *The language of native Spanish- and English-speaking schizotypal college students*. Unpublished doctoral dissertation. Boston: University of Massachusetts.

Peterson, C., Jesso, B., & McCabe, A. (1999). Encouraging narratives in preschoolers: An intervention study. *Journal of Child Language, 26,* 49–67.

Peterson, C., & McCabe, A. (1983). *Developmental psycholinguistics*. New York: Plenum.

Preece, A. (1987). The range of narrative forms conversationally produced by young children. *Journal of Child Language, 14,* 353–373.

Rodino, A., Gimbert, C., Pérez, C., Craddock-Willis, K., & McCabe, A. (1991, October). "Getting your point across: Contrastive sequencing in low-income African American and Latino children's personal narrative." Paper presented at the 16th Annual Conference on Language Development. Boston: Boston University.

Rollins, P. R., McCabe, A., & Bliss, L. S. (2000). Culturally sensitive assessment of narrative skills in children. *Seminars in Speech and Language, 21*(3), 223–234.

Sánchez, J. (2001). *Mi Libro De Historias Bribris, 1st ed.* San José, CR: Lara Segura & Associates.

Sánchez, L. (2006). Kechwa and Spanish bilingual grammars: Testing hypotheses on functional interference and convergence. *The International Journal of Bilingual Education and Bilingualism, 9*(5), 535–556.

Schieffelin, B. B., & Ochs, E. (1986). Language socialization. *American Review of Anthropology, 15,* 163–191.

Scollon, R., & Scollon, S. B. K. (1981). *Narrative, literacy, and face in interethnic communication*. Norwood, NJ: Ablex.

Sebastián, E., & Slobin, D. I. (1994). Development of linguistic forms: Spanish. In R. A. Berman & D. I. Slobin (Eds.), *Relating events in narrative: A cross-linguistic developmental study* (pp. 239–284). Hillsdale, NJ: Erlbaum.

Shiro, M. (2003). Genre and evaluation in narrative development. *Journal of Child Language, 30,* 165–195.

Shorris, E. (1992). *Latinos: A biography of the people*. New York: Norton.

Silva, M. (1996). *"Princesses, cousins, and other good things": A look at the oral narrative structures of Mexican American children*. Unpublished qualifying paper (data and manuscript). Boston: Harvard University.

Silva, M., & McCabe, A. (1996). Vignettes of the continuous and family ties: Some Latino American traditions. In A. McCabe (Ed.), *Chameleon readers: Teaching children to appreciate all kinds of good stories* (pp. 116–136). New York: McGraw-Hill.

Snow, C. E., Tabors, P., Nicholson, P., & Kurland, B. (1995). SHELL: Oral language and oral literacy skills in kindergarten and first-grade children. *Journal of Research in Childhood Education, 10,* 37–48.

Snow, C. E., Porche, M. V., Tabors, P. O., & Harris, S. R. (2007). *Is literacy enough: Pathways to academic success for adolescents*. Baltimore: Brookes.

Starks, D. (2006). The changing roles of language and identity in the New Zealand Niuean community: Findings from the Pasifika languages of Manukau Project. *The International Journal of Bilingual Education and Bilingualism, 9*(3), 374–391.

Stein, N., & Glenn, C. (1979). An analysis of story comprehension in elementary school children In R. Freedle (Ed.), *New directions in discourse processing, Vol. 2* (pp. 238–267). Hillsdale, NJ: Ablex.

Steward, S. (2000). Salsa: Cubans, Nuyoricans and the global sound. In S. Broughton & M. Ellingham (Eds.), *World Music*, 488–506. *Volume 2: Latin & North America, Caribbean, India, Asia and Pacific* (pp. 488–506). London: Rough Guides Ltd.

Steward, S., & Harvey, S. (2000). Dominican Republic: Merengue attacks. In S. Broughton & M. Ellingham (Eds.), *World Music, Volume 2: Latin & North America, Caribbean, India, Asia and Pacific* (pp. 414–420). London: Rough Guides Ltd.

Stone, D. (1949). *The Boruca of Costa Rica.* Papers of the Peabody Museum of American Archaeology and Ethnology, Harvard University, Vol. XXVI.

Stone, D. (1962). *The Talamancan Tribes of Costa Rica.* Peabody Museum of Archeology and Ethnology, Harvard University, Vol. XLIII-2.

Sweeney, P., & Rosenberg, D. (2000). Venezuela: Salsa con gasolina. In S. Broughton & M. Ellingham (Eds.), *World Music, Volume 2: Latin & North America, Caribbean, India, Asia and Pacific,* (pp. 624–630). London: Rough Guides Ltd.

Tabors, P. O., Snow, C. E., & Dickinson, D. K. (2001). Homes and schools together: Supporting language and literacy development. In D. K. Dickinson & P. O. Tabors (Eds.), *Beginning literacy with language,* pp. 313–334.

Torres, L. (1997). *Puerto Rican discourse: A sociolinguistic study of a New York Suburb.* Mahwah, NJ: Erlbaum.

Uccelli, P. (This volume, 2008). *Evaluation and temporality: The use of structural evaluation in Andean Spanish-speaking children's narratives.* Manuscript. Harvard Graduate School of Education.

Uchikoshi, Y. (2005). Narrative development in bilingual kindergarteners: Can *Arthur* help? *Developmental Psychology, 41*(3), 464–478.

Vaughn, S., Linan-Thompson, S., Pollard-Durodola, S. D., Mathes, P. G., & Hagan, E. C. (2006). Effective interventions for English-language learners (Spanish-English) at risk for learning difficulties. In D. K. Dickinson & S. B. Neuman (Eds.), *Handbook of early literacy research,* Vol. 2 (pp. 185–197). New York: Guilford.

Zentella, A. C. (1985). The fate of Spanish in the United States: The Puerto Rican experience. In N. Wolfson & J. Manes (Eds.), *Language of inequality* (pp. 134–150). Albany, NY: State University of New York Press.

Zentella, A. C. (1997). *Growing up bilingual: Puerto Rican children in New York.* Malden, MA: Blackwell Publishers.

PART THREE

NARRATIVE LINKS TO LITERACY AND OTHER
SCHOOL ACHIEVEMENTS

ALISON BAILEY

The third and final part of this book focuses on the link between oral narration and literacy acquisition for Spanish-speaking children in the United States. Much has been made of this link within the predominantly monolingual English-speaking population and, to some degree, the extent to which it is replicated in other populations of students, such as atypically developing children, African American students, and low-income students. Less is known about how the narrative discourse knowledge of Spanish-English bilingual students plays a role in their later literacy development and overall school achievement, yet it is critical that we know more about this heterogeneous population of students. Children who come to school speaking a language other than English (most often Spanish) are the fastest growing segment of the public school population, and these students are among the most vulnerable to school failure (Batalova, Fix, & Murray, 2007).

Two of the three chapters in this part, the first by Sparks and the second by Bailey, Moughamian, and Dingle, empirically explore the links between oral narrative and formal schooling experiences and outcomes. Chapter 11 focuses on the very first encounters of U.S. schooling by young Latino children with an investigation of four-year-olds in a Head Start program. Their mothers were predominantly U.S. mainland and Puerto Rican born. The mothers were requested to reminisce with their children in order to elicit a series of personal narratives. Children were also prompted for independent personal narratives by the researcher. Sparks finds that Latino mothers' use of elaboration appears to be present in different degrees and in different contexts than is found in conversations between European-American, middle-class parents and children in previous studies. Nevertheless, parent elaboration was linked to children's inclusion of critical contextual information in their independent narration in Spanish with important implications for children's preschool classroom experiences.

A case study of one child and his mother illustrates in some detail the facilitative role of mothers in preschoolers' narratives.

Chapter 12 continues the theme of a narrative–school performance link with a study of early elementary school-age children who are receiving both English- and Spanish-language instruction in a two-way bilingual program. First- through third-grade students from predominantly Mexican and Central American family backgrounds were requested to provide independent personal narratives in both English and Spanish about home- and school-related topics. Highpoint analyses of narrative macrostructure along with a grammaticality and productivity measure revealed that performance on the latter did not appear to constrain students' macrostructural abilities in either Spanish-language or English language narration. To broaden and add depth to definitions of the success of bilingual programming, the role of narrative discourse skills in both languages for positive school experiences and academic outcomes is explored.

An important recommendation made by both studies is for the creation of effective measures of Spanish-language narration. Sparks calls for new assessments that are specific to Latino narration that will capture individual variation and what is typical and atypical in development. Bailey et al. document the frustration of finding existing analytical approaches less useful for characterizing the organization of students' Spanish-language narratives than the organization of their English-language narratives.

In Chapter 13, Beck summarizes the work of this book and discusses the educational implications of the socioculturally based studies of Spanish-speaking children's narrative development. She goes on to conclude with a number of key implications suggested by the studies of the cognitive and linguistic aspects of Spanish-language narration.

REFERENCE

Batalova, J., Fix, M., & Murray, J. (2007, March). *Measures of change: The demography and literacy of adolescent ELLs: A report to Carnegie Corporation of NY*. Washington, DC: National Center on Immigrant Integration Policy, Migration Policy Institute.

11

Latino Mothers and Their Preschool Children Talk About the Past: Implications for Language and Literacy

ALISON SPARKS

Key words: narration, Latino children, parent–child reminiscing, reminiscing style, language development, literacy

ABSTRACT

This chapter explores the ways that Latino mothers and their preschool children reminisce. Parent–child conversations about past events were examined for level of maternal elaboration, and children's independent narratives were analyzed for the presence of elements that are thought to characterize Latino children's narrative forms. A qualitative analysis of talk between a single mother and her child was undertaken to examine other possible strategies that Latino caregivers use to engage their children in conversations about the past. The relationship between maternal elaboration and the child's provision of contextualizing elements in independent narration points to talk about misbehavior as a culturally salient context for reminiscing. Implications for developing narrative structure and literacy in the preschool classroom are discussed.

INTRODUCTION

Recounting the day's events at dinner, telling stories about a summer vacation, detailing the events that led to an emergency room visit – all are forms of talk that occur in family conversation. From the earliest age, children learn to tell tales that are valued by those among whom they live and grow (Miller, Potts, Fung, Hoogstra, & Mintz, 1990), they come to recognize rhetorical patterns that occur regularly in the chatter they hear daily (Heath, 1986), and they become skilled narrators of personal stories in ways that are recognizable to those with whom they talk (Hymes, 1972). Although engaging in discussion about the past may be a form of talk found in all cultures, specific genres of storytelling and rhetorical strategies are valued and learned within particular cultural groups (Miller, Fung, & Koven, 2007).

During the last 25 years, researchers from across the social sciences have focused on understanding the ways that children learn to narrate significant events in their life to others. Their work has looked closely at working-class families in South Baltimore, Maryland (Miller, 1986; Miller & Sperry, 1988), both White and African American working-class families in the rural Carolinas (Heath, 1983); and middle-class families in North America (McCabe & Peterson, 1991) and New Zealand (Newcombe & Reese, 2004). Miller and Sperry (1988) found that children were able to share their renditions of past events by $2\frac{1}{2}$ years old and even at this early age, they were able to express views about the content of their stories with evaluative comments. The critical role of parents has been well documented in middle-class families where caregivers are prone to shaping the child's early attempts at narration into concise, chronologically accurate accounts of real events. These parents use conversational strategies that frame the child's attention by focusing on a single topic and talking extensively about this subject with the child (e.g., Heath, 1983).

Developmental psychologists have taken a microanalytic approach to conversational interaction in order to understand how children learn to talk about the past. Related work by McCabe and Peterson (1991) and Fivush and Fromhoff (1988) focused on the caregiver's role in helping children to narrate past events. Both studies discovered that not all English-speaking, European American middle-class parents talk about the past in structurally similar ways. Using semi-naturalistic methods, Fivush and Fromhoff asked parents to talk about particular past events with their child. They found that some parents used an elaborative style in conversation that is characterized by asking many open-ended questions that invite the child to participate in reminiscing. These caregivers engage their child in constructing a story about the past by meeting responses with confirmations of the child's utterances and continuing to ask questions that provide more information about the event. Other parents displayed what Fivush and Fromhoff (1988) called a *repetitive style*. These parents asked more yes and no questions, added little descriptive information, and tended to ask the same question repeatedly, leaving the child with a much more restricted range of possible responses.

McCabe and Peterson (1991) asked parents to record conversations about past events as they occurred naturally within the home. The results were remarkably similar to those reported by Fivush and Fromhoff (1988): Parents were observed to use a topic-extending style as they reminisced with their child, much like the elaborative group; others used a topic-switching style, similar to the repetitive style found in the work of Fivush and Fromhoff (1988). McCabe and Peterson (1991) followed the same children, examining their independent narrations at 42 months of age. They found that children of the topic-extending/elaborative parents produced more extended personal narratives than the children of parents who had used a topic-switching style in conversation. In another longitudinal study, Reese, Haden, and Fivush (1993) also found that the children of elaborative mothers showed concurrent links between the mother's elaboration and the child's memory at 40 months of age. Longitudinal effects were observed for the same children recalling more memory information in mother–child conversations when they were followed up on at 58 and 70 months of age. These results suggest that parents who use an elaborative style have children who display more robust language and memory skills in their narratives. The strongest evidence for the relationship between specific language practices and children's narrative production comes from an intervention study with low-income families by Peterson, Jesso, and McCabe (1999). Mothers who participated in the intervention were taught to ask open-ended questions and to encourage their child to continue to narrate by affirming utterances and responding with requests such as "Tell me more." The children of these mothers showed improvement in vocabulary by the end of the intervention period and, 1 year later, they produced richer narratives than the children in the control group.

The exhaustive ethnographic work undertaken by Heath in the U.S. rural South during the 1970s describes the ways that children from two working-class communities were socialized into the language practices of their parents (Heath, 1983). This work is often cited for Heath's observations on the mismatch between what working-class children learn about language use at home and what teachers expect of them at school. Yet, in the same work, Heath described language acquisition in the local mainstream, middle-class community, and her descriptions of their conversational practices fit remarkably well with those displayed by the elaborative parents found in more recent work in developmental psychology. From Heath's broad sociocultural perspective, the elaborative style used by middle-class parents can be viewed as a rehearsal space for developing the discursive tools needed in formal educational settings; these parents take the role of facilitator during the child's attempts at narration and, as they do so, they are honing both the language and memory skills that prepare children for entering school and succeeding there. Heath's observations are further borne out in a study by Reese (1995), in which the practices of elaborative parents were shown to predict print knowledge; the children who participated more in early-memory conversations with their parents displayed stronger language and literacy skills in the preschool years. Bailey and Moughamian (2007) found similar links between a mother's earlier elaborative support of her child's personal narratives and reading skill at the end of first grade.

Yet, the varied rhetorical styles that children acquire at home are not all equally valued when children enter the academic world of formal schooling (Michaels, 1981). Children from a diversity of backgrounds come to school with a rich heritage of talk and storytelling often unrecognized or unrecognizable to teachers and students from mainstream backgrounds. Although their ways may not be immediately understood by those who are fluent in mainstream modes of communication, they deserve to be acknowledged as part of the rich tradition of discourse practices from the many ethnic and cultural groups found in the

United States. If classrooms are to provide the opportunity for all children to communicate their competence through talk and storytelling, then researchers must continue to explore the variety of ways that children are socialized through language.

Little attention has been given to talk in Latino families. This is surprising, given the importance of conversation in the Latino culture and the growing number of Latinos in the United States. By 2050, one of every four Americans will have Latino ancestry (U.S. Bureau of the Census, 2004). The National Head Start Bureau reported that 34% of the children enrolled in Head Start in 2006 were from Latino families (U.S. Department of Health and Human Services, 2007) – making them the largest minority group in this nationwide program, just ahead of African Americans, who represented 31% of the children in Head Start classrooms. The numbers only increase as Latino children move on to public schools. The decade between 1993 and 2003 saw a 4.7 million increase in students attending public school throughout the United States, and 3 million of those children were from Latino families (Fry, 2006). Latino children have become the fastest growing minority in public schools today.

When talking about Latino children, it is important to remember that they do not reflect a group with a homogeneous linguistic profile. A sociolinguist who documents language usage in the Chicano community from the Southwest region of the United States observed three linguistic groups: monolingual Spanish, monolingual English, and bilinguals (Sánchez, 1996). In other words, being Latino is not synonymous with being bilingual. However, Sánchez notes that among Latinos, being bilingual is most common, with individuals displaying varying degrees of proficiency in the two languages. Although she concentrates her scholarship on the Southwest, other scholars have observed similar patterns in Latino communities throughout the United States (e.g., Zentella, 1997). It is not surprising, then, that when Latino children enter school, they bring with them varying degrees of competence in both the English and the Spanish language.

A slowly emerging body of work on conversations between Latino parents and their children suggests that participation in talk about the past is guided by different conceptions of story (Silva & McCabe, 1996) and perhaps different roles for those who engage in those conversations. Yet, there is little work comparing the conversational strategies used by Latino parents with those that have been observed in conversations between White middle-class children and their parents. In the only study to compare Latino and European American mothers' reminiscing styles, Melzi (2000) contrasts working-class mothers of European American and Central American background. She found significant differences between the mothers' styles for supporting their child's participation in talk about the past. The European American mothers in her sample actively structured the children's talk with a preponderance of close-ended questions that helped the child focus on a single event and narrate a sequentially organized story. The Central American mothers, by contrast, showed a preference for open-ended questions but appeared to be more focused on maintaining a conversation while giving the child greater latitude to recall diverse past events in narrating the story.

Others who have studied Latino children's independent narrations have proposed some defining characteristics for Latino narratives. Silva and McCabe (1996), for instance, claim that the stories told by Latino children are characterized by a strong concern with family members and relationships within the family. The preoccupation with a sequential order of events – prominent in the conception of narrative for many other groups (Labov & Waletsky, 1967; Polanyi, 1982) – is less apparent in the stories told by Latino children. This may be related to the kind of scaffolding provided by Latino parents in conversations with their children. For example, in Eisenberg's (1985) study of two young Mexican children talking with their family, she noted that the adults did not use conversational strategies that demanded temporal organization in the child's responses. Silva and McCabe (1996) examined the stories told by Latino children and found that the narrators were more concerned with the details of the story than with an accurate sequential account of specific component events; that is, their recounting of past experience highlighted a strong sense of family, with a preference for description and evaluation over a temporally ordered retelling of events.

Still, we remain in the early stages of documenting the ways that Latino families talk and how their expressions convey meaning within the family setting. As Latino children become the largest minority in public school today, it is even more important that the repertoire of language and discourse practices they take with them to the classroom become the focus of our investigations. Toward that end, I examine the home context in which children learn to narrate stories and, in turn, tell their own from a sample of low-income Latino families recruited in Worcester, Massachusetts. Specifically, I focus on the use of elaboration by Latino mothers as they reminisce with their preschool children and on the possible links between parent elaboration and children's independent narrations. The analysis of the children's independent narratives also considers whether they include elements that are said to characterize Latino narrative.

This study was undertaken to determine whether parent provision of elaboration as it has been observed and measured in middle-class samples is useful for describing parent–child reminiscing in Latino families from a low-income community. It is important to acknowledge the possible limitations of using elaboration as it has been observed in White middle-class samples within another cultural context. Comparing talk in Latino families to models derived from work on samples from other cultural groups may restrict the potential for finding unique patterns of discourse within the conversations examined herein. Thus, I focus on a conversation between a single mother and her child talking about the past in an attempt to uncover discourse practices that may be unique to Latino families. Finally, narrative assessment of preschool children is considered in light of the observations made here.

THE STUDY

Participants and Procedures

The juxtaposition of linguistic, national, and ethnic identities within the Latino culture was strongly felt in the activity of deciding just who from a larger sample of families would be included in the group discussed here. After much deliberation, 23 families with a primary caretaker of Latino origins were included; for the purposes of this study, it seemed important to include the person who spent more time with their child than any other member of the family. The primary caretakers, all female, reported their place of birth as follows: Puerto Rico (9), urban centers in the Northeastern United States (12), the Dominican Republic (1), and Colombia (1). The conversations examined are from the initial child assessment and home visit conducted as part of a longitudinal intervention study of parent–child interactions and children's language and literacy outcomes. Families with 4-year-old children (mean age of 4 years, 3 months) were recruited at Head Start preschools in Worcester, Massachusetts, at the beginning of the academic years 2003, 2004, and 2005.

The linguistic profiles of the families included were also constrained by the focus of the larger study from which these data originated. Although many bilingual families were included in the larger sample (i.e., more than 50% bilingual), participants were told that they needed to feel comfortable talking and reading to their child in English in order to participate. Thus, the Latino families who participated in this study were capable of engaging in conversation and reading in English, although many of them also spoke Spanish to their child. Of the 23 parents interviewed, 6 reported both English and Spanish as the primary language spoken at home, 12 claimed English as the primary home language, and 5 reported Spanish. The parent reports suggest different degrees of bilingualism, with some children learning two languages simultaneously and others learning sequentially, with English introduced in the preschool classroom. Even those who reported English as their main vehicle for communication most likely live in an environment in which children are regularly exposed to the Spanish language through relatives, friends, and the extended community. The children in this sample received a normal range of scores on the Peabody Picture Vocabulary Test-III (Dunn & Dunn, 1997), with a mean of 93 and a range of 73–121. For many of these children, this is only a partial view of their receptive language; an assessment of receptive vocabulary in both Spanish and English would have shown more adequately the full range of their lexical knowledge (Gutiérrez-Clellen, 1999).

At a home visit completed by two researchers, the caregivers were interviewed about language and literacy practices, and the children completed a battery of measures for language and literacy. As part of the assessment, children told personal-injury stories to one of the examiners. During the interview, parents were asked to make a list of significant past events from their child's life. The events needed to be special in some way, standing apart from the routine experience of everyday life. They were also limited by who had participated in the experience: some of the memories were shared by the caregiver and child, whereas others were from events that had occurred in the child's life away from the parent. At the end of the home visit, a videotape was made of the parent reading two books to the child and talking about four past events (i.e., one shared, one unshared, a misbehavior, and a good behavior) from the list made by the parent during the interview. There was a considerable amount of missing data for the good-behavior event, so it was omitted from these analyses.

PARENT USE OF ELABORATION IN TALK ABOUT THE PAST

To explore the kind of structure employed by Latino parents in talk with their children, their past-event conversations were coded using a 5-point scale designed to measure the level of parent elaboration in past-event talk (adapted from Haden, 1998, and Laible, 2004). This scale was chosen for ease of use but, most important, because it is a valid indicator of maternal reminiscing style (Laible, 2004) that enables direct coding from videotape. Remember that in the elaborative style, the parent facilitates the child's reporting of past experience by asking open-ended wh-questions and confirming the child's attempts at narrating past events; at the other end, parents ask predominantly yes and no questions or questions that have a limited set of answers for which the parent may already have a specific response from the child in mind. To capture the entire spectrum, this scale ranges from a conversational style centered on wh-questions, introduction of new information, no repetitions, and few yes and no questions to one that is based on yes and no questions, repetitions, very little introduction of new information, and no wh-questions (see the appendix for a description of this coding scheme). Two independent raters coded 25% of the interactions from the videotapes. Reliability was assessed with the Shrout-Fleiss (Shrout & Fleiss, 1979) interclass correlation; the average reliability across the three conversational contexts was 0.85. The remaining videotapes were completed by one coder.

Table 11.1 shows the descriptive statistics for the narrative coding of two past events and a misbehavior event. The results were similar for all three event types. The mean was 3.26 for the shared event, 2.95 for the unshared event, and 2.12 for the misbehavior event. A 3 on this coding scheme is midway between the

Table 11.1. *Descriptive statistics for coding past-event conversations for elaborativeness in parental conversational style*

Event type	N	Minimum	Maximum	Mean	Standard deviation
Shared	19	2	5	3.26	1.24
Unshared	22	1	5	2.95	1.25
Misbehavior	17	1	4	2.12	0.86

two styles in which parents ask a balance of open-ended and closed elaborative questions in conversation with their child. Although parents fall closer to the low-elaborative side of this scheme in the misbehavior event, when the three conversational contexts are combined, they received a mean of 2.88. As a group, then, the parental contributions to the conversations do not appear to fall at one extreme or the other in this coding scheme. Although there was a range of scores in all contexts, the overall tendency for the parents is to fall in the middle on this coding scheme designed to explore the extent of elaboration used by parents in past-event conversation with children. Using the same coding scheme on a sample of middle-class caregivers reminiscing with their child about a good-behavior and a bad-behavior event, parents received a higher mean of 3.68 with a full range of scores from 1 to 5 (Laible, 2004). Maternal elaboration, as observed in this Latino sample, appears to be present in differing degrees in different contexts than in the conversations between White, middle-class parents and children.

CHILDREN TELL PERSONAL STORIES OF THEIR OWN

The children's independent narratives, told to a researcher, were another source for exploring reminiscing in Latino families. During the home visit, the children engaged in a drawing activity and were then asked to talk about a personal injury, when they were either stung by a bee or hurt on the playground (adapted from Peterson & McCabe, 1983, and Reese & Newcombe, 2007). These narratives were coded for the presence of temporal and contextualizing markers – two features reflecting the temporal aspects of narrative not thought to be typically present in the narratives of Latino children (Silva & McCabe, 1996) – using the contextual and temporal dimensions from the Narrative Coherence Coding Scheme (NaCCS; Reese, Haden, Baker-Ward, Bauer, Fivush, & Ornstein, manuscript in preparation). The personal-injury stories were coded for temporal coherence according to a 4-point scale; those at the low end included no information about temporal order and those at the high end showed clear temporal organization throughout most of the narrative. The same stories were coded for contextual coherence according to a 4-point scale: at the low end of the scale, no information about time or location is provided; at the high end, both time and place are

Table 11.2. *Descriptive statistics for coding temporal and context coherence in child personal-injury stories*

Coherence type	N	Minimum	Maximum	Mean	Standard deviation
Context	18	0	1	0.33	0.48
Temporal	18	0	3	0.50	0.98

specifically mentioned. Two coders independently coded 25% of the narrative transcripts. Reliability was assessed with Cohen's Kappa; the average reliability on the temporal dimension was 0.85 and on the contextual dimension it was 0.82. The remaining transcripts were completed independently by one coder.

Table 11.2 presents the descriptive statistics for temporal and contextual coherence in personal-injury stories told by children to an unfamiliar listener. The temporal dimension appears to be low, with a mean of 0.5 but with a range of 0 to 3 on a 4-point scale. This is consistent with what we know about Latino children's narrative production. In most narratives, there was either no provision of temporal order or close to none, with only a few providing full temporal information. In contrast, the contextual dimension was largely absent from these narratives. The mean of 0.33 and a range of 0 to 1 on a 4-point scale indicate that there was little context provided in the personal-injury stories and little variation across the sample. Yet, using the same coding scheme on 4-year-old children's independent narratives from several European American middle-class samples resulted in the same low levels of coherence on these dimensions (Reese et al., manuscript in preparation). This could be interpreted in several ways. Children in this Latino sample are from families with a modest to high degree of familiarity with the English language, and it may be that as the level of comfort with a language increases, so will the use of dominant discourse practices. Thus, the children's provision of temporal and contextual information may be similar to their middle-class peers as a reflection of their acculturation to mainstream ways of talking, or middle-class children may use lower levels of context and temporality in their independent narratives than they would in past-event conversations with caregivers who assist them in constructing their stories to include these dimensions.

LINKS BETWEEN PARENT–CHILD REMINISCING AND
CHILDREN'S STORYTELLING

To further explore whether parental elaboration is fully capturing the variability that is present in both parent–child reminiscing and children's independent narratives, Pearson correlations were run between the child-coherence variables and maternal-elaboration coding (Table 11.3). Maternal elaboration was not

Table 11.3. *Pearson correlations between coherence variables*
and maternal elaboration in three contexts

Maternal elaboration	Shared	Unshared	Misbehavior
Context coherence	0.30	0.11	0.48*
Temporal coherence	−0.16	−0.28	−0.34

* p < .05; remained significant after controlling for child's age, language, and
mother's level of education.

significantly correlated with the child's provision of temporal order in the independent narratives. This finding is consistent with observations made by both
Melzi (2000) and Eisenberg (1985): Latino parents did not use the kinds of questions that demand temporal organization in their child's response. If it is the
case that independent narratives told by Latino children display similar levels of
contextual and temporal organization to middle-class children peers, they have
learned to include these elements in their narratives from other conversational
resources. This alerts us to the importance of expanding investigations into the
social origins of narrative skill beyond talk between parents and children to
include siblings, extended family members, and any community members who
regularly engage in conversation with young children.

The lack of correlations in the shared and unshared past events is another
indicator that maternal elaboration may not be typical in these particular conversations. Eisenberg (1986) also noted that two Mexican American mothers
she studied were much less engaged in discussion of past events than has been
observed in American middle-class parents. However, in this sample, the misbehavior event appears to be an exception. The strong correlation between
maternal elaboration in the misbehavior event and child provision of context
(r = .48, p < .05) in independent narratives remained significant even when
controlling for child age, language, and maternal level of education. The correlation established a relationship between caregivers who were more elaborative in
discussing the misbehavior event and children who provided relative strangers
with higher levels of context – including provision of time and place – in their
independent narratives. In fact, in the cases in which the caregiver is highly
elaborative in the misbehavior context, these mothers introduce the topic of
misconduct by referring to both time and place. One mother began the discussion with, "Remember earlier today when we went to the store?"; another asked,
"Do you remember in the old house when you guys wrote on the wall?" These
parents are modeling the importance of contextual information at the outset of
a story and the children appear to be generalizing the contextualizing elements
in their independent narrations.

Research conducted by Harwood, Miller, and Irizarry (1995) on differences in
child-rearing goals and values between lower- and middle-class Puerto Rican and

European American mothers provides a useful perspective for understanding the role of talk about misbehavior in the Latino families in this sample. The researchers found that Puerto Rican mothers expressed concern for teaching children respect and proper demeanor in social relationships; these mothers placed high value on the importance of maintaining relationships with others and acceptance by the community, whereas the European American mothers interviewed placed strong emphasis on the importance of independence and individual achievement. This finding was consistent across social class in both groups. Thus, conversations about misbehavior may be an expression of the socialization goals that Latino mothers hold for their children, serving as a way for parents to educate their children about proper conduct. In this regard, parents reminisce as a way of instructing their child in appropriate forms of behavior.

Wang (2001) made comparable observations in a study focusing on mother–child reminiscing in American and Chinese middle-class families: She observed that Chinese mothers put more emphasis on social norms and behavioral expectations than American mothers. Similarly, Miller, Wiley, Fung, & Liang (1997) found that Taiwanese parents talked far more about misbehavior events than their American counterparts as a didactic tool for socializing children into norms for good behavior. For Latinos, then, talk about a misbehavior event may be a more culturally salient context for reminiscing than other types of shared and/or unshared past events.

Nevertheless, maternal elaboration may not be the only dimension for characterizing Latino parents' reminiscing style. Focusing on internal variation among Latino mothers in this sample may be another way to account for individual differences in their child's narrative skills. The following conversational analysis between a Puerto Rican mother and her 4-year-old son is intended to explore whether elaboration is a primary dimension for characterizing the ways that she engages her son in dialogue and to uncover the extent to which other socializing practices may guide their participation in past-event talk. During the interview, this mother reported that she was born in Puerto Rico and that the primary language spoken at home is English. This was consistent with the videotape made during the home visit in which no code-switching into Spanish was observed on the part of the mother or the child.

Miguel and His Mother Recall Making Cookies

In this conversation, the mother discussed a shared past event and a misbehavior event with her son. She received a score of 2 on the elaboration scale for both events. To receive a 2 on this scale, parents ask some open-ended questions, but they comprise a small proportion of the total. During the talk, the child plays with several dinosaurs and, eventually, the figures become characters in their discussion. The mother sits comfortably on the living room couch and invites her son to sit next to her while they chat:

[Note: "xxx" is for unintelligible utterances; underlined text indicates talk that takes place at the same time.]

Mother:	Let's have a little talk.
Miguel:	xxx xxx
Mother:	OK. Remember when we had those cookie [sic]?
Miguel:	Yes.
Mother:	What did you like best about making those cookie [sic]?
Miguel:	I liked I liked making more than I got.
Mother:	Did you remember the recipe? Because if you don't know the recipe we can't make it no more.
Miguel:	I know the recipe.
Mother:	Yeah. What is it?
Miguel:	All you need is milk.
Mother:	Ah-huh.
Miguel:	And and sugar
Mother:	Huh, you remember!
Miguel:	And, and what? And what again?
Mother:	Did we put eggs?
Miguel:	Yes.
Mother:	I think so, right?
Miguel:	Yes.
Mother:	OK. We made them all right?
Miguel:	Yeah.

After asking if he remembers making cookies, this mother asks her son to recall what he enjoyed most about baking cookies with her. Neither the mother's questions nor the child's response invoke the where or when of the story. Rather, the two of them together begin to reconstruct the recipe. Miguel asserts that he remembers the recipe and begins to list the ingredients. When he falters after listing milk and sugar, his mother helps him by asking if eggs were included. There are no references to context or order of events as the mother and son recall the recipe together. She begins the conversation with an open-ended question, "What did you like best about making those cookie?" but quickly narrows the scope of her inquiry to the list of ingredients for the cookie recipe.

This mother could be characterized as low in elaboration, as observed in the score of 2 she received on the elaboration scale. In the beginning, she asks two open-ended questions, but the conversation quickly narrows to a specific request for the ingredients in a recipe. On the lower end of the elaboration dimension, the caregiver structures the conversation with just this kind of narrow focus with specific answers in mind. Nevertheless, in this case, a singular focus on the elaborative dimension misses much of what is actually taking place between mother and son. Miguel's mother does not simply rely on a combination of open- and closed-ended questions to engage her child in conversation. By shifting the level of analysis from text to interaction, it is possible to uncover another set of meanings in the past-event conversations scrutinized here (for a discussion of the importance of this methodological issue, see Gumperz & Hymes, 1972, and Miller, Fung, & Koven, 2007).

In this conversation, a request to remember a past event is enacted as mother and son coconstruct a list of ingredients for a cookie recipe. The context of the event is not deemed significant enough to be explicitly stated nor is there reference to temporal order. Yet, the two are highly engaged in talk that takes its shape less through the mother's use of wh-questions and more by means of a familiar conversational genre (i.e., teasing), which facilitates the act of both mother and son recalling the cookie recipe together. She increases her child's desire to demonstrate his ability to remember the recipe by teasing him about why he needs to remember: She suggests that if he cannot remember how to make the cookies, they will not be able to bake them again. She says, "Because if you don't know the recipe, we can't make it no more." He responds immediately and demonstrates that he is well acquainted with baking cookies.

How does teasing work to increase his desire to participate in the conversation? In Eisenberg's study (1986) of two Spanish-speaking Mexican girls during their second year growing up in California, women – more than other members of the family – were observed teasing children. Eisenberg found that teasing was used to control the behavior of children and at the same time engage in fun and amusement with them.

Miller (1986) found similar uses for teasing as a means to secure obedience and direct a child's attention. In this conversation, the mother challenges her son to remember the recipe and then adds a mock threat: If he cannot recall, they will not make more cookies. Her challenge and mock threat and her son's subsequent counterclaim comprise a typical discourse structure for teasing (Miller, 1986). The teasing formula must be familiar and recognized by both participants or the antagonism of the challenge would be interpreted as an angry attack. The ease with which Miguel's mother draws him into the topic and keeps him playfully involved throughout is proof that the boy does not take the threat literally but rather understands that his mother is lightheartedly testing his ability to remember the recipe more than she is threatening to boycott their baking together.

Another important feature of the conversation that alerts the child to the playful aspect of his mother's request is the contextualization cues (Gumperz, 1982). These cues combine with the text to alert the audience to the way in which the words are to be understood; they serve as commentary on the text. In this conversation, the mother uses a higher pitch in her voice and exaggerated facial gestures as cues to send the message to Miguel that her request is in the realm of play – the test of memory is an amusement they will engage in together. The child uses the mother's extratextual cues to alert him to the fact that the threat is not literal and the task of remembering the recipe together is a playful interaction as well.

The conversation then quickly shifts to another past event that is closely related to the topic of making cookies. The move to another past event could be interpreted as the need to switch topics due to a limited ability to elaborate on the cookie-making subject. However, Melzi (2000) has suggested that the Latino caregivers in her sample introduced more than one topic – often two – as a way of elaborating on a single narrative and, by doing so, encouraging their child to incorporate related events within the framework of recalling a single past event. A similar strategy is observed in the following excerpt:

Mother:	Yeah. We still have some. You can only have one.
Miguel:	Oh yeah.
Mother:	But not every day.
Miguel:	I'm gonna just jump in that thing [referring to the cookie jar] and close that thing and locked it and eat all the cookies.
Mother:	Hah. Oh-oh. You gotta ask first before you jump in that cookie jar and eat all those cookies.
Miguel:	That clawie [name for the dinosaur] he'll be open it and went in there and ate all xxx <u>xxx.</u>
Mother:	<u>Oh he did.</u> I thought you did.
Miguel:	He did.
Mother:	I think I remember you sneaking in the cookie jar and getting a cookie.
Miguel:	No, pretend that [referring to the dinosaurs].
Mother:	And then you said only eat one but you eat two, remember?

In this sequence, Miguel's mother takes on a more explicitly didactic tone, beginning with setting limits on the number of cookies her son should be eating. The admonition to eat only one cookie leads to a contested memory, one in which his mother remembers that Miguel ate two cookies from the cookie jar without her knowledge. Miller (1986) notes that teasing and contested memories are closely related, so it is not surprising that a similar discourse pattern emerges here. Miguel sustains the rhetorical frame of the teasing interaction by reasserting himself with a counterclaim. He readjusts the limits his mother just set in place; he is going to get right into the cookie jar and eat every last one of them and the dinosaur is going to accompany him in this endeavor. Miguel switches time frame mid-sentence, as indicated by the initial verb in the future tense, followed by two verbs in the past tense. He transitions from telling his mother what he and the dinosaur plan to do to reporting on what the dinosaur has already done ("That clawie, <u>he'll open</u> it and <u>went</u> in there and <u>ate</u> all xxx xxx."). This gives his mother the pretext for drawing her son back to the realm of real past events ("Oh, he did. I thought you did."); she goes on to accuse him of sneaking two cookies from the cookie jar. Miguel again claims that he did no such thing and attempts to draw her attention back to the dinosaurs. But his mother is not distracted and continues to describe the cookie-jar heist.

There is a remarkable fluidity in the shift to this related episode. Again, the mother uses paralinguistic cues to alert the child to the fact that she is not angry, but she persists with this topic in order to send a strong message – he should not have eaten the cookies without consulting her. In this instance, Miguel's mother does not use wh-questions to support her child's participation, yet she plays the stronger part in controlling the direction of the conversation. She begins this section by telling Miguel that he can eat only one cookie at a time, and she ends it by asserting her view of what took place in their disputed memory. She is able to engage her son in talk about a past transgression as a way of encouraging compliance with parental ideals for appropriate behavior, but her goal is accomplished through a discourse structure that embeds a serious social message within a playful framework.

Miguel continues to play with the dinosaur figure and introduces another one to play the role of brother. This allows his mother to initiate talk about a misbehavior event, in which Miguel had hit his brother. She does so by joining him in the pretend dinosaur play and re-creating the scene between her two sons. The same rhetorical pattern for teasing is once again repeated with a challenge, mock threat, and the child's counterclaim, although the mother's initial challenge is less explicit than the one she uses in the beginning of the conversation.

[Note: Relevant action and contextualization cues are noted to the right of the dialogue.]

Miguel:	Wait. We need this one too.	[referring to the dinosaurs].
Mother:	Oh, why?	
Miguel:	Because, because this pretend this is the brother.	
Mother:	Oh, that's the brother.	
Miguel:	Yeah, he don't know how to eat.	
Mother:	Oh, that's his brother.	[increased pitch]
Miguel:	Yeah.	
Mother:	And what do the brothers do?	[increased pitch]
Miguel:	They all, they all.	
Mother:	Are they hitting each other?	[increased pitch]
Miguel:	No, no, no, no, no. He's walking where, he's getting the cookie but he's he's already eating there and they're eating a cookie.	[makes eating noises]
Mother:	Oh, let me see his brother.	[picks up dinosaur]
	OK, brother, I gonna hit you.	
	Pew. Haah.	[increased pitch]
	I'm gonna tell my mom.	[increased pitch]
	Oh, I remember a brother that hit his brother. What's his name?	

Miguel:	xxx.	
Mother:	You not going to tell me? Why?	[leaning toward Miguel, wide-eyed].
Miguel:		[shakes his head no]
Mother:	<u>Oh, come on.</u>	
Miguel:	<u>Poo. Poo.</u>	
Mother:	Isn't his name Miguel?	
Miguel:	No.	
Mother:	Oh yeah, Miguel hit Jakey. Remember you hit Jakey right here.	
Miguel:	No.	
Mother:	And Jakey was upset.	
Miguel:	No. No. I was just pretend and I just pretend I, I grabbed and put him like that	
Mother:	Oh. Come here. I saw Jakey say, "Ma, Miguel hit me again." Remember?	[Miguel acts out the event; mother shows mock surprised facial gesture]
Miguel:	No. OK. Pretend <u>that</u>	
Mother:	<u>Did you</u> say sorry to him?	
Miguel:	No. I was I was just I was jus. It wasn't for real.	
Mother:	Oh. It wasn't for real?	[mock surprised face]
Miguel:	I was just pretending.	
Mother:	Oh, you was pretending you hit him? Jakey was serious. He told me it hurt.	[Miguel pretends to hit his mother on the arm and she laughs and grins.
Miguel:	Did that hurt?	
Mother:	What? Sit over here?	
Miguel:	I was just playing with him.	
Mother:	OK. Alright.	

Miguel pretends that the dinosaurs are brothers and states that one of them does not know how to eat. When his mother replies, "Oh, that's his brother" and asks, "What do the brothers do?," she increases the pitch of her voice as a cue to let her son know that she is challenging him to recall an event that does not please her. There is no explicit request to remember, but the intent is clear in her use of extratextual cues. The high pitch sets off this part of the conversation, marking out the text as distinct from what takes place before. When she then asks, "Are they hitting each other?," Miguel knows that she has fallen out of their pretense and now makes reference to real-life events. He understands that she mockingly asks if the dinosaur brothers hit one another. She challenges him to recall a real event, a fight he had with his brother. His response, "No, no, no, no, no," serves as a vehement counterclaim and testimony to his recognition of his mother's intent. Although Miguel tries to remain within the pretend world of dinosaurs eating cookies, his mother again uses her high-pitched voice to act out the real-life scene with the dinosaurs in their lap. She then leans forward with an exaggerated surprised expression and asks him why he is not going to tell her what happened. Again, the overstated gesture comments on her words: Yes, she wants to talk about something that displeases her, but this is a difficult conversation that is taking place within a playful frame.

As in the last segment, the structure of this conversation does not rely heavily on the use of wh-questions. This may also be a function of the fact that the two are engaged in reconstructing a contested memory in which each has a different version of the events that took place. Again, the mother plays an important part in maintaining the overall structure of the past-event conversation. Later in the conversation, Miguel tries to convince his mother that he was only pretending when he hit his brother. At the level of discourse, the mother employs the same strategies found in the teasing format to engage her child in a conversation in which there is a strong social message about acceptable and unacceptable ways to behave. However, this time, after a long dispute about what took place between the brothers, she accepts his assertion that he was only pretending and meant no harm to his brother. Her acceptance of his explanation is punctuated with a laugh and a big grin; although she has allowed his version of the past to prevail, she has also conveyed a message of disapproval for the way Miguel treated his brother.

In a comparison between stories about past transgressions in middle-class families in the United States and China, Miller et al. (1997) found that Chinese parents use disputed past events to explicitly instruct their child about normative behaviors in social contexts, whereas parents in the United States revisited past wrongdoings to entertain and affirm strengths in their child's character. Like the Chinese parents, this mother introduces the misbehavior events to remind her son about proper rules of conduct. Yet, while doing this, she maintains a unique tone in which she appears to be more interested in checking his memory of the event to find out if Miguel had apologized to his brother. She does not explicitly delineate rules for proper conduct nor does she include a didactic coda as did Chinese parents in some of their narratives. In fact, Miguel's version of events prevails in the end when she accepts his assertion that he was only pretending to fight. It may be that Latino parents have a unique way of using stories to instruct while maintaining a playful, lighthearted tone in the conversation. This is especially evident in the way this mother allows her son to move freely from the pretend world of dinosaurs to the real world in which a disagreement is unfolding between them. Her skill at incorporating her son's fantasy play into a message about past misbehavior typifies this combination of a serious theme that is folded into a playful context.

Many defining elements that have been observed in talk among Latinos are present in the conversation examined (Melzi, 2000; Silva & McCabe, 1996). The importance of family relationships is strongly felt throughout but especially in the misbehavior event that focuses on the relationship between Miguel and his brother. As mother and son reminisce, the stories do not emerge within a linear time frame, nor do the speakers provide contextualizing information to anchor the narratives to time or place. The seamless transition from one past event to the next, without explicit textual notation, can be seen as a prominent feature of a storytelling style that is not concerned with temporal order. This particular feature, closely related to the topic-associating style (Michaels, 1981) observed in African American children, appears to be a natural part of this mother's narrative repertoire. She also introduces an episode that is related to the shared past event that begins her conversation with Miguel, a similar strategy to one observed by Melzi (2000) in conversations between Central American mothers and their children. Although the focus here has been primarily on maternal contributions to this conversation, Miguel's responses do not resemble the past-event talk found in middle-class children in conversations with their parents. Silva and McCabe (1996) note that the stories they gathered from Latino children might not be considered narratives at all when judged from a perspective rooted in middle-class European North American expectations about story and narration.

The conversation between Miguel and his mother was examined to explore how their talk reflects the cultural patterns found in conversations among Latinos. What is unknown at this point is how much this conversation reflects the idiosyncratic relationship between a mother and her son. An examination of the narratives produced by the entire sample, including this mother and son, revealed that on the whole, Latino caregivers did not use strategies that could be interpreted as good exemplars of the elaborative style. Because this analysis rests on a talk between a single parent and her child, these observations only suggest what may be regular features in talk among Latino family members. Clearly, analysis of a large sample from naturally occurring data is needed to see whether the prevalence of teasing and talk about disputed events is a routine part of conversations in Latino families.

The strong connections between child narrative production and literacy are well established (Dickinson & Tabors, 2001; Griffin, Hemphill, & Camp, 2004; Heath, 1983; Paul & Smith, 1993; Reese, 1995). The earliest narrative forms are learned in the context of family conversations; however, the cross-cultural study of narrative development has made it apparent that the oral-language demands on children as they enter school are not all learned at home (Heath, 1986). When children come from culturally and linguistically diverse backgrounds, the structure of their narratives differs from mainstream expectations of well-formed stories (McCabe & Rollins, 1994). Exploring talk in Latino families can be a means for understanding the language and narrative skills that Latino children take with them to preschool as they embark on the beginning of their formal educational experience.

The results presented herein suggest that children of Latino heritage from a low-income background do not enter formal schooling with a repertoire of narrative skills that are compatible with expectations in many preschool class-rooms. Latino parents in this sample were not highly elaborative in past-event talk and their child's independent narrations do not show a strong concern for the temporal or contextual aspects of their recalled experiences. Thus, we should not expect Latino children to be accustomed to a style of narrative interaction in which adults ask questions that facilitate a sequentially ordered, "topic-centered" narrative form – the hallmarks of narratives produced by middle-class children (Michaels, 1981). The mismatch in expectations between home and school may be a contributing factor to the over-enrollment of low-income minority children in special-education classes (Artiles & Trent, 1994). This is also consistent with previous research that found that child narratives lacking temporal order or explicit connections between events may be mistaken as a symptom of language impairment (Westby, Van Dongen, & Maggart, 1989) rather than a cultural dif-ference. Others have made similar observations in classrooms in which teachers are unable to make sense of stories told in culturally different genres and thus judge a child's performance as incoherent or off topic (Michaels, 1981; Silva & McCabe, 1996).

Preschool classrooms should be a place where children learn to participate in a variety of experiences that will promote development of narrative skill. Teachers should expect children to demonstrate a range of narrative styles and promote learning of targeted skills designed to support those who may be less familiar with forms of narration practiced at school (Gutiérrez-Clellan, Peña, & Quinn, 1995). The classroom offers a variety of contexts for exposing Latino children to sequentially ordered narrative structure, including but not limited to storybook reading, show and tell or sharing time, and any context for discussion of upcoming and past events. However, it is just as important for teachers to acknowledge and build on the narrative practices that chil-dren carry with them to the preschool classroom. Silva and McCabe (1996) note the importance for Latino children of engaging in personal storytelling as part of classroom curriculum. Forms of teasing, as they have been observed in conversation herein and elsewhere, are not likely patterns of discourse to be found in a preschool classroom between teachers and children. Wiley, Rose, Burger, & Miller (1998) note that whereas teasing promotes a way for young children to defend their own perspective, it is probably not a form of expression that is deployed in the classroom setting. Nevertheless, I am proposing that teasing may be an effective strategy for engaging some Latino children in narrative forms of conversation if the teacher or other professionals are sensitive to which children might enjoy this kind of playful interaction. I have observed Latino teachers in the Head Start program who are quite skillful at using teasing as a way to increase child participation in conversation in the preschool classroom.

A critical goal for future research is to develop assessments that distinguish between normal variation in the narrative forms of Latino children and those produced by Latino children at risk for language impairment. Assessments using middle-class models as a normative reference do not accurately discern between children with normally developing language skills and those who have a language disorder. There is still much to discover about the ways that Latino children learn to narrate their experiences at home and how their rich linguistic heritage contributes to language learning and the acquisition of literacy.

APPENDIX: CODING SCHEME FOR ELABORATIVENESS IN PARENTAL CONVERSATIONAL STYLE

1 = The information that the parent introduces is in the form of yes and no questions or repetitions. Parent asks no open-ended questions.

2 = The parent introduces or requests several new pieces of information about the event in question (e.g., in about 20% to 30% of her conversational turns). These new pieces of information, however, are most often in the form of yes and no questions or statements and may be repeated frequently. The level of repetition may thus be high. The parent asks some open-ended questions but they comprise only a small proportion of her total questions.

3 = The parent introduces or requests new ideas or pieces of information about the event on approximately half of her conversational turns (20% to 60% of the time). There may be moderate amounts of repetition. The parent asks the child a balance of open-ended questions and yes and no questions.

4 = The parent introduces or requests a new piece of information about the event discussed on the majority of her conversational turns. There may be several incidences of repetition. The majority of the questions asked of the child are open-ended, although there may be a few that are not open-ended.

5 = The parent introduces new information or requests information on most conversational turns. Almost all of the questions that the mother asks of the child are open-ended. There are few, if any, yes and no questions or repetitions. The parent provides or requests information about most aspects of the event (what happened, where, when, who). The conversation is relatively lengthy.

ACKNOWLEDGMENTS

This research was made possible through a grant to Elaine Reese and Wendy Grolnick from the National Institute of Child Heath and Human Development (#HD 42115). Many thanks are extended to Diana Leyva and Alana Roughan for coding the parent–child narratives. I would like to express appreciation to all of the families from Head Start of Worcester, Massachusetts, who participated in the study. I am especially grateful to Elaine Reese for guidance and suggestions throughout the preparation of this manuscript. Portions of this chapter were presented at the biennial meeting of the International Society for Behavioral Development in Melbourne, Australia, in 2006 and the Georgetown University Round Table in 2008.

REFERENCES

Artiles, A. J., & Trent, S. (1994). Over-representation of minority students in special education: A continuing debate. *Journal of Special Education, 27*, 410–437.

Bailey, A. L., & Moughamian, A. C. (2007). Telling stories their way: Narrative scaffolding with emergent readers and readers. *Narrative Inquiry, 17*(2), 203–229.

Bialystok, E., & Herman, J. (1999). Does bilingualism matter for early literacy? *Bilingualism: Language and Cognition, 2*, 35–44.

Dickinson, D. K., & Tabors, P. O. (2001). *Beginning literacy with language: Young children learning at home and school.* Cambridge: Paul H. Brookes.

Dunn, L. M., & Dunn, L. M. (1997). Peabody Picture Vocabulary Test (3rd ed.). Circle Pines, MN: American Guidance Service, Inc.

Eisenberg, A. (1985). Learning to describe past experiences in conversation. *Discourse Processes, 8*, 177–204.

Eisenberg, A. (1986). Teasing: Verbal play in two Mexican homes. In B. B. Schieffelin & E. Ochs (Eds.), *Language socialization across cultures* (pp. 182–198). New York: Cambridge University Press.

Fivush, R., & Fromhoff, F. A. (1988). Style and structure in mother–child conversations about the past. *Discourse Processes, 11*, 337–355.

Fry, R. (2006). The changing landscape of American public education: New students, new schools. Washington, D.C: Pew Research Center Publications, Pew Hispanic Center.

Goswami, U. (2001). Early phonological development and the acquisition of literacy. In S. B. Neuman & D. K. Dickinson (Eds.), *Handbook of early literacy research* (pp. 111–125). New York: Guilford Press.

Griffin, T., Hemphill, L., & Camp, L. (2004). Oral discourse in the preschool years and later literacy skills. *First Language, 24*, 123–147.

Gumperz, J. J. (1982). *Discourse strategies.* Cambridge: Cambridge University Press.

Gumperz, J. J., & Hymes, D. H. (Eds.) (1972). *New directions in sociolinguistics: The ethnography of communication.* New York: Holt, Rinehart.

Gutiérrez-Clellen, V. F. (1999). Language choice in intervention with bilingual children. *American Journal of Speech Language Pathology, 8*, 291–301.

Gutiérrez-Clellen, V. F., Peña, E., & Quinn, R. (1995). Accommodating cultural differences in narrative style: A multicultural perspective. *Topics in Language Disorders, 15*, 54–67.

Haden, C. A. (1998). Reminiscing with different children: Relating maternal stylistic consistency and sibling similarity in talk about the past. *Developmental Psychology, 34,* 99–114.

Harwood, R. L., Miller, J. G., & Irizarry, N. L. (1995). *Culture and attachment: Perceptions of the child in context.* New York: Guilford Press.

Heath, S. B. (1983). *Ways with words: Language, life, and work in communities and classrooms.* New York: Cambridge University Press.

Heath, S. B. (1986). Taking a cross-cultural look at narratives. *Topics in Language Disorders, 7,* 84–94.

Hymes, D. H. (1972). Models of the interaction of language and social life. In J. J. Gumperz & D. H. Hymes (Eds.) (1972). *New directions in sociolinguistics: The ethnography of communication.* New York: Holt, Rinehart.

Labov, W., & Waletsky, J. (1967), Narrative analysis: Oral versions of personal experiences. In J. Helm (Ed.), *Essays on the verbal and visual arts* (pp. 12–44). Seattle, WA: University of Washington Press.

Laible, D. (2004). Mother–child discourse in two contexts: Links with child temperament, attachment security and socioemotional competence. *Developmental Psychology, 40,* 979–992.

McCabe, A., & Peterson, C. (1991). Getting the story: A longitudinal study of parental styles in eliciting narratives and developing narrative skill. In A. McCabe & C. Peterson (Eds.), *Developing narrative structure* (pp. 217–253). Hillsdale, NJ: Erlbaum.

McCabe, A., & Rollins, P. R. (1994). Assessment of preschool narrative skills. *American Journal of Speech-Language Pathology, 3,* 45–56.

Melzi, G. (2000). Cultural variations in the construction of personal narratives: Central American and European American mothers' elicitation styles. *Discourse Processes, 30,* 153–177.

Metsala, J. L. (1999). Young children's phonological awareness and nonword repetition as a function of vocabulary development. *Journal of Educational Psychology, 91,* 3–19.

Michaels, S. (1981). "Sharing time": Children's narrative styles and differential access to literacy. *Language and Society, 10,* 423–422.

Miller, P. J. (1986). Teasing as language socialization and verbal play in a White working-class community. In B. B. Schieffelin & E. Ochs (Eds.), *Language Socialization Across Cultures* (pp. 199–212). Cambridge: Cambridge University Press.

Miller, P. J., Fung, H., & Koven, M. (2007). Narrative reverberations: How participation in narrative practices co-creates persons and cultures. In S. Kitayama & D. Cohen (Eds.), *Handbook of cultural psychology.* New York: Guilford Press.

Miller, J. M., Potts, R., Fung, H., Hoogstra, L., & Mintz, J. (1990). Narrative practices and the social construction of self in childhood. *American Ethnologist, 17,* 292–311.

Miller, P. J., & Sperry, L. (1988). Early talk about the past: The origins of conversational stories of personal experience. *Journal of Child Language, 15,* 293–315.

Miller, P. J., Wiley, A. R., Fung, H., & Liang, C. H. (1997). Personal storytelling as a medium of socialization in Chinese and American families. *Child Development, 68,* 557–568.

Newcombe, R., & Reese, E. (2004). Evaluations and orientations in mother–child narratives as function of attachment security: A longitudinal study. *International Journal of Behavioral Development, 28,* 230–245.

Paul, R., & Smith, R. L. (1993). Narrative skills in four-year-olds with normal, impaired, and late-developing language. *Journal of Speech and Hearing Research, 36*, 592–598.

Peterson, C., Jesso, B., & McCabe, A. (1999). Encouraging narratives in preschoolers: An intervention study. *Journal of Child Language, 26*, 49–67.

Peterson, C., & McCabe, A. (1983). *Developmental psycholinguistics: Three ways to look at a child's narrative.* New York: Plenum.

Polanyi, L. (1982). Linguistic and social constraints on storytelling. *Journal of Pragmatics, 6*, 509–524.

Reese, E. (1995). Predicting children's literacy from mother–child conversations. *Cognitive Development, 10*, 381–405.

Reese, E., & Fivush, R. (1993). Parental styles of talking about the past. *Developmental Psychology, 29*, 596–606.

Reese, E., Haden, K. A., Baker-Ward, L., Bauer, P. J., Fivush, R., & Ornstein, P. (manuscript in preparation). Narrative Coherence Coding Scheme (NaCCS).

Reese, E., Haden, C. A., & Fivush, R. (1993). Mother–child conversations about the past: Relationships of style and memory over time. *Cognitive Development, 8*, 403–430.

Reese, E. & Newcombe, R. (2007). Training mothers in elaborative reminiscing enhances children's autobiographical memory and narrative. *Child Development, 78*, 1153–1170.

Sánchez, R. (1996). Our linguistic and social context. In J. Amastae & L. Elias-Olivares (Eds.), *Spanish in the United States: Sociolinguistic aspects* (pp. 9–46). New York: Cambridge University Press.

Shrout, P. E. & Fleiss, J. L. (1979). Interclass correlations: Uses in assessing rater reliability. *Psychological Bulletin, 86*, 420–428.

Silva, M. J., & McCabe, A. (1996). Vignettes of the continuous and family ties: Some Latino American traditions. In A. McCabe, *Chameleon readers: Teaching children to appreciate all kinds of good stories.* New York: McGraw-Hill.

U.S. Bureau of the Census (2004). *U.S. interim projections by age, race, sex, and Hispanic origins.* www.census.gov.

U.S. Department of Health and Human Services, Head Start Bureau (2007). Head Start program fact sheet, 2007 [Data file]. Available from U.S. Department of Health and Human Services Web site, http://www.hhs.gov.

Wang, Q. (2001). "Did we have fun?": American and Chinese mother–child conversations about shared emotional experiences. *Cognitive Development, 16*, 693–715.

Westby, C. E., Van Dongen R., & Maggart, Z. (1989). Assessing narrative competence. *Seminars in Speech and Language, 10*, 63–76.

Whitehouse Initiative on Educational Excellence for Hispanic Americans (1999). Latinos in education: Early childhood, elementary, secondary, undergraduate, graduate. (ERIC Document Reproduction Service No. ED 449288.)

Wiley, A., Rose, A., Burger, L., & Miller, P. (1998). Constructing autonomous selves through narrative practices: A comparative study of working-class and middle-class families. *Child Development, 69*, 833–847.

Williams, K. T. (1997). *Expressive Vocabulary Test.* Circle Pines, MN: American Guidance Service.

Zentella, A. C. (1997). *Growing up bilingual: Puerto Rican children in New York.* Malden, MA: Blackwell.

12

The Contribution of Spanish-Language Narration to the Assessment of Early Academic Performance of Latino Students

ALISON L. BAILEY, ANI C. MOUGHAMIAN, AND MARY DINGLE

Key words: Bilingual education, two-way bilingual programs, school-age children, Spanish-language narration, literacy, academic achievement

ABSTRACT

Evaluations of bilingual programming have largely looked to students' academic performance as the measure of success. This study ascertains the role of Spanish-language narrative abilities in the academic achievement of Spanish-dominant first- through third-grade students, as well as in other developments related to school environments (e.g., attitudes toward school and metalinguistic awareness). Specifically, we asked three questions: (1) What are the Spanish-language narrative abilities of school-age bilingual children?; (2) How do children's Spanish-language and English-language narrative abilities compare?; and (3) What are the relationships between Spanish-language narrative abilities and school achievement, both narrowly and broadly defined? Spanish- and English-language personal narratives were elicited from 20 Spanish-dominant students enrolled in a two-way bilingual program in California. The children came from predominantly low- and middle-income Mexican- and Central American–heritage families. Elicitation prompts included stories about participation in school and their community. Spanish narratives were analyzed at the microstructural level for grammatical accuracy, complexity, and productivity. The macrostructural sophistication of both Spanish and English narratives was examined using highpoint analysis. Results suggest that most of the Spanish narratives were grammatically complex and contained few grammatical errors, but far fewer were as structurally sophisticated as the English-language narratives. Narrative ability was related to measures of students' oral Spanish-language abilities, English-language-arts skills, and level of metapragmatic awareness in English. Understanding these and other relationships is particularly important with Latino children whose school dropout rates cannot be explained by academic performance alone. The study underscores the importance of children's native-language discourse abilities to both their success *in* U.S. schools and measuring the success *of* their schools.

INTRODUCTION

Studies of the efficacy of bilingual programs in the United States have typically looked to students' academic performance as a measure of success, particularly performance in English language arts (ELA). In terms of current state and federal accountability for student learning, the No Child Left Behind (2001) legislation requires schools to show adequate yearly progress in English, mathematics, and science. For students who are receiving literacy instruction in a different first language, their English language skills must still be assessed and reported. Although schools may be required to administer assessments of language arts and other academic achievements in the first language (e.g., the Spanish Assessment of Basic Education, 2nd edition; McGraw-Hill, 2006), for students enrolled in bilingual programs, these results are not part of the formal accountability calculation for determining a school's success in teaching (Mayer, 2007). This is, in fact, logical when one considers that K-12 assessments of academic achievement may be rare or do not exist at all in low-incidence languages. English-language learners are thus eligible to take accommodated versions of a state's standards-based academic achievement tests that include translated assessments, where available, and use of bilingual dictionaries or glossaries during testing (Rivera, Collum, Shafer Willner, & Sia, 2006).

Such a focus on academic achievement in the content areas of ELA and mathematics, among others, may overshadow the successes of bilingual programming in other important areas of student growth and development. For example, bilingual programs that foster strong first- and second-language skills may promote the development of metalinguistic abilities in balanced bilingual students that are known to be related to literacy in both languages (e.g., August & Hakuta, 1997). In addition, an education that leverages a student's confidence and familiarity with his or her first language into the necessary self-esteem and positive attitude toward schooling will likely lead to engaged and sustainable learning for the student (e.g., Marsh, Trautwein, Lüdtke, Köller, & Baumer, 2005).

Moreover, the accountability focus, with its reliance on large-scale assessment of ELA and mathematics, may even miss more subtle but equally important student gains within these same content areas. For example, students' metapragmatic skills, or knowledge of how to organize and use language appropriately in different contexts, clearly comprise a critical language skill. However, these skills typically go unmeasured in large-scale ELA assessment due to the constraints of whole-group paper-and-pencil test administration. In this chapter, we explore three main questions that together may ultimately contribute a solution for how best to measure the success of bilingual instruction. By exploring the nature of Spanish-language narration in 20 elementary-school age bilingual children and then relationships between their Spanish-language narration and various measures of school-related ability and attitudes, we aim to both broaden existing definitions and measurement of success in bilingual programming and to deepen our understanding of the processes of language and literacy acquisition in bilingual students so they can be more precisely measured and also included in evaluations of bilingual schooling. This understanding includes the relationship between Spanish discourse skills, such as narrative, and English-language discourse abilities. Specifically, we ask (1) What are the Spanish-language narrative abilities of school-age bilingual children?; (2) How do children's Spanish-language and English-language narrative abilities compare?; and (3) What are the relationships between Spanish-language narrative abilities and school achievement, both narrowly and broadly defined?

To address the first two questions, we conducted highpoint analysis (Peterson & McCabe, 1983), closely examining the macrostructural organization of the Spanish- and English-language narratives of 20 Spanish-dominant first-through third-grade bilingual students. The Spanish-language narratives were also analyzed at the microstructural level for length and grammatical complexity and accuracy in Spanish. To address the third question, we employed an array of available standardized assessments of Spanish-language proficiency and academic achievement in ELA and mathematics, as well as a school-developed measure of feelings about school, researcher-developed metalinguistic- and metapragmatic-awareness measures, and we conducted highpoint analysis of the students' English-language narratives for comparative purposes.

In the following sections, we briefly outline the current situation of bilingual education in the United States and review existing literature of development of Spanish-English bilingual narration. Drawing on findings from the literature, we then propose ways to broaden and add depth to a definition of successful bilingual instruction.

The Current Context of U.S. Bilingual Schooling

Opponents of bilingualism who were instrumental in passing state initiatives in California in 1998, in Arizona in 2000, and in Massachusetts in 2002 to reduce bilingual programming have traditionally argued that the cost of bilingual education is a drain on state financial resources (e.g., Porter, 1990), that bilingual education goes against the melting-pot ideal of mainstream America (e.g., Citrin, 1990), and that taking courses in a native language hinders the process of becoming proficient in English (e.g., Unz, 2000). In his comprehensive review of the English-only movement and attacks on bilingual education, Crawford (2000, p. 6) characterized the tactics of the movement as "promoting English-only laws in the name of national unity" (p. 1). Proponents of English-only, he further argues, have claimed that "Language diversity inevitably leads to language conflict, ethnic hostility, and political separatism *à la Québec* (playing to paranoia of all stripes)."

Studies of the effects of English-only instruction in the form of Structured English Immersion (SEI) have subsequently been mixed. For example, in California, claims of student gains in English have been made (e.g., White, 2006), but other studies show no such results (e.g., the Civil Rights Project, 2002; Rolstad, Mahoney, & Glass, 2005) or show the study of favorable SEI results to be methodologically flawed (MacSwan, 2006). (See also Zehr, 2006, for a recent overview of the current policy and political ramifications of bilingual versus English-only programming and the mixed results associated with SEI.)

One fact that is clear, however, is that studying the success of English-only programming on academic achievement will not reveal anything about the success of bilingual programming on academic achievement nor the effects of learning two languages on English-language acquisition. To accomplish this, all language skills and the academic achievements of bilingual students need to be examined comprehensively.

Contrary to popular misconception, bilingual instruction did not disappear with the introduction of the English-only mandates. Bilingual education continued with parental waivers (i.e., parents must sign a wavier form requesting that their child be placed in a bilingual program). In the Los Angeles Unified School District in California, for example, a full 48% of English-language-learning students received bilingual programming in the 2005–2006 school year (MacSwan, 2006). Moreover, there has been an increase in the number of students enrolled in two-way or dual-language bilingual programs with emphasis on language enrichment, use of native-speaker models for second-language learning, and simultaneous or sequential teaching of content material using the two languages. The main goal of two-way bilingual programs is to have students acquire a second language while fostering the continued growth of their first language. In California, where approximately 1.6 million children are officially designated as English-language learners, the number of two-way bilingual classrooms has grown from just 95 in 1998 when Proposition 227, the English-only initiative, was passed, to 197 classrooms in 2005 (California Department of Education, 2006).

Nationally, the number of two-way bilingual programs reported to the Center for Applied Linguistics in 2006 was 338, up from 150 just 10 years earlier (Center for Applied Linguistics, 2006). The children in the current study were participants of just such a program in which their teachers were fluent Spanish speakers, educated and trained in methods to teach a second language in a two-way bilingual program. All literacy instruction was provided in a student's dominant language, either English or Spanish, with the second language taught through additional language lessons and other content lessons throughout the day.

Development of Spanish-English Bilingual Narration

There have been a number of studies in the past 10 to 15 years that examined Spanish-language narrative style and development (e.g., Gutiérrez-Clellen, Peña, & Quinn, 1995; McCabe & Bliss, 2004; Rodino, Gimbert, Pérez, Craddock-Willis, & McCabe, 1991; Silva & McCabe, 1996). From this research, studies have shown narratives produced by Spanish-speaking children to be organized around the description of personal relationships and connections between individuals (e.g., clear lines of relationship established between the narrator and the people or family pets about whom they narrate) rather than to structure their stories based on event sequences (Rodino et al., 1991; Silva & McCabe, 1996). In a review of studies, Fiestas and Peña (2004) report additional hallmarks of Spanish-language narration in young children, including a bias toward providing accounts of family history, use of the present-progressive verb form, and – for those children from whom bilingual data have been available – greater use of adverbial clauses in their Spanish-language narratives compared with their English-language narratives.

To date, however, there have been few within-child studies of the development of Spanish- and English-language narrative abilities. The studies of young bilingual children by McCabe and Bliss (2005), Pearson (2002), Uccelli and Páez (2007) and Fiestas and Peña (2004) are notable exceptions. This research has revealed that Spanish story organization predicts children's English narrative performance (Pearson, 2002; Uccelli & Páez, 2007). Fiestas and Peña's (2004) investigation of 4- to 7-year-old bilinguals found greater use of adverbial clauses in the children's Spanish-language narratives than in their English-language narratives. These studies have predominantly relied on story generation from pictures used as prompts, as well as the classic narrative elicitation picture-book selection, *Frog where are you?*, by Mayer (1969). However, these picture elicitation techniques while focused on fictional story generation, do not necessarily elicit impersonal oral narratives (McCabe & Bliss, 2008); indeed, some of the children in the Fiestas and Peña (2004) study interpreted the picture prompts as an opportunity to provide a personal narrative rather than a fictional story. Clearly, there is still great need for further investigation of the bilingual narrative abilities of children, including the abilities of older school-age children, across a range of narrative genres.

Like Champion, McCabe, and Colinet (2003), whose focus was a different student population (i.e., Haitian American), we expect there to be a positive relationship between narrative structure and literacy. Although studies have shown a connection between narrative and literacy for monolingual English-speaking children (e.g., Catts & Kamhi, 1999; Griffin, Hemphill, Camp, & Wolf, 2004), we must also be receptive to the fact that there might not be any connection between narrative ability and literacy skill in other school-age populations. For example, Champion et al. (2003) found that there was no relationship between narrative and literacy for some African American students in some of the studies they reviewed. This finding may be the same for Spanish-speaking students because the narrative structures of these students do not correspond with the structure of many storybooks encountered in school and for which young (monolingual) English-speaking children's early oral-narrative experiences prepare them (Deckner, Adamson, & Bakeman, 2006; NICHD Early Child Care Research Network, 2005; Reese, 1995; Sénéchal & LeFevre, 2002; Snow, Burns, & Griffin, 1998; Wells, 1986).

One reason narrative may have a close predictive tie to literacy is the similarity between the cognitive and metalinguistic demands placed on the narrator when telling a story and the demands placed on a reader or writer when making sense of or creating comprehensible text (e.g., Snow et al., 1998; Bailey & Moughamian, 2007). Not all discourse-level skills place the same demands on the speaker as studies in the atypical arena have revealed. Indeed, within the field of atypical language development, children have been found to be more intelligible and fluent during dialogic discourse with a partner (e.g., conversation) than during monologic discourse (e.g., narration), although pertinently for language development, their Mean Length of Utterances (MLUs) are longer in narration (Wagner, Nettelbladt, Sahlen, & Nilholm, 2000). Moreover, the conceivably lesser cognitive and linguistic demands placed on children during conversation may explain the fewer communication breakdowns or dysfluencies (e.g., repairs, abandoned utterances) during conversation than during narration (MacLachlan & Chapman, 1988).

Much as Peña, Bedore, and Rappazzo (2003) found the need to consider Spanish bilingual children's vocabulary knowledge by assessing both languages, we argue for the need to examine the discourse-level skills – particularly abilities in the demanding narrative genre – of school-age children in both languages for the information they yield, not only about oral language development but also about their ties to literacy.

The recent National Literacy Panel reviewed studies that address the relationship between first-language oral proficiency and second-language literacy (August & Shanahan, 2006). Although the few available studies that have examined this important topic show positive relationships between oral language skills in a first language and students' later reading abilities in English, their focus has been primarily on word (e.g., phonological processing) and sentence-level (e.g., grammatical knowledge) connections, rather than discourse skills (Genesee & Geva, 2006). Moreover, the National Literacy Panel did not identify any studies investigating the relationship between first- and second-language narrative abilities (Geva & Genesee, 2006; but see Miller et al., 2006). The Panel called for more research in this area, stressing, "To assess a language-minority child's language, literacy and content knowledge, we need to understand the linguistic and psychological structures that he or she has in both the minority and majority languages and how they interact" (García, McKoon, & August,

2006, p. 593). They go on to point out that experts "warn that data from oral language proficiency measures in English should not be the only basis for exit decisions [i.e., exit from bilingual programs to mainstream classrooms]" (p. 595). Collectively, the research reviewed herein makes it evident that there is much room for further research of the relationship between narration in Spanish and in English and the role it plays in the academic outcomes of children being schooled bilingually in the United States.

Broadening the Definition of Successful Bilingual Education

Student self-concept (i.e., how students perceive their own competence) has an impact on academic achievement. Indeed, student self-concept has been found to be both a cause and an effect of academic achievement (Marsh et al., 2005; Wigfield & Karpathian, 1991). Students with greater confidence in themselves are more successful academically and, as children mature, their academic self-concept becomes more strongly correlated with their performance on academic achievement tests (Guay, Marsh, & Boivin, 2003). Previous work by Imbens-Bailey with Armenian American bilingual students examined the role of attitudes toward Armenian language, culture, and schooling and found that those students who had greater Armenian language skills (including oral narrative skills) through formal Armenian schooling had a more positive attitude about both their Armenian and mainstream American cultural experiences, including their schooling experiences (Imbens-Bailey, 1995, 1996, 2000). These studies, however, did not include any measures of student academic performance in English, so it is not possible to determine what effects their bilingualism had on attitudes and school outcomes. However, taken together with the previous studies of self-esteem effects on academic outcomes, this work suggests that a potentially powerful additional argument in support of bilingual education may lie in showing a role for attitude toward school and perceived academic competence in the eventual school success of bilingual children (see also chapter 10, this volume).

Exploring this possible argument may be particularly fruitful in the case of Latino children, whose dropout rate in later school years cannot be explained by their academic performance alone (Valencia, 2002). That is, these children are often doing well in school – they may even be high achievers – yet they may later drop out of school. For some students, reasons for dropping out may not be related to poor school performance but rather due to issues of motivation, self-esteem, and attitudes toward the school environment (Phinney, Baumann, & Blanton, 2001; Stevenson, Chen, & Uttal, 1990). Gándara (2005) reports that only 60% of the Hispanic population between 18 and 24 years old complete high school compared with 84% of the White population. In part, this gap may be explained by factors related to demotivating schooling practices, including continued under-representation of Latino students in gifted and talented programs and the lack of demanding curricula for higher achieving Latino students. It is important, therefore, that schools attend to children's attitudes about their learning environment. In the case of bilingual programming, this entails fostering an environment that can lead to the learning of two languages in an additive and cognitively stimulating context – that is, in circumstances in which the child is not being asked to give up his or her first language in the process of acquiring a second nor prevented from using both languages for learning in school.

Adding Depth to the Definition of Successful Bilingual Education

When we talk of adding depth to the definition of successful bilingual education, we are really referring to ways in which we can add greater precision or accuracy to our measurement of the efficacy of bilingual programming. This relies upmost on a better understanding of bilingual students. Arguments for bilingual education have included the cognitive and metacognitive advantages that have been found in balanced bilinguals (August & Hakuta, 1997; Ben-Zeev, 1977; Bialystok, 2001; Cook, 2005; Díaz & Klingler, 1991; Hakuta & Díaz, 1985). Also, an increasing number of studies have shown that children transition to literacy much more quickly and successfully if they are first taught to read and write in their dominant spoken language (Willig, 1985; Yelland, Pollard, & Mercuri, 1993) and are similarly more successful if they are taught content-area material in their dominant language (Bialystok & Cummins, 1991; Verhoeven, 1994). Learning to be literate in Spanish and English may be mutually beneficial to the acquisition of the two languages (Miller et al., 2006). At the very least, Spanish literacy does not appear to interfere with the development of English literacy skills. For example, Bayley & Schecter (2005) found that students who maintained literacy skills in Spanish wrote narratives in English as competently as their monolingual English-speaking peers.

Differences in the linguistic and cognitive experiences of students who have more than one language might make them different learners from monolingual students, and the way in which we teach bilingual students should capitalize on the advantages they have as a result of their bilingualism. As Cook (2005, p. 53) points out, "L2 [second language] users have different language abilities and knowledge and different ways of thinking from monolingual native speakers. Rather than encouraging the students to approximate native English speakers as much as possible, teaching should try to make them independent L2 users who can function across two languages with mental abilities the monolingual native speaker cannot emulate."

An example of differences between the linguistic abilities of bilinguals and monolinguals (beyond simply speaking two languages, of course) can be taken from the work of Viberg (2001). She reported that bilingual children had a tendency to give more detailed and concrete versions of stories they read in both

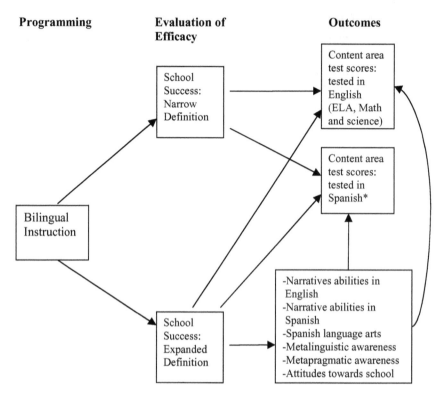

* Tested in Spanish but currently not used for school accountability.

Figure 12.1. The role of Spanish-language narrative-ability outcomes in the measurement of bilingual program efficacy.

their Swedish and second-language narrative retellings than their monolingual counterparts. The monolingual children tended to give briefer, more condensed retellings of the stories they read.

From the review of the different literatures that we have brought to bear on the role of narrative abilities in two languages for educational outcomes, we can hypothesize relationships between the various factors in the form of a conceptual model. The model in Figure 12.1 shows the relationships between narrative abilities in both Spanish and English and a broad array of both academic and prosocial outcomes related to school. The outcomes under the expanded definition of school success are also hypothesized to be intercorrelated, as well as related to the traditionally narrower set of measures of bilingual programming efficacy such as standardized ELA, mathematics, and science test scores – assessments that Miller et al. (2006) call *decontextualized* in contrast with the more *contextualized* measures of narrative discourse elicited during a one-on-one conversational protocol (e.g., Peterson & McCabe, 1983). Narrative is a genre of language not readily sampled and analyzed in a standardized testing format.

The current study was able to obtain standardized scores for the content areas tested in English for Spanish-language proficiency, and scores on a measure of students' attitudes toward school. We also sampled speech to create measures of students' narrative abilities in Spanish and English, and created measures of metalinguistic and metapragmatic awareness. The current study, however, is limited by the number of Spanish-dominant students enrolled in the focal two-way bilingual program. With just 20 students, our investigations of the hypothesized relationships between these factors is qualitative and primarily exploratory in nature. Specifically, the purpose of the current study is to begin to create profiles of Spanish-dominant first- through third-grade students to ascertain the role of their Spanish-language narrative abilities in their academic achievement and other indicators of their development in the school environment.

METHOD

Participants

Twenty Spanish-dominant Latino students (11 girls and 9 boys) in the first through third grades took part in the study. Language dominance was determined by the Pre-Language Assessment Scales in English and in Spanish (Duncan & De Ávila, 1986a, 1986b) at kindergarten entry (see the following section for details). Students were enrolled in a two-way bilingual program that was designed to provide instruction to both Spanish- and English-dominant students in two multigrade clusters: a kindergarten–first-grade cluster (five students in the study were first-graders from this cluster) and a second-grade third-grade cluster (eight students in the study were second-graders and seven were third-graders from this cluster) (Stipek, Ryan, & Alarcón, 1997, 2001) . English-dominant children with whom these children came into contact had been randomly assigned by the school to either the two-way bilingual program or an English-only classroom.

The school was situated in a large urban area of Southern California and served as a university laboratory school. Human subjects informed-consent procedures were followed; school data provided demographic information and recent academic achievement scores. The children predominantly came from families of Mexican and Central American (e.g., Salvadorian) heritage, with most born in the United States to foreign-born parents. Half of the sample came from families with an annual household income below $14,900; the other half came from families with an annual household income between $15,000 and $49,000 (in 1998 U.S. dollars).

Procedures

Several oral narratives were elicited in both Spanish and English from each of the children. The students were interviewed one-on-one by two interviewers in two identical sessions: one session in English with an English-only–speaking interviewer or with a bilingual Spanish-English interviewer, and one session in Spanish with the bilingual Spanish-English interviewer. With few students in the study, no attempt to counterbalance the order was made, and most students received the interview in English followed by the Spanish interview. The interviews were conducted with students in a room adjacent to their classroom. The interviewers used the techniques of Peterson and McCabe (1983) to conversationally elicit oral personal narratives from the students by first modeling a narrative of a past event from their own life (e.g., a brief tale about a naughty pet) in either English or Spanish. Students were then asked to tell a similar story from their own past experiences. After this initial warm-up exchange, eight additional narrative prompts were read aloud to each student (see the Appendix). The prompts asked the students to tell stories about their participation in cultural, family, and school activities and events. The same protocol was read to each student, and he or she was encouraged to respond to each prompt and tell as much about the events as possible. If a student could not respond to a prompt, the interviewer moved on to a subsequent prompt. There were no time or length limitations imposed on the children's narrations. The interviewers used general prompts to encourage elaboration (e.g., "Can you tell me a bit more about what happened?") and, if necessary, asked students to clarify the events of the narrative. It was noticeable that the children switched back to English frequently during the interviews in Spanish, so the interviewer often needed to remind students to tell their stories in Spanish. Students averaged approximately five English-language narratives and just two or three Spanish-language narratives. The interviews in Spanish and English were audiotaped for later verbatim transcription.

The oral narratives were initially categorized thematically as cultural, family-related, or school-related. Narratives that could not be coded thematically by one of the three categories fell under a miscellaneous category. To provide a fuller account of the Spanish-language narratives we were interested in profiling, we analyzed these narratives at both macrostructural and microstructural levels, whereas the English-language narratives were coded only at the macrostructural level for comparative purposes.

At the macrostructural level, we analyzed each clause of the narratives using highpoint analysis (Peterson & McCabe, 1983). The highpoint analysis used a rating scale of 0–7 points. *Nonnarrative* (rated 0) responses contained no past-event clauses. *One-Event* and *Two-Event* narratives contained one and two past-event clauses, respectively (rated 1 and 2, respectively). *Miscellaneous* narratives contained several past-event clauses, but there was no logical or causal sequence to the clauses (rated 3). *Leapfrog* narratives involved a causal string of events, but clauses appeared to be in an illogical order and/or omitted key events (rated 4). *Chronological* narratives were a simple "laundry list" of ordered events (rated 5). *End-at-highpoint* narratives were sequentially ordered but ended prematurely at the climax or highpoint (concentration of evaluative comments) of the story (rated 6). *Classic* narratives contained orientation information and a well-ordered sequence of past-event clauses that came to a climax, and they provided a resolution to the climatic events of the story (rated 7).

The longest Spanish-language narratives were then further analyzed for microstructural elements using a scoring rubric that focused on the grammatical complexity, accuracy, and productivity of the students' narratives. The rubric was used to rate narratives from the most unsophisticated uses of Spanish (e.g., isolated lexical items) in brief responses, through sentence fragments and simple sentence structures often in short accounts about past events, to complex and accurate sentence structures often in longer account of past events. This scoring rubric was on a scale of 1–13 points. Scores on this Spanish-narrative ability measure were used to group students into low-, medium-, and high-ability groups (see Results section for details).

At a third session with the students, we administered a researcher-developed metacognitive assessment in English and a school-developed questionnaire of attitudes about the school environment and perceived academic performance. The metacognitive assessment provided subscale scores for metalinguistic and metapragmatic awareness. The 28 metalinguistic items included the ability to give formal definitions; the ability to manipulate phonemes, syllables, and morphemes in compound words; and the ability to uncouple word referents from their semantic component. For example, the classic Piagetian "sun–moon" reversal task required the child to say whether or not it is dark outside and if the moon is now called the sun and vice versa. The metapragmatic-awareness subsection contained seven items that focused primarily on the usage of two languages (e.g., being able to articulate when they used Spanish, to whom, and why).

We administered the Feelings About School (FAS) questionnaire, which uses Likert scales of 0–5 for students to rate 16 questions. The questions are designed to measure attitude toward the academic environment, including the student's perceived academic performance (Stipek, 2000). Examples of these questions include "How much does your teacher care for you?" "How good will you be in reading in the third grade?" and "How fun are the things that you do in school?" Available from the school database were standardized assessment scores for Spanish-language proficiency (i.e., Pre-Language Assessment Scales: Spanish, or Pre-LAS Spanish) and English language proficiency (i.e., Pre-LAS English) at kindergarten entry for 18 students who began school in that grade (i.e., one high-ability and one medium-ability Spanish narrator did not start school at kindergarten); ELA performance on the Stanford Achievement Test Series: Ninth Edition (i.e., SAT-9, Harcourt Brace, 1996); and mathematics performance (SAT-9) for second and third grades only (N = 15). The Pre-LAS Spanish and English are measures of oral language skills (i.e., listening and speaking) expressed as proficiency levels 1–5. The SAT-9 assessments are norm-referenced achievement tests for which stanine scores on a scale of 0–9 were available.

Reliability

Reliability for the highpoint analysis of narratives was calculated on a randomly selected set of 12 narrative transcripts (6 Spanish, 6 English). Simple inter-rater agreement between two coders was 0.75 and Cohen's Kappa was 0.65. The three disagreements were resolved by consensus. All 20 Spanish-language optimal narratives were coded for microstructural features by two coders. Simple reliability was 0.90, with a Cohen's Kappa of 0.83. Again, any disagreements were resolved by consensus.

RESULTS AND DISCUSSION

Spanish-Language and English-Language Narrative Abilities

Addressing our first research question, "What are the Spanish-language narrative abilities of school-age bilingual children?," we examined both microstructural and macrostructural characteristics of the students' narratives. The findings from the microanalytical measure that focused on grammaticality and productivity were used to group students by ability. The distribution of scores was trimodal; therefore, we created three main groups of students for further analyses. There was a clear positive skew in the distribution, with many students scoring perfect scores of 13 points on the microstructural measure to form the high-ability group. A medium-ability group was formed that included students with scores skewed toward the higher values, leaving very few low-scoring students to form a low-ability group (Table 12.1).

Specifically, half of the students (five girls, five boys) demonstrated the ability to tell Spanish-language narratives using multiple past-tense clauses with complex syntactic structures that contained very few grammatical errors. An example is "... *Regreso mi tarea y tuve un buen día*"; "*I return my homework and I had a good day.*" However, the use of *regreso* here is an Anglicism; *regreso* means "to come back," not "to return (an object)" (the semantically correct verb in this context would be *devolver*). Another seven students (six girls, one boy) in the sample also organized their personal stories into multiple past-tense events using grammatically accurate sentences, but they showed less complexity and more repetition in the syntactic structure of their utterances (e.g., "*Y hicimos los libros unos libros y después fuimos a educación física y después fuimos a la clase*"; "*and we made the books, some books and then we went to physical education and then we went to class*"). Three students (all male) gave responses with grammatically simple if accurate utterances (e.g., "*Me puse mis roller blades y yo me yo um corrí y me caí*"; "*I put on my roller blades and I, I um ran and I fell*"). Overall, these students' responses tended to be composed of just a few short utterances.

Children across the two grade clusters were distributed across the Spanish-language narrative grammaticality/productivity ability groupings, with two of

Table 12.1. *Summary of narrative performances by ability group (Total N = 20)*

Spanish-language narrative ability group[a]	Grade level	Spanish-language narrative macrostructural rating[b]	English-language narrative macrostructural rating[b]
High (N = 10)			
Maritza	1	Classic	Chronological
Martín	2	Classic	Chronological
Javier	3	Classic	Chronological
Sally	3	End-at-highpoint	End-at-highpoint
Joanna	2	Chronological	Classic
Christine	1	Chronological	Classic
Yolanda	3	Chronological	Chronological
Ralph	3	Chronological	Classic
Kyle	2	Chronological	Classic
Harry	3	One-event	End-at-highpoint
Medium (N = 7)			
Adriana	2	Chronological	Chronological
Héctor	2	Chronological	Classic
Melinda	2	Chronological	Classic
Sonia	3	Chronological	Classic
Jayne	1	Chronological	Classic
Julisa	3	Chronological	Chronological
Valencia	1	Two-event	Chronological
Low (N = 3)			
Alberto	2	End-at-highpoint	Classic
Kiko	2	One-event	Chronological
Lorenzo	1	Non-narrative	Leapfrog

[a] Ability group based on grammatical complexity, accuracy and overall productivity.
[b] Highpoint category of highest rated narrative.

the five first-graders in each of the high- and medium-ability groups and one in the low-ability group; three of the eight second-graders in each of the high- and medium-ability groups and two in the low-ability group; and five of the seven third-graders in the high-ability group and two in the medium-ability group (see Table 12.1).

Results of the highpoint analysis also presented in Table 12.1 suggested that just three students (all in the high-ability group) told Spanish-language narratives that fit the definition of classic narrative structure. One student told an end-at-highpoint narrative. The best level of narrative response in Spanish for the majority of students (i.e., 11) was a chronological story with no highpoint. These were evenly dispersed across the high- and medium-ability Spanish-narrative grammaticality/productivity groups. Several of these stories had characteristics reminiscent of prior research on the nature of Spanish-language narratives (e.g., Silva & McCabe, 1996); that is, they contained intricate details about relationships between characters rather than just focusing on the organization of macrostructures (e.g., "*... había una niña. Era mi amiga y ella fue conmigo a agarrar mi perro. Y después ella me dijo que había un hombre que robaba a los niños*". "*There was a girl. She was my friend and she went with me to get my dog. And then she told me there was a man who robbed the children.*"). The best response from one high-ability student was essentially nonnarrative in structure with just one past-tense event in each of the otherwise grammatically complex and accurate responses to the narrative prompts. One medium-ability-group student's best performance was with a two-event narrative. Conversely, one low-ability-group student, whose story was grammatically simplistic, came close to telling a story with classic narrative structure, ending prematurely at the highpoint. The responses to narrative prompts of the remaining two low-ability-group students did not demonstrate any narrative macrostructure. One was categorized as a one-event story and one contained no past-tense clauses to create even a minimal narrative.

Highpoint analyses revealed information not only about the students' macrostructural abilities in their Spanish-language narratives but also interesting comparisons with their narrative-discourse abilities in English, allowing us to address our second research question: "How do children's Spanish-language and English-language narrative abilities compare?" Triple the number of children produced a classic narrative in English (9) compared with the number who produced a classic narrative in Spanish (3). Fourteen of the children had English-language narratives rated as macrostructurally more sophisticated than their Spanish-language narratives. Four children had the same best performance: One ended her stories in both languages on the highpoint; three were categorized as telling chronological narratives in both languages. Just three remaining children told classic narratives in Spanish but only chronological narratives in English; all were in the Spanish-narrative grammaticality/productivity high-ability group. There were no children in the sample who told classic narratives in both languages. Thus, overall, the children's macrostructural abilities were stronger when they told stories in English than when they told them in Spanish. In the following paragraphs, we extensively use excerpts from many of the children's narratives to illustrate these findings in more detail.

Among the best organized Spanish-language narratives in this study was Martín's story about the end of a tiring day. Although his stories in English were chronological narratives, his Spanish narrative about an everyday event was much more sophisticated. In his English narratives, he tended to describe long lists of events. In his Spanish narrative, the events lead to a highpoint. In this narrative, he has to stay up late to finish his homework; the next day he is tired (crisis point) but resolves this by sleeping in the car on the way to school. When he arrives at school, he has rested, and he turns in his homework and has a good day.

Un día en mi casa estaba haciendo mi tarea
[One day in my house I was doing my homework]
Y estaba cansado y eran las doce de la noche
[And I was tired and it was twelve at night]
Y después en la [sic] proxima día lo tenía de [sic] regresar
[And then in the next day I had to return]
Y estaba todo cansado queriéndome dormir
[And I was all tired wanting to sleep]
Y luego ya no tenía sueño porque me dormí en el carro
[And then I was no longer sleepy because I slept in the car]
Regreso [sic] mi tarea y tuve un buen día
[I backed [= returned] my homework and I had a good day]

Javier is another student whose Spanish-language narration was more elaborate than his English-language narration. His English narratives were heavily prompted by the researcher and were only strings of events. He eventually moved to more developed narratives that revolved around an incident that needed a resolution, but he did not fully develop the resolution. His most elaborated Spanish narrative followed a similar format, but the level of detail and evaluation was much greater. The narrative described hiking down a hill toward a river with his father. The resolution was more fully developed, and it was closer to the classic narrative structure (*"Y cuando por fin llegamos abajo, llegamos allá cerca de donde estaban los mangos... Entonces, estuvimos todos bien sudados y entonces nos regaló un mango alguien." "And when we finally got to the bottom and ended up where there were mangos.... Then, we were all sweaty and then someone gave us mangos."*)

Maritza was the third student whose Spanish narrative abilities exceeded (slightly) her English narrative abilities. In the following excerpt, she told a story to the interviewer about her mother stepping on a piece of aluminum foil that had been in the hot sun. She chose to tell this story twice, once in Spanish and once in English. It is worth noting that the English narrative does not contain as much detail as the Spanish narrative. However, this was not because it was a repeat of the same story; rather, the English narrative was actually produced in an earlier session with a different interviewer.

Spanish narrative:

Cuando mi mamá era chiquita no vio el papel de aluminio y estaba solita en la calle.
[When my mom was little she did not see the aluminum paper and she was by herself in the street.]
Y después lo pisó, pero ella no lo vio pero estaba ahí.
[And then she stepped on it, but she did not see it, but it was there.]
Porque el sol estaba brillando, estaba bien caliente.
[Because the sun was shining, it was very hot.]

Y lo pisó.
[And she stepped on it.]

Y después se peló todo el pie.
[And later the whole foot peeled.]

Y después se tenía que ir con el doctor.
[And later she had to go to the doctor.]

English narrative:

My mommy, when she was little, she went outside to the yard and there was
   like, it was pretty hot in Puerto Rico.
And there was like aluminum foil, but she didn't see it and she stepped on it.
And it peeled off her like whole foot.

Alberto is one of the many students who was rated as telling a classic narrative
in English – in this case, about fighting with local boys when visiting family in
Mexico. However, he told a much less sophisticated narrative in Spanish that
borrowed the English term *roller blades* and needed prompting by the interviewer
(I) to even reach a highpoint (i.e., getting "a very big scrape" that "had a lot of
blood").

English narrative:

. . . Mexico, Guadalajara.
We were in a line.
And the boys were devils there, because they always fight with me and
I didn't want to use my karate on them.
So one day they got me really mad and they hit me, so I hit them back.
And then they fell and they landed on the wood on the bed.
They never behave theirselves [sic].

Spanish narrative:

Pues, una vez yo estaba jugando afuera y yo me puse mis roller blades.
[Well, one time I was playing outside and I put on my roller blades.]

Y yo, me . . . yo um corrí y me caí.
[And I, I um ran and I fell.]

I: And then what happened?

A: *Y yo* [unintelligible] *y un raspado muy grande y tenía mucha sangre.*
[And I [unintelligible] and a very big scrape and it had a lot of blood.]

As reported, several Spanish- and even English-language narratives were
identified as being chronological. They primarily contained a list of events rather
than being organized around a highpoint in the story. For example, Sonia's

response to a prompt to tell in Spanish about an event at school elicited the following, excerpted from a much longer list of complicating actions conjoined with "*y*" that never reach a highpoint:

Y después fuimos a jugar afuera.
[And then we went to play outside.]

Y jugué con mis amigas.
[And I played with my friends.]

Y jugué hand ball.
[And I played hand ball.]

Y después fui a la clase.
[And then we went to class.]

Y um, y después hicimos terminamos la historia.
[And, um, and then we made finished the story.]

Similarly, Adriana told several chronological stories in Spanish and English, providing few evaluative comments or resolutions that would have been typical of classic narrative structure. For example, in a story about her last birthday, she listed a series of events that she was involved in at school, such as making a necklace for her mother and then finding a bird in her backpack. She also told a story about Christmas, which was her grandmother's birthday, but again she was only able to provide a series of actions, including eating cake, playing with friends, and eating.

The least sophisticated narratives in the study were produced by two students who appeared to have difficulty responding to the narrative elicitation prompts in both Spanish and English. For example, after much prompting, Lorenzo provided the following sentence in Spanish:

Hola, ¿cómo estás? Si tú puedes, si tú quieres jugar conmigo?
[Hi, how are you? If you can, if you want to play with me?]

Consequently, he did not tell a story; rather, he gave words that he knew in Spanish and sometimes created a sentence. The sentences were seemingly unrelated and not about any personal experience he had had in the past.

Similarly, Lorenzo's English narratives were confusing and predominantly in the structurally unsophisticated leapfrog pattern. He sometimes provided lists of things, such as when he listed all the presents he had received for Christmas and how he had spent 100 dollars on several items, rather than developing these past experiences into a series of connected events. In a story about a wedding he attended, Lorenzo told us:

It was so fun 'cause sometimes, once when I was about to leave he had ice.
And then he attacked me with the ice.
And sometimes he hit me though right here, or sometime over here.

But I throw them back and sometimes they hit them.
It's like an army. But they didn't know I was doing them.
We were smashing and smashing and sometimes we slipped.

He continued to talk about the ice fight, but then moved on to another topic without finishing the story about the wedding. It appeared that Lorenzo did not understand linear story structure very well in either English or Spanish.

Academic Abilities of the Three Spanish Narrative-Ability Groups

To address our third research question, "What are the relationships between Spanish-language narrative abilities and school achievement, both narrowly and broadly defined?," we examined in depth with this modest sample the patterns in bilingual narrative abilities, academic performance, and attitude toward schooling. We first report correlations between the continuous variables measuring language ability, academic achievement, metacognition subtypes, and attitudes for the group of students as a whole. We then use ability groupings on the Spanish narrative grammaticality/productivity measure to describe how well students were doing according to the standardized assessments of school achievement (e.g., SAT-9 ELA and mathematics scores) – the narrow definition of bilingual success described in the model in Figure 12.1. Finally, we examine the ability groups in depth to also include the students' narrative skills, metalinguistic and metapragmatic awareness, and feelings about school in the definition of success.

There were significant positive correlations between the Spanish-language grammaticality/productivity measure and the students' Pre-LAS Spanish scores at the point they had entered kindergarten ($r = .562$, $p = .02$), as well as their current year SAT-9 ELA scores ($r = .587$, $p = .02$) (among the second- and third-grade students only), and their metapragmatic skills in English ($r = .809$, $p < .001$), lending support to the model in Figure 12.1 that these relationships are important to consider in the development and measurement of Spanish-language discourse-level skills of bilingual students. Another important positive correlation among these variables was found between the metalinguistic and metapragmatic measures in English ($r = .530$, $p = .02$), which, as a moderate correlation, suggests that conscious reflection on language knowledge is related to – but not the same as – reflection on language usage in this sample of children. Furthermore, there was a correlation between SAT-9 ELA and mathematics scores ($r = .802$, $p < .001$), which is a strong correlation found in the general population of students (Reynolds, 1991). The FAS measure was positively correlated with both the Pre-LAS English and the metalinguistic measure ($r = .523$, $p = .03$; $r = .534$, $p = .02$, respectively). That is, those children with higher English language awareness and higher oral English abilities (as measured by a standardized assessment) rated their school environment and their scholastic

Table 12.2. *Summary scores (mean and SD), school achievement measures and attitude by ability group (Total N = 20)*

Spanish narrative-ability Group	Oral language skills in Spanish[a]	Oral language skills in English[a]	ELA abilities[b]	English-language mathematics abilities[b]	Metalinguistic/metapragmatic abilities in English[c]	FAS rating[d]
High (N = 10)	4.2	3.7	5.6	5.5	29.7 (6.1)/	4.5
	(0.83)	(1.1)	(1.6)	(1.9)	7.4 (0.52)	(0.48)
Medium (N = 7)	3.3	3.7	5	4.6	25.1 (7.8)/	4.5
	(1.9)	(0.52)	(1.4)	(2.1)	6.7 (.49)	(0.30)
Low (N = 3)	2.7	2.0	2.5	4	26.3 (9.5)/	4.1
	(0.58)	(1.0)	(0.71)	(0)	5.3 (1.5)	(0.36)

[a] Mean Pre-LAS level in Spanish and English at kindergarten (N = 18).
[b] Mean SAT-9 stanine score for second- and third-graders only (N = 15).
[c] Mean score; maximum scores are 45 and 8 for the metalinguistic and metapragmatic subsections, respectively.
[d] FAS mean Likert scale value (1–5).

performance high, and those students with lower English language awareness and abilities rated them low. This suggests that children's oral English-language skills (but not their oral Spanish-language skills) and their degree of awareness of language as an object of reflection may play a role in how well they regard their school environment and rate their scholastic performance. Although the students in this study were in a two-way bilingual program, their school was still predominantly populated by English-dominant – in fact, English-only – students and teachers, and many out-of-classroom activities such as assemblies and school trips were conducted in English-dominant environments, which may impact how well students who are less proficient in English and metalinguistically aware will fare in two-way programs.

Considering the narrowest definition of success in bilingual programming, Table 12.2 shows that the three Spanish-narrative ability groups differed by standardized achievement outcomes in ELA and mathematics. There was a positive trend: the higher the ability group, the better the average performance of the students on these assessments. No statistical analyses were attempted, given the small numbers of students in each group.

When we add several of the measures proposed in the model in Figure 12.1, we see that these also differentiate the ability groups in ways not dissimilar to the standardized measures but with some intriguing anomalies that warrant further discussion and eventual study (see Table 12.2). The mean standardized oral language skills in Spanish and English when students had been kindergarteners also differed by ability group. It is not surprising that the low-ability group had the lowest standardized scores on the Spanish measure, but it is surprising that the low-ability group should also have had the lowest English language scores when they entered school. Conceivably, these students could have been among the most imbalanced bilinguals in the sample and had poorer Spanish-language skills than English-language skills, including poorer narrative abilities in Spanish than in English as they moved up the grades. However, we know from the previous discussion about narrative abilities that these students tended to have poor narrative abilities in both English and Spanish. Relatively impoverished language skills in both languages are a phenomenon documented by Hakuta (1986) among young Spanish-English bilingual children of Puerto Rican origin growing up in New Haven, Connecticut. We must be cautious, however, because subsequent research revealed the linguistic and pedagogical complexities as well as the ethnical dangers of surmising that a bilingual child is "semilingual" (e.g., MacSwan, 2000). In the future, it will be useful to carefully explore the role of narrative-discourse abilities in the identification of children with developmental difficulties in both languages, relative to their other language abilities (e.g., lexical development and syntactic knowledge). However, this is outside the scope of the current chapter.

It is important to note that with some of the additional outcome measures, the medium-ability group sometimes patterned after the high-ability group and sometimes after the low-ability group. Specifically, this group had comparable mean Pre-LAS English scores and mean FAS ratings, and they also showed a similar distribution of abilities in organizing the macrostructures of their English-language stories to the high-ability group (see Table 12.1). However, in another key outcome (i.e., metalinguistic awareness), the medium-ability group patterned after the low-ability group. These findings may reflect the fact that the relationships between Spanish narrative ability (as captured by grammaticality and productivity) and these additional outcomes and narrative measures are only most salient at the extremes of narrative ability; however, a study with a larger sample is needed to further investigate this interpretation. We now examine all of these outcomes in greater detail within the context of each Spanish narrative-ability group. (Note that all names are pseudonyms.)

Spanish Narrative High-Ability Group

Martín, Christine, and Javier have some similar characteristics. They each scored 13 (the highest score) on the Spanish narrative grammaticality/productivity ability measure, although Christine's best English-language narrative was structurally more sophisticated than her Spanish narratives, whereas the opposite was true for the boys. All three told many stories in response to our prompts. In notes about Martín, the interviewer wrote, "quiet but self-assured and willing to tell a multitude of stories." Notes for Christine indicate that she was "engaged." Javier was described as very comfortable in responding to our prompts, and a student who provided thoughtful answers. Their FAS ratings also showed similar patterns (4.4, 3.3, and 4.5, respectively). These three students felt very positive about their relationships with teachers and students at school but rated their academic abilities as low. Christine's metalinguistic-awareness score was below the mean for her ability group (21), although her metapragmatic-awareness score was only slightly below the mean (7). For comparison, Martín's metalinguistic-awareness score was 28 and Javier's was 36; their metapragmatic-awareness scores were both 8. Joanna's profile mirrors that of Christine's with the exceptions that she told only two narratives in total, one in each language, and she had a higher FAS rating (4.19).

Yolanda and Maritza are two other students who both scored 13 on their Spanish narratives. In Spanish, Maritza told classic narratives, whereas Yolanda told chronological narratives. They both felt very positive about all aspects of school, evinced by very high FAS scores (4.8 and 5.0). Yolanda also had the highest metalinguistic score of the group (37) and a high metapragmatic-awareness score (8). Maritza's scores were not as high as Yolanda's scores; her metalinguistic-awareness score was 26 and her metapragmatic-awareness score was 7. Their English-language narratives were chronological recountings of past events, some with a slight hint of highpoint, and most centered on their home and family. Yolanda told chronological stories in Spanish about the dogs at her house, one in which the dogs got out and she was crying as she began to look for them. Her father caught them and the story ended (e.g., *and he started to chase him and he went inside one thing, but he caught him*).

Una vez se escaparon los perros
[One time the dogs escape]

Y yo estaba llorando y después fuimos a buscarlos
[And I was crying and then we went to look for them]

Y una señora que vivía en una calle dijo que los vio
[And a woman that lived in a street said that she saw them]

Y fuimos a una calle y ahí vimos a mi perro y había otro que era de nosotros
[And we went to a street and there we saw my dog and there was another dog that was ours]

Y le tenía miedo a mi papá porque mi papá es muy estricto con los perros
[And he was scare of my dad because my dad is very strict with the dogs]

Y lo empezó a perseguir y él se fue dentro de una cosa, pero lo cachó
[And he started to chase him and he went inside one thing, but he caught him]

I: Oh, ¿a los dos perros?
I: Both dogs?

Y: Uh huh.

When asked about her language skills, Sally reported that she spoke both English and Spanish and that she was able to read and write in Spanish as well.

Sally also received a high score of 4.6 on the FAS measure, indicating that she liked school and felt like a competent student. Despite her low metalinguistic- and metapragmatic-awareness skills – as demonstrated by her scores of 24 and 7, respectively – Sally was a fairly capable storyteller both grammatically (scoring 13 on the ability measure) and with her use of macrostructure, as the following excerpt from a Spanish-language narrative shows. Sally told a story about a trip to her grandmother's house for Easter. Sally was clearly able to use complex sentences in her narrative. She produced an end-at-highpoint narrative with a final evaluative comment that her cousin would not share the eggs she had found:

> *Fuimos a la casa de mi abuela con mis padres y mis primos.*
> [I went to my grandmother's house with my parents and my cousins.]
>
> *Mi prima y yo fuimos afuera.*
> [My cousin and I went outside.]
>
> *Y buscamos huevos. Mi prima agarró mucho[s] y no los quería compartir.*
> [And we looked for eggs. My cousin found a lot but she did not want to share them.]

Sally was also a relatively competent storyteller in English, consistently telling end-at-highpoint narratives.

Harry, Ralph, and Kyle, similar to Sally, all had high scores on the FAS measure (4.9, 4.3, and 4.8, respectively). Harry, like Sally, also scored relatively poorly on the metacognitive assessments (29 on the metalinguistic and 7 on the metapragmatic tests). Harry's ability to tell a narrative in English matched Sally's as well, as he also told an end-at-highpoint narrative for his optimal narrative response. However, both Ralph and Kyle differed somewhat from these two previous students. Both boys received far higher scores on the metacognitive assessments, with both receiving a score of 36 on the metalinguistic-awareness assessment and Ralph an 8 and Kyle a 7 on the metapragmatic-awareness assessment. Additionally, they proved to have higher narrative skills in English because they both told classic narratives in that language. Kyle used reported speech in his story about a trip to the hospital when he said, "*I was crying and crying so they took me to the hospital. By the time I went there, I said 'Mommy, I want my bottle.'*" He also provided a resolution to his story when he concluded: "*They gave me a shot and they took a test. Like a three- or two-year-old test 'cause I hit my head really hard. But I was okay.*"

However, neither Kyle nor Ralph was able to provide a classic narrative in Spanish. Their narratives provided a chronological series of events that had occurred. Harry was even less capable of utilizing classic-narrative structure in his Spanish narratives. He was unwilling to tell stories when prompted and responded to the prompts with single sentences rather than a story. Although he was able to use complex sentences in Spanish, he did not put them together into a cohesive story.

Spanish Narrative Medium-Ability Group

Julisa and Héctor were rated a 12 and an 11, respectively, on their Spanish narratives. The researcher commented that Julisa was engaged and thoughtful in her responses to the narrative prompts; Héctor was much more reluctant to participate. Julisa rated academics slightly lower than other items on the FAS ratings. Héctor had a very high overall rating on the FAS but rated his relationships with others and his writing ability slightly lower than other items. They both had the same metalinguistic score (27) and similar metapragmatic scores, with Julisa scoring 7 and Héctor scoring 6.

Julisa's narratives were very well developed although not quite classic narratives. Her Spanish narrative was about being hit on a bridge. She ended up at the nurse's office with her mother and her father, who was a doctor. She was able to go on with her day but, at a soccer game later that afternoon, she was almost hit by a ball in the same place. The story has great detail and emotion, but a highpoint and resolution are not well developed. Her English-language narratives also contained great dramatic elements but again are still rated as chronological in form (e.g., "my brother was going to say watch out and he split his leg and cut himself right here and he let the dog loose . . . and then my mom was outside . . . and my dad got him and put him back inside").

Héctor (H) told a story that was among the best developed English-language narratives of this sample of students, although this was an outlier among his other less-developed stories. His English narrative about being stuck in a tree was dramatic (e.g., *I was yelling and yelling*) and had a well-developed highpoint (e.g., *then my legs got numb*) and an appropriate resolution (e.g., *until they came back and said, "okay, we'll get you down"*). It was a short but coherent, well-structured story. His Spanish narrative was not nearly as well developed and, instead of a dramatic event, it was a description of a trip to the beach where he saw a sea lion. The story was a chronological series of events told in simple sentences (e.g., *and then I got on the boat and then we saw another sea lion and we went home*).

English narrative:

My next-door neighbor he has kids and we go tree climbing.
We go all the way up to the top.
Once my friend he pulled me all the way up to the top
and they went back inside the house and forgot that I was in the tree.
I was yelling and yelling, but they didn't hear me because they were inside.
Then my legs got numb.

I was there for like 45 minutes, until they came back and said "OK, we'll get you down."

Spanish narrative:

H: *Cuando fui a la playa vi un...*
[When I went to the beach I saw a...]

H: How do you say sea lion in Spanish?

I: *Animal de la mar,* I don't know.
[Sea animal, I don't know.]

H: *Vi un animal del mar y era una foca.*
[I saw a sea animal and it was a sea lion.]

Y la toqué y entonces vi los barcos en la playa.
[And I touched it and then I saw the boats in the beach.]

Y entonces me subí a un barco.
[And then I got in a boat.]

Y entonces vimos otra foca y nos fuimos a la casa.
[And then we saw another sea lion and we went home.]

Adriana, Melinda, Sonia, and Jayne all scored 12 on the Spanish discourse assessment because they were able to use several complex sentences, although not with great accuracy. These narratives were also all categorized as chronological stories. Where Adriana also told chronological stories in English, Melinda, Sonia, and Jayne told classic narratives in English. However, these girls scored similarly on the FAS measure (between 4.2 and 4.7). They had relatively high metalinguistic-awareness scores (between 28 and 35) and all scored above the average, with 7 points on the metapragmatic-awareness measure. Adriana scored much lower on these measures, with a scores of 15 on the metalinguistic-awareness measure and 6 on the metapragmatic-awareness measure.

To conclude this group, we profile Valencia, who was described as a friendly, engaged student. She scored 11 on the Spanish discourse assessment, telling a two-event story in Spanish using several relatively simple but accurate sentences. Her English-language narratives were rated as chronological, suggesting they were longer stories but not necessarily any more structurally sophisticated than her best two-event Spanish-language story. Her FAS rating of 4.0 is lower than the mean for this group. Valencia's metalinguistic-awareness score was low at 14 points; however, her metapragmatic-awareness score was quite high at 7.

Spanish Narrative Low-Ability Group

Alberto is an interesting case within this sample of 20 students because his profile of abilities showed that his low score of 8 on the Spanish narrative grammaticality/productivity measure did not preclude him from forming a rel-atively well-organized narrative in Spanish (rated as end-at-highpoint). This high macrostructural performance is more consistent with students in the medium- and high-ability groups as are his scores on the FAS (4.5) and for the metalinguistic- and metapragmatic-awareness measures (37 and 7, respec-tively). His English narratives also included one classic linear narrative, although this was an anomaly because most of his stories were sufficiently disorganized to be categorized as leapfrog narratives.

Kiko also had a low rating (7) on his Spanish narratives. He rated a large number of FAS items very low but was given a high rating to the items that related to a positive relationship with his teacher, to gain an overall score of 4.0. His metalinguistic- and metapragmatic-awareness scores were 19 and 5, respectively. Researcher comments about this student began very positively (i.e., "very excited and engaged") but the second and third times we met with Kiko he was bored and seemed reluctant to participate. He particularly did not want to speak in Spanish, and the narrative he told was very short and negative in theme (*"Un día aho [= no había] nada . . . porque estaba muy oscuro. Muchos carros chocaron."*; *"One day [there] was nothing . . . because it was very dark. Many cars crashed."*). His English narratives were longer and chronologically organized but with little evaluation or development of a highpoint. One of his stories was about a game he called "butt ball." Participants of this game would sit on a wall with their "butt" hanging out and someone would try to hit them with a hard ball. This came at the end of a series of narrative prompts and, although it is the most developed narrative, it contained little evaluative commentary or highpoint development (e.g., *"And we were like sneaking like this on the wall so no could see us to this market. And we got another ball and we kept playing."*).

Lorenzo was able to use one isolated simple sentence in his Spanish narrative but received a score of only 5 points because the majority of his utterances were sentence fragments. He scored much lower (3.8) on the FAS measure than any of the other students. He scored relatively low on the measures of metacognition, with scores of 23 on the metalinguistic-awareness measure and 4 on the metapragmatic-awareness measure, the lowest score of this sample. Lorenzo's responses to the narrative prompts were poorly structured in both Spanish (categorized as nonnarrative) and English (categorized as leapfrog).

General Discussion

Many of the stories told to us in Spanish followed a chronological sequence of events (several with a focus on relationship details) rather than the classic linear form which characterized many of the English-language narratives with their incorporation of orientation, complicating actions, evaluative highpoint, and resolution. By the age of 6 years, the most common form of narrative for the mostly European American children who have been studied is the classic linear narrative (e.g., McCabe and Rollins, 1994; see also chapter 10, this volume). This difference in findings for the Spanish-language narratives of first-through third-grade students in this study may be due to cultural differences in preferred narrative style or the fact that the Spanish-language skills of these students, although exceeding their English-language skills at school entry, had not continued to develop sufficiently to support the extended discourse abilities used in organizing narration. This was not a simple inability to organize language at levels beyond the sentence because 8 of the 11 students who gave chronological narratives in Spanish were capable of classic narrative structure in English.

Further research needs to investigate why narrative macrostructural abilities do not seem to transfer across a bilingual child's two languages; that is, do cultural differences in style preference play a role, or is there a threshold of language ability needed in each of the child's languages in order to independently produce classic narrative structure in each language? A third possibility, is that the overwhelming number of Spanish-language narratives characterized as chronological in the highpoint analysis are not being served by this particular approach to understanding narrative development. We suspect that highpoint analysis may be failing to capture the organization of these students' Spanish-language narratives and thus may prove to be less useful to researchers and educators in this context. In the future, we need to explore ways in which organizational structures can be characterized in more revealing ways for these narratives.

Our findings also suggested different kinds of diversity *within* the Spanish-narrative ability groups. First, grade level did not seem to be a strong determinant of ability group status, with first- and second-grade students grouped with third grade students in both the high- and medium-ability groups that were formed on the basis of the grammaticality and productivity of the students' Spanish-language narratives (see Table 12.1). Second, not only did it appear that these microstructural abilities were largely unrelated to grade, but they did not seem to be prerequisite for demonstrating mature narrative macrostructure. This was generally the case with Spanish-language narration; chronological narratives are prevalent in both the high- and medium-ability groups, and this was particularly true of English-language narration, with classic and chronological narratives represented in each of the three Spanish-narrative ability groups. This finding echoes that of Uccelli and Páez (2007) who found that narrative structure was a separate construct from the other language measures in the narratives of their kindergarten and first-grade bilinguals.

Our investigations of the hypothesized relationships between Spanish- and English-language narrative abilities, academic achievement, and other indicators of development in the school environment were qualitative and primarily exploratory in nature. However, the results of the current study, by describing the profiles of 20 Spanish-dominant first- through third-grade students, are suggestive of the nuanced roles of different types of information in measuring success in bilingual programs and revealed, among other things, that Spanish-narrative ability was related to measures of other Spanish-language abilities, ELA skills, and level of metapragmatic awareness in English.

By including Spanish-language narratives in the students' profiles of language ability, we can use narrative as a tool to parlay what we know of their Spanish-language development into their English-language development and academic achievement outcomes. The study revealed that different information was yielded by employing both microstructural and macrostructural analyses. Information about the grammaticality and productivity of narratives along with knowledge of the students' ability to organize stories using macrostructural components (e.g., orientation, complicating action, evaluation, and resolution) provided complementary profiles of their narrative-discourse abilities. Students with good linguistic skills in Spanish (i.e., the ability to accurately use multiclause sentences and complex syntactic structures) were not always able to tell well-organized personal stories.

Although much has been made of children's ability in their first language as a sound basis for and a good predictor of literacy in a second language, little attention has been given to which aspects of oral-language ability will prepare children for the positive transfer of cross-linguistic skills (Genesee & Geva, 2006). This study suggests that we cannot take for granted that students' syntactic knowledge of Spanish means that they have knowledge of the discourse-level skills that have been found to be related to later reading comprehension in monolingual English students (Griffin et al., 2004; Snow et al., 1998).

CONCLUSION

Discourse-level abilities in Spanish should be part of judging the success of a bilingual program. The criteria for success of a bilingual program can be spelled out with the model proposed in Figure 12.1. However, there are a number of limitations with the current study that necessitate further study, and many of these have been mentioned throughout the chapter. Moreover, in the future, we need to study the diversity of narrative types (i.e., fictional compositions and retellings as well as personal narratives) because each will give complementary information on narrative abilities. The relationship of the different types of narrative discourse to literacy skills may also vary due to the cognitive and linguistic demands of the task. For example, Fiestas and Peña's (2004) study findings suggest that the degree of contextual support differs in different storytelling contexts. Contextual support is high if a child is retelling a story or generating a fictional story from pictures, whereas contextual support is low (as in the current study) when a child is telling a factual, personal narrative from memory alone. Thus, oral narratives produced in the former manner may not be as highly correlated with literacy, a decontextualized use of language (e.g., Snow et al., 1998), as personal narratives may be.

As previously mentioned, with only 20 students in the current study, our investigations of the hypothesized relationships between these factors – by necessity – have been primarily qualitative and exploratory. A future study with more students and information on all relevant measures (e.g., including tests scores for mathematics and science in Spanish) that are missing from the current data set is necessary to pursue these hypotheses more fully and in statistically sophisticated ways.

However, the findings of this study have underscored the importance of children's native-language discourse-level abilities to school success and adjustment. Studying relationships among these factors is critical, particularly in the case of Latino children whose rate of dropout in later school years cannot be explained by English academic performance alone. Often, Latino students initially do well in school yet drop out later, possibly due to issues of self-esteem and attitudes toward schooling (Phinney et al., 2001; Stevenson et al., 1990). Gándara (2005) pointed out that good-quality bilingual schooling, among other remedies, could play a role in reversing this trend among Latino youth. Moreover, she has called for the recognition of gifted and talented Latino students *within* a multilingual context. The needs of these students, who may be vulnerable to dropping out not because of poor test scores but rather because of lack of opportunity or meaningful preparation, have largely gone unaddressed. "Today's definitions [of gifted and talented] are narrow and overly dependent on developed academic skills. They also fail to account adequately for cultural and linguistic differences in the expression of ability and the inadequacy of most teachers and standardized tests to recognize and measure high ability or talent in Latino students" (Gándara, 2005, p. 31). Broadening and adding depth to the definitions of the success of bilingual programming and the success of the students that it serves in the ways we have described and proposed in this chapter should go toward ameliorating the concerns that educators have in meeting the needs of all Latino students, including the highest achieving students.

The addition of an affective measure in this study also revealed important information about student motivation and academic self-perception. We might go so far as to propose that future content analysis of oral narratives collected in both languages of bilinguals be used to help ascertain students' attitudes toward school, their bilingual language programs, and their general academic progress. The focus on the relational aspects of the stories by Latino narrators (Silva & McCabe, 1996) may make narrative data very suited to this use because they may reveal attitudes toward teachers, classmates, and family and the ways in which they might support a child's schooling experiences. For example, these elements are present in the following personal narrative by Melinda, which tells of her involvement in a school play about the tradition of *Día de los Muertos* (Day of the Dead):

M: We did a show about the *Día de los Muertos.*

I: Oh, tell me what was the show about? What is *Día de los Muertos* about?

M: Well, it is when people die and, um, like people already been like already inside what's it called? The thing where they put them in it?

I: The coffin?

M: Yeah, and um and so I think, um, well we were talking about it, about it to the little children and, um, so we were teaching the children of the little class, the kindergarten about the *Día de los Muertos.* So I thought that was a good idea and I was proud of myself and the kids.

I: You were proud of yourself and the kids? What part did you play?

M: Well, I played the one with myself when I was "Oxside" [character in story?] and, Um, I was telling a story and I was a little girl that always wanted to have her wish. And the other ones are the gods, the boys were the gods and the girls. Some of the boys and some of the girls were, um, the, my aunts and my uncles and my . . . like that.

I: Oh, people that had died?

M: Yeah, so I was the. . . . Well, I felt like I was the special one in my thoughts, but some of the people, the family of the kids that were doing the show were here and my mom too. She was really proud of me.

In this narrative, Melinda makes several evaluative comments about the children in her school who are Latino, European American, and of several other ethnicities, as well as her mother's support for her participation in this culturally relevant play. These suggest a positive attitude toward her educational experience. This contrasted with the information yielded by simply knowing her FAS score of 4.69. Although this measure tells us that Melinda scored highly on the 5-point scale, giving a combination of 4 and 5 points to the 16 questions about school, it does not offer us the richness of affective detail that personal stories can (Imbens-Bailey, 1997). Mining the affective content of children's narratives about their educational, linguistic, and cultural experiences could deepen our understanding of their self-reported ratings of school and academic performance, as well as add explanatory information to our interpretations of their academic achievements overall.

We end on a cautionary note from Minami (2002, p. 234), a scholar of bilingualism and himself a bilingual: "As researchers, we should not blindly believe that being bilingual is advantageous in all areas of cognitive development. Or, more generally, rather than simply believing that bilinguals have an advantage over monolinguals or vice versa, it is meaningful to understand in what kinds of cognitive domains we can identify bilingual advantage (and this eventually leads to the discussion of the efficacy of bilingual education programs)." Point taken. Thus, we should endeavor to leverage what we know about the Spanish-language skills (including narrative-discourse abilities) of bilingual students when we evaluate their success in U.S. schools, as well as when we evaluate the success of these students' schools in meeting their needs.

Warm up: Pet Story

Interviewer told a story of a pet being naughty; the children were prompted to tell whether something similar had happened to them.

Culture

Have you ever been on a trip where you needed to speak Spanish?
Can you tell me something you did once with friends on the weekend?

Family

Have you ever visited your grandparents? (Or, have your grandparents ever visited you?) Can you tell me about one of your (their) visits?

School

Have you ever celebrated any festivals here at school? Can you tell me about one?
What happened on your last birthday at school?
Tell me about your favorite memory of school.
Tell me about your worst memory of school.

ACKNOWLEDGMENT

Support for the collection of the data reported herein was provided to the first author of this chapter by the former Urban Education Study Center at the University of California at Los Angeles (now CONNECTIONS).

REFERENCES

August, D., & Hakuta, K. (1997). *Improving schooling for language-minority children: A research agenda.* Washington, DC: National Academy Press.

August, D., & Shanahan, T. (2006). *Developing literacy in second-language learners: Report of the National Literacy Panel on language minority children and youth.* Mahwah, NJ: Lawrence Erlbaum Associates.

Bailey, A. L., & Moughamian, A. C. (2007). Telling stories their way: Narrative scaffolding with emergent readers and readers. *Narrative Inquiry, 17*(2), 203–229.

Bayley, R. & Schecter, S. R. (2005). Spanish maintenance and English literacy: Mexican descent children's Spanish and English narratives. In K.Denham & A. C. Lobeck (Eds.) *Language in the schools: Integrating linguistics knowledge into K-12 teaching* (pp. 121–137). Mahwah, NJ: LEA.

Ben-Zeev, S. (1977). The influence of bilingualism on cognitive strategy and cognitive development. *Child Development, 48*, 1009–1018.

Bialystok, E. (2001). *Bilingualism in development: Language, literacy, and cognition.* New York: Cambridge University Press.

Bialystok, E., & Cummins, J. (1991). Language, cognation, and education of bilingual children. In E. Bialystok (Ed.), *Language processing in bilingual children.* Cambridge: Cambridge University Press.

California Department of Education (2006). *Two-way immersion programs in California.* Retrieved on 2/26/07 from http://www.cde.ca.gov/sp/el/ip/resources.asp.

Catts, H., & Kamhi, A. (1999). Causes of reading disabilities. In H. Catts and A. Kamhi (Eds.), *Language and reading disabilities* (pp. 95–127). Boston: Allyn & Bacon.

Center for Applied Linguistics (2006). *Directory of two-way bilingual immersion programs in the U.S.* Retrieved on 2/26/07 from http://www.cal.org/twi/directory.

Champion, T., McCabe, A. K., & Colinet, Y. (2003). The whole world could hear: The structure of Haitian American children's narratives. *Imagination, Cognition and Personality, 22*(4), 381–400.

Citrin, J. (1990). Language politics and American identity. *Public Interest, 99*, 97–104.

Civil Rights Project (2002). *What works for the children? What we know and don't know about bilingual education.* Cambridge, MA: Harvard University.

Cook, V. (2005). Basing teaching on the L2 user. In E. Llurda (Ed.), *Non-native language teachers: Perceptions, challenges, and contributions to the profession* (pp. 47–61). New York: Springer.

Crawford, J. (2000). *At war with diversity: U.S. language policy in an age of anxiety.* Clevedon, UK: Multilingual Matters.

Deckner, D. F., Adamson, L. B., & Bakeman, R. (2006). Child and maternal contributions to shared reading: Effects on language and literacy development. *Applied Developmental Psychology, 27*, 31–41.

Díaz, R., & Klingler, C. (1991). Toward an explanatory model of the interaction between bilingualism and cognitive development. In E. Bialystok (Ed.), *Language processing in bilingual children.* Cambridge: Cambridge University Press.

Duncan, S. E., & De Ávila, E. A. (1986a). *Pre-Language Assessment Scales.* Monterey, CA: CTB/McGraw-Hill.

Duncan, S. E., & De Ávila, E. A. (1986b). *Pre-Language Assessment Scales: Spanish.* Monterey, CA: CTB/McGraw-Hill.

Fiestas, C. E., & Peña, E. D. (2004). Narrative discourse in bilingual children: Langauge and task effects. *Language, Speech and Hearing Services in Schools, 35*, 155–168.

Gándara, P. (2005). *Fragile futures: Risk and vulnerability among Latino high achievers.* Princeton, NJ: Educational Testing Service.

García, G. E., McKoon, G., & August, D. (2006). Language and literacy assessment of language-minority students. In D. August & T. Shanahan (Eds.), *Developing literacy in second-language learners: Report of the National Literacy Panel on language minority children and youth.* Mahwah, NJ: Lawrence Erlbaum Associates.

Genesee, F., & Geva, E. (2006). Cross-linguistic relationships in working memory, phonological processes and oral language. In D. August & T. Shanahan (Eds.), *Developing literacy in second-languagelLearners: Report of the National Literacy Panel on language minority children and youth.* Mahwah, NJ: Lawrence Erlbaum Associates.

Geva, E., & Genesee, F. (2006). First-language oral proficiency and second-language literacy. In D. August & T. Shanahan (Eds.), *Developing literacy in second-language learners: Report of the National Literacy Panel on language minority children and youth.* Mahwah, NJ: Lawrence Erlbaum Associates.

Griffin, T, Hemphill, L., Camp, L., & Wolf, D. P. (2004). Oral discourse in the preschool years and later literacy skills. *First Language, 24,* 123–147.

Guay, F., Marsh, H. W., & Boivin, M. (2003). Academic self-concept and academic achievement: Developmental perspectives on their causal ordering. *Journal of Educational Psychology, 95*(1), 124–136.

Gutiérrez-Clellen, V. F, Peña, E., & Quinn, R. (1995). Accommodating cultural differences in narrative style: A multicultural perspective: *Topics in Language Disorders, 15*(4), 54–67.

Hakuta, K. (1986). *Mirror of language: The debate on bilingualism.* New York: Basic Books.

Hakuta, K., Bialystok, E., & Cummins, J. (1991). Language, cognition and education of bilingual children. In E. Bialystok (Ed.), *Language processing in bilingual children.* Cambridge: Cambridge University Press.

Hakuta, K., & Díaz, R. (1985). The relationship between bilingualism and cognitive ability: A critical discussion and some new longitudinal data. In K. E. Nelson (Ed.), *Children's Language, Vol. 5.* Hillsdale, NJ: Lawrence Erlbaum Associates.

Harcourt Brace (1996). *Stanford Achievement Test Series.* Ninth Edition [SAT-9]. San Antonio, TX. Author.

Imbens-Bailey, A. L. (1995). Oral proficiency and literacy in an ancestral language: Implications for ethnic identity. Unpublished dissertation.

Imbens-Bailey, A. L. (1996). Ancestral language acquisition: Implications for aspects of ethnic identity among Armenian American children and adolescents. *Journal of Language and Social Psychology, 15,* 422–443.

Imbens-Bailey, A. L. (1997). When sentences are not enough: Narrative data and cultural identity. *Journal of Narrative and Life History, 7,* 343–351.

Imbens-Bailey, A. L. (2000). Language background and ethnic identity: A study of bilingual and English-only-speaking children of Armenian descent. In E. Olshtain & G. Harenczyk (Eds.), *Language, identity and immigration.* Jerusalem: Magnes.

MacLachlan, B. G., & Chapman, R. S. (1988). Communication breakdowns in normal and language-learning–disabled children's conversation and narration. *Journal of Speech and Hearing Disorders, Vol. 53,* 2–7.

MacSwan, J. (2000). The threshold hypothesis, semilingualism, and other contributions to a deficit view of linguistic minorities. *Hispanic Journal of Behavioral Sciences, 22*(1), 3–45.

MacSwan, J. (2006). *Review of immersion, not submersion, Vol. III.* Great Lakes Center for Education Research and Practice. Retrieved on December 14, 2006, from http:/www.greatlakescenter.org.

Marsh, H. W., Trautwein, U., Lüdtke, O., Köller, O.,& Baumer, J. (2005). Academic self-concept, interest, grades, and standardized test scores: Reciprocal effects models of causal ordering. *Child Development, 76*(2), 397–416.

Mayer, J. (2007). Policy needs: What federal and state governments need from language research. In A. L. Bailey (Ed.), *Language demands of school: Putting academic English to the test.* New Haven, CT: Yale University Press.

McCabe, A., & Bliss, L. S. (2008). A comparison of personal versus fictional narratives in children with language impairment. *American Journal of Speech-Language Pathology, 17,* 1–13.

McCabe, A., & Bliss, L. S. (2005). Narratives from Spanish-speaking children with impaired and typical language development. *Imagination, Cognition and Personality, 24*(4), 331–346.

McCabe, A. & Rollins, P. (1994), Assessment of preschool narrative skills. *American Journal of Speech-Language Pathology, 4,* 45–56.

McGraw-Hill (2006). *Spanish Assessment of Basic Education.* 2nd edition. Monterey, CA: Author.

Mayer, M.,(1969). *Frog, Where are You?* New York: Dial Books.

Miller, J. F., Heilmann, J., Nockerts, A., Iglesias, A., Fabiano, L., & Francis, D. J. (2006). Oral language and reading in bilingual children. *Learning Disabilities Research and Practice, 21*(1), 30–43.

Minami, M. (2002). Review of bilingualism in development: Language, literacy, and cognition. *Bilingual Research Journal, 26*(3), 229–235.

NICHD Early Child Care Research Network (2005). Pathways to reading: The role of oral language in the transition to reading. *Developmental Psychology, 41*(2), 428–442.

No Child Left Behind Act (2001). Pub. L. No. 107–110, 115 Stat. 1425.

Pearson, B. (2002). Narrative competence among monolingual and bilingual school children in Miami. In D.K. Oller & R. E. Eilers (Eds.). *Language and literacy in bilingual children* (pp. 135–174). Clevedon, UK: Multilingual Matters.

Peña, E., Bedore, L.M., & Rappazzo, C. (2003). Comparison of Spanish, English, and bilingual children's performance across semantic tasks. *Language, Speech, and Hearing Services in Schools, 34*(1), 5–16.

Peterson, C., & McCabe, A. (1983). *Developmental psycholinguistics.* New York: Plenum.

Phinney, J. S., Baumann, K., & Blanton, S. (2001). Life goals and attributions for expected outcomes among adolescents from five ethnic groups. *Hispanic Journal of Behavioral Sciences, 23*(4), 363–377.

Porter, R. P. (1990). *Forked-tongue: The politics of bilingual education.* New York: Basic Books.

Reese, E. (1995). Predicting children's literacy from mother–child conversations. *Cognitive Development, 10,* 381–405.

Reynolds, A. (1991). Early schooling of children at risk. *American Educational Research Journal, 28*(2), 392–422.

Rivera, C., Collum, E., Shafer Willner, L., & Sia, Jr., J. K. (2006). An analysis of state assessment policies addressing the accommodation of English-language learners. In C. Rivera & E. Collum (Eds.), *A national review of state assessment policy and practice for English-language learners.* Mahwah, NJ: Lawrence Erlbaum Associates, Inc.

Rodino, A. M., Gimbert, C., Pérez, C., Craddock-Willis., K., & McCabe, A. K. (October, 1991). *"Getting your point across"*: *Contractive sequencing in low-income African American and Latino children's personal narratives.* Paper presented at the 16th Annual Boston University Conference on Language Development, Boston, MA.

Rolstad, K., Mahoney, K., & Glass, G. V. (2005). The big picture: A meta-analysis of program effectiveness research on English language learners. *Educational Policy, 19,* 572–594.

Sénéchal, M., & LeFevre, J. (2002). Parental involvement in the development of children's reading skill: A five-year longitudinal study. *Child Development 73*(2), 445–460.

Silva, M. J., & McCabe, A. (1996). Vignettes of the continuous and family ties: Some Latino American traditions. In A. McCabe (Ed.), *Chameleon readers: Teaching children to appreciate all kinds of good stories.* New York: McGraw-Hill.

Snow, C. E., Burns, M. S., & Griffin, P. (Eds.) (1998). *Preventing reading difficulties in young children.* Washington, DC: National Academy Press.

Stevenson, H. W., Chen, C., & Uttal, D. H. (1990). Beliefs and achievement: A study of Black, White, and Hispanic children. *Child Development, 61,* 508–523.

Stipek, D. (2000). Feelings About School Measure. In A. L. Bailey et al. (2000), *The literacy development checklist: Manual.* Los Angeles, CA: UC Regents.

Stipek, D., Ryan, R., & Alarcón, R. (1997). *Developing a bilingual program for young children: An ongoing process.* Unpublished manuscript. Los Angeles: Seeds University Elementary School, University of California.

Stipek, D., Ryan, R., & Alarcón, R. (2001). Bridging research and practice to develop a two-way bilingual program. *Early Childhood Research Quarterly, 16,* 133–149.

Uccelli P. & Páez, (2007). Narrative and vocabulary development of bilingual children from Kindergarten to first grade: Developmental changes and associations among English and Spanish skills. *Language, Speech, and Hearing Services in Schools, 38,* 225–236.

Unz, R. (2000). Lingua Franca: It's past time for New York to scrap bilingual ed. *City Journal.* Retrieved on 3/26/07 from http://www.city-journal.org/html/10_4_sndgs06. html.

Valencia, R. (2002). *Chicano school failure and success: Past, present and future (2nd edition).* New York: Routledge, Falmer.

Verhoeven, L. (1994). Transfer in bilingual development: The linguistic interdependence hypothesis revisited. *Language Learning, 44,* 381–415.

Viberg, Å. (2001). Age-related and L2-related features in bilingual narrative development in Sweden. In L. Verhoeven & S. Strömqvist (Eds.), *Narrative development in a multilingual context* (pp. 87–128). Amsterdam/Philadelphia: John Benjamins.

Wagner, R. C., Nettelbladt, U., Sahlen, B., & Nilholm, C. (2000). Conversation versus narration in preschool children with language impairment. *International Journal of Language & Communication Disorders, 35*(1), 83–93.

Wells, C. G. (1986). *The meaning makers: Children learning language and using language to learn.* Portsmouth, NH: Heinemann.

White, D. (2006). *Immersion, not submersion, Vol. III.* Arlington, VA: Lexington Insititute.

Wigfield, A., & Karpathian, M. (1991). Who am I and what can I do? Children's self-concepts and motivation in achievement situations. *Educational Psychologist, 26*(3), 233–261.

Willig, A. (1985). A meta-analysis of selected studies on the effectiveness of bilingual education. *Review of Educational Research, 55,* 269–317.

Yelland, G. W., Pollard, J., & Mercuri, A. (1993). The metalinguistic benefits of limited contact with a second language. *Applied Psycholinguistics, 14*(4), 423–444.

Zehr, M. J. (2006). Guides avoid bilingual vs. English-only issue. *Education Week, 26*(11), 20–22.

13

Cultural Variation in Narrative Competence and Its Implications for Children's Academic Success

SARAH W. BECK

Key Words: Cultural variation, narrative style, Latino children, academic discourse, academic success

ABSTRACT

This concluding chapter ties together and comments on themes from the preceding chapters, situating these themes in the broader context of current research on Latino children's experiences with academic discourse in schools. In the first half of the chapter, the findings presented in this book are situated within the important socioculturally based tradition of research on differences between the narrative styles of ethnic and linguistic minorities and those of middle-class, European American children, and the impact that such differences have had on the academic experiences of linguistic and cultural-minority children in U.S. schools. For example, qualitative investigations have shown that children from working-class, African American backgrounds tend to employ narratives that are associative in form rather than organized around a single topic. Narratives told in this topic-associating style tend to be negatively received by teachers, with the likely consequence that their tellers may grow to doubt their capacity for success at school-based language tasks. In the second half of the chapter, I discuss the ways in which the cognitive and linguistic skills implicated in narrative competence may provide a foundation for mastery of other modes of academic discourse and reasoning. I argue that in-depth studies of narrative competence and variations in narrative style such as those presented in this book are essential to deepening our understanding of children's preparedness for academic success. Finally, I advocate incorporating education about various forms of discourse competence into professional development for teachers and offer some suggestions as to what might constitute such an education.

INTRODUCTION

As I was composing this chapter, the U.S. public was engaged in a fierce and divisive debate on a Senate bill that would have enacted a major overhaul of the immigration system, allowing undocumented immigrants to embark on a path to legal employment and eventual citizenship and establishing a new visa category for undocumented workers who perform essential services. Senate aides reported that just prior to the Senate vote, the number of messages delivered by telephone and email to Capitol Hill offices reached a level not seen since the impeachment of Bill Clinton, and that many of the messages were angry and even threatening (Zeleny, 2007). Public discourse around the bill – which the Senate ultimately failed to pass – in the run-up to the vote was characterized by the same tone that had marked the debate since the bill was first introduced in May 2005. Immigrants and their supporters, who favored a more generous policy toward immigration, cited the eagerness of immigrants to assume U.S. citizenship and to participate actively in civic life as justification for their stance. By contrast, those who endorsed more stringent legislation maintained that immigrants resist complete integration into the fabric of social life in the United States, that they maintain their own cultures and languages, and thus contribute to the fragmentation of social and cultural life. A particularly revealing anecdote appeared in a report from the State of Arizona, where one in eight adult voters is Latino. Many residents expressed concern that immigrants from Mexico are overburdening schools and contributing to "cultural disintegration"; as one European American schoolteacher put it: "You want to stay here and get an education, get benefits, and you still want to say 'Viva Mexico'? It was a slap in the face." (Kirkpatrick, 2006). Remarks such as these indicate how closely beliefs about cultural assimilation are linked to people's attitudes toward immigrants. As educators, we need to be especially mindful of how such attitudes affect teachers' perceptions of students from non–European American backgrounds and to work toward a more nuanced and detailed understanding of the ways in which cultural practices and values that non mainstream children bring to school intersect with the values and practices endorsed by schools and other mainstream institutions.

Latino students represent the greatest percentage of the school population of any ethnic group other than White: 20%, in contrast to 16% for African Americans and 7% total for other racial/ethnic groups (National Center for Education Statistics, 2007). Also, of all ethnic groups, Latino children are the most likely to speak a language other than English at home (National Center for Education Statistics, 2007). Thus, their presence as an ethnic and linguistic group will likely have a major impact on the context of language and literacy education in the United States.

Calculations by the U.S. Census Bureau reveal that along with Asian Americans, Latinos are the largest growing minority group. Latinos also comprise a substantial percentage of the immigrant population: Mexicans alone constitute roughly a third of the annual immigration flow into the United States (Passel & Suro, 2005). These increases, however, have brought no concurrent improvement in the educational and economic circumstances of Latinos or of language-minority students in general. Differences in high school dropout rates among Latino immigrants, nonimmigrants, and Whites are striking: according to the most recent available data, from 2005. Latinos born outside of the United States (which, for this analysis, included the 50 states and the District of Columbia) constituted 7% of the population aged 16 to 24 years; they represented 27% of the dropouts in this age group. Latino students (both immigrant and native-born) also continue to have much higher dropout rates than White or Black students (National Center for Education Statistics, 2007). According to recent statistics, the likelihood of failing to complete high school is also associated with language background: Whereas 10% of students who spoke English at home dropped out of high school, 18% of language minority students who spoke English very well, 31% of those who spoke English well and 51% of those who spoke English with difficulty had dropped out (National Center for Education Statistics, 2004). In other words, the greater the difficulty a student has with speaking English, the more likely that student is to drop out.

Inspired by these sobering statistics, this chapter aims to make two central points: First, if educators do not increase their knowledge of cultural variation in discourse styles and the implications of this variation, they may dismiss or denigrate the discourse competence of students from nonmainstream backgrounds. Second, I argue that narrative is an especially important genre of discourse in which to explore such variation because the skills required to succeed at telling stories are the same as or similar to skills required to succeed in other domains of schooling. Although economic factors undoubtedly influence the wide gap in achievement between Latino and European American students, it is important for educators to consider the ways in which culturally based differences between home and school discourses might influence Latino children's success in school. Teachers and school personnel are unable to change the demographic factors that contribute to income differences between Latino families and European American families. However, when equipped with sufficient background knowledge about their students' home life and cultural background, teachers can influence the degree to which Latino children (like students from any nonmainstream culture) are able to participate in authentic, intellectually engaging academic experiences, thus increasing the likelihood that they will master the discourses of schooling (Moll, Amanti, Neff, & González, 1992; Wong-Fillmore & Snow, 2000).

THE IMPORTANCE OF SOCIOCULTURAL PERSPECTIVES ON DISCOURSE AND LEARNING

Although prominent scholars have argued that certain minority ethnic groups fail to achieve academically due to what Fordham and Ogbu (1986) call "the burden of acting white," in this chapter I take a position similar to that of Ogbu's critics, who have argued that pursuing academic achievement is entirely compatible with maintaining a positive ethnic identity. For example, Conchas (2001) illustrated how Latino students in a racially diverse career academy were able to maintain both optimism about their academic and professional prospects *and* a strong sense of their ethnic identity as Latinos because teachers and students in the academy shared high expectations and common goals for students' academic work. As some of Ogbu's critics have maintained, the reason ethnic minority students do not succeed in school is not because of a cultural disposition toward failure but rather because schools marginalize students who do not adopt mainstream ways of speaking, thinking, and acting (Flores-Gonzales, 2003).

Decades' worth of richly descriptive research has illustrated the many ways in which discourse styles in general and styles of narrative in particular vary from one culture to another. Arguably, the most often cited study is Heath's (1983) ethnography of differences in communicative practices among working-class Whites, working-class Blacks, and mainstream middle-class families of both races. Noting that the variations among these groups cannot be captured by the simple dichotomy of "oral" and "literate" discourse styles, Heath (1983) pointed out several discernible differences among all three groups: For example, unlike middle-class "Maintown" parents, working-class "Roadville" parents did not extend or allow children to apply the content or structure of children's books to everyday life; in more current terms, they did not encourage what are now called "text-to-world" connections (Harvey & Goudvis, 2000). Like the mainstream parents, Roadville parents asked the children a lot of known-answer "what" questions similar to the kinds of questions that teachers ask students. Because Roadville parents placed great emphasis on children's recognition and mastery of literal content of stories, including the identification of letters and words, their children tended to do very well in the first years of elementary school but then lagged behind their middle-class peers as they were faced with more challenging inferential and analytical comprehension tasks. The working-class Black children of "Trackton," by contrast, were socialized by their parents into highly poetic, metaphorical ways of talking and telling stories. Yet, because the discourse practices of this community did not include the asking of known-answer questions (as in Roadville and Maintown), Trackton children tended to flounder when confronted by such questions in school because their metaphorical, associative responses to teachers' questions were viewed as distracting and inappropriate. Heath (1983) goes to great length to document the "backstory" that accounts for why children from these two nonmainstream groups fail in school, showing that the degree of alignment between home or community language practices and those of school has a strong association with children's success in school.

Subsequent theorizing about the nature of cultural practices underscores the point that Heath herself was trying to make: that these differences in language practices should not be attributed to the ethnicity or race of their practitioners but rather to the ways in which language use is interwoven with "ways of living, eating, sleeping, worshiping, using space, and filling time" (Heath, 1983, p. 3). A recent and useful redefinition of the term *culture* is as follows: Culture is not a static trait that can be ascribed to a particular race or ethnic group but rather a set of practices that have evolved over time under specific historical circumstances (Gutiérrez & Rogoff, 2003). This perspective on cultural differences has important implications for teachers: Rather than assuming that students are familiar with a particular way of speaking or thinking because of their participation in a certain ethnic group, teachers need to take the time to investigate the actual discourse backgrounds of students – such as their familiarity with certain ways of telling stories, making jokes, or presenting an argument – in order to create a bridge from the known patterns of discourse to new patterns. It is important for teachers to remember that the discourses of schooling have also evolved over time and as part of historical traditions, which make these discourses relatively more powerful but intrinsically no more valuable or better than discourses that evolved in nondominant cultural contexts.

Studies of the discourse patterns of students who belong to nondominant cultural groups are direly needed if we are to address the marginalization of these students in school contexts. Cross-cultural perspectives on discourse research have demonstrated the presence of alternative discourse conventions in both narrative and persuasive genres. For example, Michaels (1981) noticed a dominant pattern of topic-associating narratives styles among African American kindergarteners during "sharing-time" narrative performances in classrooms, which she contrasted with the topic-centered stories that White children told in the same context. The topic-centered narratives were characterized by linear plot development – a clear beginning, middle, and end in which a straightforward sequence of events led to a conclusion (Michaels & Cazden, 1986). Topic-centered stories represent the canonical structure typically privileged in school settings, in both oral and written modes, which may explain why the European American children's stories were more favorably received than those of the African American children in Michaels and Cazden's research. In a follow-up investigation based on Michaels' work, Hyon and Sulzby (1994) found that although African American children in their sample of 48 kindergarteners produced both topic-centered *and* topic-associating styles, the canonical topic-centered style was dominant in this group. They suggest that this difference may be due to the difference in the context of narrative production between their study and Michaels' study: Michaels' data were collected in a group classroom setting, in which the teacher required students to tell a story about something that had happened to them personally and also allowed clarifying interruptions by the teacher herself and other students. In contrast, Hyon and Sulzby (1994) elicited their narratives in a one-to-one interview setting, without interruption from the adult interlocutor, and encouraged students to tell any story they wished, without requiring that it be based on personal experience. In this context, "storybook" stories – that is, those borrowed from published children's books – were accepted as valid narrative productions. According to the authors, this less restrictive context allowed a more diverse collection of narrative styles to emerge. One implication of this explanation is that teachers need to establish classroom routines that provide students with supportive contexts for telling stories in a style that is familiar to them so that they will have the opportunity to demonstrate their best possible narrative performance. Taken together, this line of research on African American children's narratives styles highlights the need to question assumptions about the relationship between ethnic or racial group membership and discourse style, consistent with Gutiérrez and Rogoff's (2003) assertion that culture and ethnicity are not synonymous. That is, preferred discourse styles are a product of the cultural practices to which children are exposed rather than some kind of essential trait associated with one's ethnicity or race.

Another compelling illustration of how discourse preferences are associated with cultural practices rather then ethnic-group membership can be found in Farr's (1993) ethnolinguistic study of Mexican Americans in Chicago. She observed that in this community, standards for effective persuasive discourse varied depending on the listeners' place of origin and degree of exposure to other culturally based discourse norms. In her ethnographic study, she described and contrasted two communicative events, one in which a Mexican-born speaker addressed a primarily Mexican-born audience and one in which a different Mexican-born speaker addressed a Mexican American (American-born) audience. Both speakers employed the same figurative language and the parallelism characteristic of oral poetry in their speech, yet they were evaluated very differently by their different audiences. The predominantly Mexican-born audience responded favorably to this style of presentation, whereas the primarily Mexican American audience expressed impatience with the speaker's indirect and emotional style. The ethnicity of audience members and speakers was the same in both communicative contexts: Mexican; what differed was the extent to which audience members had been exposed to other cultural (i.e., European American) standards for persuasive speech.

The many parameters of narrative competence offer multiple ways in which culture may influence narrative structure and content. Narrative competence involves a set of related and interdependent skills, including vocabulary knowledge, mastery of the syntactic and morphological structures required to show temporal relationships among different events, audience awareness, and ability to understand and represent the intentions of human agents in a story. Thus, narrative competence can vary according to task circumstances and purposes. Some research suggests, for example, that children demonstrate different patterns of competence in using evaluative devices in fictional narratives and in personal narratives (Shiro, 2003). For example, high-socio-economic status (SES) and low-SES children showed a statistically significant difference in their use of evaluative devices in fictional narratives, and a similar difference between first- and fourth-grade high-SES children's use of such devices. Yet age and SES-related differences in use of evaluative devices on the personal-narrative task were not statistically significant. Stories are told in different ways for different purposes, and what counts as a "successful" narrative depends on the expectations of the audience and the conventions of the social context in which the narrator tells the story.

THE ROLE OF NARRATIVE IN CHILDREN'S EXPERIENCE OF SCHOOLING

Narrative studies, particularly those that involve young children, are an excellent place to begin an investigation into culturally based discourse variation because narrative tends to be the first discourse genre that children acquire (Applebee, 1978; Bruner, 1990). Narrative may not be essentially easier to master than informational genres (Bailey, in press), and evidence suggests that young children may be equally proficient at narrative and explanatory genres in informal conversational settings (Beals & Snow, 1994). Yet, most of the discourse that children encounter in the early years of schooling is narrative in nature (Duke, 2000), and school contexts for young children tend to give greater support to the development of narrative than to expository writing (Kamberelis & Bovino, 1999). Thus, the knowledge about narrative that children bring with them to school can serve as an important foundation for acquiring school-based knowledge.

Narrative is important to children's school experiences for two reasons: (1) because narrative is a fundamental tool for establishing and maintaining social relationships; and (2) because the skills involved in successful narrative production are similar or related to the skills involved in other important academic types of performances. Bruner (1986, p. 14) argued that narrative is a fundamental organizing framework that humans use to make sense of their experience. As such, narrative has two facets: the "landscape of action" – in which the events of a story take place, in which the story is structured – and "the landscape of consciousness," in which the human intentions that motivate these events are presented and explored. These two landscapes must be merged in order for a story to be coherent and meaningful: A storyteller must be able to organize events according to a certain logic, which depends on an understanding of human motivation and mental states. Yet, Bruner's model should not be taken to mean that structure is the primary or exclusive vehicle for meaning-making. Cross-cultural analyses of narratives have identified the important role that seemingly unstructured narratives play in the tellers' and listeners' construction of meaning (Ochs & Capps, 2004). As Ochs and Capps (2004, p. 4) put it:

> All narrative exhibits tension between the desire to construct an overarching storyline that ties events together in a seamless explanatory framework and the desire to capture the complexities of the events experienced, including haphazard details, uncertainties, and conflicting sensibilities among protagonists.

These authors depict the tension within narrative as a tension between narrative as a stable genre, with canonical expectations for structure and theme, and narrative as a way of sorting out one's relationships within the world – as a cultural tool that mediates thinking (Wertsch, 1998). Success at mastering the "genre" of narrative in contexts that require narrative performances is certainly important to children's academic success. At the same time, equally important is students' ability to use narrative as a means to construct identities in social situations. From the latter perspective, narrative can also be said to serve an "interactional" function. As Wortham (2001) argued, narratives can reveal as much about the relationship between the teller and the audience as about the teller. This dual function of narrative has been compellingly illustrated in Martínez-Roldán's (2003) study of a 7-year-old bilingual Latina student, Isabela, whose narrative ability allowed her not only to participate successfully and appropriately in the classroom literature discussions but also to develop and maintain multiple identities in the classroom. She possessed an academic identity of a talented storyteller, capable of varying her style of speaking according to context and audience and employing narrative as a form of response to literature, as well as a strong cultural identity as a recent immigrant from Mexico, which she transmitted in the content of her narratives, sharing experiences from her native country and in the United States. A close analysis of one of these narratives, told to an audience of Spanish-dominant peers and their bilingual teacher, reveals how Isabela employs a range of discourse strategies such as code-switching, quoting, and parallelism to create a coherent narrative – while also negotiating her identity as a recent immigrant to the United States, seeking a sense of place and self in this new environment. Her peers' and teacher's responses to this compelling story encourage her to elaborate with details about her place of origin in Mexico and her experiences with language discrimination and to explain how her use of language is connected to her sense of self. As Martínez-Roldán (2003, p. 518) sums up the meaning of her story, "for Isabela, identity, place and language were intertwined in narrative." Her analysis of Isabela's use of narratives highlights the important social function that narrative can play in establishing both personal and collective understandings of shared cultural experiences. Such understandings are essential to the development of positive academic identities, particularly for students from nonmainstream and language-minority backgrounds. It is important that this research employed both structural and content analyses to arrive at these conclusions. Multiple modes of inquiry into the characteristics and effects of narratives are necessary if we are to fully appreciate the role that narrative plays in students' school experiences. As Champion, Katz, Muldrow, and Dail (1999) argued, different approaches to analysis, such as content analysis and event analysis, can provide important perspectives on children's narrative competence, including the extent to which they employ narratives to develop social identities and portray cultural practices.

Whereas narrative plays a significant role in socializing individuals as members of cultural communities, it also serves important institutional purposes.

Perhaps because of narrative's central role in human cognition, telling and writing stories is a typical school activity for young children, and the narrative genre is typically central to the writing workshop model of teaching literacy that has gained increasing popularity in K-12 schools since the late 1980s (Calkins, 1994). However, narrative competence may be more than an end in itself: There is good reason to suspect that the skills required to tell a good story can also be recruited for other important academic tasks. Empirical research has documented relationships between certain narrative skills and other abilities involved in literate achievement. For example, the ability to employ evaluation devices in spoken narratives at the age of 5 years has been shown to be correlated with reading comprehension abilities at the age of 8 years (Griffin, Hemphill, Camp, & Wolf, 2004). The same research demonstrated that younger children's ability to tell a well-structured story and to elaborate on plot details was related to higher holistic assessments of their narrative skill at the later age. These authors also found a relationship between early skill at producing narrative and expository texts and later narrative competence, suggesting that the "information-funneling" (p. 143) strategies that writers employ in expository texts may be an important foundation for early narrative production. Students' ability to tell a coherent story also seems to be related to certain measures of reading comprehension: Empirical research has found that children with lower than average comprehension skills tended to tell stories that were poorly structured and lacking a "main point" (Cain & Oakhill, 1996). Based on this and similar results, reading researchers have theorized that sensitivity to story structure and narrative coherence may be strongly implicated in comprehension development (Perfetti, Landi, & Oakhill, 2005).

These empirical findings are unsurprising given the range of skills that contribute to narrative performance. Consider what a young child needs to be able to do in order to construct a complete and coherent story, as follows:

- She must be able to assess her audience's expectations and adjust the content of the narrative to meet the audience's needs (Hudson & Shapiro, 1991). (As Fivush and Hamond [1990] pointed out, even preschool-aged children show the ability to consider a listener's perspective and background knowledge when relating past events.)
- He must employ pronoun referents accurately so that the audience is not confused about each character's role in the story (Hudson & Shapiro, 1991).
- She must assume a perspective as narrator, which involves selecting certain events as more significant than others and arranging these events to make a point (Berman & Slobin, 1994).
- He must be able to recognize which elements of the story are most significant and employ evaluative strategies (e.g., intensifiers, repetition, and prosodic stress) (Peterson & McCabe, 1983) and foregrounding/backgrounding techniques (Berman & Slobin, 1994) to highlight these elements for his audience.

- She must be able to organize the macrostructure of a narrative (Hudson & Shapiro, 1991) in such a way as to emphasize the highpoint of the narrative (Labov & Waletsky, 1967).

These skills are also potentially useful for academic literacy tasks that involve nonnarrative discourse genres. For example, managing pronoun reference is a syntactic ability that transcends genre: Whether a student is writing a report or delivering a persuasive speech, his ability to manage these grammatical devices will affect how well he can craft a cohesive and coherent text (Halliday & Hasan, 1976). The ability able to employ descriptive and evaluative terms for character traits is important skill for the written interpretation of literary texts (Beach, 1999). Evaluative adjectives (e.g., radical, pivotal, and primary) are also an important resource for students learning to construct analytic arguments about causality, a written genre that is highly valued in the subject of history (Coffin, 2004). It has also been demonstrated that even children in second grade are able to incorporate experienced-based narrative accounts in support of paradigmatic claims in conversational classroom discourse (Kurth, Kidd, Gardner, & Smith, 2002).

Historical analysis is one kind of school-based task that draws on narrative modes of understanding. Attributing human-like intentions to collective entities, such as ethnic groups or nations, is one way in which students can develop and demonstrate their interpretation of historical conflict, as in the following example, which is an excerpt from a 10th-grade female Latina student's document-based essay on the causes of World War I. The student's task was to take evidence from a set of numbered documents, all of which were historical primary sources, and use it in support of an explanation for the causes of the war. This essay, which was scored by the teacher with the same scale and criteria used to assess this type of writing on the New York State Regents Exam, received a score of 4.25 on a 5-point scale; thus, it represents a fairly competent writing performance in the teacher's judgment:

> In World War I Archduke Ferdinand was assassinated by a Serbian. . . . The Austrians were highly upset with the Serbians. In Document 3, the Austrians were setting rules for the Serbians. If the Serbians repressed this order of the Austrians, the Austrians would of declared war with them. The Russians did not want the Serbians to be imperialized by the Austrians because the Russions [sic] had a common bond of Eastern Orthodox religion with the Serbians and both nations spoke the same language. Imperialism is when one Nation, country, etc. tries to take over another nation for their own personal reasons. So Russia didn't want that to happen to Serbia because Serbia and Russia were like cousins. When Russia heard that Austria-Hungary declared war on Serbia, the Tsar started mobilizing his army.

This excerpt illustrates how a narrative framework for understanding relationships can support students' understandings of a historical situation. As evidenced by her use of relational terms such as "common bond" and "like cousins," as well as descriptions of emotional and mental states ("highly upset" and "for their own personal reasons"), this student appears to be employing a cause-and-effect narrative framework coupled with insight into human motivation to articulate her understanding of the factors that initiated a major global event.

An approach to analyzing school discourse that is grounded in Systemic-Functional-Linguistics (SFL) has pointed out the many ways in which narrative discourse differs from the expository and argument genres that prevail in advanced academic discourse in secondary and post-secondary education (Schleppegrell, 2004). In summary, this approach maintains that teachers' over-reliance on narrative modes of discourse in the early years and/or with students who come to school with limited exposure to academic genres of speaking and writing inhibits the academic development of those students. I will not argue against this position here; I do propose, however, that it may be advantageous to educators to consider how narrative ways of thinking can provide students with access to basic forms of historical understanding. For example, one of the expectations for historical discourse is that students be able to demon-strate their knowledge of historical situations by telling or writing historical recounts and accounts. According to the SFL framework, responding to this expectation requires students to employ verbs that illustrate what are called "material processes" as well as "verbal and mental processes to construct points of view" (Schleppegrell, 2004, p. 128). Material processes are indicated by verbs of action, and verbal and mental processes are indicated by verbs of speaking and thinking, respectively. We can see examples of the use of these kinds of verbs in the student's World War I essay discussed previously: the student coor-dinates mental ("want"), verbal ("declared," "heard"), and material ("assassi-nated," "mobilizing") processes in an account that illustrates cause-and-effect relationships.

In more sophisticated forms of historical analysis, recounting strategies can be employed in the service of or arguing for a particular position on history. Consider this one sentence from a high-scoring essay on a statewide history exam (the New York State Regents, U.S. History), which was written in response to a prompt asking the student to discuss isolationist stances toward Europe prior to World War II. The author of the essay in which this sentence appeared took an anti-isolationist stance and used evaluative and interpretive markers to reinforce the thesis that the United States made the right decision in entering the war. The first sentence of the concluding paragraph is written in a register typical of narrative in that it employs verbal and material processes (i.e., verbs that denote speech and action) to *imply* an interpretive position that is elsewhere explicitly stated in the essay:

> The millions of voices that cried out against war were silenced as Japanese bombs were dropped on Pearl Harbor.

In this sentence, the vivid phrase, "millions of voices... cried out against the war," represents the isolationist position against which the author of this essay argued. Note that the author employs a concrete image to represent this abstract concept – the kind of image that would be equally appropriate in a narrative account of this important episode from World War II. The phrase, "were silenced," implies the author's view that the bombing of Pearl Harbor rendered the isolationist stance impractical and naïve. The use of material and verbal processes, which are typical register features of the narrative genre, thus assists the writer in performing the task of interpreting experience that is central to historical writing (Schleppegrell, 2004).

Researchers who analyze discourse from an SFL perspective emphasize that many of the features of advanced academic discourse, such as exposition and argument, are markedly different in form and function from the features that characterize narrative genres (e.g., recounts, imaginative narratives, and personal narratives). Neither students nor teachers should be led to believe that narrative performances will suffice to convey or facilitate the kinds of higher order reasoning that sophisticated forms of academic literacy require. The point that I am making, rather, is that narrative ways of knowing are a potential foundation for these later, more advanced forms. It is true that longitudinal and cross-sectional research on children's writing development has documented increased mastery of expository text features as students progress through secondary school. For example, a greater frequency of adversative and sequential conjunctions (e.g., *however, finally*) and a lower frequency of temporal and causal conjunctions (e.g., *then, because*) was found in 12th graders' writing as compared to 6th graders' writing (Crowhurst, 1990). However, this research has concentrated mainly on syntax, with little attention to how such grammatical features map onto or index ways of knowing and thinking that are involved in particular genres. Although these grammatical structures may be demonstrably more complex than the sentence-level grammatical structures found in narratives, there is still no empirical basis for suggesting that narrative is essentially easier to comprehend or produce than expository text. Indeed, literary narratives, the register of which is typically replete with temporal and causal connections, also employ figurative language and nuanced vocabularies of evaluation that can be just as challenging to writers and readers as informational text, if not more so. As Lee (1995) argued, culturally based familiarity with certain kinds of discourse strategies and linguistic tactics can be a significant resource for interpreting literary texts. Although teachers who are familiar with and able to draw on this cultural knowledge as an instructional resource may have an advantage in helping their students to acquire sophisticated literary reading skills, all teachers can acquire some degree of this knowledge with the right kind of training and support. *Chameleon Readers* (McCabe, 1995), a text designed for a teacher-education course in children's literature or reading methods, is one useful resource for this purpose.

A CHALLENGE TO LITERACY EDUCATORS AND RESEARCHERS

The issues I have raised in this chapter are relevant to all teachers of literacy in a global society. By "teachers of literacy," I mean not only those whose primary mandate is to instruct learners in the skills of decoding and comprehension but also any teacher whose curriculum involves inducting students into the ways of speaking and writing that are most appropriate for understanding and representing knowledge in a particular content area. Policy makers and school administrators are simultaneously decrying the low literacy levels of students in U.S. schools and exhorting teachers and students to achieve higher academic standards. Even as the cultural and linguistic heritage of children in U.S. schools becomes increasingly diverse, educational researchers are also becoming more aware of the special challenges that English-language learners face in mastering advanced forms of literacy in English (Schleppegrell & Colombi, 2002). These circumstances heighten the need for research that systematically documents the diverse range of discourse competencies that students bring with them to school, as well as proposals for how to build a bridge to academic literacy from this competence.

When students from different cultures come into contact with one another within the institutional context of a school, they bring with them a complex variety of internalized standards for discourse performance. It falls to their teachers to sort out what these standards are and how to reconcile them into a body of common knowledge that students can rely on to analyze and carry out performances in a variety of discourses. Reflecting on the work of the teachers who were her co-researchers, Heath (1983, p. 368) wrote:

> The teachers described here learned to bring some of the ways Trackton and Roadville children shaped experience and expressed knowledge into classrooms. They worked to enable the children to elaborate the similarities and differences among different cultural groups, and times, places, and styles. The cultural patterns of all involved expanded, and as this book is completed, some of Roadville's and Trackton's young adults are using that expanded knowledge to make life choices.

One important service that research of the kind presented in this book can provide is to highlight the many ways in which young narrators from a range of different cultural backgrounds may show competence in constructing a story. As August (2006) has argued, citing recent data from the U.S. National Center for Education Statistics, the amount of professional development available for teachers of English-language learners is insufficient to meet the current needs of these students., For example, in the three years prior to a national survey of educational resources in the U.S., it was found that only 12.5% of U.S. teachers who work with students designated as Limited English Proficient had received 8 or more hours of in-service professional development on how to provide instruction for this type of student, (National Center for Education Statistics, 2002).

Put another way, 87.5% of teachers working with Limited English Proficient students had received fewer that 8 hours of relevant professional development over three years – hardly enough time to provide them with sufficient education in how to address differences in discourse styles in their teaching.

Once the obstacle of increasing the time spent on language-related professional development for teachers is overcome, the content focus of this training needs to be adjusted in ways that will allow for education about cultural variation in discourse forms to be added to – if not incorporated within – the currently popular focus on development of strategies and skills for academic success. This focus is often enacted through modeling of expertise and successful performances through such techniques as cognitive apprenticeships, in which teachers raise awareness of their own strategies as readers and writers and then model these strategies for students, as in WestEd's Strategic Literacies Initiative (Schoenbach, Greenleaf, Cziko, & Hurwitz, 1999) or the Pathways Project from the Santa Ana, California, public schools (Olson & Land, 2007). Another popular approach, known as "Genre Study," is to analyze successful examples of written genres in order to highlight the qualities that make these models exemplary (Lattimer, 2003). Such methods are premised on the assumption that improving students' literacy performance requires making the components of successful performance at a literacy task visible and explicit to learners, and they have indeed shown demonstrable success in improving learners' performance. Teacher educators and professional developers can build on this record of success by relating state-of-the-art conceptions of expertise in literate practices to "everyday" literate practices from different cultural traditions. An example of this type of bridging between "expert" and "everyday" skills can be found in Lee's (1995) description of a culturally based cognitive apprenticeship for teaching sophisticated literary reading strategies to African American students. Her model draws on spoken-discourse strategies familiar to the students from their everyday experience, which included ways of using figurative language and double entendres in the cultural practice of "signifying." In her instruction, Lee demonstrated the strategies she used for interpreting literary texts by "thinking aloud" about her interpretations and noting explicitly when she was relying on culturally based linguistic knowledge. In addition to quantitative evidence of the gains her students made in their literary knowledge as a result of this technique, her study provides a compelling descriptive account of how culturally based knowledge and practices can be merged into an instructional framework based on cognitive strategies.

A similar approach could be applied to the study of discourse production – for example, the reading and writing of narratives. In such a scenario, teachers could read narratives from learners of different cultural backgrounds and analyze the different strengths of each in terms of structure, lexical features, and narrator's stance. It would also be productive for discussion to generate ideas about how the features of these sample narratives index types of competence related to school-based literacy tasks. For example, a narrative that stands out as exemplary in the use of evaluative devices to indicate characters' emotional states may index an ability to show empathy for fictional characters, an important skill in the development of literary understanding.

Once teachers have expanded their understanding of variations in discourse competence, how can they apply it to classroom instruction? Here, it is useful to draw on the notion of cognitive transfer. In a classic article based on a review of research on expertise in different domains, Perkins and Salamon (1988) identified instructional strategies that can be useful in promoting transfer of knowledge and skills from one context to a context that is noticeably different in terms of audience expectations and contextual constraints. To encourage such transfer, teachers need to engage in "explicit mindful abstraction of patterns" (p. 27) or "general principles" (p. 28) that are illustrated in one context and explain how those patterns or principles are applied to a new context.[1] To envision how this might play out in literacy teaching, imagine a situation in which a third-grade teacher wants to develop students' proficiency in composing written personal narratives for students with little experience in this kind of writing. This might mean having students take turns telling the kind of story with which they are most comfortable and familiar, rather than demanding a prescribed story form (e.g., a story about a scary incident that really happened or a fictional story that they read about in a book).

Teachers of children in multicultural schools occupy a special position in that they are both challenged by and privileged with the necessity of helping students to learn from differences among one another's culturally based patterns of communication. It is incumbent on teachers to model behaviors that demonstrate an attitude of respect for and interest in the discourse styles that children bring to school and to encourage children to refine those styles as part of their apprenticeship to academic discourse. Such behaviors include, for example, attentive listening and prompts for elaboration. Experimental research has shown that children assigned to highly elaborative interviewers produce narratives containing more features of conventional narrative discourse than those of children assigned to low-elaborative conditions (Cain, Eaton, Baker-Ward, & Yen, 2005). However, teachers are unlikely to demonstrate interest and request elaboration unless they perceive all students as having stories worth telling and are open to recognizing many forms of narrative competence. It is here that the obligations of researchers and teacher educators become apparent: The more systematically researchers describe, analyze, and predict the ways in which the

---

[1] Perkins and Salamon distinguish between low-road transfer, transfer to a similar context, and high-road transfer, to a much different context and task type. For the sake of illustration here, transfer from oral informal narratives to formal written narratives is presumed to be high-road transfer, although that classification is certainly open to further investigation and debate.

discourse practices of different cultural groups relate to the types of discourses involved in academic achievement, the better informed teachers will be about the tools at their disposal to facilitate this achievement.

REFERENCES

Applebee, A. (1978). *The child's concept of story: Ages two to seventeen.* Chicago: University of Chicago Press.

August, D. (2006). Demographic overview. In D. August and T. Shanahan (Eds.), *Developing literacy in second-language learners* (pp. 43–49). Mahwah, NJ: Lawrence Erlbaum Associates.

Bailey, A. L. (in press). From *Lambie* to *Lambaste*: The conceptualization, operationalization, and use of academic language in the assessment of ELL students. In K. Rolstad (Ed.), *Rethinking school language.* Mahwah, NJ: Lawrence Erlbaum Associates.

Beach, R. (1999). Evaluating students' response strategies in writing about literature. In C. Cooper & L. Odell (Eds.), *Evaluating writing: The role of teachers' knowledge about text, learning and culture.* Urbana, IL: NCTE.

Beals, D., & Snow, C. (1994). Thunder is when the angels are upstairs bowling: Narratives and explanations at the dinner table. *Journal of Narrative and Life History, 4*(4) 331–352.

Berman, R., & Slobin, D. (1994). Relating events in narrative: A cross-linguistic developmental study. Hillsdale, NJ: Erlbaum.

Bruner, J. (1986). *Actual minds, possible worlds.* Cambridge, MA: Harvard University Press.

Bruner, J. (1990). *Acts of meaning.* Cambridge, MA: Harvard University Press.

Cain, W. J., Eaton, K. L., Baker-Ward, L., & Yen, G. (2005). Facilitating low-income children's narrative performances through interviewer elaborative style and reporting condition. *Discourse Processes, 40*(3), 193–208.

Cain, K., & Oakhill, J. (1996). The nature of the relationship between comprehension skill and the ability to tell a story. *British Journal of Development Psychology, 14,* 187–201.

Calkins, L. M. (1994). *The art of teaching writing* (2nd Ed.). Portsmouth, NH: Heinemann.

Champion, T. B., Katz, L., Muldrow, R., & Dail, R. (1999). Storytelling and storymaking in an urban preschool classroom: Building bridges from home to school culture. *Topics in Language Disorders, 19,* 52–67.

Coffin, C. (2004). Learning to write history: The role of causality. *Written Communication, 21*(3), 261–289.

Conchas, G. Q. (2001) Structuring failure and success: Understanding the variability in Latino school engagement. *Harvard Educational Review, 71*(3), 475–504.

Crowhurst, M. (1990). The development of persuasive/argumentative writing. In R. Beach & S. Hynds (Eds.), *Developing discourse practices in adolescence and adulthood* (pp. 200–223). Norwood, NJ: Ablex.

Duke, N. K. (2000). 3.6 minutes per day: The scarcity of informational texts in first grade. *Reading Research Quarterly, 35*(2) 202–224.

Farr, M. (1993). Essayist literacy and other verbal performances. *Written Communication, 10*(1), 4–38.

Fivush, R., & Hamond, N. R. (1990). Autobiographic memory across the preschool years: Towards reconceptualizing childhood amnesia. In R. Fivush & J. A. Hudson (Eds.), *Knowing and remembering in young children* (pp. 223–248). New York: Cambridge University Press.

Flores-Gonzales, N. (2003). Popularity versus respect: School structure, peer groups, and Latino academic achievement. *International Journal of Qualitative Studies in Education, 18*(5), 625–642.

Fordham, S., & Ogbu, J. (1986). Black students' school success: Coping with the burden of "acting White." *Urban Review, 18*, 176–206.

Griffin, T. M., Hemphill, L., Camp., L., & Wolf, D. P. (2004). Oral discourse in the preschool years and later literacy skills. *First Language, 24*(71), 123–147.

Gutiérrez, K. D., & Rogoff, B. (2003). Cultural ways of learning: Individual traits or repertoires of practice. *Educational Researcher, 32*(5), 19–25.

Halliday, M. A. K., & Hasan, R. (1976). *Cohesion in English.* New York: Longman.

Harvey, S., & Goudvis, A. (2000). *Strategies that work: Teaching comprehension to enhance understanding.* Portland, ME: Stenhouse.

Heath, S. B. (1992). What no bedtime story means: Narrative skills at home and at school. *Language in Society, 11*, 49–76.

Heath, S. B. (1983, reprinted 1996). *Ways with words.* New York: Cambridge University Press.

Hudson, J. A., and Shapiro, L. R. (1991). From knowing to telling: The development of children's scripts, stories, and personal narratives. In A. McCabe & C. Peterson (1991), *Developing narrative structure* (pp. 89–136). Hillsdale, NJ: Lawrence Erlbaum.

Hyon, S., & Sulzby, E. (1994). African American kindergarteners' narratives: Topic-centered and topic-associating styles. *Linguistics and Education, 6*, 121–152.

Kamberelis, G., & Bovino, T. (1999). Cultural artifacts as scaffolds for genre development. *Reading Research Quarterly, 34* (2), 138–170.

Kirkpatrick, D. (2006, April 17). Demonstrations on immigration are hardening a divide. *The New York Times, Section A,* Column *1*, p. 16.

Kurth, L., Kidd, R., Gardner, R., & Smith, E. (2002). Student use of narrative and paradigmatic forms of talk in elementary science conversations. *Journal of Research in Science Teaching, 39*(9) 793–818.

Labov, W., & Waletsky, J. (1967). Narrative analysis: Oral versions of personal experience. In J. Helm (Ed.), *Essays on the verbal and visual arts.* Seattle, WA: University of Washington Press.

Lattimer, H. (2003). *Thinking through genre: Units of study in reading and writing workshops, Grades 4-12.* Portland, ME: Stenhouse.

Lee, C. (1995). A culturally based cognitive apprenticeship: Teaching African American high school students skills in literary interpretation. *Reading Research Quarterly, 30*(4), 608–630.

Martínez-Roldán, C. M. (2003). Building worlds and identities: A case study of the role of narratives in bilingual literature discussions. *Research in the Teaching of English, 3*(4), 491–526.

McCabe, A. (1995). *Chameleon readers: Teaching children to appreciate all kinds of good stories.* New York: McGraw Hill.

Michaels, S. (1981). "Sharing time:" Children's narrative styles and differential access to literacy. *Language in Society, 10*, 423–442.

Michaels, S., & Cazden, C. (1986). Teacher-child collaboration as oral preparation for literacy. In B. B. Schiefflin and P. Gilmore (Eds.), *The acquisition of literacy: Ethnographic perspectives* (pp. 132–154). Norwood, NJ: Ablex.

Moll, L., Amanti, C., Neff, D., & González, N. (1992). Funds of knowledge for teaching: Using a qualitative approach to connect homes and classrooms. *Theory into Practice, 31*(2), 132–141.

National Center for Education Statistics (2002). School and Staffing Survey: 1999–2000: Overview of the data for public, private, public charter, and Bureau of Indian Affairs Elementary and Secondary Schools. (Report 2002-313). Washington, DC: U.S. Department of Education, Office of Educational Research and Improvement. Retrieved April 26, 2008 from http://nces.ed.gov/pubs2002/2002313.pdf.

National Center for Education Statistics (2004). Language minorities and their educational and labor market indicators – Recent trends. (Report 2004-009). Washington, DC: U.S. Department of Education, Institute of Education Sciences. Retrieved April 26, 2008 from http://nces.ed.gov/pubs2004/2004009.pdf.

National Center for Education Statistics (2007). The condition of education, 2007. (Report 2007-064). Washington, DC: U.S. Department of Education, Institute of Education Sciences. Retrieved April 26, 2008 from http://nces.ed.gov/pubs2007/2007064.pdf.

Olson, C. B., & Land, R. (2007). A cognitive strategies approach to reading and writing instruction for English-language learners in secondary school. *Research in the Teaching of English, 41*(3), 269–303.

Passel, J., & Sturo, R. (2005). Rise, peak and decline: Trends in U.S. immigration, 1992–2004. Washington, DC: Pew Hispanic Center.

Perfetti, C., Landi, N., & Oakhill, J. (2005). The acquisition of reading comprehension skill. In M. J. Snowling & C. Hulme (Eds.), *The science of reading: A handbook*. Oxford, UK: Blackwell.

Perkins, D., & Salamon, G. (1988). Teaching for transfer. *Educational Leadership, 46*(1), 22–32.

Peterson, C., & McCabe, A. (1983). *Developmental psycholinguistics: Three ways of looking at a child's narrative*. New York: Plenum Press.

Schleppegrell, M. J. (2004). *The language of schooling: A functional linguistics perspective*. Mahwah, NJ: Lawrence Erlbaum.

Schleppegrell, M. J., & Colombi, M. C. (Eds.) (2002). *Developing advanced literacy in first and second languages: Meaning with power*. Mahwah, NJ: Lawrence Erlbaum.

Schoenbach, R., Greenleaf, C., Cziko, C., & Hurwitz, L. (1999). *Reading for understanding*. San Francisco: Jossey-Bass.

Shiro, M. (2003). Genre and evaluation in narrative development. *Journal of Child Language, 30*, 165–195.

Snow, C. (1991). Diverse conversational contexts for the acquisition of various language skills. In J. Miller (Ed.), *Research on child language disorders* (pp. 105–124). Austin, TX: Pro-Ed.

Wertsch, J. (1998). *Mind as action*. New York: Oxford University Press.

Wong-Fillmore, L., & Snow, C. E. (2000). What teachers need to know about language. Washington, DC: Center for Applied Linguistics.

Wortham, S. (2001). *Narratives in action.* New York: Teachers College Press.

Zeleny, J. (2007, June 27). Immigration bill prompts some menacing responses. *New York Times,* Section A, Column O, p. 18.

For EU product safety concerns, contact us at Calle de José Abascal, 56–1°,
28003 Madrid, Spain or eugpsr@cambridge.org.

www.ingramcontent.com/pod-product-compliance
Ingram Content Group UK Ltd.
Pitfield, Milton Keynes, MK11 3LW, UK
UKHW042144130625
459647UK00011B/1175